October 14, 2001

Lisa Marie' Bridal
Shower

Much Love
Mom

America's Favorite Brand Name
Light Cooking

Nutritional Analysis: Nutritional information is given for the recipes in this publication. Each analysis is based on the food items in the ingredient list, except ingredients labeled as "optional" or "for garnish." When more than one ingredient choice is listed, the first ingredient is used for analysis. If a range for the amount of an ingredient is given, the nutritional analysis is based on the lowest amount. Foods offered as "serve with" suggestions are not included in the analysis unless otherwise stated.

Microwave Cooking: Microwave ovens vary in wattage. Use the cooking times as guidelines and check for doneness before adding more time.

The publisher would like to thank the following companies and organizations for the use of their recipes in this publication: Alpine Lace Brands, Inc.; A.1.® Steak Sauce; Birds Eye®; California Prune Board; Colorado Potato Administrative Committee; Delmarva Poultry Industry, Inc.; Dole Food Company, Inc.; EGG BEATERS® Healthy Real Egg Substitute; Equal® sweetener; FLEISCHMANN'S® Original Spread; GREY POUPON® Mustard; Guiltless Gourmet®; Healthy Choice®; Hershey Foods Corporation; MOTT's® Inc., a division of Cadbury Beverages Inc.; National Honey Board; Perdue Farms Incorporated; The Procter & Gamble Company; Sauder's Penn Dutch Eggs; The J.M. Smucker Company; USA Rice Federation.

The HEALTHY CHOICE® recipes contained in this book have been tested by the manufacturers and have been carefully edited by the publisher. The publisher and the manufacturers cannot be held responsible for any ill effects caused by the errors in the recipes, or by spoiled ingredients, unsanitary conditions, incorrect preparation procedures or any other cause.

America's Favorite Brand Name
Light Cooking

PUBLICATIONS INTERNATIONAL, LTD.

America's Favorite Brand Name
Light Cooking

Introduction   **6**

Appetizers & Beverages   10

Breakfast & Brunch   **54**

Soups & Chilies   94

Salads   120

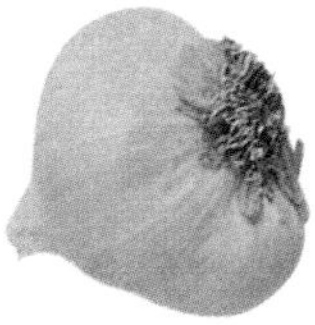

Sandwiches & Wraps   **150**

Meat Entrées   **168**

Poultry Entrées   **186**

Seafood Entrées   **212**

Pasta   230

Side Dishes & Vegetables   **260**

Cookies & Brownies   296

Cakes & Pies   **312**

More Desserts   **342**

Index   **374**

Metric Conversion Chart   **384**

Introduction

Today, people everywhere are more aware than ever before about the importance of maintaining a healthful lifestyle. In addition to proper exercise, this includes eating foods that are lower in fat, sodium and cholesterol. The goal of this cookbook is to provide today's cook with easy-to-prepare recipes that taste great, yet easily fit into your dietary goals. Eating well is a matter of making smarter choices about the foods you eat. Preparing these recipes is your first step toward making smart choices a delicious reality.

A Balanced Diet

The U.S. Department of Agriculture and the Department of Health and Human Services have developed a Food Guide Pyramid to illustrate how easy it is to eat a healthier diet. It is not a rigid description, but rather a general guide that lets you choose a healthful diet that's right for you. It calls for eating a wide variety of foods to get the nutrients you need and, at the same time, the right amount of calories to maintain a healthy weight.

Food Guide Pyramid
A Guide to Daily Food Choices

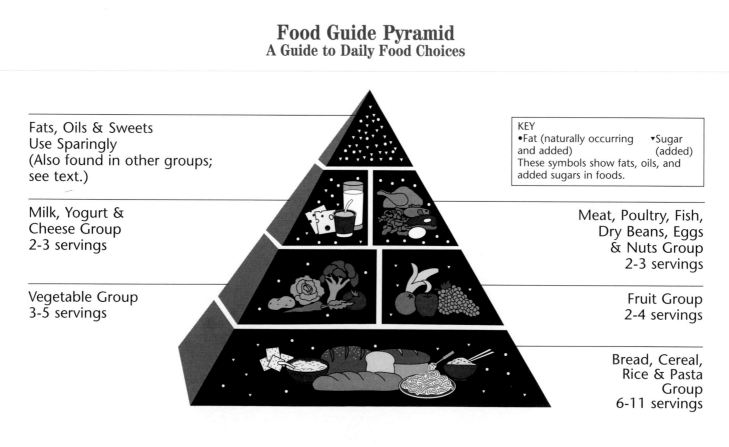

Fats, Oils & Sweets
Use Sparingly
(Also found in other groups; see text.)

KEY
•Fat (naturally occurring ▾Sugar and added) (added)
These symbols show fats, oils, and added sugars in foods.

Milk, Yogurt & Cheese Group
2-3 servings

Meat, Poultry, Fish, Dry Beans, Eggs & Nuts Group
2-3 servings

Vegetable Group
3-5 servings

Fruit Group
2-4 servings

Bread, Cereal, Rice & Pasta Group
6-11 servings

The number of servings, and consequently, the number of calories a person can eat each day, is determined by a number of factors, including age, weight, height, activity level and gender. Sedentary women and some older adults need about 1,600 calories each day. For most children, teenage girls, active women and many sedentary men, 2,000 calories is about right. Teenage boys, active men and some very active women use about 2,800 calories each day. Use the chart below to determine how many servings you need for your calorie level.

Personalized Food Group Servings for Different Calorie Levels*

	1600	2000	2800
Bread Group Servings	6	8	11
Vegetable Group Servings	3	4	5
Fruit Group Servings	2	3	4
Milk Group Servings	2-3**	2-3**	2-3**
Meat Group Servings (ounces)	5	6	7

*Numbers may be rounded
**Women who are pregnant or breast-feeding, teenagers and young adults to age 24 need 3 or more servings.

Lower Fat for Healthier Living

It is widely known that most Americans' diets are too high in fat. A low fat diet reduces your risk of getting certain diseases and helps you maintain a healthy weight. Studies have shown that eating more than the recommended amount of fat (especially saturated fat) is associated with increased blood cholesterol in some adults. A high blood cholesterol level is associated with increased risk for heart disease. A high fat diet may also increase your chances for obesity and some types of cancer.

Nutrition experts recommend diets that contain 30% or less of total daily calories from fat. The "30% calories from fat" goal applies to a total diet over time, not to a single food, serving of a recipe or meal. To find the approximate percentage of calories from fat use this easy 3-step process:

 Multiply the grams of fat per serving by 9 (there are 9 calories in each gram of fat), to give you the number of calories from fat per serving.

 Divide by the total number of calories per serving.

 Multiply by 100%.

For example, imagine a 200 calorie sandwich that has 10 grams of fat. To find the percentage of calories from fat, first multiply the grams of fat by 9:

$$10 \times 9 = 90$$

Then, divide by the total number of calories in a serving:

$$90 \div 200 = .45$$

Multiply by 100% to get the percentage of calories from fat:

$$.45 \times 100\% = 45\%$$

You may find doing all this math tiresome, so an easier way to keep track of the fat in your diet is to calculate the total grams of fat appropriate to your caloric intake, then keep a running count of fat grams over the course of a day.

Defining "Fat-Free"

It is important to take the time to read food labels carefully. For example, you'll find many food products on the grocery store shelves making claims such as "97% fat free." This does not necessarily mean that 97% of the calories are from fat (or that only 3 percent of calories come from fat). Often these numbers are calculated by weight. This means that out of 100 grams of this food, 3 grams are fat. Depending on what else is in the food, the percentage of calories from fat can be quite high. You may find that the percent of calories from fat can be as high as 50%.

Nutritional Analysis

Every recipe in this cookbook is followed by a nutritional analysis that lists certain nutrient values for a single serving.

- The analysis of each recipe includes all the ingredients that are listed in that recipe, except ingredients labeled as "optional" or "for garnish."

- If a range is given in the yield of a recipe ("Makes 6 to 8 servings" for example), the lower yield was used to calculate the per serving information.

- If a range is offered for an ingredient ("¼ to ⅛ teaspoon" for example), the first amount given was used to calculate the nutritional information.

- If an ingredient is presented with an option ("2 cups hot cooked rice or noodles" for example), the first item listed was used to calculate the nutritional information.

- Foods shown in photographs on the same serving plate and offered as "serve with" suggestions at the end of a recipe are not included in the recipe analysis unless they are listed in the ingredient list.

- Meat should be trimmed of all visible fat since this is reflected in the nutritional analysis.

- In recipes calling for cooked rice or noodles, the analysis was based on rice or noodles that were prepared without added salt or fat unless otherwise mentioned in the recipe.

The nutritional information that appears with each recipe was calculated by an independent nutrition consulting firm or submitted in part by the participating companies and associations. Every effort has been made to check the accuracy of these numbers. However, because numerous variables account for a wide range of values in certain foods, all analyses that appear in this book should be considered approximate.

The recipes in this publication are not intended as a medically therapeutic program, nor as a substitute for medically approved diet plans for people on fat, cholesterol or sodium restricted diets. You should consult your physician before beginning any diet plan. The recipes offered here can be a part of a healthy lifestyle that meets recognized dietary guidelines. A healthy lifestyle includes not only eating a balanced diet, but engaging in proper exercise as well.

All the ingredients called for in these recipes are generally available in large supermarkets, so there is no need to go to specialty or health food stores. You'll also see an ever-increasing amount of reduced fat and nonfat products available in local markets. Take advantage of these items to reduce your daily fat intake even more.

Cooking Healthier

When cooking great-tasting low fat meals, you will find some techniques or ingredients are different from traditional cooking. Fat, in the form of oil, butter, margarine and shortening is used in nearly every type of recipe. Because fat plays an important role in cooking and baking, it is difficult to merely omit it. It acts as a flavor enhancer and gives food a distinctive and desirable texture. So, instead of taking it out completely, several techniques are employed to make up for the loss of flavor and texture. These techniques include:

- Investing in nonstick bakeware and using nonstick cooking spray to reduce the need for added oil.

- Incorporating applesauce or other puréed fruit into baked goods to create a texture similar to high-fat foods.

- "Sautéing" vegetables in a small amount of broth to further reduce the need for oil.

- Using herbs, spices and flavorful vegetables in a variety of combinations to highlight the natural flavor of food, making up for the lack of fat.

- Choosing alternative protein sources, such as dried beans or tofu in recipes. Often, meat is included in a recipe as an accent flavor rather than the star attraction.

These methods for reducing fat can benefit recipes in two ways: 1) by reducing the overall amount of fat in the recipe and 2) by boosting the nutritional content of the recipe when fruits and vegetables replace high fat ingredients. These are all simple changes that you can easily make when you start cooking light and healthy!

Appetizers & Beverages

Five-Layered Mexican Dip

½ cup low fat sour cream
½ cup GUILTLESS GOURMET® Salsa
    (medium)
1 jar (12.5 ounces) GUILTLESS
    GOURMET® Bean Dip (Black or
    Pinto, mild or spicy)
2 cups shredded lettuce
½ cup chopped tomato
¼ cup (1 ounce) shredded sharp
    Cheddar cheese
    Chopped fresh cilantro and cilantro
    sprigs (optional)
1 large bag (7 ounces) GUILTLESS
    GOURMET® Baked Tortilla Chips
    (yellow, white or blue corn)

Mix together sour cream and salsa in small
bowl. Spread bean dip in shallow glass
bowl. Top with sour cream-salsa mixture,
spreading to cover bean dip.* Just before
serving, top with lettuce, tomato and
cheese. Garnish with cilantro, if desired.
Serve with tortilla chips.   *Makes 8 servings*

*Dip may be prepared to this point; cover and
refrigerate up to 24 hours.*

**Nutritional Information per Serving (⅔ cup dip,
20 chips):** *Calories: 199, Total Fat: 4 g,
Cholesterol: 8 mg, Sodium: 425 mg*

Señor Nacho Dip

4 ounces nonfat cream cheese
½ cup (2 ounces) shredded reduced-fat
    Cheddar cheese
¼ cup mild or medium chunky salsa
2 teaspoons 2% low-fat milk
4 ounces baked tortilla chips or
    assorted fresh vegetable dippers

1. Combine cream cheese and Cheddar
cheese in small saucepan; stir over low heat
until melted. Stir in salsa and milk; heat
thoroughly, stirring occasionally.

2. Transfer dip to small serving bowl. Serve
with tortilla chips. Garnish with hot peppers
and cilantro, if desired.   *Makes 4 servings*

Nutritional Information per Serving: *Calories: 181,
Total Fat: 4 g, Cholesterol: 11 mg, Sodium: 629 mg*

Olé Dip: Substitute reduced-fat Monterey
Jack cheese or taco cheese for Cheddar
cheese.

Spicy Mustard Dip: Omit tortilla chips.
Substitute 2 teaspoons spicy brown or
honey mustard for salsa. Serve with fresh
vegetable dippers or pretzels.

Five-Layered Mexican Dip

Shrimp Dip with Crudités

1 can (6 ounces) cooked shrimp, drained, divided
½ cup reduced-fat cream cheese, softened
⅓ cup plus 1 tablespoon thinly sliced green onions, divided
3 tablespoons light or fat-free Caesar salad dressing
2 teaspoons prepared horseradish
¼ teaspoon salt
2 red or yellow bell peppers, cut into 2×1-inch pieces
4 large carrots, peeled and diagonally sliced ¼ inch thick
10 crispbread or other low-fat crackers

1. Reserve several shrimp for garnish. Combine remaining shrimp, cream cheese, ⅓ cup green onions, salad dressing, horseradish and salt in medium bowl; mix well. Transfer to serving dish; top with reserved shrimp and remaining 1 tablespoon green onions. Cover and chill at least 30 minutes before serving.

2. Serve with bell peppers, carrots and crackers. *Makes 10 servings*

Nutritional Information per Serving: *Calories: 127, Total Fat: 4 g, Cholesterol: 37 mg, Sodium: 217 mg*

Green Pea Mockamole

1 package (16 ounces) frozen petit peas
4 green onions
½ cup lightly packed fresh cilantro
2 tablespoons lemon juice
½ cup GUILTLESS GOURMET® Salsa (medium)
Fresh cilantro sprigs (optional)
1 large bag (7 ounces) GUILTLESS GOURMET® Baked Tortilla Chips (yellow, white or blue corn)

Cook peas according to package directions; drain. Place peas, onions, ½ cup cilantro and juice in food processor or blender; process until smooth. Transfer to serving bowl; gently stir in salsa to combine. Garnish with cilantro sprigs, if desired. Serve warm with tortilla chips or cover and refrigerate until ready to serve. *Makes 12 servings*

Nutritional Information per Serving (¼ cup dip, 12 chips): *Calories: 96, Total Fat: 1 g, Cholesterol: 0 mg, Sodium: 171 mg*

Black Bean Salsa

1 can (15 ounces) black beans, rinsed and drained
1 cup frozen corn, thawed
1 large tomato, chopped
¼ cup chopped green onions
2 tablespoons chopped fresh cilantro
2 tablespoons lemon juice
1 tablespoon vegetable oil
1 teaspoon chili powder
¼ teaspoon salt
6 (6-inch) corn tortillas

1. Combine beans, corn, tomato, green onions, cilantro, lemon juice, oil, chili powder and salt in medium bowl; mix well.

2. Preheat oven to 400°F. Cut each tortilla into 8 wedges; place on ungreased baking sheet. Bake 6 to 8 minutes or until edges begin to brown. Serve tortilla wedges warm or at room temperature with salsa.
Makes 6 servings

Nutritional Information per Serving: *Calories: 161, Total Fat: 4 g, Cholesterol: 0 mg, Sodium: 351 mg*

Shrimp Dip with Crudités

Toasted Ravioli with Fresh Tomato-Basil Salsa

  1 package (9 ounces) refrigerated cheese ravioli
    Nonstick olive oil-flavored cooking spray
  ¾ cup plain dry bread crumbs
  2 tablespoons grated Parmesan cheese
  1 teaspoon dried basil leaves
  1 teaspoon dried oregano leaves
  ¼ teaspoon black pepper
  2 egg whites
    Fresh Tomato-Basil Salsa (recipe follows)

1. Cook ravioli according to package directions, omitting salt. Rinse under cold running water until ravioli are cool; drain well.

2. Preheat oven to 375°F. Spray large nonstick baking sheet with cooking spray.

3. Combine bread crumbs, cheese, basil, oregano and pepper in medium bowl.

4. Beat egg whites lightly in shallow dish. Add ravioli; toss lightly to coat. Transfer ravioli, a few at a time, to crumb mixture; toss to coat evenly. Arrange on prepared baking sheet. Repeat with remaining ravioli. Spray tops of ravioli with cooking spray.

5. Bake 12 to 14 minutes or until crisp. Meanwhile, prepare Fresh Tomato-Basil Salsa; serve with ravioli. Garnish, if desired.

Makes 8 servings

Fresh Tomato-Basil Salsa

  1 pound fresh tomatoes, peeled and seeded
  ½ cup loosely packed fresh basil leaves
  ¼ small onion (about 2×1-inch piece)
  1 teaspoon red wine vinegar
  ¼ teaspoon salt

1. Combine ingredients in food processor; process until finely chopped but not smooth.

Makes about 1 cup

Nutritional Information per Serving: *Calories: 167, Total Fat: 5 g, Cholesterol: 29 mg, Sodium: 337 mg*

Venezuelan Salsa

  1 mango, peeled, pitted and diced
  ½ medium papaya, peeled, seeded and diced
  ½ medium avocado, peeled, pitted and diced
  1 carrot, finely chopped
  1 small onion, finely chopped
  1 rib celery, finely chopped
    Juice of 1 lemon
  3 cloves garlic, minced
  2 tablespoons chopped cilantro
  1 jalapeño pepper, finely chopped*
  1½ teaspoons ground cumin
  ½ teaspoon salt

*Jalapeño peppers can sting and irritate the skin. Wear rubber gloves when handling peppers and do not touch eyes.

Combine all ingredients in medium bowl. Refrigerate several hours to allow flavors to blend. Serve with baked tortilla chips, carrot and celery sticks or apple wedges.

Makes 10 servings

Nutritional Information per Serving: *Calories: 52, Total Fat: 2 g, Cholesterol: 0 mg, Sodium: 117 mg*

Toasted Ravioli with Fresh Tomato-Basil Salsa

Layered White Bean and Tuna Dip

Whole Wheat Pita Toasts (recipe follows)
1¼ cups plain nonfat yogurt
2 tablespoons dry reduced-fat Ranch dressing mix
1 medium cucumber, seeded and finely chopped
1 can (6 ounces) solid white tuna packed in water, drained and flaked
⅓ cup chopped red onion
¼ cup chopped celery
1 can (15 ounces) Great Northern beans, rinsed and drained
2 medium cloves garlic, minced
½ teaspoon dried oregano leaves
¼ cup chopped tomato, drained
1 green onion with top, sliced
2 tablespoons halved radish slices (optional)
2 tablespoons slivered pitted black olives (optional)
2 medium yellow squash or zucchini, sliced ½ inch thick (about 28 slices)

1. Prepare Whole Wheat Pita Toasts; set aside.

2. Combine yogurt and dressing mix in medium bowl; stir until well blended. Measure out 1 cup yogurt mixture. Place in separate medium bowl; stir in cucumber. Cover; chill up to 4 hours.

3. Stir tuna, red onion and celery into remaining yogurt mixture. Cover; chill up to 4 hours.

4. Place beans in medium bowl; mash lightly with fork. Stir in garlic and oregano. Cover; chill up to 4 hours.

5. When ready to serve, spread bean mixture onto bottom of 9-inch pie plate or shallow serving dish; top with layers of tuna mixture and cucumber mixture. Sprinkle with tomato, green onion, radishes and olives, if desired. Serve with pita toasts and squash slices. Garnish, if desired.

Makes 8 servings

Whole Wheat Pita Toasts

4 (6-inch) whole wheat pita bread rounds
Nonstick olive oil-flavored cooking spray
1 tablespoon plus 1½ teaspoons olive oil
¼ teaspoon garlic powder
¼ teaspoon salt

1. Preheat oven to 400°F.

2. Carefully split each pita bread round horizontally in half to form 2 rounds. Cut each round into 4 wedges. (You should have 32 wedges.)

3. Place wedges, cut sides up, on large nonstick baking sheets; coat wedges with cooking spray. Brush with oil. Combine garlic powder and salt in small bowl; sprinkle evenly onto wedges.

4. Bake 5 to 8 minutes or until wedges are crisp and golden brown.

Makes 32 toasts

Nutritional Information per Serving (4 toasts, ¼ cup dip): *Calories: 128, Total Fat: 2 g, Cholesterol: 5 mg, Sodium: 322 mg*

Artichoke Dip

1 (14-ounce) can non-marinated
    artichoke hearts, chopped
1 can HEALTHY CHOICE® Recipe
    Creations™ Cream of Roasted
    Garlic Condensed Soup
1 cup fat free cream cheese
½ cup *each* fat free shredded Parmesan
    cheese, HEALTHY CHOICE® Fat Free
    Shredded Mozzarella Cheese,
    sliced green onions and roasted
    red bell peppers
¼ teaspoon black pepper
⅛ teaspoon crushed red pepper
    (optional)
    Salt (optional)
    Vegetable cooking spray

In medium bowl, combine artichoke hearts,
soup, cream cheese, Parmesan cheese,
mozzarella cheese, green onions, roasted
peppers, black pepper, red pepper and salt.
Spread mixture in 2-quart baking dish
sprayed with vegetable cooking spray.

Cover and bake at 400°F 20 minutes or until
bubbly. Serve with pita or bagel chips for
dipping. *Makes 8 servings*

Nutritional Information per Serving: *Calories: 80,
Total Fat: <1 g, Sodium: 565 mg*

Berry Good Dip

8 ounces fresh or thawed frozen
    strawberries
4 ounces nonfat cream cheese,
    softened
¼ cup reduced-fat sour cream
1 tablespoon sugar

1. Place strawberries in food processor or
blender container; process until smooth.

2. Beat cream cheese in small bowl until
smooth. Stir in sour cream, strawberry purée
and sugar; cover. Refrigerate until ready to
serve.

3. Spoon dip into small serving bowl.
Garnish with orange peel, if desired. Serve
with assorted fresh fruit dippers or angel
food cake cubes. *Makes 6 servings*

Nutritional Information per Serving: *Calories: 47,
Total Fat: 1 g, Cholesterol: 7 mg, Sodium: 120 mg*

Cowboy Caviar

    Nonstick cooking spray
2 teaspoons olive oil
1 small eggplant (about ¾ pound),
    peeled and chopped
1 cup chopped onion
1 jalapeño pepper, seeded and finely
    chopped* (optional)
1 can (15 ounces) salsa-style chunky
    tomatoes, undrained
1 can (15 ounces) black-eyed peas,
    rinsed and drained
1 teaspoon ground cumin
½ cup minced fresh cilantro
    Baked tortilla chips

*Jalapeño peppers can sting and irritate the skin. Wear
rubber gloves when handling peppers and do not touch
eyes.*

1. Coat large nonstick skillet with cooking
spray. Add oil; heat over medium heat. Add
eggplant, onion and jalapeño pepper, if
desired; cook and stir 10 minutes or until
vegetables are tender.

2. Stir in tomatoes with juice, black-eyed
peas and cumin. Cook 5 minutes, stirring
frequently. Remove from heat; stir in
cilantro.

3. Serve with tortilla chips.
Makes 16 servings

**Nutritional Information per Serving (4 chips,
¼ cup salsa):** *Calories: 107, Total Fat: 3 g, Cholesterol: 0 mg,
Sodium: 272 mg*

Roasted Eggplant Spread

1 large eggplant
1 can (14½ ounces) diced tomatoes, drained
½ cup finely chopped green onions
½ cup chopped fresh parsley
2 tablespoons red wine vinegar
1 tablespoon olive oil
3 cloves garlic, finely chopped
½ teaspoon salt
½ teaspoon dried oregano leaves
2 pita breads

1. Preheat oven to 375°F.

2. Place eggplant on baking sheet. Bake 1 hour or until tender, turning occasionally. Remove eggplant from oven. Let stand 10 minutes or until cool enough to handle.

3. Cut eggplant lengthwise in half; remove pulp. Place pulp in medium bowl; mash with fork until smooth. Add tomatoes, onions, parsley, vinegar, oil, garlic, salt and oregano; blend well. Cover eggplant mixture; refrigerate 2 hours.

4. Preheat broiler. Split pita breads horizontally in half to form 4 rounds. Stack rounds; cut into sixths to form 24 wedges. Place wedges on baking sheet. Broil 3 minutes or until crisp.

5. Serve eggplant mixture with warm pita bread wedges. Garnish with lemon and lime slices, if desired. *Makes 4 servings*

Nutritional Information per Serving (6 pita bread wedges, ½ cup eggplant spread): *Calories: 134, Total Fat: 3 g, Cholesterol: 0 mg, Sodium: 347 mg*

Vegetable-Topped Hummus

1 can (about 15 ounces) chick-peas, rinsed and drained
2 tablespoons tahini
2 tablespoons lemon juice
1 clove garlic
¾ teaspoon salt
1 tomato, finely chopped
2 green onions, finely chopped
2 tablespoons chopped parsley

1. Combine chick-peas, tahini, lemon juice, garlic and salt in food processor; process until smooth.

2. Combine tomato, green onions and parsley in small bowl.

3. Place chick-pea mixture in medium serving bowl; spoon tomato mixture evenly over top. Serve with wedges of pita bread or assorted crackers. *Makes 8 servings*

Nutritional Information per Serving: *Calories: 82, Total Fat: 3 g, Cholesterol: 0 mg, Sodium: 429 mg*

Roasted Eggplant Spread

Nutty Carrot Spread

6 ounces fat-free cream cheese, softened
2 tablespoons frozen orange juice concentrate, thawed
¼ teaspoon ground cinnamon
1 cup shredded peeled carrots
¼ cup finely chopped pecans, toasted
¼ cup raisins
36 party pumpernickel bread slices, toasted, or melba toast rounds

1. Combine cream cheese, orange juice concentrate and cinnamon in small bowl; stir until well blended. Stir in carrots, pecans and raisins.

2. Spread about 1 tablespoon cream cheese mixture onto each bread slice.

Makes 18 servings

Nutritional Information per Serving (2 pieces): *Calories: 68, Total Fat: 1 g, Cholesterol: 2 mg, Sodium: 149 mg*

Crostini

¼ loaf whole wheat baguette (4 ounces)
4 plum tomatoes
1 cup (4 ounces) shredded part-skim mozzarella cheese
3 tablespoons prepared pesto sauce

1. Preheat oven to 400°F. Slice baguette into 16 very thin, diagonal slices. Slice each tomato vertically into four ¼-inch slices.

2. Place baguette slices on nonstick baking sheet. Top each with 1 tablespoon cheese, then 1 slice tomato. Bake about 8 minutes or until bread is lightly toasted and cheese is melted. Remove from oven; top each crostini with about ½ teaspoon pesto sauce. Serve warm.   *Makes 8 servings*

Nutritional Information per Serving: *Calories: 83, Total Fat: 3 g, Cholesterol: 9 mg, Sodium: 159 mg*

Tuscan White Bean Crostini

2 cans (15 ounces each) Great Northern or cannellini beans, rinsed and drained
½ large red bell pepper, finely chopped *or* ⅓ cup finely chopped roasted red bell pepper
⅓ cup finely chopped onion
⅓ cup red wine vinegar
3 tablespoons chopped parsley
1 tablespoon olive oil
2 cloves garlic, minced
½ teaspoon dried oregano leaves
¼ teaspoon black pepper
18 French bread slices, about ¼ inch thick

1. Combine beans, bell pepper and onion in large bowl.

2. Whisk together vinegar, parsley, oil, garlic, oregano and black pepper in small bowl. Pour over bean mixture; toss to coat. Cover; refrigerate 2 hours or overnight.

3. Arrange bread slices in single layer on large nonstick baking sheet or broiler pan. Broil, 6 to 8 inches from heat, 30 to 45 seconds or until bread slices are lightly toasted. Remove; cool completely.

4. Top each toasted bread slice with about 3 tablespoons bean mixture.

Makes 6 servings

Nutritional Information per Serving: *Calories: 317, Total Fat: 4 g, Cholesterol: 0 mg, Sodium: 800 mg*

Nutty Carrot Spread

Bruschetta

1 cup thinly sliced onion
½ cup chopped seeded tomato
2 tablespoons capers
¼ teaspoon black pepper
3 cloves garlic, finely chopped
1 teaspoon olive oil
4 slices French bread
½ cup (2 ounces) shredded reduced-fat
    Monterey Jack cheese

1. Spray large skillet with nonstick cooking spray. Heat over medium heat until hot. Add onion. Cook and stir 5 minutes. Stir in tomato, capers and pepper. Cook 3 minutes.

2. Preheat broiler. Combine garlic and oil in small bowl; brush bread slices with mixture. Top with onion mixture; sprinkle with cheese. Place slices on baking sheet. Broil 3 minutes or until cheese melts.

Makes 4 servings

Nutritional Information per Serving: *Calories: 90, Total Fat: 2 g, Cholesterol: 0 mg, Sodium: 194 mg*

Marinated Artichoke Cheese Toasts

1 jar (8 ounces) marinated artichoke
    hearts, drained
½ cup (2 ounces) shredded reduced-fat
    Swiss cheese
⅓ cup finely chopped roasted red
    peppers
⅓ cup finely chopped celery
1 tablespoon plus 1½ teaspoons
    reduced-calorie mayonnaise
24 melba toast rounds
    Paprika

1. Rinse artichokes under cold running water; drain well. Pat dry with paper towels. Finely chop artichokes; place in medium bowl. Add cheese, peppers, celery and mayonnaise; mix well.

2. Spoon artichoke mixture evenly onto melba toast rounds; place on large nonstick baking sheet or broiler pan. Broil, 6 inches from heat, about 45 seconds or until cheese mixture is hot and bubbly. Sprinkle with paprika. Transfer to serving plate.

Makes 12 servings

Nutritional Information per Serving (2 toasts): *Calories: 57, Total Fat: 1 g, Cholesterol: 4 mg, Sodium: 65 mg*

Crab Toasts

1 can HEALTHY CHOICE® Recipe
    Creations™ Cream of Celery with
    Sautéed Onion & Garlic Condensed
    Soup
12 ounces crabmeat or surimi seafood,
    flaked
¼ cup *each* chopped celery and sliced
    green onions
1 tablespoon lemon juice
½ teaspoon salt (optional)
⅛ teaspoon grated lemon peel
1 French bread baguette
⅓ cup fat free shredded Parmesan
    cheese
    Paprika

In medium bowl, combine soup, crabmeat, celery, onions, lemon juice, salt and lemon peel; mix well. Cut baguette diagonally into ½-inch slices; arrange slices on 2 cookie sheets. Broil 5 inches from heat 2 minutes or until toasted, turning once.

Spread 1 tablespoon crab mixture on each baguette slice. Top with Parmesan cheese; sprinkle with paprika. Broil 5 inches from heat 2 minutes or until lightly browned.

Makes about 30 appetizers

Nutritional Information per Serving: *Calories: 50, Total Fat: 1 g, Sodium: 220 mg*

Bruschetta

Mediterranean Pita Pizzas

1 cup drained and rinsed canned
    cannellini beans
2 teaspoons lemon juice
2 medium cloves garlic, minced
2 (8-inch) pita bread rounds
1 teaspoon olive oil
½ cup thinly sliced radicchio or escarole
    lettuce (optional)
½ cup chopped seeded tomato
½ cup finely chopped red onion
¼ cup (1 ounce) crumbled feta cheese
2 tablespoons thinly sliced pitted black
    olives

1. Preheat oven to 450°F.

2. Place beans in small bowl; mash lightly
with fork. Stir in lemon juice and garlic.

3. Arrange pita bread rounds on ungreased
baking sheet; brush tops with oil. Bake 6
minutes.

4. Spread bean mixture evenly onto pita
rounds to within ½ inch of edges. Arrange
remaining ingredients evenly on pita rounds.
Bake 5 minutes or until topping is
thoroughly heated and crust is crisp. Cut
into quarters. Serve hot.

Makes 8 servings

Nutritional Information per Serving: *Calories: 98,
Total Fat: 3 g, Cholesterol: 7 mg, Sodium: 282 mg*

Black Bean Quesadillas

Nonstick cooking spray
4 (8-inch) flour tortillas
¾ cup (3 ounces) shredded reduced-fat
    Monterey Jack or Cheddar cheese
½ cup rinsed and drained canned black
    beans
2 green onions with tops, sliced
¼ cup minced fresh cilantro
½ teaspoon ground cumin
½ cup salsa
2 tablespoons plus 2 teaspoons nonfat
    sour cream

1. Preheat oven to 450°F. Spray large
nonstick baking sheet with cooking spray.
Place 2 tortillas on prepared baking sheet;
sprinkle each with half the cheese.

2. Combine beans, green onions, cilantro
and cumin in small bowl; mix lightly. Spoon
bean mixture evenly over cheese; top with
remaining tortillas. Coat tops with cooking
spray.

3. Bake 10 to 12 minutes or until cheese is
melted and tortillas are lightly browned. Cut
into quarters; top each wedge with 1
tablespoon salsa and 1 teaspoon sour cream.
Transfer to serving plate.

Makes 8 servings

Nutritional Information per Serving: *Calories: 105,
Total Fat: 4 g, Cholesterol: 8 mg, Sodium: 259 mg*

Mediterranean Pita Pizzas

South-of-the-Border Nachos

4 ounces low-fat tortilla chips
    Nonstick cooking spray
¾ cup chopped onion
2 jalapeño peppers, seeded and
    chopped*
3 cloves garlic, finely chopped
2 teaspoons chili powder
½ teaspoon ground cumin
1 boneless skinless chicken breast
    (about 6 ounces), cooked and
    chopped
1 can (14½ ounces) Mexican-style
    diced tomatoes, drained
1 cup (4 ounces) shredded reduced-fat
    Monterey Jack cheese
2 tablespoons black olives, chopped

Jalapeño peppers can sting and irritate the skin. Wear rubber gloves when handling peppers and do not touch eyes.

1. Preheat oven to 350°F. Place chips in 13×9-inch baking pan.

2. Spray large nonstick skillet with cooking spray; heat over medium heat until hot. Add onion, peppers, garlic, chili powder and cumin. Cook 5 minutes or until vegetables are tender, stirring occasionally. Stir in chicken and tomatoes.

3. Spoon tomato mixture, cheese and olives over chips. Bake 5 minutes or until cheese melts. Serve immediately.

Makes 4 servings

Nutritional Information per Serving: *Calories: 226, Total Fat: 7 g, Cholesterol: 34 mg, Sodium: 273 mg*

Taco Chicken Nachos

2 small boneless skinless chicken
    breasts (about 8 ounces)
1 tablespoon plus 1½ teaspoons taco
    seasoning mix
1 teaspoon olive oil
¾ cup nonfat sour cream
1 can (4 ounces) diced green chilies,
    drained
¼ cup minced red onion
1 bag (8 ounces) baked nonfat tortilla
    chips
1 cup (4 ounces) shredded reduced-fat
    Cheddar or Monterey Jack cheese
½ cup chopped tomato
¼ cup pitted black olive slices
    (optional)
2 tablespoons chopped fresh cilantro

1. Bring 2 cups water to a boil in small saucepan. Add chicken. Reduce heat to low; cover. Simmer 10 minutes or until chicken is no longer pink in center. Remove from saucepan; cool. Chop chicken.

2. Combine taco seasoning mix and oil in small bowl; mix until smooth paste forms. Stir in sour cream. Add chicken, green chilies and onion; mix lightly.

3. Preheat broiler. Arrange tortilla chips on small ovenproof plates or large platters; cover chips with chicken mixture and cheese. Broil, 4 inches from heat, 2 to 3 minutes or until chicken mixture is hot and cheese is melted. Sprinkle evenly with tomatoes, olives, if desired, and cilantro.

Makes 12 servings

Nutritional Information per Serving: *Calories: 148, Total Fat: 3 g, Cholesterol: 20 mg, Sodium: 431 mg*

Bell Pepper Nachos

Nonstick cooking spray
1 medium green bell pepper
1 medium yellow or red bell pepper
2 Italian plum tomatoes, seeded and
  chopped
⅓ cup finely chopped onion
1 teaspoon chili powder
½ teaspoon ground cumin
1½ cups cooked white rice
½ cup (2 ounces) shredded reduced-fat
  Monterey Jack cheese
¼ cup chopped fresh cilantro
2 teaspoons jalapeño pepper sauce *or*
  ¼ teaspoon hot pepper sauce
½ cup (2 ounces) shredded reduced-fat
  sharp Cheddar cheese

1. Spray large nonstick baking sheets with cooking spray; set aside.

2. Cut bell peppers into 2×1½-inch strips; cut strips into bite-sized triangles (each bell pepper strip should yield 2 or 3 triangles).

3. Spray large nonstick skillet with cooking spray. Add tomatoes, onion, chili powder and cumin. Cook over medium heat 3 minutes or until onion is tender, stirring occasionally. Remove from heat. Stir in rice, Monterey Jack cheese, cilantro and pepper sauce.

4. Top each pepper triangle with about 2 tablespoons rice mixture; sprinkle with Cheddar cheese. Place on prepared baking sheets; cover with plastic wrap. Refrigerate up to 8 hours before serving.

5. When ready to serve, preheat broiler. Remove covers from baking sheets; discard. Place baking sheets under broiler. Broil, 6 to 8 inches from heat, 3 to 4 minutes (or bake at 400°F 8 to 10 minutes) or until cheese is bubbly and rice is heated through. Transfer to serving plate.   *Makes 8 servings*

Nutritional Information per Serving (3 pieces): *Calories: 100, Total Fat: 3 g, Cholesterol: 9 mg, Sodium: 165 mg*

Mexican Roll-Ups

6 uncooked lasagna noodles
¾ cup prepared guacamole
¾ cup chunky salsa
¾ cup (3 ounces) shredded nonfat
  Cheddar cheese
Additional salsa (optional)

1. Cook lasagna noodles according to package directions, omitting salt. Rinse under cold running water until cool; drain.

2. Spread 2 tablespoons guacamole onto each noodle; top each with 2 tablespoons salsa and 2 tablespoons cheese.

3. Roll up noodles jelly-roll fashion. Cut each roll-up in half to form two equal-size roll-ups. Serve immediately with additional salsa.   *Makes 12 servings*

Nutritional Information per Serving: *Calories: 40, Total Fat: 1 g, Cholesterol: 2 mg, Sodium: 218 mg*

Black Bean Tostadas

1 cup rinsed and drained canned black beans, mashed
2 teaspoons chili powder
Nonstick cooking spray
4 (8-inch) corn tortillas
1 cup washed torn romaine lettuce leaves
1 cup chopped seeded tomato
½ cup chopped onion
½ cup plain nonfat yogurt
2 jalapeño peppers, seeded and finely chopped*

Jalapeño peppers can sting and irritate the skin. Wear rubber gloves when handling peppers and do not touch eyes.

1. Combine beans and chili powder in small saucepan. Cook 5 minutes over medium heat or until heated through, stirring occasionally.

2. Spray large nonstick skillet with cooking spray. Heat over medium heat until hot. Sprinkle tortillas with water; place in skillet, one at a time. Cook 20 to 30 seconds or until hot and pliable, turning once.

3. Spread bean mixture evenly over tortillas; layer with lettuce, tomato, onion, yogurt and peppers. Garnish with cilantro, sliced tomatoes and peppers, if desired. Serve immediately. *Makes 4 servings*

Nutritional Information per Serving: *Calories: 146, Total Fat: 2 g, Cholesterol: 1 mg, Sodium: 466 mg*

Roasted Garlic & Spinach Spirals

1 whole head fresh garlic
3 cups fresh spinach leaves
1 can (15 ounces) white beans, rinsed and drained
1 teaspoon dried oregano leaves
¼ teaspoon black pepper
⅛ teaspoon ground red pepper
7 (7-inch) flour tortillas

1. Preheat oven to 400°F. Trim top of garlic just enough to cut tips off center cloves; discard. Moisten head of garlic with water; wrap in foil. Bake 45 minutes or until garlic is soft and has a mellow garlicky aroma; cool. Remove garlic from skin by squeezing between fingers and thumb; place in food processor.

2. Rinse spinach leaves; pat dry with paper towels. Remove stems; discard. Finely shred leaves by stacking and cutting several leaves at a time. Place in medium bowl.

3. Add beans, oregano, black pepper and red pepper to food processor; process until smooth. Add to spinach; mix well. Spread mixture evenly onto tortillas; roll up. Trim ½ inch off ends of rolls; discard. Cut rolls into 1-inch pieces. Transfer to serving plates. *Makes 10 servings*

Nutritional Information per Serving (4 pieces):
Calories: 139, Total Fat: 2 g, Cholesterol: 0 mg, Sodium: 293 mg

Black Bean Tostada

Rock 'n' Rollers

4 (6- to 7-inch) flour tortillas
4 ounces Neufchâtel cheese, softened
⅓ cup peach preserves
1 cup (4 ounces) shredded nonfat
    Cheddar cheese
½ cup packed washed fresh spinach
    leaves
3 ounces thinly sliced regular or
    smoked turkey breast

1. Spread each tortilla evenly with 1 ounce Neufchâtel cheese; cover with thin layer of preserves. Sprinkle with Cheddar cheese.

2. Arrange spinach leaves and turkey over Cheddar cheese. Roll up tortillas; trim ends. Cover and refrigerate until ready to serve.

3. Cut "rollers" crosswise in half or diagonally into 1-inch pieces.

Makes 8 servings

Nutritional Information per Serving: *Calories: 339, Total Fat: 10 g, Cholesterol: 48 mg, Sodium: 505 mg*

Sassy Salsa Rollers: Substitute salsa for peach preserves and shredded iceberg lettuce for spinach leaves.

Ham 'n' Apple Rollers: Omit peach preserves and spinach leaves. Substitute lean ham slices for turkey. Spread tortillas with Neufchâtel cheese as directed; sprinkle with Cheddar cheese. Top each tortilla with about 2 tablespoons finely chopped apple and 2 ham slices; roll up. Continue as directed.

Cinnamon-Raisin Roll-Ups

4 ounces Neufchâtel cheese, softened
½ cup shredded carrot
¼ cup golden or regular raisins
1 tablespoon honey
¼ teaspoon ground cinnamon
4 (7- to 8-inch) whole wheat or regular
    flour tortillas
8 thin apple wedges (optional)

1. Combine Neufchâtel cheese, carrot, raisins, honey and cinnamon in small bowl; mix well.

2. Spread tortillas evenly with Neufchâtel mixture, leaving ½-inch border around edge of each tortilla. Place 2 apple wedges down center of each tortilla, if desired; roll up. Wrap in plastic wrap. Refrigerate until ready to serve.

Makes 4 servings

Nutritional Information per Serving: *Calories: 240, Total Fat: 9 g, Cholesterol: 25 mg, Sodium: 127 mg*

California Rolls

1 cup reduced-fat ricotta cheese
2 (11-inch) flour tortillas
1 tomato, thinly sliced
2 cups torn spinach leaves
1 cup chopped onion
½ teaspoon dried oregano leaves
½ teaspoon dried basil leaves
1 cup alfalfa sprouts
4 ounces sliced turkey breast

Spread cheese evenly over tortillas to within ¼ inch of edges. Layer tomato, spinach, onion, oregano, basil, alfalfa sprouts and turkey over ⅔ of each tortilla. Roll up tortillas. Wrap in plastic wrap; refrigerate 1 hour. Cut crosswise into 10 slices.

Makes 4 servings

Nutritional Information per Serving: *Calories: 209, Total Fat: 4 g, Cholesterol: 28 mg, Sodium: 233 mg*

Rock 'n' Rollers

Greek Spinach-Cheese Rolls

1 loaf (1 pound) frozen bread dough
1 package (10 ounces) frozen chopped
     spinach, thawed and squeezed dry
¾ cup (3 ounces) crumbled feta cheese
½ cup (2 ounces) shredded reduced-fat
     Monterey Jack cheese
4 green onions, thinly sliced
1 teaspoon dried dill weed
½ teaspoon garlic powder
½ teaspoon black pepper

1. Thaw bread dough according to package directions. Spray 15 muffin cups with nonstick cooking spray; set aside. Roll out dough on lightly floured surface to 15×9-inch rectangle. (If dough is springy and difficult to roll, cover with plastic wrap and let rest 5 minutes to relax.) Position dough so long edge runs parallel to edge of work surface.

2. Combine spinach, cheeses, green onions, dill weed, garlic powder and pepper in large bowl; mix well.

3. Sprinkle spinach mixture evenly over dough to within 1 inch of long edges. Starting at long edge, roll up snugly, pinching seam closed. Place seam side down; cut roll with serrated knife into 1-inch-wide slices. Place slices cut sides up in prepared muffin cups. Cover with plastic wrap; let stand 30 minutes in warm place until rolls are slightly puffy.

4. Preheat oven to 375°F. Bake 20 to 25 minutes or until golden. Serve warm or at room temperature. Rolls can be stored in refrigerator in airtight container up to 2 days.   *Makes 15 servings (1 roll each)*

Nutritional Information per Serving: *Calories: 111, Total Fat: 3 g, Cholesterol: 8 mg, Sodium: 267 mg*

Bean Tortilla Pinwheels

8 corn tortillas (6 inches each)
1 cup GUILTLESS GOURMET® Bean Dip
     (Black or Pinto, mild or spicy)

To soften tortillas, stack 4 tortillas and wrap in damp paper towel. Microwave on HIGH 20 seconds. Or, to soften tortillas in oven, preheat oven to 300°F. Wrap tortillas in foil. Bake 10 minutes.

Spread 2 tablespoons bean dip on each tortilla and roll up tightly. Evenly place toothpicks through rolls, using 6 toothpicks per tortilla. Carefully cut between toothpicks to maintain round shape and obtain 6 pinwheels per tortilla. Serve immediately.
Makes 48 pinwheels

Nutritional Information per Serving (1 bean pinwheel): *Calories: 14, Total Fat: trace, Cholesterol: 0 mg, Sodium: 24 mg*

Nacho Pinwheels: Substitute 1 cup GUILTLESS GOURMET® Nacho Dip (mild or spicy) for the bean dip. Prepare as directed.

Bean & Nacho Pinwheels: Replace ½ cup bean dip with ½ cup GUILTLESS GOURMET® Nacho Dip (mild or spicy). Soften tortillas as directed. Spread each tortilla with 1 tablespoon bean dip and 1 tablespoon nacho dip. Roll up and cut as directed.

Greek Spinach-Cheese Rolls

Turkey-Broccoli Roll-Ups

2 pounds broccoli
⅓ cup nonfat sour cream
¼ cup reduced-calorie mayonnaise
2 tablespoons frozen orange juice
    concentrate, thawed
1 tablespoon Dijon mustard
1 teaspoon dried basil leaves
1 pound smoked turkey, very thinly
    sliced

1. Trim large leaves and tough ends of lower stalks from broccoli; discard. Wash broccoli. Cut stalks lengthwise, including florets, to form approximately 40 (3-inch) spears.

2. Arrange broccoli spears in single layer in large, shallow microwavable dish. Add 1 tablespoon water. Cover dish tightly with heavy-duty plastic wrap; vent. Microwave at HIGH 6 to 7 minutes or just until broccoli is crisp-tender, rearranging spears after 4 minutes. Carefully remove plastic wrap; drain broccoli. Immediately place broccoli in cold water to prevent additional cooking; drain well. Pat dry with paper towels.

3. Combine sour cream, mayonnaise, orange juice concentrate, mustard and basil in small bowl; mix well.

4. Cut turkey slices into 2-inch-wide strips. Spread sour cream mixture evenly onto strips. Place 1 broccoli piece at short end of each strip. Starting at short end, roll up tightly (allow broccoli floret to protrude from one end). Place on serving platter; cover with plastic wrap. Refrigerate until ready to serve.   *Makes 20 servings*

Note: To blanch broccoli on stove top, bring small amount of water to a boil in saucepan. Add broccoli spears; cover. Simmer 2 to 3 minutes or until broccoli is crisp-tender; drain. Cool; continue as directed.

Nutritional Information per Serving (2 pieces):
*Calories: 51, Total Fat: 1 g, Cholesterol: 10 mg,
Sodium: 259 mg*

Egg Rolls

Sweet and Sour Sauce (recipe
    follows)
Nonstick cooking spray
3 green onions, finely chopped
3 cloves garlic, finely chopped
½ teaspoon ground ginger
½ pound boneless skinless chicken
    breasts, cooked and finely
    chopped
2 cups bean sprouts, rinsed and
    drained
½ cup shredded carrots
2 tablespoons reduced-sodium soy
    sauce
¼ teaspoon black pepper
8 egg roll wrappers
2 teaspoons vegetable oil

1. Prepare Sweet and Sour Sauce.

2. Spray large nonstick skillet with cooking spray. Heat over medium-high heat until hot. Add onions, garlic and ginger. Cook and stir 1 minute. Add chicken, bean sprouts and carrots. Cook and stir 2 minutes. Stir in soy sauce and pepper. Cook and stir 1 minute. Remove skillet from heat. Let mixture stand 10 minutes or until cool enough to handle.

3. Brush edges of egg roll wrappers with water. Spoon filling evenly down centers of wrappers. Fold ends over fillings; roll up jelly-roll fashion.

4. Heat oil in another large nonstick skillet over medium heat until hot. Add rolls. Cook 3 to 5 minutes or until golden brown, turning occasionally. Serve hot with Sweet and Sour Sauce.   *Makes 4 servings*

Sweet and Sour Sauce

1 cup water
½ cup sugar
½ cup white vinegar
¼ cup tomato paste
4 teaspoons cornstarch

Combine all ingredients in small saucepan. Bring to a boil over high heat, stirring constantly. Boil 1 minute, stirring constantly. Cool. *Makes about 1½ cups*

Nutritional Information per Serving (2 Egg Rolls): *Calories: 335, Total Fat: 5 g, Cholesterol: 48 mg, Sodium: 465 mg*

Roasted Eggplant Rolls

2 medium eggplants (¾ pound each)
2 tablespoons lemon juice
1 teaspoon olive oil
4 tablespoons (2 ounces) fat-free cream cheese
2 tablespoons nonfat sour cream
1 green onion, minced
4 sun-dried tomatoes (packed in oil), drained and minced
1 clove garlic, minced
¼ teaspoon dried oregano leaves
⅛ teaspoon black pepper
16 medium spinach leaves, washed, stemmed and dried
1 cup bottled spaghetti sauce

1. Preheat oven to 450°F. Spray 2 nonstick baking sheets with nonstick cooking spray; set aside. Trim ends from eggplants; cut lengthwise into ¼-inch-thick slices. Discard outside slices that are mostly skin. (You will have about 16 slices.)

2. Combine lemon juice and olive oil in small bowl; brush lightly over both sides of eggplant slices. Arrange slices in single layer on baking sheets. Bake 10 to 12 minutes or until slightly golden brown on bottom. Turn slices over and bake 10 to 12 minutes more or until golden on both sides and tender. (Slices may not brown evenly; turn slices as they brown. Some very dark spots will occur.) Transfer slices to plate; cool.

3. Meanwhile, stir cream cheese in small bowl until smooth. Add sour cream, green onion, tomatoes, garlic, oregano and pepper; stir until blended.

4. Place eggplant slices on work surface; spread about 1 teaspoon cream cheese mixture evenly over each slice. Arrange spinach leaves on top leaving ½-inch border. Roll up, beginning at narrower end; lay rolls seam side down on serving platter. (If making ahead, cover and refrigerate up to 2 days. Bring to room temperature before serving.) Serve with warm spaghetti sauce.
Makes 8 servings (2 rolls each)

Nutritional Information per Serving: *Calories: 77, Total Fat: 3 g, Cholesterol: 0 mg, Sodium: 213 mg*

Jicama & Shrimp Cocktail with Roasted Red Pepper Sauce

2 large red bell peppers
6 ounces (about 24 medium-large) shrimp, cleaned
1 medium clove garlic
1½ cups fresh cilantro sprigs
2 tablespoons lime juice
2 tablespoons orange juice
½ teaspoon hot pepper sauce
1 small jicama (about ¾ pound), peeled and cut into strips
1 plum tomato, halved, seeded and thinly sliced

1. Place bell peppers on broiler pan. Broil, 4 to 6 inches from heat, about 6 minutes, turning every 2 to 3 minutes or until all sides are charred. Transfer peppers to paper bag; close bag tightly. Let stand 10 minutes or until peppers are cool enough to handle and skins are loosened. Peel peppers; cut in half. Remove cores, seeds and membranes; discard.

2. Add shrimp to large saucepan of boiling water. Reduce heat to medium-low; simmer, uncovered, 2 to 3 minutes or until shrimp turn pink. Drain shrimp; rinse under cold running water. Cover; refrigerate until ready to use.

3. Place peppers and garlic in food processor; process until peppers are coarsely chopped. Add cilantro, lime juice, orange juice and pepper sauce; process until cilantro is finely chopped but mixture is not puréed.

4. Combine jicama, shrimp and tomato in large bowl. Add bell pepper mixture; toss to coat evenly. Serve over lettuce.

Makes 8 servings

Nutritional Information per Serving: *Calories: 69, Total Fat: 1 g, Cholesterol: 42 mg, Sodium: 120 mg*

Smoked Salmon Appetizers

¼ cup reduced-fat or fat-free cream cheese, softened
1 tablespoon chopped fresh dill *or* 1 teaspoon dried dill weed
⅛ teaspoon ground red pepper
4 ounces thinly sliced smoked salmon or lox
24 melba toast rounds or other low-fat crackers

1. Combine cream cheese, dill and pepper in small bowl; stir to blend. Spread evenly over each slice of salmon. Starting with short side, roll up salmon slices jelly-roll fashion. Place on plate; cover with plastic wrap. Chill at least 1 hour or up to 4 hours before serving.

2. Using a sharp knife, cut salmon rolls crosswise into ¾-inch pieces. Place pieces, cut side down, on serving plate. Garnish each piece with dill sprig, if desired. Serve cold or at room temperature with melba rounds. *Makes about 2 dozen appetizers (3 appetizers per serving)*

Nutritional Information per Serving: *Calories: 80, Total Fat: 2 g, Cholesterol: 6 mg, Sodium: 241 mg*

Jicama & Shrimp Cocktail with Roasted Red Pepper Sauce

Sesame Chicken Salad Wonton Cups

Nonstick cooking spray
20 (3-inch) wonton wrappers
1 tablespoon sesame seeds
2 small boneless skinless chicken breasts (about 8 ounces)
1 cup fresh green beans, cut diagonally into ½-inch pieces
¼ cup reduced-calorie mayonnaise
1 tablespoon chopped fresh cilantro (optional)
2 teaspoons honey
1 teaspoon reduced-sodium soy sauce
⅛ teaspoon ground red pepper

1. Preheat oven to 350°F. Spray miniature muffin pan with nonstick cooking spray. Press 1 wonton wrapper into each muffin cup; spray with nonstick cooking spray. Bake 8 to 10 minutes or until golden brown. Cool in pan on wire rack before filling.

2. Place sesame seeds in shallow baking pan. Bake 5 minutes or until lightly toasted, stirring occasionally. Set aside to cool.

3. Meanwhile, bring 2 cups water to a boil in medium saucepan. Add chicken. Reduce heat to low; cover. Simmer 10 minutes or until chicken is no longer pink in center, adding green beans after 7 minutes. Drain.

4. Finely chop chicken. Place in medium bowl. Add green beans and remaining ingredients; mix lightly. Spoon lightly rounded tablespoonful of chicken mixture into each wonton cup.

Makes 10 servings

Nutritional Information per Serving (2 filled wonton cups): *Calories: 103, Total Fat: 3 g, Cholesterol: 18 mg, Sodium: 128 mg*

Spiced Sesame Wonton Crisps

20 (3-inch square) wonton wrappers, cut in half
2 teaspoons olive oil
½ teaspoon paprika
½ teaspoon ground cumin or chili powder
¼ teaspoon dry mustard
1 tablespoon sesame seeds

1. Preheat oven to 375°F. Coat 2 large nonstick baking sheets with nonstick cooking spray.

2. Cut each halved wonton wrapper into 2 strips; place in single layer on prepared baking sheets.

3. Combine 1 tablespoon water, oil, paprika, cumin and mustard in small bowl; mix well. Brush oil mixture evenly onto wonton strips; sprinkle evenly with sesame seeds.

4. Bake 6 to 8 minutes or until lightly browned. Remove to wire rack; cool completely. Transfer to serving plate.

Makes 8 servings

Nutritional Information per Serving (10 pieces): *Calories: 75, Total Fat: 2 g, Cholesterol: 3 mg, Sodium: 116 mg*

Sesame Chicken Salad Wonton Cups

Apricot-Chicken Pot Stickers

2 cups plus 1 tablespoon water,
    divided
2 small boneless skinless chicken
    breasts (about 8 ounces)
2 cups chopped finely shredded
    cabbage
½ cup all-fruit apricot preserves
2 green onions with tops, finely
    chopped
2 teaspoons soy sauce
½ teaspoon grated fresh ginger
⅛ teaspoon black pepper
30 (3-inch) wonton wrappers
    Prepared sweet & sour sauce
    (optional)

1. Bring 2 cups water to boil in medium saucepan. Add chicken. Reduce heat to low; simmer, covered, 10 minutes or until chicken is no longer pink in center. Remove from saucepan; drain.

2. Add cabbage and remaining 1 tablespoon water to saucepan. Cook over high heat 1 to 2 minutes or until water evaporates, stirring occasionally. Remove from heat; cool slightly.

3. Finely chop chicken. Add to saucepan along with preserves, green onions, soy sauce, ginger and pepper; mix well.

4. To assemble pot stickers, remove 3 wonton wrappers at a time from package. Spoon slightly rounded tablespoonful of chicken mixture onto center of each wrapper; brush edges with water. Bring 4 corners together; press to seal. Repeat with remaining wrappers and filling.

5. Spray steamer with nonstick cooking spray. Assemble steamer so that water is ½ inch below steamer basket. Fill steamer basket with pot stickers, leaving enough space between them to prevent sticking.

6. Cover; steam 5 minutes. Transfer pot stickers to serving plate. Serve with prepared sweet & sour sauce, if desired.

Makes 10 servings (3 pot stickers each)

Nutritional Information per Serving: *Calories: 145, Total Fat: 1 g, Cholesterol: 17 mg, Sodium: 223 mg*

Cocktail Stuffed Mushrooms

30 to 40 medium-size mushrooms
1 (14-ounce) package HEALTHY
    CHOICE® Low Fat Polska Kielbasa
    Vegetable cooking spray
¾ cup minced onion
½ cup minced fresh parsley
2 teaspoons minced garlic
½ teaspoon ground fennel
½ teaspoon salt (optional)
¼ teaspoon black pepper
⅛ teaspoon crushed red pepper
1 can HEALTHY CHOICE® Recipe
    Creations™ Cream of Roasted
    Garlic Condensed Soup
⅓ cup fat free shredded Parmesan
    cheese

Wash mushrooms well. Remove stems and mince; set caps aside. In food processor, process Kielbasa until ground. In large nonstick skillet sprayed with vegetable cooking spray, sauté minced mushroom stems, Kielbasa, onion, parsley, garlic, fennel, salt, black pepper and red pepper. Cook until onion is tender.

Remove skillet from heat; add soup to meat mixture and blend well. Fill mushroom caps, dividing meat mixture evenly among caps. Sprinkle with Parmesan cheese. Bake at 400°F 20 to 22 minutes.

Makes 20 servings

Nutritional Information per Serving: *Calories: 45, Total Fat: 1 g, Sodium: 310 mg*

Apricot-Chicken Pot Stickers

Southern Crab Cakes with Rémoulade Dipping Sauce

10 ounces fresh lump crabmeat
1½ cups fresh white or sourdough bread crumbs, divided
¼ cup chopped green onions
½ cup nonfat or reduced-fat mayonnaise, divided
2 tablespoons coarse grain or spicy brown mustard, divided
¾ teaspoon hot pepper sauce, divided
1 egg white, lightly beaten
2 teaspoons olive oil, divided
Lemon wedges

1. Preheat oven to 200°F. Combine crabmeat, ¾ cup bread crumbs and green onions in medium bowl. Add ¼ cup mayonnaise, 1 tablespoon mustard, ½ teaspoon pepper sauce and egg white; mix well. Using ¼ cup mixture per cake, shape eight ½-inch-thick cakes. Roll crab cakes lightly in remaining ¾ cup bread crumbs.

2. Heat large nonstick skillet over medium heat until hot; add 1 teaspoon oil. Add 4 crab cakes; cook 4 to 5 minutes per side or until golden brown. Transfer to serving platter; keep warm in oven. Repeat with remaining 1 teaspoon oil and crab cakes.

3. To prepare dipping sauce, combine remaining ¼ cup mayonnaise, 1 tablespoon mustard and ¼ teaspoon pepper sauce in small bowl; mix well.

4. Serve warm crab cakes with lemon wedges and dipping sauce.

Makes 8 servings

Nutritional Information per Serving: *Calories: 81, Total Fat: 2 g, Cholesterol: 30 mg, Sodium: 376 mg*

Crab Canapés

⅔ cup nonfat pasteurized process cream cheese product, softened
2 teaspoons lemon juice
1 teaspoon hot pepper sauce
1 package (8 ounces) imitation crabmeat or lobster, flaked
⅓ cup chopped red bell pepper
2 green onions with tops, sliced
64 cucumber slices (about 2½ medium cucumbers cut ⅜ inch thick) or melba toast rounds

1. Combine cream cheese, lemon juice and pepper sauce in medium bowl; mix well. Stir in crabmeat, bell pepper and green onions; cover. Chill until ready to serve.

2. When ready to serve, spoon 1½ teaspoons crab mixture onto each cucumber slice. Place on serving plate; garnish with parsley, if desired. *Makes 16 servings*

Nutritional Information per Serving (4 pieces): *Calories: 31, Total Fat: trace, Cholesterol: 5 mg, Sodium: 178 mg*

Southern Crab Cakes with Rémoulade Dipping Sauce

Crown of Salmon Appetizer

1 can HEALTHY CHOICE® Recipe Creations™ Cream of Celery with Sautéed Onion & Garlic Condensed Soup, divided
2 pounds deboned and skinned halibut or other firm white fish, cut into 1-inch cubes
¼ teaspoon dried thyme leaves
⅛ teaspoon ground nutmeg
  Vegetable cooking spray
6 ounces smoked salmon (lox), thinly sliced
¼ cup nonfat milk
1½ tablespoons lemon juice

In food processor, combine half the soup, fish, thyme and nutmeg. Process 30 seconds or until mixture resembles thick pudding. Generously spray 1-quart ring mold with vegetable cooking spray. Press salmon slices into bottom and side of mold. Carefully spoon mousse into ring mold without moving salmon slices. Gently bang mold on flat surface to remove any air bubbles.

Cover mold with wax paper sprayed with vegetable cooking spray; cover waxed paper with flat lid. Place ring mold in roasting pan. Pour hot water into pan to reach two-thirds up side of mold. Bake at 350°F 1 hour. Mousse is done when it is springy to the touch and shrinks from side of mold. Let stand 10 minutes to cool before unmolding.

In small saucepan, combine remaining soup, milk and lemon juice; mix well. Simmer until heated through. Unmold ring onto serving platter. Fill center of ring with favorite green vegetable or salad. Spoon sauce around outside of mousse ring. Serve with toasted bread rounds or crackers.

Makes 12 servings

Nutritional Information per Serving: *Calories: 140, Total Fat: 3½ g, Sodium: 480 mg*

Peppered Shrimp Skewers

16 (12-inch) wooden skewers
⅓ cup teriyaki sauce
⅓ cup ketchup
2 tablespoons dry sherry or water
2 tablespoons reduced-fat peanut butter
1 teaspoon hot pepper sauce
¼ teaspoon ground ginger
32 fresh large shrimp (about 1½ pounds)
2 large yellow bell peppers
32 sugar snap peas, trimmed

1. To prevent burning, soak skewers in water at least 20 minutes before assembling kabobs.

2. Coat rack of broiler pan with nonstick cooking spray; set aside.

3. Combine teriyaki sauce, ketchup, sherry, peanut butter, pepper sauce and ginger in small saucepan. Bring to a boil, stirring constantly. Reduce heat to low; simmer, uncovered, 1 minute. Remove from heat; set aside.

4. Peel and devein shrimp, leaving tails intact.

5. Cut each bell pepper lengthwise into 4 quarters; remove stems and seeds. Cut each quarter crosswise into 4 equal pieces. Thread 2 shrimp, bell pepper pieces and sugar snap peas onto each skewer; place on prepared broiler pan. Brush with teriyaki sauce mixture.

6. Broil, 4 inches from heat, 3 minutes; turn over. Brush with teriyaki sauce mixture; broil 2 minutes longer or until shrimp turn pink. Serve with any remaining teriyaki sauce mixture. Transfer to serving plates.

Makes 16 servings

Nutritional Information per Serving: *Calories: 69, Total Fat: 1 g, Cholesterol: 66 mg, Sodium: 258 mg*

Mini Beef & Potato Kabobs

1 large Colorado Russet Potato, baked
1 green bell pepper, cut into ¾-inch cubes
1 small onion, cut into wedges
½ pound beef tenderloin, cut into ¾-inch cubes
Bamboo skewers

MARINADE:

¼ cup olive oil
¼ cup balsamic vinegar
1 tablespoon snipped fresh thyme
1 tablespoon snipped fresh basil
1 tablespoon snipped fresh parsley
1 clove garlic, minced
½ teaspoon sugar
½ teaspoon salt
½ teaspoon black pepper

Cut baked potato lengthwise into quarters, then cut crosswise into ¾-inch chunks. Drop bell pepper and onion wedges into boiling water 1 to 2 minutes; drain. For marinade, combine olive oil, vinegar, herbs, garlic, sugar, salt and black pepper in large bowl. Add meat, onion and potato; toss to coat well. Cover and chill several hours or overnight. Soak bamboo skewers in hot water 5 minutes. Thread meat, potato, bell pepper and onion on skewers. Grill over medium-high heat 5 to 7 minutes, turning once. Or, broil 5 to 6 inches from heat 5 to 7 minutes or to desired doneness.

Makes 4 servings

Nutritional Information per Serving: *Calories: 281, Total Fat: 18 g, Cholesterol: 35 mg, Sodium: 304 mg*

Favorite recipe from **Colorado Potato Administrative Committee**

Southwest Barbecue Kabobs

1 cup beer
¾ cup A.1.® Steak Sauce
2 cloves garlic, crushed
2 teaspoons chili powder
1 teaspoon ground cumin
1½ pounds round steak, cut into ½-inch strips
3 small red or green bell peppers, cut into 1-inch pieces
1 teaspoon cornstarch

In small bowl, combine beer, steak sauce, garlic, chili powder and cumin. Pour marinade over sliced steak in nonmetal dish. Cover; refrigerate 2 hours, stirring occasionally.

Remove steak from marinade; reserve marinade. Thread steak and pepper pieces alternately onto 6 skewers. In small saucepan, heat reserved marinade and cornstarch to a boil. Grill or broil kabobs, 4 inches from heat source, 15 minutes or until done, turning and brushing often with marinade. Heat remaining marinade to a boil; serve with kabobs.

Makes 6 appetizer servings

Nutritional Information per Serving: *Calories: 198, Total Fat: 4 g, Cholesterol: 71 mg, Sodium: 624 mg*

Soft Pretzels

1 package (16 ounces) hot roll mix,
    plus ingredients to prepare mix
1 egg white
2 teaspoons water
2 tablespoons *each* assorted coatings:
    grated Parmesan cheese, sesame
    seeds, poppy seeds, dried oregano
    leaves

1. Prepare hot roll mix according to package directions.

2. Preheat oven to 375°F. Spray baking sheets with nonstick cooking spray; set aside.

3. Divide dough equally into 16 pieces; roll each piece with hands to form a rope, 7 to 10 inches long. Place on prepared cookie sheets; form into desired shape (hearts, wreaths, pretzels, snails, loops, etc.).

4. Beat together egg white and water in small bowl until foamy. Brush onto dough shapes; sprinkle each shape with 1½ teaspoons of one of the coatings.

5. Bake until golden brown, about 15 minutes. Serve warm or at room temperature.

Makes 8 servings

Nutritional Information per Serving: *Calories: 214, Total Fat: 6 g, Cholesterol: 20 mg, Sodium: 315 mg*

Fruit Twists: Omit coatings. Prepare dough and roll into ropes as directed. Place ropes on lightly floured surface. Roll out, or pat, each rope into rectangle, ¼ inch thick; brush each rectangle with about 1 teaspoon spreadable fruit or preserves. Fold each rectangle lengthwise in half; twist into desired shape. Bake as directed.

Cheese Twists: Omit coatings. Prepare dough and roll into rectangles as directed in Fruit Twists. Sprinkle each rectangle with about 1 tablespoon shredded Cheddar or other flavor cheese. Fold dough rectangles, shape and bake as directed for Fruit Twists.

Oven-Fried Tex-Mex Onion Rings

½ cup plain dry bread crumbs
⅓ cup yellow cornmeal
1½ teaspoons chili powder
⅛ to ¼ teaspoon ground red pepper
⅛ teaspoon salt
1 tablespoon plus 1½ teaspoons
    margarine, melted
2 medium onions (about 10 ounces),
    sliced ⅜ inch thick
2 egg whites

1. Preheat oven to 450°F. Spray large nonstick baking sheet with nonstick cooking spray; set aside.

2. Combine bread crumbs, cornmeal, chili powder, pepper and salt in medium shallow dish; mix well. Stir in margarine and 1 teaspoon water.

3. Separate onion slices into rings. Place egg whites in large bowl; beat lightly. Add onions; toss lightly to coat evenly. Transfer to bread crumb mixture; toss to coat evenly. Place in single layer on prepared baking sheet.

4. Bake 12 to 15 minutes or until onions are tender and coating is crisp.

Makes 6 servings

Nutritional Information per Serving: *Calories: 111, Total Fat: 4 g, Cholesterol: 0 mg, Sodium: 184 mg*

Soft Pretzels

Herbed Potato Chips

Nonstick olive oil-flavored cooking
 spray
2 medium-sized red potatoes (about
 ½ pound), unpeeled
1 tablespoon olive oil
2 tablespoons minced fresh dill, thyme
 or rosemary *or* 2 teaspoons dried
 dill weed, thyme or rosemary
¼ teaspoon garlic salt
⅛ teaspoon black pepper
1¼ cups nonfat sour cream

1. Preheat oven to 450°F. Spray large
nonstick baking sheets with cooking spray;
set aside.

2. Cut potatoes crosswise into very thin
slices, about ¹⁄₁₆ inch thick. Pat dry with
paper towels. Arrange potato slices in single
layer on prepared baking sheets; coat
potatoes with cooking spray.

3. Bake 10 minutes; turn slices over. Brush
with oil. Combine dill, garlic salt and pepper
in small bowl; sprinkle evenly onto potato
slices. Continue baking 5 to 10 minutes or
until potatoes are golden brown. Cool on
baking sheets.

4. Serve with sour cream.

Makes about 60 chips

**Nutritional Information per Serving (10 chips,
about 3 tablespoons sour cream):** *Calories: 76,
Total Fat: 2 g, Cholesterol: 0 mg, Sodium: 113 mg*

Potato Skins with Cheddar Melt

4 medium-size Idaho baking potatoes
 (about 2 pounds)
4 slices lean turkey bacon
2 tablespoons vegetable oil
2 cups (8 ounces) shredded ALPINE
 LACE® Reduced Fat Cheddar
 Cheese
¼ cup fat free sour cream
2 tablespoons finely chopped chives or
 green onions
1 tablespoon minced jalapeño pepper

1. Place a piece of foil on the bottom rack of
the oven and preheat the oven to 425°F.
Scrub the potatoes well and pierce the skins
a few times with a sharp knife. Place the
potatoes directly on the middle oven rack
and bake for 1 hour or until soft.

2. Meanwhile, in a small skillet, cook the
bacon over medium heat until crisp. Drain
on paper towels, then crumble the bacon.

3. Using a serrated knife, cut the potatoes in
half lengthwise. With a small spoon, scoop
out the pulp, leaving a ¼-inch-thick shell.
(Save the potato pulp for another use.) Cut
the skins into appetizer-size triangles.

4. Place the skins on a baking sheet, brush
the insides with the oil and bake for 15
minutes or until crisp.

5. Remove the skins from the oven, sprinkle
with the cheese and return to the oven for 5
minutes or until the cheese melts. Top the
skins with the sour cream, then sprinkle with
the chives, jalapeño pepper and bacon.

Makes about 24 appetizers

Nutritional Information per Serving: *Calories: 58,
Total Fat: 3 g, Cholesterol: 7 mg, Sodium: 147 mg*

Herbed Potato Chips

S'More Gorp

2 cups honey graham cereal
2 cups low-fat granola cereal
2 cups crispy multi-bran cereal squares
2 tablespoons reduced-calorie margarine
1 tablespoon honey
¼ teaspoon ground cinnamon
¾ cup miniature marshmallows
½ cup dried fruit bits or raisins
¼ cup mini semisweet chocolate chips

1. Preheat oven to 275°F.

2. Combine cereals in nonstick 15×10×1-inch jelly-roll pan. Melt margarine in small saucepan; stir in honey and cinnamon. Pour margarine mixture evenly over cereal mixture; toss until cereals are well coated. Spread mixture evenly onto bottom of pan.

3. Bake 35 to 40 minutes or until crisp, stirring after 20 minutes. Cool completely.

4. Add marshmallows, fruit bits and chocolate chips; toss to mix.

Makes 16 servings

Nutritional Information per Serving: *Calories 137, Total Fat: 3 g, Cholesterol: trace, Sodium: 138 mg*

Trail Mix Truffles

⅓ cup dried apples
¼ cup dried apricots
¼ cup apple butter
2 tablespoons golden raisins
1 tablespoon reduced-fat peanut butter
½ cup low-fat granola
¼ cup graham cracker crumbs, divided
¼ cup mini chocolate chips

Blend fruit, apple butter, raisins and peanut butter in food processor until smooth. Stir in granola, 1 tablespoon crumbs, chips and 1 tablespoon water.

Place remaining crumbs in bowl. Shape tablespoonfuls mixture into balls; roll in crumbs. Cover; refrigerate until ready to serve. *Makes 8 servings*

Nutritional Information per Serving: *Calories: 121, Total Fat: 4 g, Cholesterol: 0 mg, Sodium: 14 mg*

Southwest Snack Mix

4 cups corn cereal squares
2 cups unsalted pretzels
½ cup unsalted pumpkin or squash seeds
1½ teaspoons chili powder
1 teaspoon minced cilantro or parsley
½ teaspoon garlic powder
½ teaspoon onion powder
1 egg white
2 tablespoons olive oil
2 tablespoons lime juice

1. Preheat oven to 300°F. Spray large nonstick baking sheet with nonstick cooking spray.

2. Combine cereal, pretzels and pumpkin seeds in large bowl. Combine chili powder, cilantro, garlic powder and onion powder in small bowl.

3. Whisk together egg white, oil and lime juice in separate small bowl. Pour over cereal mixture; toss to coat evenly. Add seasoning mixture; mix lightly to coat evenly. Transfer to prepared baking sheet.

4. Bake 45 minutes, stirring every 15 minutes; cool. Store in airtight container.

Makes 12 servings

Variation: Substitute ½ cup unsalted peanuts for pumpkin seeds.

Nutritional Information per Serving: *Calories: 93, Total Fat: 3 g, Cholesterol: 0 mg, Sodium: 114 mg*

S'More Gorp

50

Pleasin' Peanutty Snack Mix

4 cups whole wheat cereal squares *or*
 2 cups whole wheat and 2 cups
 corn or rice cereal squares
2 cups small pretzel twists or goldfish-
 shaped pretzels
½ cup dry roasted peanuts
2 tablespoons creamy peanut butter
1 tablespoon honey
1 tablespoon apple juice or water
2 teaspoons vanilla
 Nonstick cooking spray
½ cup raisins, dried fruit bits or dried
 cherries (optional)

1. Preheat oven to 250°F.

2. Combine cereal, pretzels and peanuts in large bowl; set aside.

3. Combine peanut butter, honey and apple juice in 1-cup glass measure or small microwavable bowl. Microwave at HIGH 30 seconds or until hot. Stir in vanilla.

4. Drizzle peanut butter mixture evenly over cereal mixture; toss lightly to evenly coat. Place mixture in single layer in *ungreased* 15×10-inch jelly-roll pan; coat lightly with cooking spray.

5. Bake 8 minutes; stir. Continue baking 8 to 9 minutes or until golden brown. Remove from oven. Add raisins, if desired; mix lightly.

6. Spread mixture in single layer on large sheet of aluminum foil to cool.

Makes 10 (⅔-cup) servings

Nutritional Information per Serving: *Calories: 174, Total Fat: 6 g, Cholesterol: 0 mg, Sodium: 349 mg*

Fruit Antipasto Platter

1 DOLE® Fresh Pineapple
2 medium, firm DOLE® Bananas, sliced
 diagonally
2 DOLE® Oranges, peeled and sliced
½ cup thinly sliced DOLE® Red Onion
½ pound low-fat sharp Cheddar cheese,
 cut into 1-inch cubes
2 jars (6 ounces each) marinated
 artichoke hearts, drained and
 halved
 DOLE® Green or Red Leaf Lettuce
½ cup fat-free or light Italian salad
 dressing

• Twist crown from pineapple. Quarter pineapple lengthwise; remove core. Cut whole fruit from skin; slice fruit into thin wedges.

• Arrange pineapple, bananas, oranges, onion, cheese and artichoke hearts on lettuce-lined platter; serve with dressing. Garnish with orange zest and fresh herbs, if desired. *Makes 10 servings*

Prep Time: 25 minutes

Nutritional Information per Serving: *Calories: 195, Total Fat: 4 g, Cholesterol: 16 mg, Sodium: 308 mg*

Citrus Cooler

2 cups fresh squeezed orange juice
2 cups unsweetened pineapple juice
1 teaspoon fresh lemon juice
¾ teaspoon vanilla extract
¾ teaspoon coconut extract
2 cups cold sparkling water

1. Combine juices and extracts in large pitcher. Stir in sparkling water; serve over ice. *Makes 8 servings*

Nutritional Information per Serving (¾ cup): *Calories: 66, Total Fat: <1 g, Cholesterol: 0 mg, Sodium: 2 mg*

Oregon Hot Apple Cider

8 whole cloves
8 cups apple cider
½ cup dried cherries
½ cup dried cranberries
3 cinnamon sticks, broken in half
1 pear, quartered, cored and sliced

1. Bundle cloves in small piece of cheesecloth. Tie cheesecloth to form small sack.

2. Combine cider, cherries, cranberries, cinnamon and cheesecloth sack in large saucepan. Heat just to a simmer; *do not boil.* Remove cheesecloth sack and discard.

3. Add pear before serving.

Makes 8 servings

Nutritional Information per Serving: *Calories: 180, Total Fat: 1 g, Cholesterol: 0 mg, Sodium: 10 mg*

Piña Colada Punch

3 cups water
10 whole cloves
4 cardamom pods
2 sticks cinnamon
1 can (12 ounces) frozen pineapple juice concentrate, thawed
1 pint low-fat piña colada frozen yogurt, softened*
1¼ cups lemon seltzer water
1¼ teaspoons rum extract
¾ teaspoon coconut extract (optional)

You may substitute pineapple sherbet for low-fat piña colada frozen yogurt. When using pineapple sherbet, use the coconut extract for a more authentic flavor.

1. Combine water, cloves, cardamom and cinnamon in small saucepan. Bring to a boil over high heat; reduce heat to low. Simmer, covered, 5 minutes; cool. Strain and discard spices.

2. Combine spiced water, pineapple juice concentrate and frozen yogurt in small punch bowl or pitcher. Stir until frozen yogurt is melted. Stir in seltzer water, rum extract and coconut extract, if desired.

Makes 12 servings

Nutritional Information per Serving: *Calories: 93, Total Fat: <1 g, Cholesterol: 2 mg, Sodium: 14 mg*

Cranberry-Lime Margarita Punch

6 cups water
1 container (12 ounces) frozen cranberry juice cocktail
½ cup lime juice
¼ cup sugar
2 cups ice cubes
1 cup ginger ale or tequila
1 lime, sliced

1. Combine water, cranberry juice, lime juice and sugar in punch bowl; stir until sugar dissolves.

2. Stir in ice cubes, ginger ale and lime; garnish with fresh cranberries, if desired.

Makes 10 servings

Nutritional Information per Serving: *Calories: 97, Total Fat: trace, Cholesterol: 0 mg, Sodium: 3 mg*

Breakfast & Brunch

Triple-Decker Vegetable Omelet

1 cup finely chopped broccoli
½ cup diced red bell pepper
½ cup shredded carrot
⅓ cup sliced green onions
1 clove garlic, minced
2½ teaspoons FLEISCHMANN'S® 70%
　　Corn Oil Spread, divided
¾ cup low fat cottage cheese
　　(1% milkfat), divided
1 tablespoon plain dry bread crumbs
1 tablespoon grated Parmesan cheese
½ teaspoon Italian seasoning
1½ cups EGG BEATERS® Healthy Real Egg
　　Substitute, divided
⅓ cup chopped tomato
　　Chopped fresh parsley, for garnish

In 8-inch nonstick skillet, over medium-high heat, sauté broccoli, bell pepper, carrot, green onions and garlic in 1 teaspoon spread until tender. Remove from skillet; stir in ½ cup cottage cheese. Keep warm. Combine bread crumbs, Parmesan cheese and Italian seasoning; set aside.

In same skillet, over medium heat, melt ½ teaspoon spread. Pour ½ cup Egg Beaters® into skillet. Cook, lifting edges to allow uncooked portion to flow underneath. When almost set, slide unfolded omelet onto ovenproof serving platter. Top with half each of the vegetable mixture and bread crumb mixture; set aside.

Prepare 2 more omelets with remaining Egg Beaters® and spread. Layer 1 omelet onto serving platter over vegetable and bread crumb mixture; top with remaining vegetable mixture and bread crumb mixture. Layer with remaining omelet. Top omelet with remaining cottage cheese and tomato. Bake at 425°F for 5 to 7 minutes or until heated through. Garnish with parsley. Cut into wedges to serve.

Makes 4 servings

Prep Time: 20 minutes

Cook Time: 30 minutes

Nutritional Information per Serving: *Calories: 124, Total Fat: 3 g, Cholesterol: 3 mg, Sodium: 363 mg*

Triple-Decker Vegetable Omelet

Western Omelet

½ cup finely chopped red or green bell
   pepper
⅓ cup cubed cooked potato
2 slices turkey bacon, diced
¼ teaspoon dried oregano leaves
2 teaspoons FLEISCHMANN'S® 70%
   Corn Oil Spread, divided
1 cup EGG BEATERS® Healthy Real Egg
   Substitute
Fresh oregano sprig, for garnish

In 8-inch nonstick skillet, over medium heat,
sauté bell pepper, potato, turkey bacon and
dried oregano in 1 teaspoon spread until
tender.* Remove from skillet; keep warm.

In same skillet, over medium heat, melt
remaining 1 teaspoon spread. Pour Egg
Beaters® into skillet. Cook, lifting edges to
allow uncooked portion to flow underneath.
When almost set, spoon vegetable mixture
over half of omelet. Fold other half over
vegetable mixture; slide onto serving plate.
Garnish with fresh oregano.

Makes 2 servings

Prep Time: 15 minutes

Cook Time: 10 minutes

*For frittata, sauté vegetables, turkey bacon and dried
oregano in 2 teaspoons spread. Pour Egg Beaters®
evenly into skillet over vegetable mixture. Cook without
stirring for 4 to 5 minutes or until cooked on bottom
and almost set on top. Carefully turn frittata; cook for
1 to 2 minutes more or until done. Slide onto serving
platter; cut into wedges to serve.*

Nutritional Information per Serving: *Calories: 147,
Total Fat: 6 g, Cholesterol: 10 mg, Sodium: 384 mg*

Italian Omelet

¼ cup chopped tomato
¼ cup (1 ounce) shredded part-skim
   mozzarella cheese
¼ teaspoon dried basil leaves
¼ teaspoon dried oregano leaves
1 teaspoon FLEISCHMANN'S® 70%
   Corn Oil Spread
1 cup EGG BEATERS® Healthy Real Egg
   Substitute
Chopped fresh parsley, for garnish

In small bowl, combine tomato, cheese,
basil and oregano; set aside.

In 8-inch nonstick skillet, over medium heat,
melt spread. Pour Egg Beaters® into skillet.
Cook, lifting edges to allow uncooked
portion to flow underneath. When almost
set, spoon tomato mixture over half of
omelet. Fold other half over tomato mixture;
cover and continue to cook for 1 to 2
minutes. Slide onto serving plate. Garnish
with parsley.   *Makes 2 servings*

Prep Time: 10 minutes

Cook Time: 10 minutes

Nutritional Information per Serving: *Calories: 119,
Total Fat: 4 g, Cholesterol: 8 mg, Sodium: 286 mg*

Western Omelet

Breakfast Burritos with Tomato-Basil Topping

1 large tomato, diced
2 teaspoons finely chopped basil *or*
⅛ teaspoon dried basil leaves
1 medium potato, peeled and
shredded (about 1 cup)
¼ cup chopped onion
2 teaspoons FLEISCHMANN'S® 70%
Corn Oil Spread
1 cup EGG BEATERS® Healthy Real Egg
Substitute
⅛ teaspoon ground black pepper
4 (8-inch) flour tortillas, warmed
⅓ cup shredded reduced-fat Cheddar
cheese

In small bowl, combine tomato and basil; set aside.

In large nonstick skillet, over medium heat, sauté potato and onion in spread until tender. Pour Egg Beaters® into skillet; sprinkle with pepper. Cook, stirring occasionally, until mixture is set.

Divide egg mixture evenly between tortillas; top with cheese. Fold tortillas over egg mixture. Top with tomato mixture.

Makes 4 servings

Prep Time: 15 minutes

Cook Time: 25 minutes

Nutritional Information per Serving: *Calories: 226, Total Fat: 6 g, Cholesterol: 5 mg, Sodium: 364 mg*

Spinach and Mushroom Enchiladas

2 packages (10 ounces each) frozen
chopped spinach, thawed
1 can (15 ounces) pinto beans, rinsed
and drained
1½ cups sliced mushrooms
3 teaspoons chili powder, divided
¼ teaspoon red pepper flakes
1 can (8 ounces) low-sodium tomato
sauce
2 tablespoons water
½ teaspoon hot pepper sauce
8 (8-inch) corn tortillas
1 cup (4 ounces) shredded Monterey
Jack cheese
Shredded lettuce (optional)
Chopped tomatoes (optional)

1. Combine spinach, beans, mushrooms, 2 teaspoons chili powder and red pepper in large skillet over medium heat. Cook and stir 5 minutes; remove from heat.

2. Combine tomato sauce, water, remaining 1 teaspoon chili powder and pepper sauce in medium skillet. Dip tortillas into tomato sauce mixture; stack tortillas on waxed paper.

3. Divide spinach filling into 8 portions. Spoon onto centers of tortillas; roll up and place in 12×8-inch microwavable dish. Spread remaining tomato sauce mixture over enchiladas.

4. Cover with vented plastic wrap. Microwave at MEDIUM (50% power) 10 minutes or until heated through. Sprinkle with cheese. Microwave at MEDIUM 3 minutes or until cheese is melted. Serve with lettuce and tomatoes, if desired.

Makes 4 servings

Nutritional Information per Serving: *Calories 385, Total Fat: 11 g, Cholesterol: 25 mg, Sodium: 741 mg*

Breakfast Burritos with Tomato-Basil Topping

Blintzes with Raspberry Sauce

1 (16-ounce) container low fat cottage
    cheese (1% milkfat)
3 tablespoons EGG BEATERS® Healthy
    Real Egg Substitute
½ teaspoon sugar
10 prepared French Breakfast Crepes
    (recipe follows)
    Raspberry Sauce (recipe follows)

In small bowl, combine cottage cheese, Egg
Beaters® and sugar; spread 2 tablespoonfuls
mixture down center of each crepe. Fold
two opposite ends of each crepe over filling,
then fold in sides like an envelope. In lightly
greased large nonstick skillet, over medium
heat, place blintzes seam-side down. Cook
for 4 minutes on each side or until golden
brown. Serve hot with Raspberry Sauce.

Makes 10 servings

Prep Time: 30 minutes

Cook Time: 45 minutes

Raspberry Sauce: In electric blender
container or food processor, purée 1 (16-
ounce) package frozen raspberries, thawed;
strain. Stir in 2 tablespoons sugar. Serve over
blintzes.

Nutritional Information per Serving: *Calories: 161,
Total Fat: 2 g, Cholesterol: 2 mg, Sodium: 231 mg*

French Breakfast Crepes

1 cup all-purpose flour
1 cup skim milk
⅔ cup EGG BEATERS® Healthy Real Egg
    Substitute
1 tablespoon FLEISCHMANN'S® 70%
    Corn Oil Spread, melted

In medium bowl, combine flour, milk, Egg
Beaters® and spread; let stand 30 minutes.

Heat lightly greased 8-inch nonstick skillet or
crepe pan over medium-high heat. Pour in
scant ¼ cup batter, tilting pan to cover
bottom. Cook for 1 to 2 minutes; turn and
cook for 30 seconds to 1 minute more. Place
on waxed paper. Stir batter and repeat to
make 10 crepes. Fill with desired fillings or
use in recipes calling for prepared crepes.

Makes 10 crepes

Prep Time: 10 minutes

Cook Time: 40 minutes

Nutritional Information per Serving (1 crepe):
Calories: 73, Total Fat: 1 g, Cholesterol: 0 mg, Sodium: 51 mg

Artichoke-Pepper Torte

2½ cups chopped water bagels (about
    3 bagels)
2 tablespoons olive oil
3 teaspoons dried chives, divided
    Vegetable cooking spray
2 (8-ounce) packages fat free cream
    cheese, softened
1 (15-ounce) container fat free ricotta
    cheese
1 can HEALTHY CHOICE® Recipe
    Creations™ Cream of Broccoli with
    Cheddar and Onion Condensed
    Soup
1 (4-ounce) container fat free egg
    substitute (equivalent to 2 eggs)
1 tablespoon salt free ground herbs
    and spices
1 teaspoon garlic salt
1 (8.5-ounce) can artichoke hearts,
    drained and chopped
1 (15-ounce) jar roasted red bell
    peppers, drained and chopped
1 cup chopped fresh basil

In medium bowl, combine bagels, oil and 1 teaspoon chives; mix well. Spray 9×2½-inch springform baking pan with vegetable cooking spray. Press bagel mixture into bottom of springform pan. Bake at 375°F 15 minutes; cool.

With electric mixer, combine cheeses, soup, egg substitute, herbs, garlic salt and remaining 2 teaspoons chives; mix well. Spread half the cheese mixture over bagel crust. Top with artichokes and half each of peppers and basil. Spread remaining cheese filling over basil; top with remaining peppers. Bake at 375°F 1 hour or until set in middle; cool. Refrigerate 6 to 8 hours or overnight. Run knife around edge of torte; remove side of pan. Top with remaining basil. Slice thinly and serve with crackers.

Makes 20 servings

Nutritional Information per Serving: *Calories: 100, Total Fat: 2 g, Sodium: 470 mg*

Asparagus-Swiss Soufflé

¼ cup unsalted butter substitute
½ cup chopped yellow onion
¼ cup all-purpose flour
½ teaspoon salt
¼ teaspoon cayenne pepper
1 cup 2% low fat milk
1 cup (4 ounces) shredded ALPINE LACE® Reduced Fat Swiss Cheese
1 cup egg substitute *or* 4 large eggs
1 cup coarsely chopped fresh asparagus pieces, cooked or frozen asparagus pieces, thawed and drained
3 large egg whites

1. Preheat the oven to 325°F. Spray a 1½-quart soufflé dish with nonstick cooking spray.

2. In a large saucepan, melt the butter over medium heat, add the onion and sauté for 5 minutes or until soft. Stir in the flour, salt and pepper and cook for 2 minutes or until bubbly. Add the milk and cook, stirring constantly, for 5 minutes or until the sauce thickens. Add the cheese and stir until melted.

3. In a small bowl, whisk the egg substitute (or the whole eggs). Whisk in a little of the hot cheese sauce, then return this egg mixture to the saucepan and whisk until well blended. Remove from the heat and fold in the drained asparagus.

4. In a medium-size bowl, using an electric mixer set on high, beat the egg whites until stiff peaks form. Fold the hot cheese sauce into the whites, then spoon into the soufflé dish.

5. Place the soufflé on a baking sheet and bake for 50 minutes or until golden brown and puffy.

Makes 8 servings

Nutritional Information per Serving: *Calories: 164, Total Fat: 9 g, Cholesterol: 13 mg, Sodium: 247 mg*

Eggs Santa Fe

2 eggs
½ cup GUILTLESS GOURMET® Black
   Bean Dip (mild or spicy)
¼ cup GUILTLESS GOURMET® Salsa
   (medium)
1 ounce (about 18) GUILTLESS
   GOURMET® Unsalted Baked Tortilla
   Chips
2 tablespoons low fat sour cream
1 teaspoon chopped fresh cilantro
   Fresh cilantro sprigs (optional)

To poach eggs, bring water to a boil in small skillet over high heat; reduce heat to medium-low and maintain a simmer. Gently break eggs into water, being careful not to break yolks. Cover and simmer 5 minutes or until desired firmness.

Meanwhile, place bean dip in small microwave-safe bowl or small saucepan. Microwave bean dip on HIGH 2 to 3 minutes or heat over medium heat until warm. To serve, spread ¼ cup warm bean dip in center of serving plate; top with 1 poached egg and 2 tablespoons salsa. Arrange 10 tortilla chips around egg. Dollop with 1 tablespoon sour cream and sprinkle with ½ teaspoon chopped cilantro. Repeat with remaining ingredients. Garnish with cilantro sprigs, if desired.

Makes 2 servings

Nutritional Information per Serving: *Calories: 217, Total Fat: 7 g, Cholesterol: 218 mg, Sodium: 430 mg*

Chile Scramble

2 tablespoons minced onion
1 teaspoon FLEISCHMANN'S® 70%
   Corn Oil Spread
1 cup EGG BEATERS® Healthy Real Egg
   Substitute
1 (4-ounce) can diced green chiles,
   drained
¼ cup whole kernel corn
2 tablespoons diced pimientos

In 10-inch nonstick skillet, over medium-high heat, sauté onion in spread for 2 to 3 minutes or until onion is translucent. Pour Egg Beaters® into skillet; cook, stirring occasionally, until mixture is set. Stir in chiles, corn and pimientos; cook 1 minute more or until heated through.

Makes 2 servings

Prep Time: 5 minutes

Cook Time: 10 minutes

Nutritional Information per Serving: *Calories: 118, Total Fat: 2 g, Cholesterol: 0 mg, Sodium: 254 mg*

Eggs Santa Fe

Mini Vegetable Quiches

2 cups cut-up vegetables (bell peppers, broccoli, zucchini and/or carrots)
2 tablespoons chopped green onions
2 tablespoons FLEISCHMANN'S® 70% Corn Oil Spread
4 (8-inch) flour tortillas, each cut into 8 triangles
1 cup EGG BEATERS® Healthy Real Egg Substitute
1 cup skim milk
½ teaspoon dried basil leaves

In medium nonstick skillet, over medium-high heat, sauté vegetables and green onions in spread until tender.

Arrange 4 tortilla pieces in each of 8 (6-ounce) greased custard cups or ramekins, placing points of tortilla pieces at center of bottom of cup and pressing lightly to form shape of cup. Divide vegetable mixture evenly among cups. In small bowl, combine Egg Beaters®, milk and basil. Pour evenly over vegetable mixture. Place cups on baking sheet. Bake at 375°F for 20 to 25 minutes or until puffed and knife inserted into centers comes out clean. Let stand 5 minutes before serving.   *Makes 8 servings*

Prep Time: 25 minutes

Cook Time: 30 minutes

Nutritional Information per Serving: *Calories: 122, Total Fat: 4 g, Cholesterol: 1 mg, Sodium: 198 mg*

Vegetable Quiche

Vegetable cooking spray
2 cups frozen diced potatoes with onions and peppers, thawed
1 can HEALTHY CHOICE® Recipe Creations™ Cream of Mushroom with Cracked Pepper & Herbs Condensed Soup, divided
1 (16-ounce) package frozen mixed vegetables (such as zucchini, carrots and beans), thawed and drained
1 cup fat free egg substitute (equivalent to 4 eggs)
½ cup fat free shredded Parmesan cheese, divided
¼ cup nonfat milk
¼ teaspoon dried dill weed

In 9-inch pie plate sprayed with vegetable cooking spray, press potatoes onto bottom and side to form crust. Spray potatoes lightly with vegetable cooking spray. Bake at 400°F 15 minutes.

In small bowl, combine half the soup, mixed vegetables, egg substitute and half the cheese; mix well. Pour egg mixture into potato shell; sprinkle with remaining cheese. Bake at 375°F 35 to 40 minutes or until set.

In small saucepan, combine remaining soup, milk and dill; mix well. Simmer 5 minutes until heated through. Serve sauce with quiche.   *Makes 6 servings*

Nutritional Information per Serving: *Calories: 113, Total Fat: 1 g, Sodium: 436 mg*

Mini Vegetable Quiches

Zucchini Mushroom Frittata

1½ cups EGG BEATERS® Healthy Real Egg
    Substitute
½ cup (2 ounces) shredded reduced-fat
    Swiss cheese
¼ cup skim milk
½ teaspoon garlic powder
¼ teaspoon seasoned pepper
    Nonstick cooking spray
1 medium zucchini, shredded (1 cup)
1 medium tomato, chopped
1 (4-ounce) can sliced mushrooms,
    drained
    Tomato slices and fresh basil leaves,
    for garnish

In medium bowl, combine Egg Beaters®, cheese, milk, garlic powder and seasoned pepper; set aside.

Spray 10-inch ovenproof nonstick skillet lightly with nonstick cooking spray. Over medium-high heat, sauté zucchini, tomato and mushrooms in skillet until tender. Pour egg mixture into skillet, stirring well. Cover; cook over low heat for 15 minutes or until cooked on bottom and almost set on top. Remove lid and place skillet under broiler for 2 to 3 minutes or until desired doneness. Slide onto serving platter; cut into wedges to serve. Garnish with tomato slices and basil. *Makes 6 servings*

Prep Time: 20 minutes

Cook Time: 20 minutes

Nutritional Information per Serving: *Calories: 71, Total Fat: 2 g, Cholesterol: 7 mg, Sodium: 147 mg*

Spinach Quiche

½ cup chopped onion
1 clove garlic, crushed
1 teaspoon FLEISCHMANN'S® 70%
    Corn Oil Spread
1 (10-ounce) package frozen chopped
    spinach, thawed and well drained
1 (9-inch) pastry crust, unbaked
1 cup EGG BEATERS® Healthy Real Egg
    Substitute
1 cup skim milk
1 tablespoon all-purpose flour
1 teaspoon dried basil leaves
¾ teaspoon liquid hot pepper
    seasoning

In medium nonstick skillet, over medium-high heat, sauté onion and garlic in spread until tender; add spinach. Spoon into bottom of pie crust; set aside.

In small bowl, combine Egg Beaters®, milk, flour, basil and liquid hot pepper seasoning; pour evenly over spinach mixture. Bake at 350°F for 45 to 50 minutes or until knife inserted in center comes out clean. Let stand 10 minutes before serving.

Makes 8 servings

Prep Time: 30 minutes

Cook Time: 50 minutes

Nutritional Information per Serving: *Calories: 156, Total Fat: 8 g, Cholesterol: 1 mg, Sodium: 234 mg*

Salmon Quiche: Prepare as above substituting 1 (7¾-ounce) can low-sodium salmon, drained and flaked, for spinach and 1 teaspoon dried dill weed for basil. Omit liquid hot pepper seasoning.

Nutritional Information per Serving: *Calories: 181, Total Fat: 10 g, Cholesterol: 10 mg, Sodium: 212 mg*

Zucchini Mushroom Frittata

Easy Brunch Frittata

1 cup small broccoli florets
2½ cups (12 ounces) frozen hash brown potatoes with onions and peppers (O'Brien style), thawed
1½ cups cholesterol-free egg substitute, thawed
2 tablespoons 2% low-fat milk
¾ teaspoon salt
¼ teaspoon black pepper
½ cup (2 ounces) shredded reduced-fat Cheddar cheese

1. Preheat oven to 450°F. Coat medium nonstick ovenproof skillet with nonstick cooking spray. Heat skillet over medium heat until hot. Add broccoli; cook and stir 2 minutes. Add potatoes; cook and stir 5 minutes.

2. Beat together egg substitute, milk, salt and black pepper in small bowl; pour over potato mixture. Cook 5 minutes or until edges are set (center will still be wet).

3. Transfer skillet to oven; bake 6 minutes or until center is set. Sprinkle with cheese; let stand 2 to 3 minutes or until cheese is melted.

4. Cut into wedges; serve with low-fat sour cream, if desired. *Makes 6 servings*

Nutritional Information per Serving: *Calories: 102, Total Fat: 2 g, Cholesterol: 7 mg, Sodium: 627 mg*

Ham and Cheese Frittata

1 tablespoon vegetable oil
1 cup chopped red onion
½ cup chopped green bell pepper
1 teaspoon minced garlic
1 cup (6 ounces) slivered ALPINE LACE® 97% Fat Free Boneless Cooked Ham
1 cup egg substitute *or* 4 large eggs
3 large egg whites
1 cup (4 ounces) shredded ALPINE LACE® Reduced Fat Cheddar Cheese, divided
¼ cup whole fresh tarragon leaves *or* 2 teaspoons dried tarragon
½ teaspoon salt
¼ teaspoon cracked black pepper
2 large plum tomatoes, thinly sliced

1. Preheat the broiler. In a large broilerproof skillet, heat the oil over medium-high heat. Add the onion, bell pepper and garlic and sauté for 5 minutes or until soft. Stir in the ham and cook 3 minutes more.

2. In a medium-size bowl, whisk the egg substitute (or the 4 whole eggs) with the egg whites until foamy; fold in ½ cup of the cheese, the tarragon, salt and black pepper. Pour over the vegetable-ham mixture.

3. Reduce the heat and cook, uncovered, for 6 minutes or just until the egg mixture is set around the edges. Arrange the tomato slices on top of the frittata, in a circle around the edge and in a cluster in the center. Sprinkle with the remaining ½ cup of cheese.

4. Slide the skillet under the broiler for 1 minute or until the frittata is set in the center. Serve immediately right from the skillet! *Makes 4 servings*

Nutritional Information per Serving: *Calories: 255, Total Fat: 12 g, Cholesterol: 34 mg*

Easy Brunch Frittata

Vegetable Strata

2 slices white bread, cubed
¼ cup shredded reduced-fat Swiss cheese
½ cup sliced carrots
½ cup sliced mushrooms
¼ cup chopped onion
1 clove garlic, crushed
1 teaspoon FLEISCHMANN'S® 70% Corn Oil Spread
½ cup chopped tomato
½ cup snow peas
1 cup EGG BEATERS® Healthy Real Egg Substitute
¾ cup skim milk

Place bread cubes evenly onto bottom of greased 1½-quart casserole. Sprinkle with cheese; set aside.

In medium nonstick skillet, over medium heat, sauté carrots, mushrooms, onion and garlic in spread until tender. Stir in tomato and snow peas; cook 1 to 2 minutes more. Spoon over cheese. In small bowl, combine Egg Beaters® and milk; pour over vegetable mixture. Bake at 375°F for 45 to 50 minutes or until knife inserted in center comes out clean. Let stand 10 minutes before serving.

Makes 6 servings

Prep Time: 15 minutes

Cook Time: 55 minutes

Nutritional Information per Serving: *Calories: 94, Total Fat: 2 g, Cholesterol: 3 mg, Sodium: 161 mg*

Breakfast Strata

1 can HEALTHY CHOICE® Recipe Creations™ Cream of Mushroom with Cracked Pepper & Herbs Condensed Soup
2 cups fat free egg substitute (equivalent to 8 eggs)
1 cup nonfat milk
¼ cup sliced green onions
1 teaspoon dry mustard
½ teaspoon salt (optional)
Vegetable cooking spray
6 slices reduced fat white bread, cut into 1-inch cubes
4 links reduced fat precooked breakfast sausage, thinly sliced

In medium bowl, combine soup, egg substitute, milk, green onions, mustard and salt; mix well. In 2-quart baking dish sprayed with vegetable cooking spray, combine bread cubes, sausage and soup mixture; toss to coat. Bake at 350°F 30 to 35 minutes or until set. *Makes 6 servings*

Nutritional Information per Serving: *Calories: 110, Total Fat: 2½ g, Sodium: 400 mg*

Vegetable Strata

Mexican Strata Olé

4 (6-inch) corn tortillas, halved, divided
1 cup chopped onion
½ cup chopped green bell pepper
1 clove garlic, crushed
1 teaspoon dried oregano leaves
½ teaspoon ground cumin
1 teaspoon FLEISCHMANN'S® 70% Corn Oil Spread
1 cup dried kidney beans, cooked in unsalted water according to package directions
½ cup (2 ounces) shredded reduced-fat Cheddar cheese
1½ cups skim milk
1 cup EGG BEATERS® Healthy Real Egg Substitute
1 cup thick and chunky salsa

Arrange half the tortilla pieces in bottom of greased 12×8×2-inch baking dish; set aside.

In large nonstick skillet, over medium-high heat, sauté onion, bell pepper, garlic, oregano and cumin in spread until tender; stir in beans. Spoon half the mixture over tortillas; repeat layers once. Sprinkle with cheese.

In medium bowl, combine milk and Egg Beaters®; pour evenly over cheese. Bake at 350°F for 40 minutes or until puffed and golden brown. Let stand 10 minutes before serving. Serve topped with salsa.

Makes 8 servings

Prep Time: 25 minutes

Cook Time: 50 minutes

Nutritional Information per Serving: *Calories: 142, Total Fat: 3 g, Cholesterol: 1 mg, Sodium: 293 mg*

Eggs Benedict

Mock Hollandaise Sauce (recipe follows)
4 eggs, divided
2 English muffins, split into halves
Fresh spinach leaves, washed and drained
8 ounces sliced lean Canadian bacon
4 tomato slices, cut ¼ inch thick
Paprika

1. Prepare Mock Hollandaise Sauce. Set aside.

2. Bring 6 cups water to a boil in large saucepan over high heat. Reduce heat to simmer. Carefully break 1 egg into small dish and slide egg into water. Repeat with remaining 3 eggs. Simmer, uncovered, about 5 minutes or until yolks are just set.

3. Meanwhile, toast muffin halves; place on serving plates. Top each muffin half with spinach leaves, 2 ounces Canadian bacon, 1 tomato slice and 1 egg. Spoon Mock Hollandaise Sauce over eggs; sprinkle with paprika.
Makes 4 servings

Mock Hollandaise Sauce

4 ounces fat-free cream cheese
3 tablespoons plain nonfat yogurt
1 tablespoon lemon juice
1 teaspoon Dijon mustard

1. Process all ingredients in food processor or blender until smooth. Heat in small saucepan over medium-high heat until hot.
Makes about ¾ cup sauce

Nutritional Information per Serving: *Calories: 237, Total Fat: 6 g, Cholesterol: 248 mg, Sodium: 1209 mg*

Scrambled Egg Burritos

Nonstick cooking spray
1 red bell pepper, chopped
5 green onions, sliced
½ teaspoon red pepper flakes
1 cup cholesterol-free egg substitute
1 tablespoon chopped fresh cilantro or parsley
4 (8-inch) flour tortillas
½ cup (2 ounces) shredded low-sodium, reduced-fat Monterey Jack cheese
⅓ cup salsa

1. Spray medium nonstick skillet with cooking spray. Heat over medium heat until hot. Add bell pepper, onions and red pepper flakes. Cook and stir 3 minutes or until vegetables are crisp-tender.

2. Add egg substitute to vegetables. Reduce heat to low. Cook and stir 3 minutes or until set. Sprinkle with cilantro.

3. Stack tortillas and wrap in paper towels. Microwave at HIGH 1 minute or until tortillas are hot.

4. Place one fourth of egg mixture on each tortilla. Sprinkle with cheese. Fold sides over to enclose filling. Serve with salsa.

Makes 4 servings

Nutritional Information per Serving: *Calories: 186, Total Fat: 4 g, Cholesterol: 6 mg, Sodium: 425 mg*

Triple Berry Breakfast Parfait

2 cups vanilla sugar-free nonfat yogurt
¼ teaspoon ground cinnamon
1 cup sliced strawberries
½ cup blueberries
½ cup raspberries
1 cup low-fat granola without raisins

1. Combine yogurt and cinnamon in small bowl. Combine strawberries, blueberries and raspberries in medium bowl.

2. For each parfait, layer ¼ cup fruit mixture, 2 tablespoons granola and ¼ cup yogurt mixture in parfait glass. Repeat layers. Garnish with mint leaves, if desired.

Makes 4 servings

Nutritional Information per Serving: *Calories: 236, Total Fat: 2 g, Cholesterol: 0 mg, Sodium: 101 mg*

Spinach-Cheddar Squares

1½ cups EGG BEATERS® Healthy Real Egg Substitute
¾ cup skim milk
1 tablespoon dried onion flakes
1 tablespoon grated Parmesan cheese
¼ teaspoon garlic powder
⅛ teaspoon ground black pepper
¼ cup plain dry bread crumbs
¾ cup shredded fat-free Cheddar cheese, divided
1 (10-ounce) package frozen chopped spinach, thawed and well drained
¼ cup diced pimientos

In medium bowl, combine Egg Beaters®, milk, onion flakes, Parmesan cheese, garlic powder and pepper; set aside.

Sprinkle bread crumbs evenly into bottom of lightly greased 8×8×2-inch baking dish. Top with ½ cup Cheddar cheese and spinach. Pour egg mixture evenly over spinach; top with remaining Cheddar cheese and pimientos.

Bake at 350°F for 35 to 40 minutes or until knife inserted in center comes out clean. Let stand 10 minutes before serving.

Makes 16 appetizer servings

Prep Time: 15 minutes

Cook Time: 40 minutes

Nutritional Information per Serving: *Calories: 39, Total Fat: 0 g, Cholesterol: 1 mg, Sodium: 134 mg*

Potato Latkes

⅔ cup EGG BEATERS® Healthy Real Egg
    Substitute
⅓ cup all-purpose flour
¼ cup grated onion
¼ teaspoon ground black pepper
4 large potatoes, peeled and shredded
    (about 4 cups)
3 tablespoons FLEISCHMANN'S® 70%
    Corn Oil Spread, divided
1½ cups sweetened applesauce
    Fresh chives, for garnish

In large bowl, combine Egg Beaters®, flour, onion and pepper; set aside.

Pat shredded potatoes dry with paper towels. Stir into egg mixture. In large nonstick skillet, over medium-high heat, melt 1½ tablespoons spread. For each pancake, spoon about ⅓ cup potato mixture into skillet, spreading into a 4-inch circle. Cook for 3 minutes on each side or until golden; remove and keep warm. Repeat with remaining mixture, using remaining spread as needed to make 12 pancakes. Serve hot with applesauce. Garnish with chives. *Makes 4 servings*

Prep Time: 20 minutes

Cook Time: 18 minutes

Nutritional Information per Serving: *Calories: 460, Total Fat: 12 g, Cholesterol: 0 mg, Sodium: 208 mg*

Apple Raisin Pancakes

2 cups all-purpose flour
2 tablespoons sugar
1 tablespoon baking powder
2 teaspoons ground cinnamon
1¾ cups skim milk
⅔ cup EGG BEATERS® Healthy Real Egg
    Substitute
5 tablespoons FLEISCHMANN'S® 70%
    Corn Oil Spread, melted, divided
¾ cup chopped apple
¾ cup seedless raisins

In large bowl, combine flour, sugar, baking powder and cinnamon. In medium bowl, combine milk, Egg Beaters® and 4 tablespoons spread; stir into dry ingredients just until blended. Stir in apple and raisins.

Brush large nonstick griddle or skillet with some of remaining spread; heat over medium-high heat. Using ¼ cup batter for each pancake, pour batter onto griddle. Cook until bubbly; turn and cook until lightly browned. Repeat with remaining batter using remaining spread as needed to make 16 pancakes.
Makes 16 (4-inch) pancakes

Prep Time: 10 minutes

Cook Time: 15 minutes

Nutritional Information per Serving (1 pancake):
Calories: 134, Total Fat: 4 g, Cholesterol: 1 mg, Sodium: 157 mg

Potato Latkes

Silver Dollar Pancakes with Mixed Berry Topping

1¼ cups all-purpose flour
2 tablespoons sugar
2 teaspoons baking soda
1½ cups buttermilk
½ cup EGG BEATERS® Healthy Real Egg
    Substitute
3 tablespoons FLEISCHMANN'S® 70%
    Corn Oil Spread, melted, divided
    Mixed Berry Topping (recipe follows)

In large bowl, combine flour, sugar and baking soda. Stir in buttermilk, Egg Beaters® and 2 tablespoons spread just until blended.

Brush large nonstick griddle or skillet with some of remaining spread; heat over medium-high heat. Using 1 heaping tablespoon batter for each pancake, spoon batter onto griddle. Cook until bubbly; turn and cook until lightly browned. Repeat with remaining batter using remaining spread as needed to make 28 pancakes. Serve hot with Mixed Berry Topping.

Makes 28 (2-inch) pancakes

Prep Time: 20 minutes

Cook Time: 20 minutes

Mixed Berry Topping: In medium saucepan, over medium-low heat, combine 1 (12-ounce) package frozen mixed berries,* thawed, ¼ cup honey and ½ teaspoon grated gingerroot (*or* ⅛ teaspoon ground ginger). Cook and stir just until hot and well blended. Serve over pancakes.

3 cups mixed fresh berries may be substituted.

Nutritional Information per Serving (4 pancakes, ¼ cup topping): *Calories: 228, Total Fat: 6 g, Cholesterol: 2 mg, Sodium: 491 mg*

Black Bean Pancakes & Salsa

1 cup GUILTLESS GOURMET® Black
    Bean Dip (mild or spicy)
2 egg whites
½ cup unbleached all-purpose flour
½ cup skim milk
1 tablespoon canola oil
    Nonstick cooking spray
½ cup fat free sour cream
½ cup GUILTLESS GOURMET® Salsa
    (medium)
    Yellow tomatoes and fresh mint
    leaves (optional)

For pancake batter, place bean dip, egg whites, flour, milk and oil in blender or food processor; blend until smooth. Refrigerate 2 hours or overnight.

Preheat oven to 350°F. Coat large nonstick skillet with cooking spray; heat over medium heat until hot. For each pancake, spoon 2 tablespoons batter into skillet; cook until bubbles form and break on pancake surface. Turn pancakes over; cook until lightly browned on other side. Place on baking sheet; keep warm in oven. Repeat to make 16 small pancakes. (If batter becomes too thick, thin with more milk.) Serve hot with sour cream and salsa. Garnish with tomatoes and mint, if desired.   *Makes 4 servings*

Nutritional Information per Serving (4 pancakes, 2 tablespoons sour cream, 2 tablespoons salsa): *Calories: 192, Total Fat: 4 g, Cholesterol: 0 mg, Sodium: 403 mg*

Silver Dollar Pancakes with
Mixed Berry Topping

PB & J French Toast

¼ cup blueberry preserves, or any
   flavor
6 slices whole wheat bread, divided
¼ cup creamy peanut butter
½ cup EGG BEATERS® Healthy Real Egg
   Substitute
¼ cup skim milk
2 tablespoons FLEISCHMANN'S® 70%
   Corn Oil Spread
1 large banana, sliced
1 tablespoon honey
1 tablespoon orange juice
1 tablespoon dry roasted unsalted
   peanuts, chopped
   Low fat vanilla yogurt (optional)

Spread preserves evenly over 3 bread slices. Spread peanut butter evenly over remaining bread slices. Press preserves and peanut butter slices together to form 3 sandwiches; cut each diagonally in half. In shallow bowl, combine Egg Beaters® and milk. In large nonstick griddle or skillet, over medium-high heat, melt spread. Dip each sandwich in egg mixture to coat; transfer to griddle. Cook sandwiches for 2 minutes on each side or until golden. Keep warm.

In small bowl, combine banana slices, honey, orange juice and peanuts. Arrange sandwiches on platter; top with banana mixture. Serve warm with a dollop of yogurt, if desired.   *Makes 6 servings*

Prep Time: 25 minutes

Cook Time: 10 minutes

Nutritional Information per Serving (without yogurt): *Calories: 242, Total Fat: 11 g, Cholesterol: 1 mg, Sodium: 262 mg*

Cinnamon French Toast

1 cup EGG BEATERS® Healthy Real Egg
   Substitute
⅓ cup skim milk
1 teaspoon ground cinnamon
1 teaspoon vanilla extract
10 (1-inch-thick) slices French bread
2 tablespoons FLEISCHMANN'S® 70%
   Corn Oil Spread, divided
   Additional FLEISCHMANN'S® 70%
   Corn Oil Spread (optional)
   Maple-flavored syrup (optional)

In small bowl, combine Egg Beaters®, milk, cinnamon and vanilla. Pour half of egg mixture into 13×9×2-inch baking pan. Arrange bread slices in pan; pour remaining egg mixture evenly over bread slices. Let stand for 15 to 20 minutes to absorb egg mixture.

In large nonstick griddle or skillet, over medium heat, melt 1 tablespoon spread. Cook half the bread slices for 3 minutes on each side or until golden. Cook remaining bread slices using remaining 1 tablespoon spread as needed. Serve topped with additional spread and syrup, if desired.
            Makes 5 servings

Prep Time: 25 minutes

Cook Time: 15 minutes

Nutritional Information per Serving (without additional spread or syrup): *Calories: 260, Total Fat: 7 g, Cholesterol: 0 mg, Sodium: 537 mg*

PB & J French Toast

Apricot-Almond Coffee Ring

1 cup dried apricots, sliced
1 cup water
3½ teaspoons EQUAL® Measure™ or
     12 packets EQUAL® sweetener or
     ½ cup EQUAL® Spoonful™
⅛ teaspoon ground mace
1 loaf (16 ounces) frozen Italian bread
     dough, thawed
⅓ cup sliced or slivered almonds,
     divided
  Skim milk
1 teaspoon EQUAL® Measure™ or
     3 packets EQUAL® sweetener or
     2 tablespoons EQUAL® Spoonful™

• Heat apricots, water, 3½ teaspoons Equal® Measure™ or 12 packets Equal® sweetener or ½ cup Equal® Spoonful™ and mace to boiling in small saucepan; reduce heat and simmer, covered, until apricots are tender and water is absorbed, about 10 minutes. Simmer, uncovered, until no water remains, 2 to 3 minutes. Cool.

• Roll dough on floured surface into 14×8-inch rectangle. Spread apricot mixture on dough to within 1 inch of edges; sprinkle with ¼ cup almonds. Roll dough up jelly-roll style, beginning with long edge; pinch edge of dough to seal. Place dough seam side down on greased cookie sheet, forming circle; pinch ends to seal.

• Using scissors, cut dough from outside edge almost to center, making cuts 1 inch apart. Turn each section cut side up so filling shows. Let rise, covered, in warm place until dough is double in size, about 1 hour.

• Brush top of dough lightly with milk; sprinkle with remaining almonds and 1 teaspoon Equal® Measure™ or 3 packets Equal® sweetener or 2 tablespoons Equal® Spoonful™. Bake coffee cake in preheated 375°F oven until golden, 25 to 30 minutes. Cool on wire rack.

Makes about 12 servings

Nutritional Information per Serving: *Calories: 154, Total Fat: 3 g, Cholesterol: 0 mg, Sodium: 180 mg*

Spicy Scones

1½ cups all-purpose flour
⅓ cup plus 1 tablespoon sugar, divided
2 teaspoons baking powder
1¼ teaspoons ground cinnamon, divided
½ teaspoon ground nutmeg
½ teaspoon baking soda
½ teaspoon salt
3 tablespoons Prune Purée (page 83)
     or prepared prune butter
1 tablespoon cold margarine
1 cup low-fat buttermilk

Preheat oven to 400°F. Coat baking sheet with vegetable cooking spray. In large bowl, combine flour, ⅓ cup sugar, baking powder, 1 teaspoon cinnamon, nutmeg, baking soda and salt. Cut in prune purée and margarine until mixture resembles coarse crumbs. Blend in buttermilk. Spoon eight mounds of batter onto prepared baking sheet. Combine remaining 1 tablespoon sugar and ¼ teaspoon cinnamon; sprinkle over batter. Bake about 15 minutes or until lightly browned. *Makes 8 scones*

Nutritional Information per Serving (1 scone): *Calories: 160, Total Fat: 2 g, Cholesterol: 5 mg, Sodium: 320 mg*

Favorite recipe from **California Prune Board**

Apricot-Almond Coffee Ring

Blueberry Lemon Scones

2⅔ cups all-purpose flour
½ cup plus 2 tablespoons sugar, divided
2½ teaspoons baking powder
1 teaspoon baking soda
½ teaspoon salt
½ cup dried blueberries
1 container (8 ounces) low-fat lemon yogurt
⅓ cup Prune Purée (page 83) or prepared prune butter
3 tablespoons butter or margarine, melted
1 tablespoon grated lemon peel
2 teaspoons vanilla
¼ teaspoon ground nutmeg

Preheat oven to 400°F. Coat baking sheet with vegetable cooking spray. In large mixer bowl, combine flour, ½ cup sugar, baking powder, baking soda and salt. Add blueberries. In small bowl, mix yogurt, prune purée, butter, lemon peel and vanilla until blended. Add to flour mixture; mix just until mixture holds together. Turn dough out onto lightly floured surface and pat into 10-inch round. Combine remaining 2 tablespoons sugar and nutmeg; sprinkle evenly over dough. Pat sugar mixture gently into dough; cut into 12 equal wedges. Place wedges on prepared baking sheet, spacing 1 inch apart. Bake in center of oven about 15 minutes or until lightly browned and cracked on top. Remove from baking sheet to wire rack to cool slightly. Serve warm.

Makes 12 scones

Variation: Substitute currants, raisins or chopped dried cherries for the blueberries.

Nutritional Information per Serving (1 scone):
Calories: 211, Total Fat: 3 g, Cholesterol: 10 mg, Sodium: 280 mg

Favorite recipe from **California Prune Board**

Orange-Pecan Scones

2½ cups all-purpose flour
½ cup sugar
1 tablespoon baking powder
1 teaspoon baking soda
¾ teaspoon salt
¼ cup Prune Purée (page 83) or prepared prune butter
2 tablespoons cold margarine or butter
1 container (8 ounces) nonfat lemon yogurt
2 tablespoons frozen orange juice concentrate, thawed
Grated peel of 1 orange
¼ cup chopped toasted pecans

Preheat oven to 400°F. Coat baking sheet with vegetable cooking spray. In large bowl, combine flour, sugar, baking powder, baking soda and salt. Cut in prune purée and margarine with pastry blender until mixture resembles coarse crumbs. Add yogurt, juice concentrate and orange peel; mix just until blended. Stir in pecans. Turn dough out onto floured surface and knead two or three times. Pat into 8-inch circle and cut into 12 equal wedges. Place wedges on prepared baking sheet, spacing 2 inches apart. Bake in center of oven 15 to 20 minutes or until lightly browned and springy to the touch. Serve warm or at room temperature.

Makes 12 scones

Nutritional Information per Serving (1 scone):
Calories: 190, Total Fat: 4 g, Cholesterol: 5 mg, Sodium: 320 mg

Favorite recipe from **California Prune Board**

Cranberry Scones

2½ cups all-purpose flour
½ cup packed brown sugar
1 tablespoon baking powder
1 teaspoon baking soda
¾ teaspoon salt
½ teaspoon ground cinnamon
¼ cup Prune Purée (recipe follows) or
   prepared prune butter
2 tablespoons cold margarine or butter
1 container (8 ounces) nonfat vanilla
   yogurt
¾ cup dried cranberries
1 egg white, lightly beaten
1 tablespoon granulated sugar

Preheat oven to 400°F. Coat baking sheet with vegetable cooking spray. In large bowl, combine flour, brown sugar, baking powder, baking soda, salt and cinnamon. Cut in prune purée and margarine with pastry blender until mixture resembles coarse crumbs. Mix in yogurt just until blended. Stir in cranberries. On floured surface, roll or pat dough to ¾-inch thickness. Cut out with 2½- to 3-inch biscuit cutter, rerolling scraps as needed, but handling as little as possible. Arrange on prepared baking sheet, spacing 2 inches apart. Brush with egg white and sprinkle with granulated sugar. Bake in center of oven about 15 minutes or until golden brown and springy to the touch. Serve warm or at room temperature.

Makes 12 scones

Prune Purée

1⅓ cups (8 ounces) pitted prunes
6 tablespoons hot water

Combine pitted prunes and hot water in container of food processor or blender.

Pulse on and off until prunes are finely chopped and smooth. Store leftovers in covered container in refrigerator up to two months. *Makes 1 cup*

Nutritional Information per Serving (1 scone):
Calories: 190, Total Fat: 2 g, Cholesterol: 0 mg, Sodium: 280 mg

Favorite recipe from **California Prune Board**

Date Bran Muffins

1½ cups 100% bran cereal
1½ cups skim milk
⅓ cup margarine, melted
1 egg
1 teaspoon vanilla
1¼ cups all-purpose flour
4¼ teaspoons EQUAL® Measure™ *or*
   14 packets EQUAL® sweetener *or*
   ½ cup plus 4 teaspoons EQUAL®
   Spoonful™
1 tablespoon baking powder
2 teaspoons ground cinnamon
½ teaspoon salt
½ cup pitted dates, chopped

• Combine cereal and milk in medium bowl; let stand 5 minutes. Stir in margarine, egg and vanilla. Add combined flour, Equal®, baking powder, cinnamon and salt, stirring just until mixture is blended. Stir in dates.

• Spoon batter into greased muffin pans; bake in preheated 375°F oven until muffins are browned and toothpicks inserted in centers come out clean, 20 to 25 minutes. Cool in pans on wire rack 5 minutes; remove from pans and cool on wire rack.

Makes 1 dozen

Nutritional Information per Serving (1 muffin):
Calories: 164, Total Fat: 6 g, Cholesterol: 18 mg, Sodium: 390 mg

Blueberry Muffins with a Twist of Lemon

1 cup all-purpose flour
1 cup uncooked rolled oats
¼ cup packed brown sugar
1 teaspoon baking powder
1 teaspoon baking soda
¾ teaspoon cinnamon, divided
¼ teaspoon salt
8 ounces lemon-flavored low-fat
    yogurt
¼ cup cholesterol-free egg substitute *or*
    2 egg whites
1 tablespoon vegetable oil
1 teaspoon grated lemon peel
1 teaspoon vanilla
1 cup fresh or frozen blueberries
1 tablespoon granulated sugar
1 tablespoon sliced almonds (optional)

1. Preheat oven to 400°F. Spray 12 (2½-inch) muffin cups with nonstick cooking spray.

2. Combine flour, oats, brown sugar, baking powder, baking soda, ½ teaspoon cinnamon and salt in large bowl.

3. Combine yogurt, egg substitute, oil, lemon peel and vanilla in small bowl; stir into flour mixture just until blended. Gently stir in blueberries. Spoon mixture into muffin cups.

4. Mix granulated sugar, remaining ¼ teaspoon cinnamon and almonds, if desired, in small bowl. Sprinkle over muffin mixture.

5. Bake 18 to 20 minutes or until lightly browned and toothpick inserted into centers comes out clean. Cool slightly on racks before serving. *Makes 12 servings*

Nutritional Information per Serving: *Calories: 125, Total Fat: 2 g, Cholesterol: 1 mg, Sodium: 198 mg*

Apple-Cinnamon Bread

⅓ cup packed brown sugar
⅓ cup granulated sugar
3 egg whites
¼ cup Prune Purée (page 83) or
    prepared prune butter
⅔ cup buttermilk
1¾ cups all-purpose flour
1 teaspoon ground cinnamon
¾ teaspoon baking powder
¾ teaspoon baking soda
½ teaspoon salt
¼ teaspoon ground nutmeg
¼ teaspoon ground cloves
¾ cup peeled and finely chopped apple
    (spooned, not packed, into cup)

Preheat oven to 375°F. Coat 8½×4½×2¾-inch loaf pan with vegetable cooking spray. In mixer bowl, beat sugars, egg whites and prune purée until well blended. Mix in buttermilk until blended. In medium bowl, combine flour, cinnamon, baking powder, baking soda, salt, nutmeg and cloves; stir into sugar mixture just until blended. Stir in apple. Spoon batter into prepared pan. Bake in center of oven 45 to 50 minutes or until toothpick inserted into center comes out clean. Cool in pan 5 minutes; remove from pan to wire rack. Cool completely before slicing. *Makes 1 loaf (12 slices)*

Nutritional Information per Serving (1 slice):
Calories: 140, Total Fat: 0 g, Cholesterol: 0 mg, Sodium: 180 mg

Favorite recipe from **California Prune Board**

Blueberry Muffins with a Twist of Lemon

Orange Fruit Bread

      2 cups all-purpose flour
  ¼ cup sugar
  1½ teaspoons baking powder
  ½ teaspoon baking soda
  ½ teaspoon salt
  ¼ cup Prune Purée (page 83) or
      prepared prune butter
  ¾ cup orange juice
  ½ cup orange marmalade
      Grated peel of 1 orange
  1 package (6 ounces) mixed dried fruit
      bits
  ¼ cup chopped toasted pecans

Preheat oven to 350°F. Coat 8½×4½×2¾-inch loaf pan with vegetable cooking spray. In mixer bowl, combine flour, sugar, baking powder, baking soda and salt. Add prune purée; beat at low speed until blended. Add juice, marmalade and orange peel. Beat at low speed just until blended. Stir in fruit bits and pecans. Spoon batter into prepared pan. Bake in center of oven about 1 hour or until toothpick inserted into center comes out clean. Cool in pan 5 minutes; remove from pan to wire rack. Cool completely. For best flavor, wrap securely and store overnight before slicing. Serve with orange marmalade, if desired.

Makes 1 loaf (12 slices)

Nutritional Information per Serving (1 slice):
Calories: 200, Total Fat: 2 g, Cholesterol: 0 mg, Sodium: 170 mg

Favorite recipe from **California Prune Board**

Pineapple Zucchini Bread

  1 cup vegetable oil
  3 eggs
  3½ teaspoons EQUAL® Measure™ *or*
      12 packets EQUAL® sweetener *or*
      ½ cup EQUAL® Spoonful™
  1 teaspoon vanilla
  2 cups shredded zucchini
  1 can (8½ ounces) unsweetened
      crushed pineapple in juice, drained
  3 cups all-purpose flour
  1½ teaspoons ground cinnamon
  1 teaspoon baking soda
  ¾ teaspoon salt
  ¾ teaspoon ground nutmeg
  1 cup raisins
  ½ cup chopped walnuts (optional)

• Mix oil, eggs, Equal® and vanilla in large bowl; stir in zucchini and pineapple. Combine flour, cinnamon, baking soda, salt and nutmeg in medium bowl; stir into oil mixture. Stir in raisins and walnuts, if desired. Spread batter evenly in 2 greased and floured 8½×4½×2½-inch loaf pans.

• Bake in preheated 350°F oven until breads are golden and toothpick inserted in centers comes out clean, 50 to 60 minutes. Cool in pans on wire rack 10 minutes; remove from pans and cool completely on wire rack.

Makes 2 loaves (about 16 slices each)

Nutritional Information per Serving (1 slice):
Calories: 134, Total Fat: 7 g, Cholesterol: 20 mg, Sodium: 97 mg

Orange Fruit Bread

Banana Walnut Bread

½ cup skim milk
2 eggs
4 tablespoons margarine, softened
7¼ teaspoons EQUAL® Measure™ *or*
  24 packets EQUAL® sweetener *or*
  1 cup EQUAL® Spoonful™
1 teaspoon vanilla
½ teaspoon banana extract
1¼ cups mashed ripe bananas (about 2 large)
1¾ cups all-purpose flour
1 teaspoon baking soda
1 teaspoon ground cinnamon
½ teaspoon salt
¼ teaspoon baking powder
⅓ cup coarsely chopped walnuts

• Beat milk, eggs, margarine, Equal®, vanilla and banana extract in large bowl with electric mixer 30 seconds; add bananas and beat on high speed 1 minute.

• Add combined flour, baking soda, cinnamon, salt and baking powder, mixing just until blended. Stir in walnuts. Spread mixture evenly in greased 8½×4½×2½-inch loaf pan.

• Bake in preheated 350°F oven until bread is golden and toothpick inserted in center comes out clean, about 60 minutes. Cool in pan on wire rack 5 minutes; remove from pan and cool on wire rack.

Makes 1 loaf (about 16 slices)

Nutritional Information per Serving (1 slice):
Calories: 127, Total Fat: 5 g, Cholesterol: 27 mg, Sodium: 199 mg

Maple-Walnut Bread

1 cup packed brown sugar
¼ cup Prune Purée (page 83) or prepared prune butter
2 egg whites
1½ teaspoons maple flavoring
¾ cup low-fat buttermilk
2 cups all-purpose flour
2 teaspoons baking powder
½ teaspoon baking soda
½ teaspoon salt
⅓ cup finely chopped, toasted walnuts

Preheat oven to 350°F. Coat 8½×4½×2¾-inch loaf pan with vegetable cooking spray. In mixer bowl, beat sugar, prune purée, egg whites and maple flavoring until well blended. Mix in buttermilk until blended. In medium bowl, combine flour, baking powder, baking soda and salt; stir into sugar mixture. Stir in walnuts. Spoon batter into prepared pan. Bake in center of oven 50 minutes or until toothpick inserted into center comes out clean. Cool in pan 5 minutes; remove from pan to wire rack. Cool completely before slicing.

Makes 1 loaf (12 slices)

Nutritional Information per Serving (1 slice):
Calories: 190, Total Fat: 2 g, Cholesterol: 1 mg, Sodium: 160 mg

Favorite recipe from **California Prune Board**

Triple-Berry Jam

4 cups fresh strawberries or thawed
    frozen unsweetened strawberries
2 cups fresh raspberries or thawed
    frozen unsweetened raspberries
1 cup fresh blueberries or thawed
    frozen unsweetened blueberries
1 package (1¾ ounces) no-sugar-
    needed pectin
2 tablespoons EQUAL® Measure™ or
    20 packets EQUAL® sweetener or
    ¾ cup plus 4 teaspoons EQUAL®
    Spoonful™

• Mash strawberries, raspberries and blueberries, by hand or with food processor, to make 4 cups pulp. Stir in pectin; let mixture stand 10 minutes, stirring frequently. Transfer to large saucepan. Cook and stir over medium heat until mixture comes to a boil. Cook and stir 1 minute more. Remove from heat; stir in Equal®. Skim off foam, if necessary.

• Immediately fill containers, leaving ½-inch headspace. Seal and let stand at room temperature until firm (several hours). Store up to 2 weeks in refrigerator or 6 months in freezer.   *Makes 8 (½-pint) jars*

**Nutritional Information per Serving
(1 tablespoon):** *Calories: 9, Total Fat: 0 g,
Cholesterol: 0 mg, Sodium: 3 mg*

Peach Preserves

2½ to 3 pounds ripe peaches (10 to 12)
2 tablespoons lemon juice
1 package (1¾ ounces) no-sugar-
    needed pectin
7¼ teaspoons EQUAL® Measure™ or
    24 packets EQUAL® sweetener or
    1 cup EQUAL® Spoonful™

• Peel, pit and finely chop peaches; measure 4 cups into saucepan. Stir in lemon juice and pectin. Let stand 10 minutes, stirring frequently. Cook and stir until boiling. Cook and stir 1 minute more. Remove from heat; stir in Equal®. Skim off foam.

• Immediately ladle into freezer containers or jars, leaving ½-inch headspace. Seal and label containers. Let stand at room temperature several hours or until set. Store up to 2 weeks in refrigerator or 6 months in freezer.   *Makes 8 (½-pint) jars*

**Nutritional Information per Serving
(1 tablespoon):** *Calories: 10, Total Fat: 0 g,
Cholesterol: 0 mg, Sodium: 3 mg*

Maple-Flavored Syrup

1 cup apple juice
2½ teaspoons cornstarch
1 tablespoon margarine
1¾ teaspoons EQUAL® Measure™ or
    6 packets EQUAL® sweetener or
    ¼ cup EQUAL® Spoonful™
1 teaspoon maple flavoring
1 teaspoon vanilla

• Combine apple juice and cornstarch in small saucepan. Cook and stir until thickened and bubbly. Cook and stir 2 minutes more. Remove from heat. Stir in margarine, Equal®, maple flavoring and vanilla. Serve over pancakes, waffles or French toast.   *Makes 1 cup*

**Nutritional Information per Serving
(1 tablespoon):** *Calories: 18, Total Fat: 1 g,
Cholesterol: 0 mg, Sodium: 9 mg*

Spiced Fruit Butter

3 pounds apples, pears or peaches
¾ cup apple juice, pear nectar or peach
    nectar
1 to 2 teaspoons ground cinnamon
½ teaspoon ground nutmeg
⅛ teaspoon ground cloves
5 teaspoons EQUAL® Measure™ *or*
    16 packets EQUAL® sweetener *or*
    ⅔ cup EQUAL® Spoonful™

• Peel and core or pit fruit; slice. Combine prepared fruit, fruit juice and spices in Dutch oven. Bring to boiling; cover and simmer until very tender, about 15 minutes. Cool slightly. Purée in batches in blender or food processor. Return to Dutch oven.

• Simmer, uncovered, over low heat until desired consistency, stirring frequently. (This may take up to 1 hour.) Remove from heat; stir in Equal®. Transfer to freezer containers or jars, leaving ½-inch headspace. Store up to 2 weeks in refrigerator or up to 3 months in freezer.   *Makes 6 (½-pint) jars*

**Nutritional Information per Serving
(1 tablespoon):** *Calories: 16, Total Fat: 0 g,
Cholesterol: 0 mg, Sodium: 0 mg*

Strawberry Jam

2 quarts fresh or frozen strawberries
1 package (1¾ ounces) no-sugar-
    needed pectin
4 tablespoons EQUAL® Measure™ *or*
    40 packets EQUAL® sweetener *or*
    1⅔ cup EQUAL® Spoonful™

• Mash strawberries to make 4 cups pulp. Combine strawberries and pectin in large saucepan. Let stand 10 minutes, stirring frequently. Cook and stir over medium heat until mixture comes to a boil. Cook and stir 1 minute more. Remove from heat; stir in Equal®. Skim off foam if necessary.

• Immediately fill containers, leaving ½-inch headspace. Seal and let stand at room temperature several hours or until set. Store up to 2 weeks in refrigerator or 6 months in freezer.   *Makes 4 (½-pint) jars*

**Nutritional Information per Serving
(1 tablespoon):** *Calories: 8, Total Fat: 0 g,
Cholesterol: 0 mg, Sodium: 0 mg*

Holiday Eggnog

2 cups skim milk
2 tablespoons cornstarch
3½ teaspoons EQUAL® Measure™ *or*
    12 packets EQUAL® sweetener *or*
    ½ cup EQUAL® Spoonful™
2 eggs, beaten
2 teaspoons vanilla
¼ teaspoon ground cinnamon
2 cups skim milk, chilled
⅛ teaspoon ground nutmeg

• Mix 2 cups milk, cornstarch and Equal® in small saucepan; heat to boiling. Boil 1 minute, stirring constantly. Mix about half of milk mixture into eggs; return egg mixture to remaining milk in saucepan. Cook over low heat until slightly thickened, stirring constantly. Remove from heat; stir in vanilla and cinnamon. Cool to room temperature; refrigerate until chilled. Stir 2 cups chilled milk into custard mixture; serve in small glasses. Sprinkle with nutmeg.
          Makes 8 (4-ounce) servings

Variation: Stir 1 to 1½ teaspoons rum or brandy extract into eggnog, if desired.

Nutritional Information per Serving: *Calories: 79,
Total Fat: 1 g, Cholesterol: 55 mg, Sodium: 79 mg*

*Left to right: Strawberry Jam,
Spiced Fruit Butter*

Strawberry Smoothie

8 ounces plain nonfat yogurt
¼ cup skim milk
1 teaspoon EQUAL® Measure™ *or*
    3 packets EQUAL® sweetener *or*
    2 tablespoons EQUAL® Spoonful™
3 cups frozen strawberries
1 cup ice cubes

• Combine yogurt, milk and Equal® in blender container. With blender running, add berries, a few at a time, through opening in lid. Blend until smooth; add ice cubes, one at a time, through opening in lid, blending until slushy. Pour into glasses.
Makes 4 (6-ounce) servings

Nutritional Information per Serving: *Calories: 82, Total Fat: 0 g, Cholesterol: 1 mg, Sodium: 58 mg*

Coffee Latte

1¼ cups regular grind espresso or other dark roast coffee
1 cinnamon stick, broken into pieces
6 cups water
2½ teaspoons EQUAL® Measure™ *or*
    8 packets EQUAL® sweetener *or*
    ⅓ cup EQUAL® Spoonful™
2½ cups skim milk
Ground cinnamon or nutmeg

• Place espresso and cinnamon stick in filter basket of drip coffee pot; brew coffee with water. Stir Equal® into coffee; pour into 8 mugs or cups.

• Heat milk in small saucepan until steaming. Process half of milk in blender at high speed until foamy, about 15 seconds; pour milk into 4 mugs of coffee, spooning foam on top. Repeat with remaining milk and coffee. Sprinkle with cinnamon before serving.
Makes about 8 (8-ounce) servings

Nutritional Information per Serving: *Calories: 31, Total Fat: 0 g, Cholesterol: 1 mg, Sodium: 46 mg*

Fitness Shake

2 cups skim milk
2 medium-size ripe bananas, cut into 1-inch pieces
½ cup nonfat dry milk powder
½ cup plain or banana nonfat yogurt
⅓ cup wheat germ
2½ teaspoons EQUAL® Measure™ *or*
    8 packets EQUAL® sweetener *or*
    ⅓ cup EQUAL® Spoonful™
1 teaspoon vanilla
Ground cinnamon (optional)

• Blend all ingredients except cinnamon in blender or food processor until smooth. Pour into glasses and sprinkle with cinnamon, if desired.
Makes 4 (8-ounce) servings

Nutritional Information per Serving: *Calories: 190, Total Fat: 2 g, Cholesterol: 4 mg, Sodium: 134 mg*

Orange Jubilee

1 small can (6 ounces) frozen orange juice concentrate
2¼ cups skim milk
1¾ teaspoons EQUAL® Measure™ *or*
    6 packets EQUAL® sweetener *or*
    ¼ cup EQUAL® Spoonful™
½ teaspoon vanilla
8 ice cubes
Ground nutmeg or cinnamon (optional)

• Process orange juice concentrate, milk, Equal® and vanilla in food processor or blender until smooth; add ice cubes and process again until smooth. Serve in small glasses; sprinkle with nutmeg or cinnamon, if desired.   *Makes 6 (4-ounce) servings*

Nutritional Information per Serving: *Calories: 94, Total Fat: 0 g, Cholesterol: 2 mg, Sodium: 49 mg*

Left to right: Strawberry Smoothie, Orange Jubilee

Soups & Chilies

Spicy Pumpkin Soup with Green Chili Swirl

1 can (4 ounces) diced green chilies,
   drained
¼ cup reduced-fat sour cream
¼ cup fresh cilantro leaves
1 can (15 ounces) solid-pack pumpkin
1 can (about 14 ounces) fat-free
   reduced-sodium chicken broth
½ cup water
1 teaspoon ground cumin
½ teaspoon chili powder
¼ teaspoon garlic powder
⅛ teaspoon ground red pepper
   (optional)

1. Combine green chilies, sour cream and cilantro in food processor or blender; process until smooth.*

2. Combine pumpkin, chicken broth, water, cumin, chili powder, garlic powder and pepper, if desired, in medium saucepan; stir in ¼ cup green chili mixture. Bring to a boil; reduce heat to medium. Simmer, uncovered, 5 minutes, stirring occasionally.

3. Pour into serving bowls. Top each serving with small dollops of remaining green chili mixture and additional sour cream, if desired. Run tip of spoon through dollops to swirl. *Makes 4 servings*

Omit food processor step by adding green chilies directly to soup. Finely chop cilantro and combine with sour cream. Dollop with sour cream mixture as directed.

Nutritional Information per Serving: *Calories: 72, Total Fat: 1 g, Cholesterol: 5 mg, Sodium: 276 mg*

Spicy Pumpkin Soup with Green Chili Swirl

Mediterranean Fish Soup

4 ounces uncooked pastina or other
small pasta
Nonstick cooking spray
¾ cup chopped onion
2 cloves garlic, minced
1 teaspoon fennel seeds
1 can (14½ ounces) no-salt-added
stewed tomatoes, undrained
1 can (about 14 ounces) fat-free
reduced-sodium chicken broth
1 tablespoon minced fresh parsley
½ teaspoon black pepper
¼ teaspoon ground turmeric
8 ounces firm, white-fleshed fish, cut
into 1-inch pieces
3 ounces raw small shrimp, peeled and
deveined

1. Cook pasta according to package
directions, omitting salt. Drain and set aside.

2. Spray large nonstick saucepan with
cooking spray. Add onion, garlic and fennel
seeds; cook over medium heat 3 minutes or
until onion is soft.

3. Stir in tomatoes, chicken broth, parsley,
pepper and turmeric. Bring to a boil; reduce
heat and simmer 10 minutes. Add fish and
cook 1 minute. Add shrimp and cook until
shrimp just begin to turn opaque.

4. Divide pasta among bowls; ladle soup
over pasta.   *Makes 4 servings*

Nutritional Information per Serving: *Calories: 209,
Total Fat: 2 g, Cholesterol: 59 mg, Sodium: 111 mg*

Black Bean Bisque with Crab

3 cups low sodium chicken broth,
defatted
1 jar (12.5 ounces) GUILTLESS
GOURMET® Black Bean Dip (mild
or spicy)
1 can (6 ounces) crabmeat, drained
2 tablespoons brandy (optional)
6 tablespoons low fat sour cream
Chopped fresh chives (optional)

Microwave Directons: Combine broth and
bean dip in 2-quart glass measure or
microwave-safe casserole. Cover with vented
plastic wrap or lid; microwave on HIGH 6
minutes or until soup starts to bubble.

Stir in crabmeat and brandy, if desired;
microwave on MEDIUM (50% power) 2
minutes or to desired serving temperature.
To serve, ladle bisque into 8 individual
ramekins or soup bowls, dividing evenly.
Swirl 1 tablespoon sour cream into each
serving. Garnish with chives, if desired.
                        Makes 8 servings

Stove Top Directions: Combine broth and
bean dip in 2-quart saucepan; bring to a
boil over medium heat. Stir in crabmeat and
brandy, if desired; cook 2 minutes or to
desired serving temperature. Serve as
directed.

Nutritional Information per Serving: *Calories: 90,
Total Fat: 1 g, Cholesterol: 22 mg, Sodium: 260 mg*

Mediterranean Fish Soup

Vietnamese Beef Soup

¾ pound boneless lean beef, such as
sirloin or round steak
3 cups water
1 can (about 14 ounces) beef broth
1 can (10½ ounces) condensed
consommé
2 tablespoons reduced-sodium soy
sauce
2 tablespoons minced fresh ginger
1 cinnamon stick (3 inches long)
4 ounces uncooked rice noodles,
⅛ inch wide
½ cup thinly sliced or julienned carrots
2 cups fresh mung bean sprouts
1 small red onion, halved and thinly
sliced
½ cup chopped cilantro
½ cup chopped fresh basil leaves
2 jalapeño peppers, stemmed, seeded
and minced* or 1 to 3 teaspoons
Chinese chili sauce or paste

*Jalapeño peppers can sting and irritate the skin. Wear rubber gloves when handling peppers and do not touch eyes.

1. Place beef in freezer 45 minutes or until firm. Meanwhile, combine water, beef broth, consommé, soy sauce, ginger and cinnamon stick in large saucepan; bring to a boil over high heat. Reduce heat to low; simmer, covered, 20 to 30 minutes. Remove cinnamon stick; discard. Meanwhile, place rice noodles in large bowl and cover with warm water; let stand until pliable, about 20 minutes.

2. Slice beef across grain into very thin strips. Drain noodles. Place noodles and carrots in simmering broth; cook 2 to 3 minutes or until noodles are tender. Add beef and bean sprouts; cook 1 minute or until beef is no longer pink.

3. Remove from heat; stir in red onion, cilantro, basil and jalapeño peppers. To serve, lift noodles from soup with fork and place in bowls. Ladle remaining ingredients and broth over noodles.

Makes 6 servings

Nutritional Information per Serving: *Calories: 180, Total Fat: 3 g, Cholesterol: 32 mg, Sodium: 800 mg*

Kansas City Steak Soup

Nonstick cooking spray
½ pound ground sirloin or ground
round beef
1 cup chopped onion
3 cups frozen mixed vegetables
1 cup sliced celery
1 can (14½ ounces) stewed tomatoes,
undrained
1 beef bouillon cube
½ to 1 teaspoon black pepper
2 cups water
1 can (10½ ounces) fat-free reduced-
sodium beef broth
½ cup all-purpose flour

1. Spray Dutch oven with cooking spray. Heat over medium-high heat until hot. Add beef and onion. Cook and stir 5 minutes or until beef is browned.

2. Add mixed vegetables, celery, tomatoes, bouillon cube, pepper and water. Bring to a boil. Whisk together beef broth and flour until smooth; add to beef mixture, stirring constantly. Return mixture to a boil. Reduce heat to low. Cover and simmer 15 minutes, stirring frequently. *Makes 6 servings*

Nutritional Information per Serving: *Calories: 198, Total Fat: 5 g, Cholesterol: 23 mg, Sodium: 598 mg*

Vietnamese Beef Soup

Moroccan Lentil & Vegetable Soup

1 tablespoon olive oil
1 cup chopped onion
4 medium cloves garlic, minced
½ cup dry lentils, sorted, rinsed and drained
1½ teaspoons ground coriander
1½ teaspoons ground cumin
½ teaspoon black pepper
½ teaspoon ground cinnamon
3¾ cups fat-free reduced-sodium chicken broth
½ cup chopped celery
½ cup chopped sun-dried tomatoes (not packed in oil)
1 medium yellow summer squash, chopped
½ cup chopped green bell pepper
½ cup chopped parsley
1 cup chopped plum tomatoes
¼ cup chopped cilantro or basil

1. Heat oil in medium saucepan over medium heat. Add onion and garlic; cook 4 to 5 minutes or until onion is tender, stirring occasionally. Stir in lentils, coriander, cumin, black pepper and cinnamon; cook 2 minutes. Add chicken broth, celery and sun-dried tomatoes; bring to a boil over high heat. Reduce heat to low; simmer, covered, 25 minutes.

2. Stir in squash, bell pepper and parsley. Continue cooking, covered, 10 minutes or until lentils are tender.

3. Top with plum tomatoes and cilantro just before serving.   *Makes 6 servings*

Nutritional Information per Serving: *Calories: 131, Total Fat: 3 g, Cholesterol: 0 mg, Sodium: 264 mg*

Spicy Lentil and Pasta Soup

2 medium onions, thinly sliced
½ cup chopped carrot
½ cup chopped celery
½ cup chopped peeled turnip
1 small jalapeño pepper, finely chopped*
2 cans (about 14 ounces each) vegetable broth
2 cups water
1 can (14½ ounces) no-salt-added stewed tomatoes, undrained
8 ounces dried lentils
2 teaspoons chili powder
½ teaspoon dried oregano leaves
3 ounces uncooked whole wheat spaghetti, broken
¼ cup minced fresh cilantro

Jalapeño peppers can sting and irritate the skin. Wear rubber gloves when handling peppers and do not touch eyes.

1. Spray large nonstick saucepan with nonstick cooking spray. Add onions, carrot, celery, turnip and jalapeño. Cook over medium heat 10 minutes or until vegetables are crisp-tender.

2. Add broth, water, tomatoes, lentils, chili powder and oregano. Bring to a boil. Reduce heat; cover and simmer 20 to 30 minutes or until lentils are tender.

3. Add pasta and cook 10 minutes or until tender.

4. Ladle soup into bowls; sprinkle with cilantro.   *Makes 6 servings*

Nutritional Information per Serving: *Calories: 261, Total Fat: 2 g, Cholesterol: 1 mg, Sodium: 771 mg*

Moroccan Lentil & Vegetable Soup

Eggplant & Orzo Soup with Roasted Red Pepper Salsa

Nonstick cooking spray
2 medium eggplants (1 pound each)
1½ cups finely chopped onions
2 cloves garlic, minced
2 cans (14.5 ounces each) low sodium
   chicken broth, defatted
1 jar (11.5 ounces) GUILTLESS
   GOURMET® Roasted Red Pepper
   Salsa
1 teaspoon black pepper
¾ cup uncooked orzo, cooked
   according to package directions

Preheat oven to 425°F. Coat baking sheet with cooking spray. Halve eggplants lengthwise and place cut side down on baking sheet. Bake about 15 to 20 minutes or until skins are wrinkled and slightly charred. Allow eggplants to cool until safe enough to handle. Peel eggplants; carefully remove and discard seeds. Finely chop eggplants; set aside.

Combine onions and garlic in 2-quart microwave-safe casserole. Cover with vented plastic wrap or lid; microwave on HIGH 5 to 6 minutes or until onions are tender. Add eggplants, broth, salsa and pepper; cover. Microwave on HIGH 6 to 8 minutes more or until soup bubbles. To serve, place ⅓ cup orzo into each of 6 individual soup bowls. Ladle 1 cup soup over orzo in each bowl.

Makes 6 servings

Stove Top Directions: Prepare eggplants as directed. Bring ¼ cup broth to a boil in 2-quart saucepan over medium-high heat. Add onions and garlic; cook and stir until onions are tender. Add eggplants, remaining broth, salsa and pepper. Return to a boil. Serve as directed.

Nutritional Information per Serving: *Calories: 181, Total Fat: 2 g, Cholesterol: 24 mg, Sodium: 281 mg*

Roman Spinach Soup

6 cups fat-free reduced-sodium chicken
   broth
1 cup cholesterol-free egg substitute
¼ cup minced fresh basil
3 tablespoons freshly grated Parmesan
   cheese
2 tablespoons lemon juice
1 tablespoon minced fresh parsley
¼ teaspoon ground white pepper
⅛ teaspoon ground nutmeg
8 cups fresh spinach, stemmed and
   chopped

1. Bring chicken broth to a boil in 4-quart saucepan over medium heat.

2. Beat together egg substitute, basil, cheese, lemon juice, parsley, pepper and nutmeg in small bowl. Set aside.

3. Stir spinach into broth; simmer 1 minute. Slowly pour egg mixture into broth mixture, whisking constantly so egg threads form. Simmer 2 to 3 minutes or until egg is cooked. Serve immediately.

Makes 8 servings

Nutritional Information per Serving: *Calories 46, Total Fat: 1 g, Cholesterol: 2 mg, Sodium: 153 mg*

Onion Soup with Pasta

Nonstick cooking spray
3 cups sliced onions
3 cloves garlic, minced
½ teaspoon sugar
2 cans (about 14 ounces each) fat-free
   reduced-sodium beef broth
½ cup uncooked small pasta stars
2 tablespoons dry sherry
¼ teaspoon salt
⅛ teaspoon black pepper
   Grated Parmesan cheese

1. Spray large saucepan with cooking spray; heat over medium heat until hot. Add onions and garlic. Cook, covered, 5 to 8 minutes or until onions are wilted. Stir in sugar; cook about 15 minutes or until onion mixture is very soft and browned.

2. Add beef broth to saucepan; bring to a boil. Add pasta and simmer, uncovered, 6 to 8 minutes or until tender. Stir in sherry, salt and pepper. Sprinkle lightly with cheese.

Makes 4 servings

Nutritional Information per Serving: *Calories 141, Total Fat: 1 g, Cholesterol: 0 mg, Sodium: 201 mg*

Pasta Meatball Soup

10 ounces lean ground sirloin
5 tablespoons acini di pepe pasta, divided
¼ cup fresh, finely crushed bread crumbs
1 egg
2 tablespoons finely chopped fresh parsley, divided
1 teaspoon dried basil leaves, divided
¼ teaspoon salt
⅛ teaspoon black pepper
1 clove garlic, minced
2 cans (about 14 ounces each) fat-free reduced-sodium beef broth
1 (8-ounce) can tomato sauce
⅓ cup chopped onion

1. Combine beef, 2 tablespoons pasta, bread crumbs, egg, 1 tablespoon parsley, ½ teaspoon basil, salt, pepper and garlic in medium bowl. Form into 28 to 30 (1-inch) meatballs.

2. Bring beef broth, tomato sauce, onion and remaining ½ teaspoon basil to a boil in large saucepan over medium-high heat. Carefully add meatballs to broth. Reduce heat to medium-low; simmer, covered, 20 minutes. Add remaining 3 tablespoons pasta; cook 10 minutes or until tender. Garnish with remaining 1 tablespoon parsley.

Makes 4 servings

Nutritional Information per Serving: *Calories: 216, Total Fat: 7 g, Cholesterol: 89 mg, Sodium: 599 mg*

Tuscany Bean & Pasta Soup

Vegetable cooking spray
½ cup chopped onion
2 cloves garlic, minced
1 can HEALTHY CHOICE® Recipe Creations™ Cream of Mushroom with Cracked Pepper & Herbs Condensed Soup
2½ cups nonfat milk
1 (15-ounce) can cannellini beans, drained and rinsed
1 cup cooked small macaroni (shells or elbow)
2 teaspoons chopped fresh parsley
½ teaspoon chili powder
½ teaspoon salt (optional)
Crumbled cooked bacon for garnish (optional)

In medium saucepan sprayed with vegetable cooking spray, sauté onion and garlic until tender. Add soup, milk, beans, macaroni, parsley, chili powder and salt; mix well. Simmer 10 minutes, stirring occasionally. Garnish with bacon, if desired.

Makes 6 servings

Nutritional Information per Serving: *Calories: 150, Total Fat: 1 g, Sodium: 410 mg*

Gazpacho

2 cups HUNT'S® Low Sodium Tomato Juice
1 (14½-ounce) can fat free, low sodium beef broth
1 can HEALTHY CHOICE® Recipe Creations™ Tomato with Garden Herbs Condensed Soup
1½ cups *each* peeled and diced cucumbers and diced green bell peppers
1¼ cups *each* shredded carrots and diced celery
½ cup sliced green onions
¼ cup chopped fresh parsley
2 cloves garlic, minced
1 tablespoon lime juice
2 teaspoons low sodium Worcestershire sauce
½ teaspoon salt (optional)
   Fat free sour cream
   Chopped cilantro

In large bowl, combine tomato juice, beef broth, soup, cucumbers, peppers, carrots, celery, green onions, parsley, garlic, lime juice, Worcestershire sauce and salt. Chill at least 2 hours to blend flavors. Top with desired amount of sour cream and cilantro.

Makes 4 to 6 servings

Nutritional Information per Serving: *Calories: 80, Total Fat: ½ g, Sodium: 210 mg*

Cioppino

1 teaspoon olive oil
1 large onion, chopped
1 cup sliced celery, with celery tops
1 clove garlic, minced
4 cups water
1 fish-flavored bouillon cube
1 tablespoon salt-free Italian herb seasoning
¼ pound cod or other boneless mild-flavored fish fillets
¼ pound small shrimp, peeled and deveined
¼ pound bay scallops
1 large tomato, chopped
1 can (10 ounces) baby clams, rinsed and drained (optional)
¼ cup flaked crabmeat or crabmeat blend
2 tablespoons fresh lemon juice

1. Heat olive oil in large saucepan over medium heat until hot. Add onion, celery and garlic. Cook and stir 5 minutes or until onion is soft. Add water, bouillon cube and Italian seasoning. Cover and bring to a boil over high heat.

2. Cut cod fillets into ½-inch pieces. Add cod, shrimp, scallops and tomato to saucepan. Reduce heat to medium-low; simmer 10 to 15 minutes or until seafood is opaque. Add clams, if desired, crabmeat and lemon juice. Heat through.

Makes 4 servings

Nutritional Information per Serving: *Calories 122, Total Fat: 2 g, Cholesterol: 75 mg, Sodium: 412 mg*

Gazpacho

Ginger Wonton Soup

4 ounces lean ground pork
½ cup reduced-fat ricotta cheese
½ tablespoon minced fresh cilantro
½ teaspoon black pepper
⅛ teaspoon Chinese 5-spice powder
20 fresh or thawed frozen wonton
    wrappers
1 teaspoon vegetable oil
⅓ cup chopped red bell pepper
1 teaspoon grated fresh ginger
2 cans (about 14 ounces each) fat-free
    reduced-sodium chicken broth
2 teaspoons reduced-sodium soy sauce
4 ounces fresh snow peas
1 can (8¾ ounces) baby corn, rinsed
    and drained
2 green onions, thinly sliced

1. Cook pork in small nonstick skillet over medium-high heat 4 minutes or until no longer pink. Cool slightly; stir in cheese, cilantro, black pepper and 5-spice powder.

2. Place 1 teaspoon filling in center of each wonton wrapper. Fold top corner of wonton over filling. Lightly brush remaining corners with water. Fold left and right corners over filling. Tightly roll filled end toward remaining corner in jelly-roll fashion. Moisten edges with water to seal. Cover and set aside.

3. Heat oil in large saucepan. Add bell pepper and ginger; cook 1 minute. Add chicken broth and soy sauce; bring to a boil. Add snow peas, baby corn and wontons. Reduce heat to medium-low and simmer 4 to 5 minutes or until wontons are tender. Sprinkle with green onions.

Makes 4 servings

Nutritional Information per Serving: *Calories: 259, Total Fat: 5 g, Cholesterol: 53 mg, Sodium: 261 mg*

Asian Noodle Soup

4 ounces dried Chinese egg noodles
3 cans (about 14 ounces each) fat-free
    reduced-sodium chicken broth
2 slices fresh ginger
2 cloves garlic, peeled and cut into
    halves
½ cup fresh snow peas, cut into 1-inch
    pieces
3 tablespoons chopped green onions
1 tablespoon chopped fresh cilantro
1½ teaspoons hot chili oil
½ teaspoon dark sesame oil

1. Cook noodles according to package directions, omitting salt. Drain.

2. Meanwhile, combine chicken broth, ginger and garlic in large saucepan; bring to a boil over high heat. Reduce heat to low; simmer about 15 minutes. Remove ginger and garlic with slotted spoon; discard.

3. Add snow peas, green onions, cilantro, chili oil and sesame oil to broth; simmer 3 to 5 minutes. Stir in noodles; serve immediately. *Makes 4 servings*

Nutritional Information per Serving: *Calories 118, Total Fat: 4 g, Cholesterol: 4 mg, Sodium: 152 mg*

Ginger Wonton Soup

Vegetable-Chicken Noodle Soup

1 cup chopped celery
½ cup thinly sliced leek (white part only)
½ cup chopped carrot
½ cup chopped turnip
6 cups fat-free reduced-sodium chicken broth, divided
1 tablespoon minced fresh parsley
1½ teaspoons fresh thyme *or*
    ½ teaspoon dried thyme leaves
1 teaspoon fresh rosemary *or*
    ¼ teaspoon dried rosemary
1 teaspoon balsamic vinegar
¼ teaspoon black pepper
2 ounces uncooked yolk-free wide noodles
1 cup diced cooked chicken

1. Place celery, leek, carrot, turnip and ⅓ cup chicken broth in large saucepan. Cover and cook over medium heat until vegetables are tender, stirring occasionally.

2. Stir in remaining chicken broth, parsley, thyme, rosemary, vinegar and pepper. Bring to a boil; add noodles. Cook until noodles are tender; stir in chicken. Reduce heat to medium. Simmer until heated through.
Makes 6 servings

Nutritional Information per Serving: *Calories: 98, Total Fat: 2 g, Cholesterol: 18 mg, Sodium: 73 mg*

Hearty Chicken and Rice Soup

10 cups chicken broth
1 medium onion, chopped
1 cup sliced celery
1 cup sliced carrots
¼ cup snipped fresh parsley
½ teaspoon dried thyme leaves
½ teaspoon cracked black pepper
1 bay leaf
1½ cups chicken cubes (about ¾ pound)
2 cups cooked rice
2 tablespoons lime juice
    Lime slices for garnish

Combine chicken broth, onion, celery, carrots, parsley, thyme, pepper and bay leaf in Dutch oven. Bring to a boil over high heat, stirring occasionally.

Reduce heat to low. Simmer, uncovered, 10 to 15 minutes. Add chicken; simmer, uncovered, 5 to 10 minutes or until chicken is cooked. Remove and discard bay leaf.

Stir in rice and lime juice just before serving. Garnish with lime slices.   *Makes 8 servings*

Nutritional Information per Serving: *Calories: 184, Total Fat: 4 g, Cholesterol: 23 mg, Sodium: 1209 mg*

Favorite recipe from **USA Rice Federation**

Vegetable-Chicken Noodle Soup

Southwest Corn and Turkey Soup

3 dried ancho chilies (each about
  4 inches long)
2 small zucchini
  Nonstick cooking spray
1 medium onion, thinly sliced
3 cloves garlic, minced
1 teaspoon ground cumin
3 cans (about 14 ounces each) fat-free
  reduced-sodium chicken broth
1½ to 2 cups (8 to 12 ounces) shredded
  cooked dark turkey meat
1 can (15 ounces) chick-peas or black
  beans, rinsed and drained
1 package (10 ounces) frozen corn
¼ cup cornmeal
1 teaspoon dried oregano leaves
⅓ cup chopped cilantro

1. Cut stems from chilies; shake out seeds. Place chilies in medium bowl; cover with boiling water. Let stand 20 to 40 minutes or until chilies are soft; drain. Cut open lengthwise and lay flat on work surface. With edge of small knife, scrape chili pulp from skin. Finely mince pulp; set aside.

2. Cut zucchini in half lengthwise; slice crosswise into ½-inch-wide pieces. Set aside.

3. Spray large saucepan with cooking spray; heat over medium heat. Add onion; cook, covered, 3 to 4 minutes or until light golden brown, stirring several times. Add garlic and cumin; cook and stir about 30 seconds or until fragrant. Add chicken broth, reserved chili pulp, zucchini, turkey, chick-peas, corn, cornmeal and oregano; bring to a boil over high heat. Reduce heat to low; simmer 15 minutes or until zucchini is tender. Stir in cilantro; ladle into bowls and serve.

Makes 6 servings

Nutritional Information per Serving: *Calories: 243, Total Fat: 5 g, Cholesterol: 32 mg, Sodium: 408 mg*

Cream of Chicken Soup

1 cup uncooked white rice
3 cans (10¾ ounces each) fat-free
  reduced-sodium chicken broth
1 skinless chicken breast (about
  6 ounces)
1 rib celery, coarsely chopped
1 carrot, thinly sliced
¼ cup coarsely chopped onion
3 sprigs fresh parsley
1¼ cups evaporated skimmed milk
¼ teaspoon dried thyme leaves
⅛ teaspoon white pepper
⅛ teaspoon ground nutmeg
2 tablespoons finely chopped fresh
  parsley
1 green onion, finely chopped

1. Cook rice according to package directions, omitting salt.

2. Meanwhile, combine chicken broth and chicken in large saucepan. Bring to a boil over high heat. Reduce heat to medium-low. Simmer 10 minutes, skimming off any foam that rises to surface. Add celery, carrot, onion and parsley sprigs. Simmer 10 minutes or until chicken is no longer pink near bone and vegetables are tender, skimming off any foam that rises to surface.

3. Remove chicken breast from saucepan. Let stand 10 minutes or until cool enough to handle. Remove chicken from bone. Cut into 1-inch pieces.

4. Add rice, chicken pieces, milk, thyme, pepper and nutmeg to saucepan. Cook over medium-high heat 8 minutes or until soup thickens, stirring constantly.

5. Top servings evenly with chopped parsley and green onion.   *Makes 4 servings*

Nutritional Information per Serving: *Calories: 326, Total Fat: 4 g, Cholesterol: 28 mg, Sodium: 173 mg*

Southwest Corn and Turkey Soup

Chicken and Dumplings Stew

2 cans (about 14 ounces each) fat-free
    reduced-sodium chicken broth
1 pound boneless skinless chicken
    breast halves, cut into bite-sized
    pieces
1 cup diagonally sliced carrots
¾ cup diagonally sliced celery
1 onion, halved and cut into small
    wedges
3 small new potatoes, unpeeled, cut
    into cubes
½ teaspoon dried rosemary
¼ teaspoon black pepper
1 can (14½ ounces) diced tomatoes,
    drained *or* 1½ cups diced fresh
    tomatoes
3 tablespoons all-purpose flour
    blended with ⅓ cup water

DUMPLINGS:
¾ cup all-purpose flour
1 teaspoon baking powder
¼ teaspoon onion powder
¼ teaspoon salt
1 to 2 tablespoons finely chopped
    parsley
¼ cup cholesterol-free egg substitute
¼ cup 1% low-fat milk
1 tablespoon vegetable oil

1. Bring chicken broth to a boil in Dutch oven; add chicken. Cover; simmer 3 minutes. Add carrots, celery, onion, potatoes, rosemary and pepper. Cover; simmer 10 minutes. Reduce heat; stir in tomatoes and dissolved flour. Cook and stir until broth thickens.

2. Combine ¾ cup flour, baking powder, onion powder and salt in medium bowl; blend in parsley. Combine egg substitute, milk and oil in small bowl; stir into flour mixture. *Do not overmix.*

3. Return broth mixture to a boil. Drop 8 tablespoons of dumpling batter into broth; cover tightly. Reduce heat; simmer 18 to 20 minutes. *Do not lift lid.* Dumplings are done when toothpick inserted comes out clean.

Makes 4 servings

Nutritional Information per Serving (2 dumplings and stew): *Calories: 422, Total Fat: 7 g, Cholesterol: 70 mg, Sodium: 968 mg*

New Orleans Pork Gumbo

1 pound pork loin roast
    Nonstick cooking spray
1 tablespoon margarine
2 tablespoons all-purpose flour
1 cup water
1 can (16 ounces) stewed tomatoes,
    undrained
1 package (10 ounces) frozen cut okra
1 package (10 ounces) frozen
    succotash
1 beef bouillon cube
1 teaspoon hot pepper sauce
1 teaspoon black pepper
1 bay leaf

1. Cut pork into ½-inch cubes. Spray large Dutch oven with cooking spray. Heat over medium heat until hot. Add pork; cook and stir 4 minutes or until pork is browned. Remove pork from Dutch oven.

2. Add margarine to Dutch oven. Stir in flour. Cook and stir until roux is browned. Whisk in water. Add pork and remaining ingredients. Bring to a boil. Reduce heat to low and simmer 15 minutes. Remove bay leaf.

Makes 4 servings

Nutritional Information per Serving: *Calories 295, Total Fat: 10 g, Cholesterol: 45 mg, Sodium: 602 mg*

Chicken and Dumplings Stew

Vegetable-Bean Chowder

Nonstick cooking spray
½ cup chopped onion
½ cup chopped celery
2 cups water
½ teaspoon salt
2 cups cubed peeled potatoes
1 cup carrot slices
1 can (15 ounces) cream-style corn
1 can (15 ounces) cannellini beans, rinsed and drained
¼ teaspoon dried tarragon leaves
¼ teaspoon black pepper
2 cups 1% low-fat milk
2 tablespoons cornstarch

1. Spray 4-quart Dutch oven or large saucepan with cooking spray; heat over medium heat until hot. Add onion and celery. Cook and stir 3 minutes or until crisp-tender.

2. Add water and salt. Bring to a boil over high heat. Add potatoes and carrots. Reduce heat to medium-low. Simmer, covered, 10 minutes or until potatoes and carrots are tender. Stir in corn, beans, tarragon and pepper. Simmer, covered, 10 minutes or until heated through.

3. Stir milk into cornstarch in medium bowl until smooth. Stir into vegetable mixture. Simmer, uncovered, until thickened.

Makes 5 servings

Nutritional Information per Serving: *Calories: 273, Total Fat: 2 g, Cholesterol: 4 mg, Sodium: 696 mg*

Double Corn & Cheddar Chowder

1 tablespoon margarine
1 cup chopped onion
2 tablespoons all-purpose flour
2½ cups fat-free reduced-sodium chicken broth
1 can (16 ounces) cream-style corn
1 cup frozen corn
½ cup finely diced red bell pepper
½ teaspoon hot pepper sauce
¾ cup (3 ounces) shredded sharp Cheddar cheese
Freshly ground black pepper (optional)

1. Melt margarine in large saucepan over medium heat. Add onion; cook and stir 5 minutes. Sprinkle onion with flour; cook and stir 1 minute.

2. Add chicken broth; bring to a boil, stirring frequently. Add cream-style corn, corn kernels, bell pepper and pepper sauce; bring to a simmer. Cover; simmer 15 minutes.

3. Remove from heat; gradually stir in cheese until melted. Ladle into soup bowls; sprinkle with black pepper, if desired.

Makes 6 servings

Double Corn, Cheddar & Rice Chowder: Add 1 cup cooked white or brown rice with corn.

Nutritional Information per Serving: *Calories: 180, Total Fat: 6 g, Cholesterol: 10 mg, Sodium: 498 mg*

Vegetable-Bean Chowder

Vegetarian Chili

1 tablespoon vegetable oil
2 cloves garlic, finely chopped
1½ cups thinly sliced mushrooms
⅔ cup chopped red onion
⅔ cup chopped red bell pepper
2 teaspoons chili powder
¼ teaspoon ground cumin
⅛ teaspoon ground red pepper
⅛ teaspoon dried oregano leaves
1 can (28 ounces) peeled whole
    tomatoes, undrained
⅔ cup frozen baby lima beans
½ cup canned Great Northern beans,
    rinsed and drained
3 tablespoons nonfat sour cream
3 tablespoons shredded reduced-fat
    Cheddar cheese

1. Heat oil in large nonstick saucepan over medium-high heat until hot. Add garlic; cook and stir 3 minutes. Add mushrooms, onion and bell pepper. Cook 5 minutes, stirring occasionally. Add chili powder, cumin, red pepper and oregano; cook and stir 1 minute. Add tomatoes and beans; reduce heat to medium-low. Simmer 15 minutes, stirring occasionally.

2. Top servings with sour cream and cheese.

Makes 4 servings

Nutritional Information per Serving: *Calories: 189, Total Fat: 5 g, Cholesterol: 3 mg, Sodium: 428 mg*

Mediterranean Chili

1 can HEALTHY CHOICE® Recipe
    Creations™ Tomato with Garden
    Herbs Condensed Soup
1 cup fat free refried beans
¼ cup water
    Vegetable cooking spray
10 ounces extra-lean ground beef
1 small eggplant, diced
½ cup *each* diced onion and diced
    green bell pepper
2 cloves garlic, minced
½ teaspoon chili powder
½ teaspoon salt (optional)

In medium bowl, combine soup, beans and water; mix well. Set aside. In large saucepan sprayed with vegetable cooking spray, cook beef until no longer pink; drain and set aside.

In same saucepan, sauté eggplant, onion, pepper, garlic, chili powder and salt over medium-high heat until vegetables are tender. Add soup mixture and beef; mix well. Simmer until hot and bubbly.

Makes 4 servings

Nutritional Information per Serving: *Calories: 220, Total Fat: 6 g, Sodium: 470 mg*

Vegetarian Chili

Texas-Style Chili

Nonstick cooking spray
1 pound lean boneless beef chuck, cut into ½-inch pieces
2 cups chopped onions
5 cloves garlic, minced
2 tablespoons chili powder
1 tablespoon ground cumin
1 teaspoon ground coriander
1 teaspoon dried oregano leaves or ground oregano
2½ cups fat-free reduced-sodium beef broth
1 cup prepared salsa or picante sauce
2 cans (16 ounces each) pinto or red beans (or one of each), rinsed and drained
½ cup chopped fresh cilantro
½ cup nonfat sour cream
1 cup chopped ripe tomatoes

1. Spray Dutch oven or large saucepan with nonstick cooking spray; heat over medium-high heat until hot. Add beef, onions and garlic; cook and stir until beef is no longer pink, about 5 minutes. Sprinkle mixture with chili powder, cumin, coriander and oregano; mix well. Add beef broth and salsa; bring to a boil. Cover; simmer 45 minutes.

2. Stir in beans; continue to simmer, uncovered, 30 minutes or until beef is tender and chili has thickened, stirring occasionally.

3. Stir in cilantro. Ladle into bowls; top with sour cream and tomatoes. Garnish with pickled jalapeño peppers, if desired.

Makes 8 servings

Nutritional Information per Serving: *Calories: 268, Total Fat: 7 g, Cholesterol: 37 mg, Sodium: 725 mg*

Turkey Chili with Black Beans

1 pound ground turkey breast
1 can (about 14 ounces) fat-free reduced-sodium chicken broth
1 large onion, finely chopped
1 green bell pepper, seeded and diced
2 teaspoons chili powder
½ teaspoon ground allspice
¼ teaspoon ground cinnamon
¼ teaspoon paprika
1 can (15 ounces) black beans, rinsed and drained
1 can (14 ounces) crushed tomatoes in tomato purée, undrained
2 teaspoons cider vinegar

1. Heat large nonstick skillet over high heat. Add turkey, chicken broth, onion and bell pepper. Cook and stir, breaking up turkey. Cook until turkey is no longer pink.

2. Add chili powder, allspice, cinnamon and paprika. Reduce heat to medium-low; simmer 10 minutes. Add black beans, tomatoes and vinegar; bring to a boil.

3. Reduce heat to low; simmer 20 to 25 minutes or until thickened to desired consistency.

Makes 4 servings

Nutritional Information per Serving: *Calories: 272, Total Fat: 2 g, Cholesterol: 75 mg, Sodium: 873 mg*

Texas-Style Chili

Salads

Italian Crouton Salad

6 ounces French or Italian bread
¼ cup plain nonfat yogurt
¼ cup red wine vinegar
4 teaspoons olive oil
1 tablespoon water
3 cloves garlic, minced
6 medium (about 12 ounces) plum
    tomatoes
½ medium red onion, thinly sliced
3 tablespoons slivered fresh basil
    leaves
2 tablespoons finely chopped parsley
12 leaves red leaf lettuce *or* 4 cups
    prepared Italian salad mix
2 tablespoons grated Parmesan cheese

1. Preheat broiler. Cut bread into ¾-inch cubes. Place in single layer on jelly-roll pan. Broil, 4 inches from heat, 3 minutes or until bread is golden, stirring every 30 seconds to 1 minute. Remove from baking sheet; place in large bowl.

2. Whisk together yogurt, vinegar, oil, water and garlic in small bowl until blended; set aside. Core tomatoes; cut into ¼-inch-wide slices. Add to bread along with onion, basil and parsley; stir until blended. Pour yogurt mixture over crouton mixture; toss to coat. Cover; refrigerate 30 minutes or up to 1 day. (Croutons will be more tender the following day.)

3. To serve, place lettuce on plates. Spoon crouton mixture over lettuce. Sprinkle with cheese. *Makes 6 servings*

Nutritional Information per Serving: *Calories: 160, Total Fat: 5 g, Cholesterol: 2 mg, Sodium: 234 mg*

Italian Crouton Salad

Chicken Caesar Salad

4 small boneless skinless chicken breast
    halves
6 ounces uncooked gnocchi or other
    dried pasta
1 package (9 ounces) frozen artichoke
    hearts, thawed
1½ cups cherry tomatoes, quartered
¼ cup plus 2 tablespoons plain nonfat
    yogurt
2 tablespoons reduced-calorie
    mayonnaise
2 tablespoons grated Romano cheese
1 tablespoon sherry or red wine
    vinegar
1 clove garlic, minced
½ teaspoon anchovy paste
½ teaspoon Dijon mustard
½ teaspoon white pepper
1 small head romaine lettuce, torn into
    bite-size pieces
1 cup toasted bread cubes

1. Grill or broil chicken breasts until no longer pink in center; set aside.

2. Cook pasta according to package directions, omitting salt. Drain and rinse well under cold water until pasta is cool; drain well. Combine pasta, artichoke hearts and tomatoes in large bowl; set aside.

3. Combine yogurt, mayonnaise, cheese, sherry, garlic, anchovy paste, mustard and white pepper in small bowl; whisk until smooth. Add to pasta mixture; toss to coat evenly.

4. Arrange lettuce on platter or individual plates. Spoon pasta mixture over lettuce. Thinly slice chicken breasts and place on top of pasta. Sprinkle with bread cubes.

Makes 4 servings

Nutritional Information per Serving: *Calories: 379, Total Fat: 8 g, Cholesterol: 56 mg, Sodium: 294 mg*

Fresh Greens with Hot Bacon Dressing

3 cups torn spinach leaves
3 cups torn romaine lettuce leaves
2 small tomatoes, cut into wedges
1 cup sliced mushrooms
1 medium carrot, shredded
1 slice bacon, cut into small pieces
3 tablespoons red wine vinegar
1 tablespoon water
¼ teaspoon dried tarragon leaves
⅛ teaspoon coarsely ground black
    pepper
¼ teaspoon EQUAL® Measure™ *or*
    1 packet EQUAL® sweetener *or*
    2 teaspoons EQUAL® Spoonful™

• Combine spinach, romaine, tomatoes, mushrooms and carrot in large bowl; set aside.

• Cook bacon in 12-inch skillet until crisp. Carefully stir in vinegar, water, tarragon and pepper. Heat to boiling; remove from heat. Stir in Equal®.

• Add spinach mixture to skillet. Toss 30 to 60 seconds or just until greens are wilted. Transfer to serving bowl. Serve immediately.
Makes 4 to 6 (1⅓-cup) servings

Nutritional Information per Serving: *Calories: 51, Total Fat 1 g, Cholesterol: 1 mg, Sodium: 74 mg*

Chicken Caesar Salad

Penne Salad with Spring Peas

1 pound penne or medium pasta
　　shells, cooked and cooled
1½ cups fresh or thawed frozen peas,
　　cooked
1 large yellow or red bell pepper,
　　sliced
½ cup sliced green onions and tops
1 cup skim milk
½ cup fat-free mayonnaise
½ cup red wine vinegar
¼ cup minced parsley
2 teaspoons drained green
　　peppercorns, crushed (optional)
1¾ teaspoons EQUAL® Measure™ or
　　6 packets EQUAL® sweetener or
　　¼ cup EQUAL® Spoonful™
Salt and pepper

• Combine pasta, peas, bell pepper and green onions in salad bowl. Blend milk and mayonnaise in medium bowl until smooth. Stir in vinegar, parsley, peppercorns and Equal®.

• Pour dressing over salad and toss to coat; season to taste with salt and pepper.

Makes 6 (1-cup) servings

Nutritional Information per Serving: *Calories: 190, Total Fat: 1 g, Cholesterol: 26 mg, Sodium: 188 mg*

Festive Potato Salad

1 can HEALTHY CHOICE® Recipe
　　Creations™ Cream of Celery with
　　Sautéed Onion & Garlic Condensed
　　Soup
½ cup plain nonfat yogurt
3 tablespoons *each* red wine vinegar
　　and sweet relish
1 tablespoon Dijon mustard
1 clove garlic, minced
½ teaspoon salt (optional)
¼ teaspoon black pepper
4 russet potatoes, peeled, cooked and
　　cut into 1-inch cubes
¾ cup sliced green onions
½ cup *each* diced red bell pepper and
　　thinly sliced celery
3 hard-boiled egg whites, chopped
½ teaspoon dry mustard

In small bowl, combine soup, yogurt, vinegar, relish, mustard, garlic, salt and black pepper. Using wire whisk, blend until smooth. Set aside.

In large bowl, combine potatoes, green onions, bell pepper, celery, egg whites and mustard. Add soup mixture and toss gently until well coated. Refrigerate at least 1 hour to blend flavors. *Makes 8 servings*

Nutritional Information per Serving: *Calories: 110, Total Fat: 1 g, Sodium: 240 mg*

Penne Salad with Spring Peas

Marinated Tomato Salad

MARINADE:

1½ cups tarragon vinegar or white wine
   vinegar
½ teaspoon salt
¼ cup finely chopped shallots
2 tablespoons finely chopped chives
2 tablespoons fresh lemon juice
¼ teaspoon ground white pepper
2 tablespoons extra-virgin olive oil

SALAD:

6 plum tomatoes, quartered vertically
2 large yellow tomatoes, sliced
   horizontally into ½-inch slices
16 red cherry tomatoes, halved
   vertically
16 small yellow pear tomatoes, halved
   vertically

1. To prepare marinade, combine vinegar
and salt in large bowl; stir until salt is
completely dissolved. Add shallots, chives,
lemon juice and white pepper; mix well.
Slowly whisk in oil until well blended.

2. Add tomatoes to marinade; toss well.
Cover and let stand at room temperature 2
to 3 hours.   *Makes 8 servings*

Nutritional Information per Serving: *Calories: 56,
Total Fat: 2 g, Cholesterol: 0 mg, Sodium: 64 mg*

Salmon and Green Bean Salad with Pasta

1 can (6¼ ounces) salmon
8 ounces small whole wheat or regular
   pasta shells
¾ cup fresh green beans, cut into
   2-inch pieces
⅔ cup finely chopped carrots
½ cup nonfat cottage cheese
3 tablespoons plain nonfat yogurt
1½ tablespoons lemon juice
1 tablespoon fresh dill
2 teaspoons grated onion
1 teaspoon prepared mustard

1. Drain salmon and separate into chunks;
set aside.

2. Cook pasta according to package
directions, including ¼ teaspoon salt; add
green beans during last 3 minutes of
cooking. Drain and rinse well under cold
water until pasta and green beans are cool.

3. Combine pasta, green beans, carrots and
salmon in medium bowl.

4. Place cottage cheese, yogurt, lemon juice,
dill, onion and mustard in blender or food
processor; process until smooth. Pour over
pasta mixture; toss to coat evenly. Garnish
as desired.   *Makes 6 servings*

Nutritional Information per Serving: *Calories: 210,
Total Fat: 3 g, Cholesterol: 15 mg, Sodium: 223 mg*

Marinated Tomato Salad

Chicken and Spinach Salad

12 ounces chicken tenders
    Nonstick cooking spray
4 cups shredded spinach leaves
2 cups washed and torn romaine
    lettuce leaves
8 thin slices red onion
2 tablespoons (1 ounce) crumbled blue
    cheese
1 large grapefruit, peeled and
    sectioned
½ cup frozen citrus blend concentrate,
    thawed
¼ cup prepared fat-free Italian salad
    dressing

1. Cut chicken tenders into 2×½-inch strips. Spray large nonstick skillet with cooking spray; heat over medium heat until hot. Add chicken tenders; cook and stir 5 minutes or until no longer pink in center. Remove from skillet.

2. Divide spinach, lettuce, onion, cheese, grapefruit and chicken among 4 salad plates. Combine citrus blend concentrate and Italian dressing in small bowl; drizzle over salads. Garnish with assorted greens, if desired. *Makes 4 servings*

Nutritional Information per Serving: *Calories: 218, Total Fat: 4 g, Cholesterol: 55 mg, Sodium: 361 mg*

Zesty Romaine and Pasta Salad

6 ounces bow tie pasta
1 cup broccoli florets
¼ cup water
¼ cup red wine vinegar
2 tablespoons sugar
1 tablespoon finely chopped fresh basil
1 tablespoon lemon juice
1 tablespoon Dijon mustard
1 clove garlic, minced
½ teaspoon black pepper
6 cups torn romaine lettuce leaves
1 can (15 ounces) kidney beans, rinsed
    and drained
1 cup carrot slices
1 small red onion, cut into halves and
    thinly sliced
½ cup grated Parmesan cheese

1. Cook pasta according to package directions, adding broccoli during last 3 minutes of cooking; drain. Rinse under cold running water until cool; drain.

2. To make dressing, whisk water, vinegar, sugar, basil, lemon juice, mustard, garlic and pepper in small bowl until well blended.

3. Combine lettuce, pasta, broccoli, beans, carrots and onion in large bowl. Add dressing; toss to coat. Sprinkle with cheese. *Makes 4 servings*

Nutritional Information per Serving: *Calories: 276, Total Fat: 2 g, Cholesterol: 0 mg, Sodium: 230 mg*

Chicken and Spinach Salad

Apple Slaw with Poppy Seed Dressing

1 cup coarsely chopped unpeeled
    Jonathan apple
1 teaspoon lemon juice
2 tablespoons nonfat sour cream
4½ teaspoons skim milk
1 tablespoon frozen apple juice
    concentrate, thawed
1 teaspoon sugar
¾ teaspoon poppy seeds
½ cup sliced carrot
⅓ cup shredded green cabbage
⅓ cup shredded red cabbage
2 tablespoons finely chopped green
    bell pepper
Additional cabbage leaves (optional)

1. Combine apple and lemon juice in resealable plastic food storage bag. Seal bag; toss to coat.

2. Combine sour cream, milk, apple juice concentrate, sugar and poppy seeds in small bowl until well blended. Add apple mixture, carrot, cabbages and pepper; toss to coat. Serve on cabbage leaves and garnish with fresh greens and carrot slice, if desired.

Makes 2 servings

Nutritional Information per Serving: *Calories: 94, Total Fat: 1 g, Cholesterol: trace, Sodium: 34 mg*

Mediterranean Pasta Salad

1 package (8 ounces) refrigerated or
    frozen cheese tortellini
1½ cups broccoli and/or cauliflower
    florets
1 can (8 ounces) DOLE® Pineapple
    Chunks, undrained
2 tablespoons balsamic or red wine
    vinegar
1 tablespoon olive or vegetable oil
¼ pound fresh link turkey sausage,
    cooked, drained and sliced
1 medium DOLE® Red, Yellow or Green
    Bell Pepper, cut into 1-inch pieces

• **Prepare** tortellini as package directs, except add broccoli during last 2 minutes of cooking.

• **Drain** pineapple; reserve ¼ cup juice.

• **Combine** reserved juice, vinegar and oil in large serving bowl.

• **Drain** tortellini and broccoli. Add tortellini, broccoli, sausage, bell pepper and pineapple to dressing; toss to evenly coat. Serve at room temperature or chilled.

• **Toss** before serving. Garnish with fresh herbs, if desired.

Makes 6 servings

Prep Time: 10 minutes

Cook Time: 20 minutes

Nutritional Information per Serving: *Calories: 184, Total Fat: 5 g, Cholesterol: 19 mg, Sodium: 290 mg*

Apple Slaw with Poppy Seed Dressing

Spicy Orzo and Black Bean Salad

2 tablespoons olive oil
2 tablespoons minced jalapeño pepper,* divided
1 teaspoon chili powder
¾ cup uncooked orzo pasta
1 cup frozen mixed vegetables
1 can (16 ounces) black beans, rinsed and drained
2 thin slices red onion
¼ cup chopped cilantro
¼ cup fresh lime juice
¼ cup fresh lemon juice
4 cups washed and torn spinach leaves
2 tablespoons crumbled blue cheese (optional)

Jalapeño peppers can sting and irritate the skin. Wear rubber gloves when handling peppers and do not touch eyes.

1. Combine oil, 1 tablespoon jalapeño and chili powder in medium bowl.

2. Bring 6 cups water and remaining 1 tablespoon jalapeño to a boil in large saucepan. Add orzo. Cook 10 to 12 minutes or until tender; drain. Rinse in cold water; drain.

3. Place frozen vegetables in small microwavable container. Cover and microwave at HIGH 3 minutes or until hot. Cover and let stand 5 minutes.

4. Add orzo, vegetables, black beans, onion, cilantro, lime juice and lemon juice to olive oil mixture in bowl. Divide spinach evenly among serving plates. Top with orzo and bean mixture. Sprinkle with blue cheese, if desired. Garnish with fresh cilantro, if desired. *Makes 4 servings*

Nutritional Information per Serving: *Calories: 356, Total Fat: 9 g, Cholesterol: 0 mg, Sodium: 467 mg*

Smoked Turkey Pasta Salad

8 ounces uncooked ditalini pasta (small tubes)
6 ounces smoked turkey or chicken breast, skin removed, cut into strips
1 can (15 ounces) light kidney beans, rinsed and drained
½ cup thinly sliced celery
¼ cup chopped red onion
⅓ cup reduced-fat mayonnaise
2 tablespoons chopped fresh chives or green onion
2 tablespoons balsamic vinegar
1 tablespoon fresh tarragon *or* 1½ teaspoons dried tarragon leaves
1 teaspoon Dijon mustard
1 clove garlic, minced
¼ teaspoon black pepper
Lettuce leaves (optional)

1. Cook pasta according to package directions, omitting salt. Drain and rinse well under cold water until pasta is cool; drain well.

2. Combine pasta with turkey, beans, celery and onion in medium bowl. Combine mayonnaise, chives, vinegar, tarragon, mustard, garlic and pepper in small bowl. Pour over pasta mixture; toss to coat evenly. Serve on lettuce leaves, if desired. *Makes 7 servings*

Nutritional Information per Serving: *Calories: 233, Total Fat: 5 g, Cholesterol: 12 mg, Sodium: 249 mg*

Spicy Orzo and Black Bean Salad

Scallop and Spinach Salad

1 package (10 ounces) spinach leaves, washed, stemmed and torn
3 thin slices red onion, halved and separated
12 ounces sea scallops
   Ground red pepper
   Paprika
   Nonstick cooking spray
½ cup prepared fat-free Italian salad dressing
¼ cup crumbled blue cheese
2 tablespoons toasted walnuts

1. Pat spinach dry; place in large bowl with red onion. Cover; set aside.

2. Rinse scallops. Cut in half horizontally (to make 2 thin rounds); pat dry. Sprinkle top side lightly with red pepper and paprika. Spray large nonstick skillet with cooking spray; heat over high heat until very hot. Add half of scallops, seasoned side down, in single layer, placing ½ inch or more apart. Sprinkle with red pepper and paprika. Cook 2 minutes or until browned on bottom. Turn scallops; cook 1 to 2 minutes or until opaque in center. Transfer to plate; cover to keep warm. Wipe skillet clean; repeat procedure with remaining scallops.

3. Place dressing in small saucepan; bring to a boil over high heat. Pour dressing over spinach and onion; toss to coat. Divide among 4 plates. Place scallops on top of spinach; sprinkle with blue cheese and walnuts. *Makes 4 servings*

Nutritional Information per Serving: *Calories: 169, Total Fat: 6 g, Cholesterol: 50 mg, Sodium: 660 mg*

Curried Salad Bombay

1 package (about 1⅓ pounds) PERDUE® FIT 'N' EASY® Fresh Skinless & Boneless Turkey Breast
½ cup reduced-sodium chicken broth
½ cup reduced-calorie mayonnaise
½ cup plain low-fat yogurt
1 tablespoon peach or mango chutney
2 to 3 teaspoons curry powder
   Salt and black pepper to taste (optional)
1 red apple, unpeeled, cored and sliced
1 green apple, unpeeled, cored and sliced
¾ cup red and/or green seedless grapes
2 tablespoons snipped fresh chives
   Curly green or Bibb lettuce

Microwave Directions: In deep 2-quart microwavable dish, place turkey breast and chicken broth. Cover with plastic wrap and microwave at HIGH 3 minutes. Reduce power to MEDIUM-HIGH (70% power) and microwave 7 minutes. Turn turkey breast over; cover with plastic wrap and microwave at MEDIUM-HIGH 7 minutes longer. Cover dish with aluminum foil and cool turkey in broth.

In medium bowl, combine mayonnaise, yogurt, chutney, curry, salt and pepper; blend well. Remove turkey from broth and cut into small cubes; add to mayonnaise mixture. Add apples, grapes and chives; toss gently to coat ingredients with dressing. Serve salad on bed of lettuce.

Makes 6 servings

Nutritional Information per Serving: *Calories: 241, Total Fat: 8 g, Cholesterol: 78 mg, Sodium: 263 mg*

Scallop and Spinach Salad

Sunburst Chicken Salad

1 tablespoon fat-free mayonnaise
1 tablespoon nonfat sour cream
2 teaspoons frozen orange juice
    concentrate, thawed
¼ teaspoon grated orange peel
1 boneless skinless chicken breast,
    cooked and chopped
1 large kiwi, thinly sliced
⅓ cup mandarin oranges
¼ cup finely chopped celery
4 lettuce leaves, washed
2 tablespoons coarsely chopped
    cashews

Combine mayonnaise, sour cream, concentrate and peel in small bowl. Add chicken, kiwi, oranges and celery; toss to coat. Cover; refrigerate 2 hours. Serve on lettuce leaves. Top with cashews.

Makes 2 servings

Nutritional Information per Serving: *Calories: 195, Total Fat: 6 g, Cholesterol: 39 mg, Sodium: 431 mg*

Spinach Tomato Salad

1 package (8 ounces) DOLE® Complete
    Spinach Bacon Salad
2 medium tomatoes, halved and cut
    into thin wedges
1 can (14 to 16 ounces) low-sodium
    kidney or garbanzo beans, drained
½ medium cucumber, thinly sliced
½ small onion, thinly sliced

• **Toss** spinach, croutons and bacon from salad bag with tomatoes, beans, cucumber and onion in medium serving bowl.

• **Pour** dressing from packet over salad; toss to evenly coat. *Makes 4 servings*

Prep Time: 10 minutes

Nutritional Information per Serving: *Calories: 210, Total Fat: 6 g, Cholesterol: 0 mg, Sodium: 423 mg*

Chicken and Fruit Salad

½ cup plain nonfat yogurt
½ to 1 teaspoon lemon-pepper
    seasoning
½ teaspoon dry mustard
¼ teaspoon garlic salt
¼ teaspoon poppy seed
1¼ teaspoons EQUAL® Measure™ *or*
    4 packets EQUAL® sweetener *or*
    3 tablespoons EQUAL® Spoonful™
1 to 2 tablespoons orange juice
4 cups torn spinach leaves
8 ounces thinly sliced cooked chicken
    breast
2 cups sliced strawberries
1½ cups thinly sliced yellow summer
    squash
1 cup halved seedless green grapes
2 medium oranges, peeled and
    sectioned
½ cup toasted pecan pieces (optional)

• Combine yogurt, lemon-pepper seasoning, mustard, garlic salt, poppy seed and Equal® in small bowl. Add enough orange juice to reach drizzling consistency; set aside.

• Line platter with spinach. Arrange chicken, strawberries, squash, grapes and orange sections over spinach. Drizzle salad with dressing. Sprinkle with pecans, if desired.

Makes 4 servings

Nutritional Information per Serving: *Calories: 202, Total Fat: 5 g, Cholesterol: 51 mg, Sodium: 380 mg*

Sunburst Chicken Salad

Penne Pasta Salad

6 cups cooked penne pasta
2 cups shredded cooked skinless
    chicken breast
1 cup chopped red onion
¾ cup *each* chopped red or green bell
    pepper and sliced zucchini
1 (4-ounce) can sliced black olives,
    drained
1 teaspoon crushed red pepper
1 teaspoon salt (optional)
1 can HEALTHY CHOICE® Recipe
    Creations™ Cream of Roasted
    Chicken with Herbs Condensed
    Soup
½ cup *each* lemon juice and fat free
    shredded Parmesan cheese
½ cup shredded fresh basil (optional)

In large bowl, combine pasta, chicken, onion, bell pepper, zucchini, olives, red pepper and salt; toss lightly. In small bowl, combine soup and lemon juice; mix well. Pour soup mixture over pasta salad; mix well. Sprinkle with Parmesan cheese and basil, if desired. *Makes 8 servings*

Nutritional Information per Serving: *Calories: 258, Total Fat: 6 g, Sodium: 380 mg*

Jalapeño Coleslaw

6 cups preshredded cabbage or
    coleslaw mix
2 tomatoes, seeded and chopped
6 green onions, coarsely chopped
2 jalapeño peppers, finely chopped*
¼ cup cider vinegar
3 tablespoons honey
1 teaspoon salt

*Jalapeño peppers can sting and irritate the skin. Wear rubber gloves when handling peppers and do not touch eyes.

1. Combine cabbage, tomatoes, green onions, jalapeños, vinegar, honey and salt in serving bowl; mix well. Cover and refrigerate until ready to serve. *Makes 4 servings*

Nutritional Information per Serving: *Calories: 98, Total Fat: <1 g, Cholesterol: 0 mg, Sodium: 564 mg*

Shredded Carrot and Raisin Salad

1 pound carrots, peeled and shredded
1½ cups thinly sliced, cored, peeled
    apples
¼ cup dark raisins
½ cup plain low-fat yogurt or sour
    cream
⅓ cup skim milk
1 tablespoon lemon juice
1½ teaspoons EQUAL® Measure *or*
    5 packets EQUAL® sweetener *or*
    3½ tablespoons EQUAL® Spoonful™
¼ teaspoon ground nutmeg
¼ teaspoon ground cinnamon

• Combine carrots, apples and raisins in large bowl. Combine remaining ingredients; spoon over carrot mixture and toss to coat. Refrigerate until chilled. *Makes 6 servings*

Nutritional Information per Serving: *Calories: 90, Total Fat: 0 g, Cholesterol: 1 mg, Sodium: 48 mg*

Penne Pasta Salad

Roasted Red Pepper, Corn & Garbanzo Bean Salad

2 cans (15 ounces each) garbanzo
   beans
1 jar (11.5 ounces) GUILTLESS
   GOURMET® Roasted Red Pepper
   Salsa
1 cup frozen whole kernel corn,
   thawed and drained
½ cup GUILTLESS GOURMET® Green
   Tomatillo Salsa
2 green onions, thinly sliced
8 lettuce leaves
   Fresh tomato wedges and sunflower
   sprouts (optional)

Rinse and drain beans well; place in 2-quart casserole. Add roasted red pepper salsa, corn, tomatillo salsa and onions; stir to combine. Cover and refrigerate 1 hour or up to 24 hours.

To serve, line serving platter with lettuce. Spoon bean mixture over top. Garnish with tomatoes and sprouts, if desired.

Makes 8 servings

Nutritional Information per Serving: *Calories: 174, Total Fat: 2 g, Cholesterol: 0 mg, Sodium: 268 mg*

Caesar Salad

12 cups torn romaine lettuce leaves
½ cup EGG BEATERS® Healthy Real Egg
   Substitute
¼ cup olive oil*
¼ cup lemon juice
1 teaspoon GREY POUPON® Dijon
   Mustard
2 cloves garlic, minced
¼ teaspoon ground black pepper
   Grated Parmesan cheese (optional)

Vegetable oil can be substituted.

Place lettuce in large bowl; set aside.

In small bowl, whisk together Egg Beaters®, oil, lemon juice, mustard, garlic and pepper until well blended. To serve, pour dressing over lettuce, tossing until well coated. Serve with Parmesan cheese, if desired.

Makes 8 servings

Prep Time: 15 minutes

Nutritional Information per Serving (without cheese): *Calories: 84, Total Fat: 7 g, Cholesterol: 0 mg, Sodium: 48 mg*

Triple Bean Salad

1 can (15½ ounces) dark kidney beans,
   drained
1 can (14½ ounces) green beans,
   drained
1 can (14½ ounces) wax beans,
   drained
¼ cup sliced green onions
¼ cup red wine vinegar
1 tablespoon olive oil
1 teaspoon EQUAL® Measure™ *or*
   3 packets EQUAL® sweetener *or*
   2 tablespoons EQUAL® Spoonful™
1 teaspoon dried basil leaves
1 small clove garlic, minced
¼ teaspoon salt
¼ teaspoon fresh ground pepper

• Combine kidney beans, green beans, wax beans, green onions, vinegar, oil, Equal®, basil, garlic, salt and pepper in large nonmetallic bowl. Mix well. Cover; refrigerate overnight. Serve chilled.

Makes 4 (1-cup) servings

Nutritional Information per Serving: *Calories: 174, Total Fat: 4 g, Cholesterol: 0 mg, Sodium: 1025 mg*

Roasted Red Pepper,
Corn & Garbanzo Bean Salad

Sweet and Sour Broccoli Pasta Salad

8 ounces uncooked pasta twists
2 cups broccoli florets
⅔ cup shredded carrots
1 medium Red or Golden Delicious apple, cored, seeded and chopped
⅓ cup plain nonfat yogurt
⅓ cup apple juice
3 tablespoons cider vinegar
1 tablespoon light olive oil
1 tablespoon Dijon mustard
1 teaspoon honey
½ teaspoon dried thyme leaves
Lettuce leaves

1. Cook pasta according to package directions, omitting salt and adding broccoli during last 2 minutes. Drain and rinse well under cold water until pasta and broccoli are cool; drain well.

2. Place pasta, broccoli, carrots and apple in medium bowl.

3. Combine yogurt, apple juice, vinegar, oil, mustard, honey and thyme in small bowl and pour over pasta mixture; toss to coat evenly.

4. Serve on individual dishes lined with lettuce. Garnish with apple slices, if desired.
Makes 6 servings

Nutritional Information per Serving: *Calories: 198, Total Fat: 3 g, Cholesterol: trace, Sodium: 57 mg*

Garlic Chicken Caesar Salad

DRESSING:
1 can HEALTHY CHOICE® Recipe Creations™ Cream of Roasted Garlic Condensed Soup
½ cup fat free, low sodium chicken broth
¼ cup balsamic vinegar
¼ cup fat free shredded Parmesan cheese, divided
1 tablespoon low sodium Worcestershire sauce

SALAD:
2 heads romaine lettuce, torn into 2-inch pieces
4 grilled boneless, skinless chicken breast halves, cut into 2-inch strips
½ cup fat free herb-seasoned croutons

In food processor or blender, combine soup, chicken broth, vinegar, 2 tablespoons Parmesan cheese and Worcestershire sauce; process until smooth. In large salad bowl, combine lettuce and 1 cup dressing; toss well to coat. Top with chicken and croutons; sprinkle with remaining 2 tablespoons cheese.
Makes 8 servings

Nutritional Information per Serving: *Calories: 130, Total Fat: 2 g, Sodium: 330 mg*

Sweet and Sour Broccoli Pasta Salad

Caribbean Cole Slaw

Orange-Mango Dressing (recipe
follows)
8 cups shredded green cabbage
1½ large mangoes, peeled, pitted and
diced
½ medium red bell pepper, thinly sliced
½ medium yellow bell pepper, thinly
sliced
6 green onions, thinly sliced
¼ cup chopped cilantro

1. Prepare Orange-Mango Dressing.

2. Combine cabbage, mangoes, bell
peppers, green onions and cilantro in large
bowl; stir gently to mix evenly. Pour in
Orange-Mango Dressing; toss gently to coat.
Serve, or store in refrigerator up to 1 day.

Makes 6 servings

Orange-Mango Dressing

½ mango, peeled, pitted and cubed
1 carton (6 ounces) plain nonfat
yogurt
¼ cup frozen orange juice concentrate
3 tablespoons fresh lime juice
½ to 1 jalapeño pepper, stemmed,
seeded and minced*
1 teaspoon finely minced fresh ginger

*Jalapeño peppers can sting and irritate the skin. Wear
rubber gloves when handling peppers and do not touch
eyes.*

1. Place mango in food processor; process
until smooth. Add remaining ingredients;
process until smooth.   *Makes about 1 cup*

Nutritional Information per Serving: *Calories: 124,
Total Fat: 1 g, Cholesterol: 1 mg, Sodium: 52 mg*

Sesame Pork Salad

3 cups cooked rice
1½ cups slivered cooked pork*
¼ pound fresh snow peas, trimmed and
julienned
1 medium cucumber, peeled, seeded
and julienned
1 medium red bell pepper, julienned
½ cup sliced green onions
2 tablespoons sesame seeds, toasted
(optional)
¼ cup chicken broth
3 tablespoons rice vinegar or white
wine vinegar
3 tablespoons soy sauce
1 tablespoon peanut oil
1 teaspoon sesame oil

*Substitute 1½ cups slivered cooked chicken for pork, if
desired.*

Combine rice, pork, snow peas, cucumber,
pepper, onions and sesame seeds, if desired,
in large bowl. Combine chicken broth,
vinegar, soy sauce and oils in small jar with
lid. Pour over rice mixture; toss lightly. Serve
at room temperature or slightly chilled.

Makes 6 servings

Nutritional Information per Serving: *Calories: 269,
Total Fat: 8 g, Cholesterol: 32 mg, Sodium: 867 mg*

Favorite recipe from **USA Rice Federation**

Caribbean Cole Slaw

Santa Fe Chicken Pasta Salad

12 ounces uncooked spiral pasta
2 cups cooked chicken breast cubes
1 medium zucchini or yellow squash,
    cut in half lengthwise, then sliced
    crosswise
1 cup GUILTLESS GOURMET® Green
    Tomatillo Salsa
1 cup drained and coarsely chopped
    artichoke hearts
½ cup chopped green onions
½ cup sliced black olives
    Lettuce leaves
    Fresh dill sprigs (optional)

Cook pasta according to package directions; drain. Place pasta in large nonmetal bowl; add chicken, zucchini, tomatillo salsa, artichoke hearts, onions and olives. Toss lightly. Refrigerate at least 6 hours before serving.

To serve, line serving platter with lettuce leaves. Top with pasta mixture. Garnish with dill, if desired.   *Makes 4 servings*

Nutritional Information per Serving: *Calories: 413, Total Fat: 5 g, Cholesterol: 45 mg, Sodium: 429 mg*

Grilled Steak and Asparagus Salad

½ cup bottled light olive oil vinaigrette
    dressing
⅓ cup A.1.® Steak Sauce
1 (1-pound) beef top round steak
1 (10-ounce) package frozen asparagus
    spears, cooked and cooled
½ cup thinly sliced red bell pepper
8 large leaves lettuce
1 tablespoon toasted sesame seeds

In small bowl, blend vinaigrette and steak sauce. Pour marinade over steak in nonmetal dish. Cover; refrigerate 1 hour.

Remove steak from marinade. Grill or broil steak, 4 inches from heat source, 10 minutes or to desired doneness, basting occasionally with marinade and turning 2 or 3 times. Thinly slice steak; arrange steak, asparagus and bell pepper on lettuce leaves. Heat marinade to a boil; pour over salad. Sprinkle with sesame seeds; serve immediately.

Makes 4 servings

Nutritional Information per Serving: *Calories: 209, Total Fat: 5 g, Cholesterol: 65 mg, Sodium: 857 mg*

Orange and Red Onion Salad

¼ cup EGG BEATERS® Healthy Real Egg
    Substitute
2 tablespoons white wine vinegar
¼ teaspoon paprika
⅓ cup vegetable oil
2 tablespoons honey
2 tablespoons orange juice
6 cups torn romaine lettuce and fresh
    spinach leaves
1 cup orange segments
⅓ cup thinly sliced red onion

In blender container, blend Egg Beaters®, vinegar and paprika just until mixed. Without turning off blender, pour in oil in a slow steady stream. Continue blending until oil is completely incorporated and mixture is smooth and thick. Pour into medium bowl; stir in honey and orange juice. Cover; chill until ready to use.

In large bowl, combine lettuce and spinach leaves, orange segments and onion. To serve, pour dressing over salad, tossing until well coated.   *Makes 6 servings*

Prep Time: 25 minutes

Nutritional Information per Serving: *Calories: 164, Total Fat: 12 g, Cholesterol: 0 mg, Sodium: 42 mg*

Santa Fe Chicken Pasta Salad

Fajita Salad

1 beef sirloin steak (6 ounces)
¼ cup fresh lime juice
2 tablespoons chopped fresh cilantro
1 clove garlic, minced
1 teaspoon chili powder
2 red bell peppers
1 medium onion
1 teaspoon olive oil
1 cup chick-peas, rinsed and drained
4 cups mixed salad greens
1 tomato, cut into wedges
1 cup salsa

1. Cut beef into 2×1×¼-inch strips. Place in resealable plastic food storage bag. Combine lime juice, cilantro, garlic and chili powder in small bowl. Pour over beef; seal bag. Let stand 10 minutes, turning once.

2. Cut peppers into strips. Cut onion into slices. Heat oil in large nonstick skillet over medium-high heat until hot. Add bell peppers and onion. Cook and stir 6 minutes or until vegetables are crisp-tender. Remove from skillet. Add beef and marinade to skillet. Cook and stir 3 minutes or until meat is cooked through. Remove from heat. Add peppers, onion and chick-peas to skillet; toss to coat with pan juices. Cool slightly.

3. Divide greens evenly among serving plates. Top with beef mixture and tomato wedges. Serve with salsa. Garnish with sour cream and sprigs of cilantro, if desired.

Makes 4 servings

Nutritional Information per Serving: *Calories: 160, Total Fat: 5 g, Cholesterol: 30 mg, Sodium: 667 mg*

Creamy Garlic Dressing

12 ounces (2 cartons) ALPINE LACE® Fat Free Cream Cheese with Garlic & Herbs
½ cup 2% low fat milk
¼ cup fat free sour cream
2 tablespoons fresh lemon juice
1 tablespoon prepared horseradish
½ teaspoon freshly ground black pepper
Radish slices (optional)

1. In a food processor or blender, process all of the ingredients for 30 seconds or until well blended. Refrigerate until ready to serve. Garnish with the radish slices, if you wish.

2. Serve this dressing over vegetable or meat salads. It's also a great sauce for grilled meat, chicken and fish. *Makes 2 cups*

Nutritional Information per Serving (2 tablespoons): *Calories: 34, Total Fat: 0 g, Cholesterol: 4 mg, Sodium: 123 mg*

Fajita Salad

Sandwiches & Wraps

Grilled Vegetable Muffuletta

10 cloves garlic, peeled
  Nonstick cooking spray
 1 tablespoon balsamic vinegar
 1 tablespoon fresh lemon juice
 1 tablespoon olive oil
 ¼ teaspoon black pepper
 1 round whole wheat sourdough bread
  loaf (1½ pounds)
 1 medium eggplant, cut crosswise into
  eight ¼-inch-thick slices
 2 small yellow squash, cut lengthwise
  into thin slices
 1 small red onion, thinly sliced
 1 large red bell pepper, seeded and
  quartered
 2 slices (1 ounce each) reduced-fat
  Swiss cheese
 8 leaves spinach

1. Preheat oven to 350°F. Place garlic in ovenproof dish. Spray garlic with cooking spray. Cover with foil; bake 30 to 35 minutes or until garlic is very soft and golden brown.

2. Place garlic, vinegar, lemon juice, olive oil and black pepper in food processor; process using on/off pulsing action until smooth. Set aside.

3. Slice top off bread loaf. Hollow out loaf, leaving ½-inch-thick shell. Reserve bread for another use.

4. Prepare coals for grilling. Brush vegetables with garlic mixture. Arrange on grid over medium coals. Grill 10 to 12 minutes or until crisp-tender, turning once. Separate onion slices into rings.

5. Layer half of eggplant, squash, onion, bell pepper, cheese and spinach in hollowed bread, pressing gently after each layer. Repeat layers with remaining vegetables, cheese and spinach. Replace bread top and serve immediately or wrap tightly with plastic wrap and refrigerate for up to 4 hours.   *Makes 6 servings*

Nutritional Information per Serving: *Calories: 422, Total Fat: 8 g, Cholesterol: 7 mg, Sodium: 721 mg*

Grilled Vegetable Muffuletta

Down Home Barbecued Beef

1 slice bacon
½ cup chopped onion
½ cup ketchup
½ cup apple juice
1 tablespoon white vinegar
1 teaspoon prepared mustard
1 teaspoon Worcestershire sauce
⅛ teaspoon salt
⅛ teaspoon ground black pepper
2½ teaspoons EQUAL® Measure™ *or*
    8 packets EQUAL® sweetener *or*
    ⅓ cup EQUAL® Spoonful™
12 ounces thinly sliced roast beef
4 kaiser rolls (optional)

• Cut bacon into 1-inch pieces; cook in medium saucepan over medium-high heat 3 to 4 minutes or until almost cooked. Add onion; cook 3 to 5 minutes or until bacon is crisp and onion is tender, stirring occasionally.

• Combine ketchup, apple juice, vinegar, mustard, Worcestershire sauce, salt and pepper; add to bacon mixture. Reduce heat; cover and simmer until flavors are blended, 15 to 20 minutes.

• Stir in Equal® and sliced beef. Serve warm on rolls, if desired. *Makes 4 servings*

Microwave Directions: Cut bacon into 1-inch pieces and place in 1½-quart microwavable casserole. Cook, uncovered, at HIGH 1 minute. Add onion and cook at HIGH 2½ to 3 minutes or until bacon is crisp and onion is tender, stirring once. Combine ketchup, apple juice, vinegar, mustard, Worcestershire sauce, salt and pepper; add to bacon mixture. Cook, covered, at HIGH 4 to 5 minutes or until boiling. Cook at MEDIUM (50% power) 8 to 10 minutes or until flavors are blended, stirring twice. Stir in Equal® and sliced beef. Serve warm.

Nutritional Information per Serving: *Calories: 223, Total Fat: 6 g, Cholesterol: 70 mg, Sodium: 542 mg*

Turkey Gyros

1 turkey tenderloin (8 ounces)
1½ teaspoons Greek seasoning
1 cucumber
⅔ cup plain nonfat yogurt
¼ cup finely chopped onion
2 teaspoons dried dill weed
2 teaspoons fresh lemon juice
1 teaspoon olive oil
4 rounds pita bread
1½ cups shredded romaine lettuce
    leaves
1 tomato, thinly sliced
2 tablespoons crumbled feta cheese

1. Cut turkey tenderloin across grain into ¼-inch slices. Place turkey slices on plate; lightly sprinkle both sides with Greek seasoning. Let stand 5 minutes.

2. Cut two-thirds of cucumber into thin slices. Finely chop remaining cucumber. Combine chopped cucumber, yogurt, onion, dill weed and lemon juice in small bowl.

3. Heat oil in large skillet over medium heat until hot. Add turkey; cook 2 minutes on each side or until cooked through. Wrap 2 pitas in paper toweling. Microwave at HIGH 30 seconds or just until warmed. Repeat with remaining pitas. Divide lettuce, tomato, cucumber slices, turkey, cheese and yogurt-cucumber sauce evenly among pitas. Fold edges over and secure with toothpicks.
Makes 4 servings

Nutritional Information per Serving: *Calories 319, Total Fat: 4 g, Cholesterol: 55 mg, Sodium: 477 mg*

Down Home Barbecued Beef

Grilled Cheese 'n' Tomato Sandwiches

8 slices whole wheat bread, divided
6 ounces part-skim mozzarella cheese, cut into 4 slices
1 large tomato, cut into 8 thin slices
⅓ cup yellow cornmeal
2 tablespoons grated Parmesan cheese
1 teaspoon dried basil leaves
½ cup EGG BEATERS® Healthy Real Egg Substitute
¼ cup skim milk
2 tablespoons FLEISCHMANN'S® 70% Corn Oil Spread, divided
1 cup low-salt tomato sauce, heated

On each of 4 bread slices, place 1 cheese slice and 2 tomato slices; top with remaining bread slices. Combine cornmeal, Parmesan cheese and basil on waxed paper. In shallow bowl, combine Egg Beaters® and milk. Melt 1 tablespoon spread in large nonstick griddle or skillet. Dip sandwiches in egg mixture; coat with cornmeal mixture. Transfer 2 sandwiches to griddle. Cook sandwiches for 3 minutes on each side or until golden. Repeat using remaining spread and sandwiches. Cut sandwiches in half; serve warm with tomato sauce for dipping.

Makes 4 servings

Prep Time: 20 minutes

Cook Time: 14 minutes

Nutritional Information per Serving: *Calories: 420, Total Fat: 18 g, Cholesterol: 35 mg, Sodium: 657 mg*

Open-Faced Eggplant Melt

1 can HEALTHY CHOICE® Recipe Creations™ Tomato with Garden Herbs Condensed Soup
¼ cup fat free, low sodium chicken broth
3 sandwich-size English muffins, split and toasted
Vegetable cooking spray
1 small eggplant, cut crosswise into 1-inch slices and grilled
½ cup roasted red bell pepper strips, drained (6 strips)
6 slices HEALTHY CHOICE® Low Fat Smoked Ham
½ cup HEALTHY CHOICE® Fat Free Shredded Mozzarella Cheese

In small bowl, combine soup and chicken broth; mix well. Set aside. Place toasted muffin halves in single layer in shallow baking dish sprayed with vegetable cooking spray. Spread 1 tablespoon soup mixture on each muffin half. Top each muffin half with 1 slice eggplant, 1 bell pepper strip and 1 slice ham.

Pour remaining soup mixture evenly over sandwiches and sprinkle with cheese. Cover and bake at 350°F 10 minutes or until cheese is melted and sandwiches are heated through.

Makes 6 servings

Nutritional Information per Serving: *Calories: 100, Total Fat: 1 g, Sodium: 360 mg*

Grilled Cheese 'n' Tomato Sandwich

Barbecued Cheese Burgers

BARBECUE SPREAD:

¼ cup reduced calorie mayonnaise
¼ cup bottled barbecue sauce
¼ cup red or green pepper hamburger relish

BURGERS:

1½ pounds ground lean turkey or ground beef round
⅓ cup bottled barbecue sauce
⅓ cup minced red onion
1 teaspoon hot red pepper sauce
½ teaspoon garlic salt
6 sesame seed hamburger buns, split
6 slices (1 ounce each) ALPINE LACE® Fat Free Pasteurized Process Skim Milk Cheese Product—For Cheddar Lovers

1. To make the Barbecue Spread: In a small bowl, stir all of the spread ingredients together until well blended. Cover and refrigerate.

2. To make the Burgers: In a medium-size bowl, mix the turkey, barbecue sauce, onion, hot pepper sauce and garlic salt. Form into 6 patties (5 inches each), about 1¼ inches thick. Cover with plastic wrap and refrigerate for at least 30 minutes or overnight.

3. To cook the Burgers: Preheat the grill (or broiler). Grill over medium-hot coals (or broil) 4 inches from the heat for 4 minutes on each side for medium or until cooked the way you like them. Place the buns alongside the burgers for the last 5 minutes to heat, if you wish. Top each burger with a slice of cheese.

4. To serve, spread the insides of the buns with the Barbecue Spread and stuff each bun with a burger.   *Makes 6 burgers*

Nutritional Information per Serving (1 burger):
Calories: 351, Total Fat: 10 g, Cholesterol: 63 mg, Sodium: 1051 mg

Maui Chicken Sandwich

1 can (8 ounces) DOLE® Pineapple Slices, undrained
½ teaspoon dried oregano leaves
¼ teaspoon garlic powder
4 boneless, skinless small chicken breast halves
½ cup light Thousand Island salad dressing
½ cup finely chopped jicama or water chestnuts
¼ teaspoon ground red pepper (optional)
4 whole grain or whole wheat sandwich rolls
DOLE® Red or Green Bell Pepper, sliced into rings, or shredded
DOLE® Iceberg Lettuce

• **Combine** undrained pineapple, oregano and garlic powder in shallow, nonmetallic dish. Add chicken; turn to coat both sides. Cover and marinate 15 minutes in refrigerator.

• **Grill** or broil chicken and pineapple, brushing occasionally with reserved marinade, 5 to 8 minutes on each side or until chicken is no longer pink in center and pineapple is golden brown. Discard any remaining marinade.

• **Combine** dressing, jicama and ground red pepper. Spread onto bottom halves of rolls. Top with chicken, bell pepper, pineapple, lettuce and top halves of rolls. Garnish with fresh fruit and mint leaves, if desired.
Makes 4 servings

Prep Time: 10 minutes

Marinate Time: 15 minutes

Grill Time: 15 minutes

Nutritional Information per Serving: *Calories: 284, Total Fat: 8 g, Cholesterol: 82 mg, Sodium: 452 mg*

Black Bean & Rice Burritos

½ cup nonfat cottage cheese
2 tablespoons soft fresh goat cheese
1½ cups cooked brown rice or long-grain rice, kept warm
3 tablespoons minced red onion
3 tablespoons chopped fresh cilantro
¼ teaspoon ground cumin
¼ cup low sodium chicken broth, defatted
8 whole wheat tortillas (6 inches each)
¾ cup GUILTLESS GOURMET® Spicy Black Bean Dip
½ cup (2 ounces) shredded low fat Monterey Jack cheese
3 cups finely shredded lettuce
½ cup GUILTLESS GOURMET® Salsa (medium)
Fresh cilantro sprigs (optional)

Preheat oven to 350°F. Place cottage and goat cheeses in medium bowl; blend with fork until smooth. Add rice, onion, chopped cilantro and cumin. Mix well; set aside.

Place broth in shallow bowl. Working with 1 tortilla at a time, dip tortilla in broth to moisten each side. Spread 1 heaping tablespoonful bean dip on tortilla, then top with 1 heaping tablespoonful rice mixture. Roll up tortilla and place in 12×8-inch baking dish, seam side down. Repeat with remaining tortillas, bean dip and rice mixture. Cover with foil.

Bake about 25 to 30 minutes or until heated through. Remove foil; top with shredded cheese. Return to oven until cheese melts. To serve, arrange burritos on plate. Top with lettuce and salsa. Garnish with cilantro sprigs, if desired.   *Makes 8 burritos*

Nutritional Information per Serving (1 burrito): *Calories: 224, Total Fat: 5 g, Cholesterol: 7 mg, Sodium: 425 mg*

Mediterranean Vegetable Sandwiches

1 small eggplant, peeled, halved and cut into ¼-inch-thick slices
Salt
1 small zucchini, halved and cut lengthwise into ¼-inch-thick slices
1 green or red bell pepper, sliced
3 tablespoons balsamic vinegar
½ teaspoon salt
½ teaspoon garlic powder
2 French bread rolls, halved

1. Place eggplant in nonaluminum colander; sprinkle eggplant with salt. Let stand 30 minutes to drain. Rinse eggplant; pat dry with paper towels.

2. Preheat broiler. Spray rack of broiler pan with nonstick cooking spray. Place vegetables on rack. Broil 4 inches from heat, 8 to 10 minutes or until vegetables are browned, turning once.

3. Combine vinegar, ½ teaspoon salt and garlic powder in medium bowl until well blended. Add vegetables; toss to coat. Divide vegetable mixture evenly between rolls. Garnish with apple slices, if desired. Serve immediately.   *Makes 2 servings*

Nutritional Information per Serving: *Calories: 178, Total Fat: 2 g, Cholesterol: 0 mg, Sodium: 775 mg*

Meatless Sloppy Joes

2 cups thinly sliced onions
2 cups chopped green bell peppers
2 cloves garlic, finely chopped
2 tablespoons ketchup
1 tablespoon mustard
1 can (15 ounces) kidney beans, rinsed, drained and slightly mashed
1 can (8 ounces) tomato sauce
1 teaspoon chili powder
   Cider vinegar
2 sandwich rolls, halved

Spray skillet with nonstick cooking spray. Add onions, peppers and garlic. Cook and stir 5 minutes over medium heat. Stir in ketchup and mustard. Add beans, sauce and chili powder. Cook 5 minutes, stirring frequently. Add ⅓ cup vinegar if dry. Serve on rolls.   *Makes 4 servings*

Nutritional Information per Serving: *Calories: 242, Total Fat: 2 g, Cholesterol: 0 mg, Sodium: 994 mg*

Huevos Ranchwich

¼ cup EGG BEATERS® Healthy Real Egg Substitute
1 teaspoon diced green chiles
1 whole wheat hamburger roll, split and toasted
1 tablespoon thick and chunky salsa, heated
1 tablespoon shredded reduced-fat Cheddar and Monterey Jack cheese blend

On lightly greased griddle or skillet, pour Egg Beaters® into lightly greased 4-inch egg ring or biscuit cutter. Sprinkle with chiles. Cook 2 to 3 minutes or until bottom of egg patty is set. Remove egg ring and turn egg patty over. Cook 1 to 2 minutes longer or until done.

To serve, place egg patty on bottom of roll. Top with salsa, cheese and roll top.
          Makes 1 sandwich

Prep Time: 10 minutes

Cook Time: 5 minutes

Nutritional Information per Serving: *Calories: 143, Total Fat: 2 g, Cholesterol: 6 mg, Sodium: 411 mg*

The Californian

3 tablespoons reduced-fat cream cheese, softened
1 tablespoon chutney
4 slices pumpernickel bread
4 leaves lettuce
¾ pound thinly sliced deli chicken breast
1⅓ cups alfalfa sprouts
1 medium mango, peeled and sliced
1 pear, cored and sliced
4 strawberries

1. Combine cream cheese and chutney in small bowl; spread about 1 tablespoon on each bread slice. Place 1 lettuce leaf over cream cheese mixture. Divide chicken evenly; place over lettuce.

2. Arrange alfalfa sprouts over chicken; arrange mango and pear slices over sprouts. Garnish each sandwich with a strawberry.
          Makes 4 servings

Nutritional Information per Serving: *Calories 318, Total Fat: 6 g, Cholesterol: 72 mg, Sodium: 304 mg*

Meatless Sloppy Joe

Turkey Burgers

1 pound ground turkey breast
1 cup whole wheat bread crumbs
1 egg white
½ teaspoon dried sage leaves
½ teaspoon dried marjoram leaves
¼ teaspoon salt
¼ teaspoon ground black pepper
1 teaspoon vegetable oil
4 whole grain sandwich rolls, split in
　half
¼ cup Cowpoke Barbecue Sauce*
　(page 186)

Or substitute prepared barbecue sauce.

1. Combine turkey, bread crumbs, egg white, sage, marjoram, salt and pepper in large bowl until well blended. Shape into 4 patties.

2. Heat oil in large nonstick skillet over medium-high heat until hot. Add patties. Cook 10 minutes or until patties are no longer pink in centers, turning once.

3. Place one patty on bottom half of each roll. Spoon 1 tablespoon Cowpoke Barbecue Sauce over top of each burger. Place tops of rolls over burgers. Serve with lettuce and tomato and garnish with carrot slices, if desired. *Makes 4 burgers*

Nutritional Information per Serving: *Calories: 319, Total Fat: 6 g, Cholesterol: 41 mg, Sodium: 669 mg*

Tarragon Chicken Salad Sandwiches

1¼ pounds boneless skinless chicken
　breasts, cooked and diced
1 cup thinly sliced celery
1 cup seedless red or green grapes, cut
　into halves
½ cup raisins
½ cup plain nonfat yogurt
¼ cup reduced-fat mayonnaise or salad
　dressing
2 tablespoons finely chopped shallots
　or onion
2 tablespoons minced fresh tarragon
½ teaspoon salt
⅛ teaspoon white pepper
6 leaves lettuce
6 whole wheat buns, split

1. Combine chicken, celery, grapes and raisins in large bowl. Combine yogurt, mayonnaise, shallots, tarragon, salt and pepper in small bowl. Spoon over chicken mixture; mix lightly.

2. Place 1 lettuce leaf in each bun. Divide chicken mixture evenly among buns.
Makes 6 servings

Nutritional Information per Serving: *Calories 353, Total Fat: 7 g, Cholesterol: 76 mg, Sodium: 509 mg*

Turkey Burger

Barbecued Pork Sandwiches

    2 pork tenderloins (about 1½ pounds
        total)
    ⅓ cup prepared barbecue sauce
    ½ cup prepared horseradish
    4 pita bread rounds, cut into halves
    1 onion, thinly sliced
    4 leaves romaine lettuce
    1 red bell pepper, cut lengthwise into
        ¼-inch-thick slices
    1 green bell pepper, cut lengthwise
        into ¼-inch-thick slices

1. Preheat oven to 400°F. Place pork
tenderloins in roasting pan; brush with
barbecue sauce.

2. Bake tenderloins 15 minutes; turn and
bake 15 minutes or until internal
temperature reaches 155°F. Cover with foil;
let stand 15 minutes.

3. Slice pork across grain. Spread horseradish
on pita bread halves; stuff with pork, onion,
lettuce and bell peppers.

Makes 4 servings

Nutritional Information per Serving: *Calories: 440,
Total Fat: 9 g, Cholesterol: 121 mg, Sodium: 628 mg*

Tuna Salad Pita Pockets

    1 can (9 ounces) tuna packed in water,
        drained
    1 cup chopped cucumber
    ¼ cup part-skim ricotta cheese
    2 tablespoons reduced-fat mayonnaise
    2 tablespoons red wine vinegar
    2 green onions, chopped
    1 tablespoon sweet pickle relish
    2 cloves garlic, finely chopped
    ½ teaspoon salt
    ¼ teaspoon black pepper
    2 rounds pita bread, halved
    1 cup alfalfa sprouts

Combine all ingredients except bread and
sprouts. Fill bread with sprouts and tuna
mixture.   *Makes 4 servings*

Nutritional Information per Serving: *Calories: 209,
Total Fat: 4 g, Cholesterol: 22 mg, Sodium: 752 mg*

Spicy Beef and Onion Sandwiches

    Nonstick cooking spray
    6 ounces beef sirloin steak, cut 1 inch
        thick
    1 medium onion, thinly sliced
    ½ cup water
    1 tablespoon mustard seeds
    1 cup sliced mushrooms
    1 tablespoon sugar
    1 tablespoon cider vinegar
    1 teaspoon olive oil
    3 kaiser rolls
    3 tablespoons spicy brown mustard

1. Spray large nonstick skillet with cooking
spray; heat over medium heat until hot. Add
beef; partially cover and cook 4 minutes on
each side or until cooked through. Remove
beef from skillet.

2. Add onion, water and mustard seeds to
skillet. Cook over medium-high heat 5
minutes or until water has evaporated. Add
mushrooms, sugar, vinegar and oil. Cook 5
minutes or until onions are browned, stirring
frequently.

3. Cut rolls crosswise in half. Spread with
mustard. Thinly slice meat; layer on rolls.
Top with onion mixture.   *Makes 3 servings*

Nutritional Information per Serving: *Calories 347,
Total Fat: 11 g, Cholesterol: 38 mg, Sodium: 541 mg*

Barbecued Pork Sandwich

Hummus Pita Sandwiches

2 tablespoons sesame seeds
1 can (15 ounces) garbanzo beans, undrained
1 to 2 cloves garlic, peeled
¼ cup loosely packed parsley
3 tablespoons fresh lemon juice
1 tablespoon olive oil
¼ teaspoon black pepper
4 rounds pita bread, cut into halves
2 tomatoes, thinly sliced
1 cucumber, sliced
1 cup alfalfa sprouts, rinsed and drained
2 tablespoons crumbled feta cheese

1. Toast sesame seeds in small nonstick skillet over medium heat until lightly browned, stirring frequently. Remove from skillet and cool. Drain garbanzo beans; reserve liquid.

2. Place garlic in food processor. Process until minced. Add garbanzo beans, parsley, lemon juice, oil and pepper. Process until almost smooth, scraping side of bowl once. If mixture is very thick, add 1 to 2 tablespoons reserved garbanzo bean liquid. Pour hummus into medium bowl. Stir in sesame seeds.

3. Spread about 3 tablespoons hummus in each pita half. Divide tomatoes, cucumber and alfalfa sprouts evenly among pitas. Sprinkle with cheese.   *Makes 4 servings*

Nutritional Information per Serving (2 pita bread halves): *Calories: 364, Total Fat: 9 g, Cholesterol: 7 mg, Sodium: 483 mg*

Mediterranean Pita Sandwiches

1 cup plain nonfat yogurt
1 tablespoon chopped fresh cilantro
2 cloves garlic, minced
1 teaspoon lemon juice
1 can (15 ounces) chick-peas, rinsed and drained
1 can (14 ounces) artichoke hearts, rinsed, drained and coarsely chopped
1½ cups thinly sliced cucumbers, cut into halves
½ cup shredded carrot
½ cup chopped green onions
4 rounds whole wheat pita bread, cut into halves

1. Combine yogurt, cilantro, garlic and lemon juice in small bowl.

2. Combine chick-peas, artichoke hearts, cucumbers, carrot and green onions in medium bowl. Stir in yogurt mixture until well blended.

3. Divide cucumber mixture among pita halves.   *Makes 4 servings*

Nutritional Information per Serving: *Calories 297, Total Fat: 3 g, Cholesterol: 1 mg, Sodium: 726 mg*

Hummus Pita Sandwich

Pinto Bean & Zucchini Burritos

6 flour tortillas (6 inches each)
¾ cup GUILTLESS GOURMET® Pinto
    Bean Dip (spicy)
2 teaspoons water
1 teaspoon olive oil
1 medium zucchini, chopped
¼ cup chopped green onions
¼ cup GUILTLESS GOURMET® Green
    Tomatillo Salsa
1 cup GUILTLESS GOURMET® Salsa
    (medium), divided
1½ cups shredded lettuce
    Fresh cilantro leaves (optional)

Preheat oven to 300°F. Wrap tortillas in foil. Bake 10 minutes or until softened and heated through. Meanwhile, combine bean dip and water in small bowl. Heat oil in large skillet over medium-high heat until hot. Add zucchini and onions. Cook and stir until zucchini is crisp-tender; stir in bean dip mixture and tomatillo salsa.

Fill each tortilla with zucchini mixture, dividing evenly. Roll up tortillas; place on 6 individual serving plates. Top with salsa. Serve hot with lettuce. Garnish with cilantro, if desired.   *Makes 6 servings*

Nutritional Information per Serving (1 burrito): *Calories: 176, Total Fat: 3 g, Cholesterol: 0 mg, Sodium: 515 mg*

Pita Pockets

1 can HEALTHY CHOICE® Recipe
    Creations™ Tomato with Garden
    Herbs Condensed Soup
¼ cup fat free sour cream
    Vegetable cooking spray
1 pound ground turkey
½ cup *each* HEALTHY CHOICE® Fat Free
    Shredded Cheddar Cheese and
    sliced green onions
½ teaspoon salt (optional)
3 pita bread rounds, cut in half to form
    pockets
1 cup *each* shredded lettuce and diced
    tomato

In small bowl, combine soup and sour cream; mix well. Set aside. In large nonstick skillet sprayed with vegetable cooking spray, cook turkey over medium-high heat until no longer pink; drain.

Add soup mixture, cheese, onions and salt to skillet; mix well. Reduce heat; cover and simmer 5 minutes or until cheese is melted. Fill pita bread pockets with turkey mixture. Garnish with lettuce and tomato.

Makes 6 servings

Nutritional Information per Serving: *Calories: 270, Total Fat: 7 g, Sodium: 430 mg*

Pinto Bean & Zucchini Burrito

Meat Entrées

Mustard-Crusted Roast Pork

3 tablespoons Dijon mustard
4 teaspoons minced garlic, divided
2 whole well-trimmed pork tenderloins (about 1 pound each)
2 tablespoons dried thyme leaves
1 teaspoon black pepper
½ teaspoon salt
1 pound asparagus spears, ends trimmed
2 red or yellow bell peppers (or one of each), cut lengthwise into ½-inch-wide strips
1 cup fat-free reduced-sodium chicken broth, divided

1. Preheat oven to 375°F. Combine mustard and 3 teaspoons garlic in small bowl. Spread mustard mixture evenly over top and sides of both tenderloins. Combine thyme, black pepper and salt in small bowl; reserve 1 teaspoon mixture. Sprinkle remaining mixture evenly over tenderloins, patting so that seasoning adheres to mustard. Place tenderloins on rack in shallow roasting pan. Roast 25 minutes.

2. Arrange asparagus and bell peppers in single layer in shallow casserole or 13×9-inch baking pan. Add ¼ cup chicken broth, reserved thyme mixture and remaining 1 teaspoon garlic; toss to coat.

3. Roast vegetables in oven alongside tenderloins 15 to 20 minutes or until thermometer inserted into center of pork registers 160°F and vegetables are tender. Transfer tenderloins to carving board; tent with foil and let stand 5 minutes. Arrange vegetables on serving platter, reserving juices in dish; cover and keep warm. Add remaining ¾ cup broth and juices in dish to roasting pan. Place over range top burner(s); simmer 3 to 4 minutes over medium-high heat or until juices are reduced to ¾ cup, stirring frequently. Carve tenderloins crosswise into ¼-inch slices; arrange on serving platter. Spoon juices over pork and vegetables.   *Makes 8 servings*

Nutritional Information per Serving: *Calories: 182, Total Fat: 5 g, Cholesterol: 65 mg, Sodium: 304 mg*

Mustard-Crusted Roast Pork

Moroccan Pork Tagine

1 pound well-trimmed pork tenderloin, cut into ¾-inch medallions
1 tablespoon all-purpose flour
1 teaspoon ground cumin
1 teaspoon paprika
¼ teaspoon powdered saffron *or* ½ teaspoon turmeric
¼ teaspoon ground red pepper
¼ teaspoon ground ginger
1 tablespoon olive oil
1 medium onion, chopped
3 cloves garlic, minced
2½ cups chicken broth, divided
⅓ cup golden or dark raisins
1 cup uncooked quick-cooking couscous
¼ cup chopped cilantro
¼ cup toasted sliced almonds (optional)

1. Toss pork with flour, cumin, paprika, saffron, pepper and ginger in medium bowl; set aside.

2. Heat oil in large nonstick skillet over medium-high heat. Add onion; cook 5 minutes, stirring occasionally. Add pork and garlic; cook 4 to 5 minutes or until pork is no longer pink, stirring occasionally. Add ¾ cup chicken broth and raisins; bring to a boil over high heat. Reduce heat to medium; simmer, uncovered, 7 to 8 minutes or until pork is cooked through, stirring occasionally.

3. Meanwhile, bring remaining 1¾ cups chicken broth to a boil in medium saucepan. Stir in couscous. Cover; remove from heat. Let stand 5 minutes or until liquid is absorbed.

4. Spoon couscous onto 4 plates; top with pork mixture. Sprinkle with cilantro and almonds, if desired. *Makes 4 servings*

Nutritional Information per Serving: *Calories: 435, Total Fat: 10 g, Cholesterol: 70 mg, Sodium: 686 mg*

Potato and Pork Frittata

12 ounces (about 3 cups) frozen hash brown potatoes
1 teaspoon Cajun seasoning
4 egg whites
2 whole eggs
¼ cup 1% low-fat milk
1 teaspoon dry mustard
¼ teaspoon black pepper
10 ounces frozen stir-fry vegetables
¾ cup chopped cooked lean pork
½ cup (2 ounces) shredded Cheddar cheese

1. Preheat oven to 400°F. Spray baking sheet with nonstick cooking spray. Spread potatoes on baking sheet; sprinkle with Cajun seasoning. Bake 15 minutes or until hot. Remove from oven. *Reduce oven temperature to 350°F.*

2. Beat egg whites, eggs, milk, mustard and pepper in small bowl. Place vegetables and ⅓ cup water in medium nonstick skillet. Cook over medium heat 5 minutes or until vegetables are crisp-tender; drain.

3. Add pork and potatoes to vegetables in skillet; stir lightly. Add egg mixture. Sprinkle with cheese. Cook over medium-low heat 5 minutes. Place skillet in 350°F oven and bake 5 minutes or until egg mixture is set and cheese is melted. *Makes 4 servings*

Nutritional Information per Serving: *Calories: 251, Total Fat: 7 g, Cholesterol: 135 mg, Sodium: 394 mg*

Moroccan Pork Tagine

Thai-Style Pork Kabobs

⅓ cup reduced-sodium soy sauce
2 tablespoons fresh lime juice
2 tablespoons water
2 teaspoons hot chili oil*
2 cloves garlic, minced
1 teaspoon minced fresh ginger
12 ounces well-trimmed pork tenderloin
1 red or yellow bell pepper, cut into ½-inch chunks
1 red or sweet onion, cut into ½-inch chunks
2 cups hot cooked rice

If hot chili oil is not available, combine 2 teaspoons vegetable oil and ½ teaspoon red pepper flakes in small microwavable cup. Microwave at HIGH 1 minute. Let stand 5 minutes to infuse flavor.

1. Combine soy sauce, lime juice, water, chili oil, garlic and ginger in medium bowl; reserve ⅓ cup mixture for dipping sauce. Set aside.

2. Cut pork tenderloin lengthwise in half; cut crosswise into 4-inch slices. Cut slices into ½-inch strips. Add to bowl with soy sauce mixture; toss to coat. Cover; refrigerate at least 30 minutes or up to 2 hours, turning once.

3. To prevent sticking, spray grid with nonstick cooking spray. Prepare coals for grilling.

4. Remove pork from marinade; discard marinade. Alternately weave pork strips and thread bell pepper and onion chunks onto eight 8- to 10-inch metal skewers.

5. Grill, covered, over medium-hot coals 6 to 8 minutes or until pork is no longer pink in center, turning halfway through grilling time. Serve with rice and reserved dipping sauce. *Makes 4 servings*

Nutritional Information per Serving: *Calories: 248, Total Fat: 4 g, Cholesterol: 49 mg, Sodium: 271 mg*

Grilled Pork Tenderloin with Apple Salsa

1 tablespoon chili powder
½ teaspoon garlic powder
1 pound pork tenderloin
2 Granny Smith apples, peeled, cored and finely chopped
1 can (4 ounces) diced mild green chilies
¼ cup lemon juice
3 tablespoons finely chopped fresh cilantro
1 clove garlic, minced
1 teaspoon dried oregano leaves
½ teaspoon salt

1. To prevent sticking, spray grid with nonstick cooking spray. Prepare coals for grilling.

2. Combine chili powder and garlic powder in small bowl; mix well. Coat pork with spice mixture.

3. Grill pork on uncovered grill over medium-high coals 30 minutes, turning occasionally, until internal temperature reaches 155°F when tested with meat thermometer in thickest part of tenderloin. Cover with foil and let rest 10 minutes before slicing.

4. To make apple salsa, combine apples, chilies, lemon juice, cilantro, garlic, oregano and salt in medium bowl; mix well.

5. Slice pork across grain; serve with salsa. *Makes 4 servings*

Nutritional Information per Serving: *Calories: 201, Total Fat: 5 g, Cholesterol: 81 mg, Sodium: 678 mg*

Thai-Style Pork Kabobs

Pork with Couscous & Root Vegetables

1 teaspoon vegetable oil
½ pound pork tenderloin, thinly sliced
2 sweet potatoes, peeled and chopped
2 medium turnips, peeled and chopped
1 carrot, sliced
3 cloves garlic, finely chopped
1 can (about 15 ounces) chick-peas, rinsed and drained
1 cup fat-free reduced-sodium vegetable broth
½ cup pitted prunes, cut into thirds
1 teaspoon ground cumin
½ teaspoon ground cinnamon
¼ teaspoon ground allspice
¼ teaspoon ground nutmeg
¼ teaspoon black pepper
1 cup uncooked quick-cooking couscous, cooked
2 tablespoons dried currants

1. Heat oil in large nonstick skillet over medium-high heat until hot. Add pork, sweet potatoes, turnips, carrot and garlic; cook and stir 5 minutes. Stir in chick-peas, vegetable broth, prunes, cumin, cinnamon, allspice, nutmeg and pepper. Cover; bring to a boil over high heat. Reduce heat to medium-low; simmer 30 minutes.

2. Serve pork and vegetables on couscous. Top servings with currants.

Makes 4 servings

Nutritional Information per Serving: *Calories: 508, Total Fat: 6 g, Cholesterol: 30 mg, Sodium: 500 mg*

Mandarin Pork Stir-Fry

1½ cups DOLE® Mandarin Tangerine Juice or Pineapple Orange Juice, divided
Vegetable cooking spray
12 ounces lean pork tenderloin or boneless, skinless chicken breast halves, cut into thin strips
1 tablespoon finely chopped fresh ginger *or* ½ teaspoon ground ginger
2 cups DOLE® Shredded Carrots
½ cup chopped DOLE® Pitted Prunes
4 DOLE® Green Onions, diagonally cut into 1-inch pieces
2 tablespoons low-sodium soy sauce
1 teaspoon cornstarch
Hot cooked rice (optional)

• **Heat** 2 tablespoons juice over medium-high heat in large, nonstick skillet sprayed with vegetable cooking spray until juice bubbles.

• **Add** pork and ginger. Cook and stir 3 minutes or until pork is no longer pink; remove pork from skillet.

• **Heat** 3 tablespoons juice in skillet. Add carrots, prunes and green onions; cook and stir 3 minutes.

• **Stir** soy sauce and cornstarch into remaining juice; add to carrot mixture in skillet. Return pork to skillet; cover. Cook 2 minutes or until heated through and sauce is slightly thickened. Serve over rice and garnish with green onions and orange peel, if desired. *Makes 4 servings*

Prep Time: 15 minutes

Cook Time: 15 minutes

Nutritional Information per Serving: *Calories: 225, Total Fat: 4 g, Cholesterol: 71 mg, Sodium: 312 mg*

Pork with Couscous & Root Vegetables

Pork Chops in Creamy Garlic Sauce

1 cup fat-free reduced-sodium chicken broth
¼ cup garlic cloves, peeled and crushed (about 12 to 15)
½ teaspoon olive oil
4 boneless pork loin chops, each about ¼ inch thick
1 tablespoon minced fresh parsley
½ teaspoon dried tarragon leaves
¼ teaspoon salt
¼ teaspoon black pepper
2 tablespoons water
1 tablespoon all-purpose flour
1 tablespoon dry sherry
2 cups cooked white rice

1. Place chicken broth and garlic in small saucepan. Bring to a boil over high heat. Cover; reduce heat to low. Simmer 25 to 30 minutes or until garlic mashes easily with fork. Set aside to cool. Purée until smooth in blender or food processor.

2. Heat olive oil in large nonstick skillet over medium-high heat. Add pork; cook 1 to 1½ minutes on each side or until browned. Pour garlic purée into skillet. Sprinkle with parsley, tarragon, salt and pepper. Bring to a boil; cover. Reduce heat to low; simmer 10 to 15 minutes or until pork is juicy and barely pink in center. Remove pork from skillet; keep warm.

3. Combine water and flour in small cup. Slowly pour flour mixture into skillet; bring to a boil. Cook and stir until mixture thickens. Stir in sherry. Serve sauce over pork and rice. *Makes 4 servings*

Nutritional Information per Serving: *Calories: 188, Total Fat: 9 g, Cholesterol: 40 mg, Sodium: 260 mg*

Moo Shu Pork

1 cup DOLE® Tropical Fruit Juice or Pineapple Juice
1 tablespoon low-sodium soy sauce
2 teaspoons sesame seed oil
2 teaspoons cornstarch
8 ounces pork tenderloin, cut into thin strips
1½ cups Oriental-style mixed vegetables
¼ cup hoisin sauce (optional)
8 (8-inch) flour tortillas, warmed
2 DOLE® Green Onions, cut into thin strips

• **Stir** juice, soy sauce, sesame seed oil and cornstarch in shallow, nonmetallic dish until blended; remove ½ cup mixture for sauce.

• **Add** pork to remaining juice mixture in shallow dish. Cover and marinate 15 minutes in refrigerator. Drain pork; discard marinade.

• **Cook** and stir pork in large, nonstick skillet over medium-high heat 2 minutes or until pork is lightly browned. Add vegetables; cook and stir 3 to 4 minutes or until vegetables are tender-crisp. Stir in reserved ½ cup juice mixture; cook 1 minute or until sauce thickens.

• **Spread** hoisin sauce onto center of each tortilla, if desired; top with moo shu pork. Sprinkle with green onions. Fold opposite sides of tortilla over filling; fold remaining sides of tortilla over filling. Garnish with slivered green onions, kumquats and fresh herbs, if desired. *Makes 4 servings*

Prep Time: 10 minutes

Marinate Time: 15 minutes

Cook Time: 10 minutes

Nutritional Information per Serving: *Calories: 256, Total Fat: 6 g, Cholesterol: 27 mg, Sodium: 374 mg*

Pork Chops in Creamy Garlic Sauce

Glazed Stuffed Pork Chops

2 medium cooking apples
3 cups prepared cabbage slaw blend
¾ cup apple cider, divided
¼ cup raisins
2 tablespoons maple-flavored pancake syrup
4 teaspoons spicy brown mustard, divided
2 lean pork chops, 1 inch thick (about 6 ounces each)
Nonstick cooking spray
2 teaspoons cornstarch

1. Quarter and core apples. Chop 6 quarters; reserve remaining 2 quarters. Combine chopped apples, slaw blend, ¼ cup apple cider, raisins, syrup and 2 teaspoons mustard in large saucepan. Cover and cook over medium heat 5 minutes or until cabbage is tender.

2. Make a pocket in each pork chop by cutting horizontally through chop almost to bone. Fill each pocket with about ¼ cup cabbage-apple mixture. Keep remaining cabbage-apple mixture warm over low heat.

3. Spray medium nonstick skillet with cooking spray; heat over medium heat until hot. Brown pork chops about 3 minutes on each side. Add ¼ cup apple cider. Reduce heat to low; cover and cook 8 minutes or until pork is barely pink in center. Remove pork from skillet; keep warm.

4. Add liquid from remaining cabbage-apple mixture to skillet. Combine remaining ¼ cup cider, 2 teaspoons mustard and cornstarch in small bowl until smooth. Stir into liquid in skillet. Simmer over medium heat until thickened. Spoon glaze over chops and cabbage-apple mixture. Slice remaining 2 apple quarters; divide between servings.

Makes 2 servings

Nutritional Information per Serving: *Calories: 490, Total Fat: 12 g, Cholesterol: 53 mg, Sodium: 227 mg*

Grilled Honey Garlic Pork Chops

¼ cup lemon juice
¼ cup honey
2 tablespoons soy sauce
1 tablespoon dry sherry
2 cloves garlic, minced
4 boneless center-cut lean pork chops (about 4 ounces each)

Combine all ingredients except pork chops in small bowl. Place pork in shallow baking dish; pour marinade over pork. Cover and refrigerate 4 hours or overnight. Remove pork from marinade. Heat remaining marinade in small saucepan over medium heat to a simmer. Grill pork over medium-hot coals 12 to 15 minutes, turning once during cooking and basting frequently with marinade, until meat thermometer registers 155 to 160°F. *Makes 4 servings*

Nutritional Information per Serving: *Calories: 248, Total Fat: 7 g, Cholesterol: 61 mg, Sodium: 604 mg*

Favorite recipe from **National Honey Board**

Beef and Broccoli

1 pound lean beef tenderloin
2 teaspoons minced fresh ginger
2 cloves garlic, minced
½ teaspoon vegetable oil
3 cups broccoli florets
¼ cup water
2 tablespoons teriyaki sauce
2 cups hot cooked white rice

1. Cut beef across grain into ⅛-inch slices; cut each slice into 1½-inch pieces. Toss beef with ginger and garlic in medium bowl.

2. Heat oil in wok or large nonstick skillet over medium heat. Add beef mixture; stir-fry 3 to 4 minutes or until beef is barely pink in center. Remove and reserve.

3. Add broccoli and water to wok; cover and steam 3 to 5 minutes or until broccoli is crisp-tender.

4. Return beef and any accumulated juices to wok. Add teriyaki sauce. Cook until heated through. Serve over rice.

Makes 4 servings

Nutritional Information per Serving: *Calories: 392, Total Fat: 11 g, Cholesterol: 95 mg, Sodium: 393 mg*

Steak Jamaican

6 tablespoons honey
⅓ cup lime juice
2 tablespoons vegetable oil
2 tablespoons prepared mustard
2 cloves garlic, minced
1 teaspoon grated lime peel
½ teaspoon salt
½ teaspoon coarsely ground black pepper
2 pounds lean top round steak
  Lime wedges

Whisk together all ingredients except steak and lime wedges in small bowl. Score steak across top and place in shallow baking pan. Pour marinade over steak; turn to coat all sides. Refrigerate 6 to 8 hours, turning occasionally. Broil 4 to 6 inches from heat source 3 minutes per side for medium rare or continue to cook to desired doneness. Slice thinly on the diagonal. Serve with lime wedges. *Makes 6 servings*

Nutritional Information per Serving: *Calories: 362, Total Fat: 10 g, Cholesterol: 98 mg, Sodium: 321 mg*

Favorite recipe from **National Honey Board**

Meatloaf Ring with Garlic Mashed Potatoes

4 large red potatoes, cubed
1 pound extra-lean ground beef
1 can HEALTHY CHOICE® Recipe Creations™ Cream of Roasted Garlic Condensed Soup, divided
3 slices fresh reduced fat white bread, processed to form crumbs
½ cup fat free egg substitute (equivalent to 2 eggs)
½ cup *each* shredded carrots and shredded zucchini
¼ cup *each* minced red bell pepper and minced onion
2 tablespoons minced fresh parsley, divided
1 teaspoon Italian seasoning
  Vegetable cooking spray
⅓ cup fat free cream cheese
½ teaspoon salt (optional)

In medium saucepan, combine potatoes and enough water to cover potatoes. Bring to a boil; cover and reduce heat to medium-high. Cook 20 to 25 minutes or until tender.

Meanwhile, combine beef, ⅓ cup soup, bread crumbs, egg substitute, carrots, zucchini, pepper, onion, 1 tablespoon parsley and Italian seasoning; mix well. In shallow round 2-quart baking dish sprayed with vegetable cooking spray, form beef mixture into ring around outer edge of dish, leaving center open. Bake at 400°F 20 to 25 minutes.

Drain potatoes; mash with potato masher. Add remaining soup, cream cheese and salt; mash until well mixed. Remove meatloaf from oven; mound potatoes in center. Place under broiler 5 minutes or until lightly browned. Sprinkle with remaining 1 tablespoon parsley. *Makes 6 servings*

Nutritional Information per Serving: *Calories: 317, Total Fat: 6 g, Sodium: 452 mg*

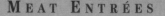

Beef Pot Roast

3 pounds beef eye of round roast
1 can (14 ounces) fat-free reduced-sodium beef broth
2 cloves garlic
1 teaspoon herbs de Provence *or* ¼ teaspoon *each* rosemary, thyme, sage and savory
4 small turnips, peeled and cut into wedges
10 ounces fresh brussels sprouts, trimmed
20 baby carrots
4 ounces pearl onions, outer skins removed
2 teaspoons cornstarch mixed with 1 tablespoon water

1. Heat large nonstick skillet over medium-high heat. Place roast, fat side down, in skillet. Cook until evenly browned. Remove roast from skillet; place in Dutch oven.

2. Pour broth into Dutch oven; bring to a boil over high heat. Add garlic and herbs de Provence. Cover tightly. Reduce heat; cook 1½ hours.

3. Add turnips, brussels sprouts, carrots and onions to Dutch oven. Cover; cook 25 to 30 minutes or until vegetables are tender. Remove meat and vegetables from Dutch oven. Arrange on serving platter; cover with foil to keep warm.

4. Strain broth; return to Dutch oven. Stir blended cornstarch mixture into broth. Bring to a boil over medium-high heat; cook and stir 1 minute or until thick and bubbly. Serve immediately with pot roast and vegetables.

Makes 6 servings

Nutritional Information per Serving: *Calories: 299, Total Fat: 7 g, Cholesterol: 79 mg, Sodium: 287 mg*

Beef & Vegetable Stir-Fry

½ cup fat-free reduced-sodium beef broth
3 tablespoons reduced-sodium soy sauce
2 teaspoons cornstarch
1 teaspoon sugar
½ teaspoon ground ginger
½ teaspoon garlic powder
½ teaspoon dark sesame oil
¼ teaspoon salt
¼ teaspoon black pepper
1 teaspoon vegetable oil
½ pound beef flank steak, cut diagonally into 1-inch slices
2 green bell peppers, thinly sliced
1 tomato, cut into wedges
8 green onions, cut into 1-inch pieces
4 cups hot cooked white rice (optional)

1. Blend beef broth, soy sauce, cornstarch, sugar, ginger, garlic powder, sesame oil, salt and black pepper in medium bowl.

2. Heat vegetable oil in wok or nonstick skillet over medium-high heat until hot. Add beef; stir-fry 3 minutes or until beef is browned. Add bell peppers, tomato and onions; stir-fry 2 minutes or until vegetables are crisp-tender.

3. Stir beef broth mixture; add to wok. Cook and stir 3 minutes or until sauce boils and thickens.

4. Serve beef mixture over hot cooked white rice, if desired. *Makes 4 servings*

Nutritional Information per Serving: *Calories: 357, Total Fat: 6 g, Cholesterol: 23 mg, Sodium: 614 mg*

Beef Pot Roast

Italian-Style Meat Loaf

1 can (6 ounces) no-salt-added tomato
    paste
½ cup dry red wine plus ½ cup water
    or 1 cup water
1 teaspoon minced garlic
½ teaspoon dried basil leaves
½ teaspoon dried oregano leaves
¼ teaspoon salt
12 ounces lean ground round
12 ounces ground turkey breast
1 cup fresh whole wheat bread crumbs
    (2 slices whole wheat bread)
½ cup shredded zucchini
¼ cup cholesterol-free egg substitute *or*
    2 egg whites

1. Preheat oven to 350°F. Combine tomato paste, wine, water, garlic, basil, oregano and salt in small saucepan. Bring to a boil; reduce heat to low. Simmer, uncovered, 15 minutes. Set aside.

2. Combine beef, turkey, bread crumbs, zucchini, egg substitute and ½ cup reserved tomato mixture in large bowl. Mix well. Shape into loaf; place into ungreased 9×5×3-inch loaf pan. Bake 45 minutes. Discard any drippings. Pour ½ cup remaining tomato mixture over top of loaf. Return to oven for 15 minutes. Place on serving platter. Cool 10 minutes before slicing.   *Makes 8 servings*

Nutritional Information per Serving: *Calories: 144, Total Fat: 2 g, Cholesterol: 41 mg, Sodium: 171 mg*

Shanghai Beef

1 can HEALTHY CHOICE® Recipe
    Creations™ Cream of Mushroom
    with Cracked Pepper & Herbs
    Condensed Soup
⅓ cup nonfat milk
1½ teaspoons teriyaki sauce
¼ teaspoon garlic powder
⅛ teaspoon crushed red pepper
    (optional)
    Vegetable cooking spray
12 ounces sirloin steak,* cut into
    2×¼-inch slices
¾ cup julienne-cut carrots
1 (8-ounce) can sliced water chestnuts,
    drained
3 dried shiitake mushrooms, soaked,
    drained and sliced *or* 1 (4-ounce)
    can sliced mushrooms, drained

Pork or chicken may be substituted for steak.

In medium bowl, mix soup, milk, teriyaki sauce, garlic powder and red pepper; set aside. Heat large nonstick skillet sprayed with vegetable cooking spray over medium-high heat 1 minute. Add steak; sauté until brown on both sides. Remove from skillet.

Add carrots, water chestnuts and mushrooms to skillet; sauté 2 to 3 minutes. Stir in soup mixture; reduce heat and cook until heated through. Return steak to skillet; heat 1 minute.   *Makes 4 servings*

Nutritional Information per Serving: *Calories: 226, Total Fat: 6 g, Sodium: 490 mg*

Italian-Style Meat Loaf

Beef Stroganoff

1 large onion, cut lengthwise, then thinly sliced
½ cup plain nonfat yogurt
½ cup reduced-fat sour cream
3 tablespoons chopped chives, divided
1 tablespoon all-purpose flour
2 teaspoons Dijon mustard
¼ teaspoon salt
⅛ teaspoon white pepper
1 teaspoon olive oil
1 pound boneless sirloin steak, cut in half lengthwise, then sliced into ¼-inch pieces
6 ounces portobello mushrooms or other fresh mushrooms, sliced
8 ounces cooked mafalda or other wide noodles
12 ounces steamed baby carrots

1. Heat large nonstick skillet over low heat; add onion. Cover; cook, stirring occasionally, 10 minutes or until tender. Remove onion from skillet. Set aside.

2. Combine yogurt, sour cream, 2 tablespoons chives, flour, mustard, salt and pepper in small bowl. Set aside.

3. Heat oil in skillet over medium-high heat. Add beef and mushrooms; cook and stir 3 to 4 minutes or until beef is lightly browned. Return onion to skillet. Reduce heat to low. Stir in yogurt mixture until well blended and slightly thickened, about 2 minutes. Serve over noodles and carrots. Sprinkle with remaining 1 tablespoon chives.

Makes 6 servings

Nutritional Information per Serving: *Calories: 179, Total Fat: 5 g, Cholesterol: 45 mg, Sodium: 190 mg*

Beef and Caramelized Onions

1 can HEALTHY CHOICE® Recipe Creations™ Cream of Mushroom with Cracked Pepper & Herbs Condensed Soup
¾ cup nonfat milk
½ cup fat free sour cream
½ teaspoon salt (optional)
1 (14-ounce) can pearl onions, drained *or* 2 cups thinly sliced onions
1 clove garlic, minced
1 tablespoon low fat margarine
1 teaspoon sugar
1 tablespoon vinegar
1 cup sliced mushrooms
12 ounces sirloin steak, cut into 2×¼-inch slices
4 cups hot cooked yolk free egg noodles
1 tablespoon minced fresh parsley

In small bowl, mix soup, milk, sour cream and salt; set aside. In nonstick skillet, sauté onions and garlic in hot margarine over medium heat until lightly brown. Add sugar; cook until golden, stirring constantly. Stir in vinegar; cook 1 minute. Remove from skillet; set aside.

Add mushrooms to skillet; sauté mushrooms until lightly brown. Remove from skillet; set aside. Add steak; sauté over high heat until browned on both sides. Remove from skillet; drain skillet. Add soup mixture to skillet; cook over low heat until heated through. Return onions, mushrooms and steak to skillet. Heat 2 minutes. *(Do not boil.)* Serve over hot cooked noodles; garnish with parsley.

Makes 6 servings

Nutritional Information per Serving: *Calories: 305, Total Fat: 5 g, Sodium: 495 mg*

Beef Stroganoff

Poultry Entrées

Chicken Fajitas with Cowpoke Barbecue Sauce

1 cup Cowpoke Barbecue Sauce (recipe follows), divided
Nonstick cooking spray
10 ounces boneless skinless chicken breasts, cut lengthwise into 1×½-inch pieces
2 green or red bell peppers, thinly sliced
1 cup sliced onion
2 cups tomato wedges
4 warm (6-inch) flour tortillas

1. Prepare Cowpoke Barbecue Sauce.

2. Spray large nonstick skillet with cooking spray. Heat over medium-high heat until hot. Brush chicken with ¼ cup barbecue sauce. Add to skillet. Cook and stir 3 minutes or until chicken is browned. Add peppers and onion. Cook and stir 3 minutes or until vegetables are crisp-tender and chicken is no longer pink. Add tomatoes. Cook 2 minutes or until heated through, stirring occasionally.

3. Serve with warm flour tortillas and remaining ¾ cup Cowpoke Barbecue Sauce. Garnish with cilantro, if desired.

Makes 4 servings

Cowpoke Barbecue Sauce

1 teaspoon vegetable oil
¾ cup chopped green onions
3 cloves garlic, finely chopped
1 can (14½ ounces) crushed tomatoes
½ cup ketchup
¼ cup water
¼ cup orange juice
2 tablespoons cider vinegar
2 teaspoons chili sauce
Dash Worcestershire sauce

Heat oil in large nonstick saucepan over medium heat until hot. Add onions and garlic. Cook and stir 5 minutes or until onions are tender. Stir in remaining ingredients. Reduce heat to medium-low. Cook 15 minutes, stirring occasionally.

Makes 2 cups

Nutritional Information per Serving: *Calories: 310, Total Fat: 6 g, Cholesterol: 36 mg, Sodium: 736 mg*

Chicken Fajita with Cowpoke Barbecue Sauce

Chicken Florentine with Lemon Mustard Sauce

2 whole boneless skinless chicken
    breasts, halved (1 pound)
¼ cup EGG BEATERS® Healthy Real Egg
    Substitute
½ cup plain dry bread crumbs
1 teaspoon dried basil leaves
1 teaspoon garlic powder
2 tablespoons FLEISCHMANN'S® Sweet
    Unsalted 70% Corn Oil Spread,
    divided
⅓ cup water
2 tablespoons GREY POUPON® Dijon
    Mustard
2 tablespoons lemon juice
1 tablespoon sugar
1 (10-ounce) package frozen chopped
    spinach, cooked, well drained and
    kept warm

Pound chicken breasts to ¼-inch thickness. Pour Egg Beaters® into shallow bowl. Combine bread crumbs, basil and garlic. Dip chicken breasts into Egg Beaters®, then coat with bread crumb mixture.

In large nonstick skillet, over medium-high heat, melt 1 tablespoon spread. Add chicken; cook for 5 to 7 minutes on each side or until browned and no longer pink in center. Remove chicken from skillet; keep warm. In same skillet, melt remaining spread; stir in water, mustard, lemon juice and sugar. Simmer 1 minute or until thickened. To serve, arrange chicken on serving platter. Top with spinach; drizzle with lemon-mustard sauce.

Makes 4 servings

Prep Time: 25 minutes

Cook Time: 15 minutes

Nutritional Information per Serving: *Calories: 278, Total Fat: 8 g, Cholesterol: 69 mg, Sodium: 468 mg*

Healthy Choice® Tangy Oven-Fried BBQ Chicken

1 cup all-purpose flour
1 tablespoon *each* garlic powder, onion
    powder and poultry seasoning
6 boneless, skinless chicken breast
    halves
½ teaspoon salt (optional)
    Vegetable cooking spray
1 can HEALTHY CHOICE® Recipe
    Creations™ Tomato with Garden
    Herbs Condensed Soup
½ cup chopped onion
¼ cup *each* low sodium Worcestershire
    sauce and packed brown sugar
2 tablespoons cider vinegar

In large bowl, combine flour, garlic powder, onion powder and poultry seasoning. Season chicken with salt. Coat chicken pieces with flour mixture and place on foil-lined baking sheet sprayed with vegetable cooking spray. Bake chicken at 350°F 20 minutes.

Meanwhile, in small saucepan, combine soup, onion, Worcestershire sauce, brown sugar and vinegar; bring to a boil over medium heat. Reduce heat to low; simmer 10 minutes. Baste chicken generously with 1 cup sauce, reserving remaining sauce. Continue baking 20 minutes or until no longer pink in center. Serve with remaining sauce for dipping. *Makes 4 to 6 servings*

Nutritional Information per Serving: *Calories: 310, Total Fat: 4 g, Sodium: 230 mg*

Chicken Florentine with Lemon Mustard Sauce

Sweet and Sour Stir-Fry

1 tablespoon vegetable oil
1 pound boneless skinless chicken breasts, cut into 3-inch strips
1 can (8 ounces) sliced water chestnuts, drained
1 cup 2×½-inch red bell pepper strips
¼ cup chopped onion
2 tablespoons cornstarch
2 tablespoons soy sauce
1 tablespoon white vinegar
1 can (8 ounces) pineapple chunks packed in juice, undrained
¼ teaspoon ground ginger
¼ teaspoon salt
1¾ teaspoons EQUAL® Measure™ or
 6 packets EQUAL® sweetener or
 ¼ cup EQUAL® Spoonful™
1 package (6 ounces) frozen pea pods

• Heat oil in wok or skillet. Add chicken; cook until chicken is no longer pink, 5 to 6 minutes. Remove and set aside. Add water chestnuts, pepper and onion to wok; cook until vegetables are tender, 3 to 4 minutes, stirring constantly.

• Combine cornstarch, soy sauce and vinegar in small bowl; stir to dissolve cornstarch. Add pineapple with juice, ginger and salt. Add to vegetable mixture; cook until sauce thickens, 2 to 3 minutes, stirring constantly.

• Stir in Equal®. Add pea pods and chicken; cook until pea pods and chicken are heated through, 2 to 3 minutes.

Makes 4 servings

Nutritional Information per Serving: *Calories: 272, Total Fat: 5 g, Cholesterol: 66 mg, Sodium: 620 mg*

Mediterranean Chicken

1 can HEALTHY CHOICE® Recipe Creations™ Tomato with Garden Herbs Condensed Soup
½ cup water
1 (2.25-ounce) can sliced black olives, drained
¼ cup golden raisins
½ teaspoon *each* garlic powder and dried oregano leaves
 Vegetable cooking spray
4 boneless, skinless chicken breasts, cut into 2×1-inch strips
1 cup sliced zucchini
½ cup thin red or green bell pepper strips
3 cups hot cooked rice

In medium bowl, mix soup, water, olives, raisins, garlic powder and oregano; set aside. In large nonstick skillet sprayed with vegetable cooking spray, sauté chicken over high heat until no longer pink in center. Remove from skillet.

Add zucchini and pepper to skillet; sauté 2 to 3 minutes. Reduce heat; stir in soup mixture. Return chicken to skillet and cook until heated through. Serve over rice.

Makes 4 servings

Nutritional Information per Serving: *Calories: 434, Total Fat: 4 g, Sodium: 395 mg*

Sweet and Sour Stir-Fry

Herb Chicken with Apples

1 can HEALTHY CHOICE® Recipe Creations™ Cream of Roasted Chicken with Herbs Condensed Soup
½ cup nonfat milk
½ teaspoon Italian seasoning
  Vegetable cooking spray
4 boneless, skinless chicken breast halves
2 medium red or green apples, cored and sliced
1 small onion, thinly sliced into rings

In small bowl, mix soup, milk and Italian seasoning; set aside. Heat large nonstick skillet sprayed with vegetable cooking spray over medium heat 1 minute. Add chicken; brown 5 minutes on each side. Remove from skillet.

Add apples and onion to skillet; cook until onion is tender. Stir in soup mixture. Return chicken to skillet; reduce heat to low. Cover and simmer 5 to 10 minutes or until chicken is no longer pink in center.

Makes 4 servings

Nutritional Information per Serving: *Calories: 242, Total Fat: 5 g, Sodium: 297 mg*

Tangy Chicken Breasts with Citrus Sage Sauce

8 boneless skinless chicken breast halves (about 2 pounds)
6 ounces frozen lemonade concentrate, thawed
½ cup honey
1 teaspoon dried sage leaves
½ teaspoon dry mustard
½ teaspoon dried thyme leaves
½ teaspoon lemon juice

Rinse chicken breasts under cold water and pat dry with paper towels; place in shallow baking dish. Combine remaining ingredients in small bowl. Pour half the sauce over chicken and bake at 350°F 20 minutes. Turn chicken and pour remaining sauce over top. Bake 15 to 20 minutes more or until chicken is no longer pink in center.

Makes 8 servings

Nutritional Information per Serving: *Calories: 246, Total Fat: 3 g, Cholesterol: 69 mg, Sodium: 62 mg*

Favorite recipe from **National Honey Board**

Chicken Stir-Fry

4 boneless, skinless chicken breast halves (about 1½ pounds)
2 tablespoons vegetable oil
2 tablespoons light soy sauce
2 tablespoons orange juice
1 tablespoon cornstarch
1 bag (16 ounces) BIRDS EYE® frozen Farm Fresh Mixtures Broccoli, Carrots & Water Chestnuts

• Cut chicken into ½-inch-thick long strips.

• In wok or large skillet, heat oil over medium-high heat.

• Add chicken; cook 5 minutes, stirring occasionally.

• Meanwhile, in small bowl, combine soy sauce, orange juice and cornstarch; blend well and set aside.

• Add vegetables to chicken; cook 5 minutes more or until chicken is no longer pink in center, stirring occasionally.

• Stir in soy sauce mixture; cook 1 minute or until heated through.   *Makes 4 servings*

Herb Chicken with Apples

Crispy Baked Chicken

8 ounces (1 cup) nonfat French onion
   dip
  Skim milk
1 cup cornflake crumbs
½ cup wheat germ
6 skinless chicken breast halves or
   thighs (about 1½ pounds)

1. Preheat oven to 350°F. Spray baking pan with nonstick cooking spray.

2. Place dip in shallow bowl; stir until smooth. Add milk, 1 tablespoon at a time, until pourable consistency is reached.

3. Combine cornflake crumbs and wheat germ on plate.

4. Dip chicken pieces in milk mixture; then roll in cornflake mixture. Place chicken in prepared pan. Bake 45 to 50 minutes or until juices run clear when pierced with fork and chicken is no longer pink near bone.

Makes 6 servings

Nutritional Information per Serving: *Calories: 267, Total Fat: 4 g, Cholesterol: 69 mg, Sodium: 373 mg*

Chicken Diablo

1 can HEALTHY CHOICE® Recipe
   Creations™ Cream of Roasted
   Garlic Condensed Soup
¾ cup salsa
¼ teaspoon ground cumin
6 boneless, skinless chicken breast
   halves
1 (14-ounce) can quartered artichoke
   hearts, drained
1 (2.25-ounce) can sliced black olives,
   drained
2 tablespoons chopped fresh cilantro
   (optional)

In medium bowl, mix soup, salsa and cumin; set aside. Arrange chicken in 13×9-inch baking dish. Bake at 350°F 20 minutes. Place artichoke hearts around chicken. Top with soup mixture; sprinkle with black olives. Continue baking 25 to 30 minutes or until chicken is no longer pink in center. Sprinkle with cilantro before serving, if desired.

Makes 6 servings

Nutritional Information per Serving: *Calories: 202, Total Fat: 4 g, Sodium: 563 mg*

Chicken Divan

1 can HEALTHY CHOICE® Recipe
   Creations™ Cream of Broccoli with
   Cheddar and Onion Condensed
   Soup
¼ cup nonfat milk
½ teaspoon salt (optional)
  Vegetable cooking spray
4 slices reduced fat white bread,
   toasted
4 boneless, skinless chicken breast
   halves, cooked
1 (10-ounce) box frozen broccoli
   spears, thawed and drained
2 tablespoons fat free shredded
   Parmesan cheese

In medium bowl, combine soup, milk and salt; mix well. In 1½-quart baking dish sprayed with vegetable cooking spray, place toast slices; top each slice with chicken breast half. Arrange broccoli spears over chicken. Pour soup mixture evenly over broccoli and sprinkle with Parmesan cheese. Cover and bake at 350°F 15 minutes or until hot and bubbly.

Makes 4 servings

Nutritional Information per Serving: *Calories: 270, Total Fat: 5 g, Sodium: 530 mg*

Crispy Baked Chicken

Roast Chicken & Potatoes Catalan

2 tablespoons olive oil
2 tablespoons lemon juice
1 teaspoon dried thyme leaves
½ teaspoon salt
¼ teaspoon ground red pepper
¼ teaspoon ground saffron *or*
    ½ teaspoon crushed saffron
    threads or turmeric
2 large baking potatoes (about
    1½ pounds), cut into 1½-inch
    chunks
4 skinless bone-in chicken breast halves
    (about 2 pounds)
1 cup sliced red bell pepper
1 cup frozen peas, thawed
    Lemon wedges

1. Preheat oven to 400°F. Spray large shallow roasting pan or 15×10-inch jelly-roll pan with nonstick cooking spray.

2. Combine oil, lemon juice, thyme, salt, ground red pepper and saffron in large bowl; mix well. Add potatoes; toss to coat.

3. Arrange potatoes in single layer around edges of pan. Place chicken in center of pan; brush both sides of chicken with remaining oil mixture in bowl.

4. Bake 20 minutes. Turn potatoes; baste chicken with pan juices. Add bell pepper; continue baking 20 minutes or until chicken is no longer pink in center, juices run clear and potatoes are browned. Stir peas into potato mixture; bake 5 minutes or until heated through. Garnish with lemon wedges. *Makes 4 servings*

Nutritional Information per Serving: *Calories: 541, Total Fat: 11 g, Cholesterol: 91 mg, Sodium: 132 mg*

Chicken with Brandied Fruit Sauce

4 broiler-fryer chicken breast halves,
    boned and skinned
½ teaspoon salt
¼ teaspoon ground nutmeg
2 tablespoons butter or margarine
1 tablespoon cornstarch
¼ teaspoon ground red pepper
    Juice of 1 orange
    Juice of 1 lemon
    Juice of 1 lime
⅓ cup orange marmalade
½ cup red seedless grapes, halved
2 tablespoons brandy

Pound chicken to ½-inch thickness with meat mallet or similar flattening utensil. Sprinkle salt and nutmeg over chicken. Place butter in large skillet and heat over medium-high heat. Add chicken; cook about 8 minutes or until chicken is brown and fork-tender, turning occasionally. Blend cornstarch and red pepper in small bowl; stir in orange, lemon and lime juices and set aside. Remove chicken to serving platter. Stir marmalade into juices remaining in skillet; heat until melted. Stir in cornstarch mixture; cook and stir until mixture boils and thickens. Add grapes and brandy. Return chicken to skillet; spoon sauce over chicken. Cook 5 minutes over low heat.

Makes 4 servings

Nutritional Information per Serving: *Calories: 300, Total Fat: 7 g, Cholesterol: 68 mg, Sodium: 414 mg*

Favorite recipe from **Delmarva Poultry Industry, Inc.**

Roast Chicken & Potatoes Catalan

Cashew Chicken

10 ounces boneless skinless chicken
    breasts, cut into 1×½-inch pieces
1 tablespoon cornstarch
1 tablespoon dry white wine
1 tablespoon reduced-sodium soy
    sauce
½ teaspoon garlic powder
1 teaspoon vegetable oil
6 green onions, cut into 1-inch pieces
2 cups sliced mushrooms
1 red or green bell pepper, thinly
    sliced
1 can (6 ounces) sliced water
    chestnuts, rinsed and drained
2 tablespoons hoisin sauce (optional)
2 cups hot cooked white rice
¼ cup roasted cashews

1. Place chicken in large resealable plastic food storage bag. Blend cornstarch, wine, soy sauce and garlic powder in small bowl. Pour over chicken pieces. Seal bag; turn to coat. Marinate in refrigerator 1 hour. Drain chicken; discard marinade.

2. Heat oil in wok or large nonstick skillet over medium-high heat until hot. Add onions; stir-fry 1 minute. Add chicken; stir-fry 2 minutes or until browned. Add mushrooms, pepper and water chestnuts; stir-fry 3 minutes or until vegetables are crisp-tender and chicken is no longer pink in center. Stir in hoisin sauce, if desired; cook and stir 1 minute or until heated through.

3. Serve chicken and vegetables over rice. Top servings evenly with cashews. Serve immediately. *Makes 4 servings*

Nutritional Information per Serving: *Calories: 274, Total Fat: 7 g, Cholesterol: 36 mg, Sodium: 83 mg*

Crispy Oven-Baked Chicken

4 boneless skinless chicken breast
    halves (about 4 ounces each)
¾ cup GUILTLESS GOURMET® Salsa
    (mild, medium or hot)
    Nonstick cooking spray
1 cup (3.5 ounces) crushed* GUILTLESS
    GOURMET® Baked Tortilla Chips
    (yellow corn, white corn or chili &
    lime)
    Cherry tomatoes and pineapple sage
    leaves (optional)

Cooking Tip: Crush tortilla chips in the original bag or between two pieces of waxed paper with a rolling pin.

Wash chicken; pat dry with paper towels. Place chicken in shallow nonmetal pan or place in large resealable plastic food storage bag. Pour salsa over chicken. Cover with foil or seal bag; marinate in refrigerator 8 hours or overnight.

Preheat oven to 350°F. Coat baking sheet with cooking spray. Place crushed chips on waxed paper. Remove chicken from salsa, discarding salsa; roll chicken in crushed chips. Place on prepared baking sheet; bake 45 minutes or until chicken is no longer pink in center and chips are crisp. Serve hot. Garnish with tomatoes and sage, if desired.

Makes 4 servings

Nutritional Information per Serving: *Calories: 237, Total Fat: 4 g, Cholesterol: 69 mg, Sodium: 272 mg*

Cashew Chicken

Skillet Chicken and Rice

1 teaspoon olive oil
2 boneless skinless chicken breast halves, 2 skinless thighs, 2 skinless legs or any combination of 6 pieces
1 large onion, chopped
1 green bell pepper, chopped
1 clove garlic, minced
½ teaspoon cumin seeds
1 can (14 ounces) no-salt-added whole tomatoes, undrained
1½ cups fat-free reduced-sodium chicken broth
¾ cup uncooked white rice
2 ounces (2 slices) turkey ham, sliced into 2-inch pieces
¼ teaspoon salt
⅛ to ¼ teaspoon ground red pepper
8 ounces frozen cut green beans, thawed

1. Heat oil in 12-inch nonstick skillet over medium-high heat. Add chicken; cook 3 minutes on each side or until browned. Remove chicken from skillet.

2. Add onion, bell pepper, garlic and cumin seeds to skillet; cook and stir 5 minutes. Stir in tomatoes, chicken broth, rice, turkey ham, salt and ground red pepper; bring to a boil.

3. Return chicken to skillet, meaty side down. Cover; reduce heat. Simmer 15 minutes. Turn chicken pieces over; place green beans over chicken. Cover; simmer 20 to 30 minutes or until chicken is no longer pink in center, rice and green beans are tender and all liquid is absorbed. Serve immediately.

Makes 6 servings

Nutritional Information per Serving: *Calories: 290, Total Fat: 7 g, Cholesterol: 77 mg, Sodium: 345 mg*

Rosemary Chicken with Asparagus Lemon Rice

¼ cup dry white wine
3 cloves garlic, minced
1 tablespoon finely chopped fresh rosemary
1 tablespoon vegetable oil
1 tablespoon low-sodium soy sauce
1 teaspoon sugar
½ teaspoon ground black pepper
6 boneless skinless chicken breast halves (about 2¼ pounds)
Vegetable cooking spray
3 cups cooked rice (cooked in low-sodium chicken broth)
10 spears asparagus, blanched and cut into 1-inch pieces (¼ pound)
1 teaspoon grated lemon peel
1 teaspoon lemon pepper
½ teaspoon salt
Lemon slices for garnish
Fresh rosemary springs for garnish

Combine wine, garlic, rosemary, oil, soy sauce, sugar and pepper in large shallow glass dish. Add chicken, turning to coat; cover and marinate in refrigerator at least 1 hour. Heat large skillet coated with cooking spray over medium-high heat until hot. Add chicken and marinade; cook 7 minutes on each side or until brown and no longer pink in center. Combine rice, asparagus, lemon peel, lemon pepper and salt in large bowl. To serve, spoon rice on individual serving plates. Cut chicken into strips; fan over rice. Garnish with lemon and rosemary.

Makes 6 servings

Nutritional Information per Serving: *Calories: 294, Total Fat: 6 g, Cholesterol: 73 mg, Sodium: 437 mg*

Favorite recipe from **USA Rice Federation**

Skillet Chicken and Rice

Spicy Marinated Chicken Kebabs over Rice

½ cup white wine
¼ cup lime juice
¼ cup vegetable oil
2 cloves garlic, minced
1 jalapeño pepper, seeded and finely chopped
2 tablespoons chopped fresh cilantro
½ teaspoon salt
½ teaspoon black pepper
1½ pounds boneless skinless chicken breasts, cut into 1-inch cubes
2 medium-size red or green bell peppers, cut into 1-inch pieces
2 medium-size yellow squash, cut into 1-inch pieces
1 medium-size red onion, cut into 1-inch pieces
12 wooden or metal skewers*
Vegetable cooking spray
3 cups hot cooked rice

*Soak wooden skewers in water before using to prevent burning. Spray metal skewers with vegetable cooking spray before using.

Combine wine, lime juice, oil, garlic, jalapeño, cilantro, salt and black pepper in gallon-size plastic resealable food bag. Add chicken, bell peppers, squash and onion. Seal; toss to coat vegetables. Marinate in refrigerator 30 to 45 minutes. Remove chicken and vegetables. Place marinade in small saucepan. Bring to a boil over medium-high heat; keep warm. Alternate chicken and vegetables on skewers. Place on broiler rack coated with cooking spray; brush with marinade. Broil 4 to 6 inches from heat 8 to 10 minutes, turning and basting frequently with marinade. Serve over hot rice. *Makes 6 servings*

Nutritional Information per Serving: *Calories: 280, Total Fat: 5 g, Cholesterol: 73 mg, Sodium: 262 mg*

Favorite recipe from **USA Rice Federation**

Chicken Enchiladas

1¾ cups fat free sour cream
½ cup chopped green onions
⅓ cup minced fresh cilantro
1 tablespoon minced fresh jalapeño chili pepper
1 teaspoon ground cumin
1 tablespoon vegetable oil
12 ounces boneless, skinless chicken breasts, cut into 3×1-inch strips
1 teaspoon minced garlic
8 flour tortillas (8-inch)
1 cup (4 ounces) shredded ALPINE LACE® Reduced Fat Cheddar Cheese
1 cup bottled chunky salsa
1 small ripe tomato, chopped
Sprigs of cilantro (optional)

1. Preheat the oven to 350°F. Spray a 13×9×3-inch baking dish with nonstick cooking spray.

2. In a small bowl, mix together the sour cream, green onions, cilantro, jalapeño pepper and cumin.

3. Spray a large nonstick skillet with the cooking spray, pour in the oil and heat over medium-high heat. Add the chicken and garlic and sauté for 4 minutes or until the juices run clear when the chicken is pierced with a fork.

4. Divide the chicken strips among the 8 tortillas, placing them down the center of the tortillas. Top with the sour cream mixture, then roll them up and place them, seam side down, in the baking dish.

5. Sprinkle with the cheese, cover with foil and bake for 30 minutes or until bubbly. Spoon the salsa in a strip down the center and sprinkle the salsa with the tomato. Garnish with the sprigs of cilantro, if you wish. Serve hot! *Makes 8 servings*

Nutritional Information per Serving (1 enchilada): *Calories: 247, Total Fat: 6 g, Cholesterol: 33 mg, Sodium: 346 mg*

Lemon Chicken with Herbs

1 can HEALTHY CHOICE® Recipe Creations™ Cream of Roasted Chicken with Herbs Condensed Soup
¼ cup nonfat milk
2 tablespoons lemon juice
2 tablespoons minced fresh parsley
Vegetable cooking spray
4 boneless, skinless chicken breast halves
½ cup sliced mushrooms
¼ cup chopped red onion

In small bowl, mix soup, milk, lemon juice and parsley; set aside. Heat large nonstick skillet sprayed with vegetable cooking spray over medium heat 1 minute. Add chicken; brown 5 minutes on each side. Remove from skillet. Add mushrooms and onion to skillet; sauté 2 to 3 minutes. Stir in soup mixture.

Return chicken to skillet; reduce heat to low. Cover and simmer 5 to 10 minutes or until chicken is no longer pink in center.

Makes 4 servings

Nutritional Information per Serving: *Calories: 209, Total Fat: 5 g, Sodium: 290 mg*

Pepper Glazed Cajun Chicken

4 broiler-fryer chicken breast halves, boned and skinned
½ to 1 teaspoon Cajun seasoning
1 tablespoon vegetable oil
¼ cup sliced green onions
6 tablespoons hot pepper jelly
¼ cup defatted chicken broth
2 tablespoons white vinegar

Sprinkle Cajun seasoning over chicken. Heat oil in large nonstick skillet over medium-high heat. Add chicken; cook about 10 minutes or until chicken is brown, turning occasionally. Remove chicken and set aside.

Add onions to drippings in skillet; cook and stir 2 minutes. Add jelly, broth and vinegar; cook and stir until jelly melts. Return chicken to pan; spoon glaze over chicken. Cover and cook over medium-low heat about 5 minutes or until chicken is fork-tender, turning occasionally. Remove chicken to serving platter. Increase heat to medium-high and cook until glaze thickens slightly. Spoon glaze over chicken.

Makes 4 servings

Nutritional Information per Serving: *Calories: 248, Total Fat: 5 g, Cholesterol: 68 mg, Sodium: 126 mg*

Favorite recipe from **Delmarva Poultry Industry, Inc.**

Skillet Chicken with Garlic & Sun-Dried Tomatoes

Vegetable cooking spray
4 boneless, skinless chicken breast halves
1½ cups thinly sliced onions
½ cup finely chopped sun-dried tomatoes
1 can HEALTHY CHOICE® Recipe Creations™ Cream of Roasted Garlic Condensed Soup
¾ cup fat free, low sodium chicken broth
¼ cup white wine
½ teaspoon salt (optional)
¼ teaspoon black pepper

In large skillet sprayed with vegetable cooking spray, cook chicken until brown on both sides. Arrange onions and tomatoes over chicken.

In small bowl, combine soup, chicken broth, wine, salt and pepper; mix well. Pour mixture over chicken. Cover and simmer 20 to 25 minutes or until chicken is no longer pink in center. *Makes 4 servings*

Nutritional Information per Serving: *Calories: 230, Total Fat: 4 g, Sodium: 450 mg*

Roast Turkey with Cranberry Stuffing

**Cranberry Stuffing (recipe follows)
1 turkey (8 to 10 pounds)**

1. Prepare Cranberry Stuffing. *Reduce oven temperature to 350°F.*

2. Remove giblets from turkey. Rinse turkey and cavity in cold water; pat dry with paper towels. Fill turkey cavity loosely with stuffing. Place remaining stuffing in casserole sprayed with nonstick cooking spray. Cover casserole; refrigerate until baking time.

3. Spray roasting pan with nonstick cooking spray. Place turkey, breast side up, on rack in roasting pan. Bake 3 hours or until thermometer inserted in thickest part of thigh registers 185°F and juices run clear.

4. Transfer turkey to serving platter. Cover loosely with foil; let stand 20 minutes. Place covered casserole of stuffing in oven; *increase oven temperature to 375°F.* Bake 25 to 30 minutes or until hot.

5. Remove and discard turkey skin. Slice turkey; garnish with fresh rosemary sprigs, if desired. *Makes 10 servings*

Cranberry Stuffing

**1 loaf (12 ounces) Italian or French bread, cut into ½-inch cubes
2 tablespoons margarine
1½ cups chopped onions
1½ cups chopped celery
2 teaspoons poultry seasoning
1 teaspoon dried thyme leaves
½ teaspoon dried rosemary
¼ teaspoon salt
¼ teaspoon black pepper
1 cup coarsely chopped fresh cranberries
1 tablespoon sugar
¾ cup fat-free reduced-sodium chicken broth**

1. Preheat oven to 375°F. Arrange bread on two 15×10-inch jelly-roll pans. Bake 12 minutes or until lightly toasted.

2. Melt margarine in large saucepan over medium heat. Add onions and celery. Cook and stir 8 minutes or until vegetables are tender; remove from heat. Add bread cubes, poultry seasoning, thyme, rosemary, salt and pepper; mix well. Combine cranberries and sugar in small bowl; mix well. Add to bread mixture; toss well. Drizzle chicken broth evenly over mixture; toss well.

Makes 10 servings

Nutritional Information per Serving (turkey and stuffing): *Calories: 439, Total Fat: 12 g, Cholesterol: 136 mg, Sodium: 445 mg*

Turkey with Mustard Sauce

**1 tablespoon butter or margarine
1 pound turkey cutlets
1 cup BIRDS EYE® frozen Mixed Vegetables
1 box (10 ounces) BIRDS EYE® frozen Small Onions with Cream Sauce
1 teaspoon spicy brown mustard**

• In large nonstick skillet, melt butter over medium-high heat. Add turkey; cook until browned on both sides.

• Add mixed vegetables, onions with cream sauce and mustard; bring to boil. Reduce heat to medium-low; cover and simmer 6 to 8 minutes or until vegetables are tender and turkey is no longer pink in center.

Makes 4 servings

Prep Time: 5 minutes

Cook Time: 15 minutes

Nutritional Information per Serving: *Calories: 218, Total Fat: 5 g, Cholesterol: 105 mg, Sodium: 299 mg*

Roast Turkey with Cranberry Stuffing

Chipotle Tamale Pie

¾ pound ground turkey breast or lean ground beef
1 cup chopped onion
¾ cup diced green bell pepper
¾ cup diced red bell pepper
4 cloves garlic, minced
2 teaspoons ground cumin
1 can (15 ounces) pinto or red beans, rinsed and drained
1 can (8 ounces) no-salt-added stewed tomatoes, undrained
2 canned chipotle chilies in adobo sauce, minced (about 1 tablespoon)
1 to 2 teaspoons adobo sauce from canned chilies (optional)
1 cup (4 ounces) low-sodium reduced-fat shredded Cheddar cheese
½ cup chopped cilantro
1 package (8½ ounces) corn bread mix
⅓ cup 1% low-fat milk
1 egg white

1. Preheat oven to 400°F.

2. Cook turkey, onion, bell peppers and garlic in large nonstick skillet over medium-high heat 8 minutes or until turkey is no longer pink, stirring occasionally. Drain fat; sprinkle mixture with cumin.

3. Add beans, tomatoes, chilies and adobo sauce, if desired; bring to a boil over high heat. Reduce heat to medium; simmer, uncovered, 5 minutes. Remove from heat; stir in cheese and cilantro.

4. Spray 8-inch square baking dish with nonstick cooking spray. Spoon turkey mixture evenly into prepared dish, pressing down to compact mixture. Combine corn bread mix, milk and egg white in medium bowl; mix just until dry ingredients are moistened. Spoon batter evenly over turkey mixture to cover completely.

5. Bake 20 to 22 minutes or until corn bread is golden brown. Let stand 5 minutes before serving. *Makes 6 servings*

Nutritional Information per Serving: *Calories: 396, Total Fat: 10 g, Cholesterol: 32 mg, Sodium: 733 mg*

Turkey and Bean Tostadas

6 (8-inch) flour tortillas
1 pound 93% fat-free ground turkey
1 can (15 ounces) chili beans in chili sauce
½ teaspoon chili powder
3 cups shredded romaine lettuce
1 large tomato, chopped
½ cup reduced-fat sour cream (optional)
¼ cup chopped fresh cilantro
¼ cup (1 ounce) shredded reduced-fat Monterey Jack cheese

1. Preheat oven to 350°F. Place tortillas on baking sheets. Bake 7 minutes or until crisp. Set aside.

2. Heat large nonstick skillet over medium-high heat until hot. Add turkey. Cook and stir until turkey is browned; drain. Add beans and chili powder. Cook 5 minutes over medium heat. Divide turkey mixture evenly among tortillas. Top with remaining ingredients. *Makes 6 servings*

Nutritional Information per Serving: *Calories: 288, Total Fat: 10 g, Cholesterol: 30 mg, Sodium: 494 mg*

Chipotle Tamale Pie

Turkey & Cheese Stuffed Potatoes

6 baking potatoes, washed and pierced
2 cups frozen vegetables (such as broccoli, cauliflower, zucchini, carrots), thawed and drained
1½ cups ½-inch reduced fat cooked turkey breast cubes
1 can HEALTHY CHOICE® Recipe Creations™ Cream of Broccoli with Cheddar and Onion Condensed Soup
½ cup *each* reduced fat sour cream and nonfat milk
¼ teaspoon *each* garlic powder and black pepper
½ cup sliced green onions

Bake or microwave potatoes to desired doneness. In medium saucepan, combine vegetables, turkey, soup, sour cream, milk, garlic powder and pepper; mix well. Simmer 5 minutes, stirring occasionally.

Cut warm potatoes lengthwise and squeeze potatoes to open. Spoon equal portions of soup mixture down centers of potatoes. Sprinkle with green onions.

Makes 6 servings

Nutritional Information per Serving: *Calories: 210, Total Fat: 4 g, Sodium: 240 mg*

Turkey and Rice Quiche

3 cups cooked rice, cooled to room temperature
1½ cups chopped cooked turkey
1 medium tomato, seeded and finely diced
½ cup skim milk
3 eggs, beaten
¼ cup sliced green onions
¼ cup finely diced green bell pepper
1 tablespoon chopped fresh basil *or* 1 teaspoon dried basil leaves
½ teaspoon seasoned salt
⅛ to ¼ teaspoon ground red pepper
Nonstick cooking spray
½ cup (2 ounces) shredded Cheddar cheese
½ cup (2 ounces) shredded mozzarella cheese

Combine rice, turkey, tomato, milk, eggs, onions, bell pepper, basil, salt and ground red pepper in 13×9-inch pan coated with nonstick cooking spray. Top with cheeses. Bake at 375°F for 20 minutes or until knife inserted near center comes out clean. To serve, cut quiche into 8 squares; cut each square diagonally into 2 triangles. Garnish as desired.

Makes 8 servings (16 triangles)

Nutritional Information per Serving (2 triangles): *Calories: 231, Total Fat: 7 g, Cholesterol: 111 mg, Sodium: 527 mg*

Favorite recipe from **USA Rice Federation**

Turkey & Cheese Stuffed Potatoes

Southwestern Turkey

1 can HEALTHY CHOICE® Recipe Creations™ Tomato with Herbs Condensed Soup
½ cup fat free sour cream
   Vegetable cooking spray
1 cup sliced green onions or yellow onion
½ cup *each* diced green chiles, frozen whole kernel yellow corn and chopped red bell pepper
2 cloves garlic, minced
1 pound turkey tenderloins, cut into thin 2-inch strips
½ teaspoon salt (optional)
   Hot cooked rice (optional)

In small bowl, combine soup and sour cream; mix well. Set aside. In large nonstick skillet sprayed with vegetable cooking spray, sauté onions, chiles, corn, pepper and garlic over medium-high heat until onions and pepper are tender.

Add turkey strips to skillet and brown evenly. Add soup mixture and salt, blending well; bring to a simmer. Reduce heat to low; cover and simmer 5 minutes. Serve with rice, if desired. *Makes 4 servings*

Nutritional Information per Serving: *Calories: 261, Total Fat: 5 g, Sodium: 301 mg*

Turkey Jambalaya

1 teaspoon vegetable oil
1 cup chopped onion
1 green bell pepper, chopped
½ cup chopped celery
3 cloves garlic, finely chopped
1¾ cups fat-free reduced-sodium chicken broth
1 cup chopped seeded tomato
¼ pound cooked ground turkey breast
¼ pound cooked turkey sausage
3 tablespoons tomato paste
1 bay leaf
1 teaspoon dried basil leaves
¼ teaspoon ground red pepper
1 cup uncooked white rice
¼ cup chopped fresh parsley

1. Heat oil in large nonstick skillet over medium-high heat until hot. Add onion, bell pepper, celery and garlic; cook and stir 5 minutes or until vegetables are tender.

2. Add chicken broth, tomato, ground turkey, turkey sausage, tomato paste, bay leaf, basil and red pepper. Stir in rice; bring to a boil over high heat, stirring occasionally. Reduce heat to medium-low; simmer, covered, 20 minutes or until rice is tender.

3. Remove skillet from heat; remove and discard bay leaf. Top servings evenly with parsley. Serve immediately.

Makes 4 servings

Nutritional Information per Serving: *Calories: 416, Total Fat: 9 g, Cholesterol: 74 mg, Sodium: 384 mg*

Southwestern Turkey

Seafood Entrées

Catfish with Tropical Fruit Salsa

1 can (15¼ ounces) DOLE® Tropical
    Fruit Salad, drained
1 can (8 ounces) low-sodium whole
    kernel corn, drained
¼ cup chopped DOLE® Red or Green
    Onions
2 tablespoons diced mild green chilies
1 tablespoon chopped fresh cilantro or
    parsley
1 pound catfish or red snapper fillets
    Vegetable cooking spray
2 tablespoons lime juice
½ teaspoon paprika

• **Chop** tropical fruit salad; stir together with corn, onions, chilies and cilantro in small bowl for salsa. Set aside.

• **Arrange** fish in single layer on broiler pan sprayed with vegetable cooking spray.

• **Broil** 4 minutes; turn fish over. Brush with lime juice; sprinkle with paprika. Broil 3 to 5 minutes more or until fish flakes easily with fork. Remove fish to serving platter. Serve with reserved tropical fruit salsa.

Makes 4 servings

Nutritional Information per Serving: *Calories: 289, Total Fat: 10 g, Cholesterol: 72 mg, Sodium: 96 mg*

Red Snapper Vera Cruz

4 red snapper fillets (1 pound)
¼ cup fresh lime juice
1 tablespoon fresh lemon juice
1 teaspoon chili powder
4 green onions with 4 inches of tops,
    sliced in ½-inch lengths
1 tomato, coarsely chopped
½ cup chopped green bell pepper
½ cup chopped red bell pepper

Microwave Directions:
1. Place red snapper in shallow microwavable baking dish. Combine lime juice, lemon juice and chili powder. Pour over snapper. Marinate 10 minutes, turning once or twice.

2. Sprinkle onions, tomato and peppers over snapper. Cover dish loosely with plastic wrap. Microwave at HIGH 6 minutes or just until snapper flakes in center, rotating dish every two minutes. Let stand, covered, 4 minutes before serving. *Makes 4 servings*

Nutritional Information per Serving: *Calories 144, Total Fat: 2 g, Cholesterol: 42 mg, Sodium: 61 mg*

Catfish with Tropical Fruit Salsa

Oven-Roasted Boston Scrod

½ cup seasoned dry bread crumbs
1 teaspoon grated fresh lemon peel
1 teaspoon dried dill weed
1 teaspoon paprika
3 tablespoons all-purpose flour
2 egg whites
1½ pounds Boston scrod or orange roughy fillets, cut into 6 (4-ounce) pieces
2 tablespoons margarine, melted
Tartar Sauce (recipe follows)
Lemon wedges

1. Preheat oven to 400°F. Spray 15×10-inch jelly-roll pan with nonstick cooking spray. Combine bread crumbs, lemon peel, dill and paprika in shallow bowl. Place flour in resealable plastic food storage bag. Beat egg whites and 1 tablespoon water together in another shallow bowl.

2. Add fish, one fillet at a time, to bag. Seal bag; turn to coat fish lightly. Dip fish into egg white mixture, letting excess drip off. Roll fish in bread crumb mixture. Place in prepared jelly-roll pan. Repeat with remaining fish fillets. Brush margarine evenly over fish. Bake 15 to 18 minutes or until fish begins to flake when tested with fork.

3. Prepare Tartar Sauce while fish is baking. Serve fish with lemon wedges and Tartar Sauce.   *Makes 6 servings*

Tartar Sauce

½ cup nonfat mayonnaise
¼ cup sweet pickle relish
2 teaspoons Dijon mustard
¼ teaspoon hot pepper sauce (optional)

1. Combine all ingredients in small bowl; mix well.   *Makes ⅔ cup*

Nutritional Information per Serving: *Calories: 215, Total Fat: 5 g, Cholesterol: 49 mg, Sodium: 754 mg*

Paella

Nonstick cooking spray
10 ounces boneless skinless chicken breasts
1 teaspoon vegetable oil
½ cup uncooked white rice
4 cloves garlic, finely chopped
½ cup sliced onion
½ cup sliced green bell pepper
1 cup fat-free reduced-sodium chicken broth
½ teaspoon ground turmeric
¼ teaspoon salt
¼ teaspoon paprika
¼ teaspoon black pepper
½ cup frozen green peas
½ cup drained canned diced tomatoes
8 ounces medium shrimp, peeled

1. Preheat oven to 350°F. Spray large skillet with cooking spray; heat over medium-high heat until hot. Add chicken. Cook 10 minutes or until chicken is no longer pink in center, turning once. Remove chicken from skillet. Cool 10 minutes or until cool enough to handle. Cut into 1-inch pieces.

2. Heat oil in large ovenproof skillet or paella pan over medium heat until hot. Add rice and garlic. Cook 5 minutes or until rice is browned, stirring occasionally. Add onion and bell pepper. Stir in chicken broth, turmeric, salt, paprika and black pepper. Stir in peas and tomatoes. Place chicken and shrimp on top of rice mixture.

3. Bake 20 minutes or until heated through. Let stand 5 minutes before serving.
                    Makes 4 servings

Nutritional Information per Serving: *Calories: 258, Total Fat: 4 g, Cholesterol: 123 mg, Sodium: 371 mg*

Oven-Roasted Boston Scrod

Snapper Veracruz

Nonstick cooking spray
1 teaspoon olive oil
¼ large onion, thinly sliced
⅓ cup low sodium fish or vegetable
   broth, defatted and divided
2 cloves garlic, minced
1 cup GUILTLESS GOURMET® Salsa
   (medium)
20 ounces fresh red snapper, tilapia, sea
   bass or halibut fillets

Preheat oven to 400°F. Coat baking dish with cooking spray. (Dish needs to be large enough for fish to fit snugly together.) Heat oil in large nonstick skillet over medium heat until hot. Add onion; cook and stir until onion is translucent. Stir in 3 tablespoons broth. Add garlic; cook and stir 1 minute more. Stir in remaining broth and salsa. Bring mixture to a boil. Reduce heat to low; simmer about 2 minutes or until heated through.

Wash fish thoroughly; pat dry with paper towels. Place in prepared baking dish, overlapping thin edges to obtain an overall equal thickness. Pour and spread salsa mixture over fish.

Bake 15 minutes or until fish turns opaque and flakes easily when tested with fork. Serve hot. *Makes 4 servings*

Nutritional Information per Serving: *Calories: 184, Total Fat: 3 g, Cholesterol: 52 mg, Sodium: 353 mg*

Hazelnut-Coated Salmon Steaks

¼ cup hazelnuts
4 salmon steaks (about 5 ounces each)
1 tablespoon apple butter
1 tablespoon Dijon mustard
¼ teaspoon dried thyme leaves
⅛ teaspoon black pepper
2 cups cooked white rice

1. Preheat oven to 375°F. Place hazelnuts on baking sheet; bake 8 minutes or until lightly browned. Quickly transfer nuts to clean dry dish towel. Fold towel; rub vigorously to remove as much of the skins as possible. Finely chop hazelnuts using food processor, nut grinder or chef's knife.

2. *Increase oven temperature to 450°F.* Place salmon in baking dish. Combine apple butter, mustard, thyme and pepper in small bowl. Brush on salmon; top each steak with nuts. Bake 14 to 16 minutes or until salmon flakes easily with fork. Serve with rice and steamed snow peas, if desired.

Makes 4 servings

Nutritional Information per Serving: *Calories: 329, Total Fat: 11 g, Cholesterol: 72 mg, Sodium: 143 mg*

Mustard-Grilled Red Snapper

½ cup Dijon mustard
1 tablespoon red wine vinegar
1 teaspoon ground red pepper
4 red snapper fillets (about
   1½ pounds)

1. To prevent sticking, spray grid with nonstick cooking spray. Prepare coals for grilling.

2. Combine mustard, vinegar and pepper in small bowl; mix well. Coat fish fillets thoroughly with mustard mixture.

3. Grill fish over medium-high heat about 4 minutes per side or until fish flakes easily when tested with fork. Serve immediately.
Makes 4 servings

Nutritional Information per Serving: *Calories 200, Total Fat: 4 g, Cholesterol: 62 mg, Sodium: 477 mg*

Snapper Veracruz

Herbed Haddock Fillets

3 slices whole wheat bread
1 clove garlic
6 chive stems
½ cup loosely packed fresh parsley
¼ cup loosely packed fresh basil
2 tablespoons fresh oregano
3 to 4 tablespoons plain nonfat yogurt
1 tablespoon olive oil
1 teaspoon Dijon mustard
4 haddock fillets (5 to 6 ounces each)

1. Preheat oven to 400°F. Tear bread into pieces; place in food processor. Process until fine crumbs are formed. Measure 1 cup crumbs and place in medium bowl.

2. Place garlic in food processor; process until minced. Add chives, parsley, basil and oregano. Process until chopped, scraping side of bowl, if necessary. Add herbs to bread crumbs.

3. Combine 3 tablespoons yogurt, olive oil and mustard in small bowl. Stir into bread crumb mixture. Stir until blended and soft ball is formed. If mixture is dry, add additional 1 tablespoon yogurt.

4. Line baking sheet with aluminum foil. Place haddock on foil. Spread herb mixture over fillets. Bake 15 minutes or until fish flakes in center.   *Makes 4 servings*

Nutritional Information per Serving: *Calories 221, Total Fat: 6 g, Cholesterol: 84 mg, Sodium: 247 mg*

Grilled Fish with Pineapple-Cilantro Sauce

1 medium pineapple (about 2 pounds), peeled, cored and cut into scant 1-inch chunks
¾ cup unsweetened pineapple juice
2 tablespoons lime juice
2 cloves garlic, minced
½ to 1 teaspoon minced jalapeño pepper
2 tablespoons minced cilantro
2 tablespoons cold water
1 tablespoon cornstarch
1 to 1½ teaspoons EQUAL® Measure™ *or* 3 to 4 packets EQUAL® sweetener *or* 2 to 3 tablespoons EQUAL® Spoonful™
Salt and black pepper
6 halibut, haddock or salmon steaks or fillets (about 4 ounces each), grilled

• Heat pineapple, pineapple juice, lime juice, garlic and jalapeño pepper to boiling in medium saucepan. Reduce heat and simmer, uncovered, 5 minutes. Stir in cilantro; heat to boiling.

• Mix cold water and cornstarch; stir into boiling mixture. Boil, stirring constantly, until thickened. Remove from heat; cool 2 to 3 minutes.

• Stir in Equal®; season to taste with salt and pepper. Serve warm sauce over fish.
Makes 6 servings

Note: Pineapple-Cilantro Sauce is also excellent served with pork or lamb.

Nutritional Information per Serving: *Calories: 185, Total Fat: 3 g, Cholesterol: 36 mg, Sodium: 159 mg*

Herbed Haddock Fillet

Fish Creole

1 pound fresh or thawed frozen
    snapper or sole fillets
1 bag (16 ounces) BIRDS EYE® frozen
    Farm Fresh Mixtures Broccoli,
    Green Beans, Pearl Onions & Red
    Peppers
1 can (16 ounces) tomato sauce
1 tablespoon dried oregano or Italian
    seasoning
1 tablespoon vegetable oil
1½ teaspoons salt

• Preheat oven to 350°F.

• Place fish in 13×9-inch baking pan.

• In large bowl, combine vegetables, tomato sauce, oregano, oil and salt.

• Pour vegetable mixture over fish.

• Bake 20 minutes or until fish flakes easily when tested with fork.   *Makes 4 servings*

Prep Time: 5 minutes

Cook Time: 20 minutes

Nutritional Information per Serving: *Calories: 211, Total Fat: 5 g, Cholesterol: 42 mg, Sodium: 1648 mg*

Salmon Steaks with Lemon Dill Sauce

½ cup finely chopped red onion
2 teaspoons FLEISCHMANN'S® 70%
    Corn Oil Spread
2 tablespoons all-purpose flour
1⅓ cups skim milk
½ cup EGG BEATERS® Healthy Real Egg
    Substitute
¼ cup lemon juice
2 teaspoons grated lemon peel
2 teaspoons dried dill weed
8 (½-inch-thick) salmon steaks
    (2 pounds)
Fresh dill sprigs, for garnish

In small saucepan, over low heat, sauté onion in corn oil spread until tender-crisp. Stir in flour; cook for 1 minute. Over medium heat, gradually stir in milk; cook, stirring until mixture thickens and boils. Boil, stirring constantly, for 1 minute; remove from heat. Whisk in Egg Beaters®, lemon juice, lemon peel and dried dill; return to heat. Cook, stirring constantly until thickened. *Do not boil.*

Meanwhile, grill or broil salmon steaks for 3 to 5 minutes on each side or until fish flakes easily when tested with fork. Top with sauce. Garnish with dill sprigs.   *Makes 8 servings*

Prep Time: 15 minutes

Cook Time: 15 minutes

Nutritional Information per Serving: *Calories: 255, Total Fat: 11 g, Cholesterol: 83 mg, Sodium: 118 mg*

Fish Creole

Oriental-Style Sea Scallops

2 tablespoons sesame or vegetable oil
1½ cups broccoli flowerets
1 cup thinly sliced onion
1 pound sea scallops
3 cups thinly sliced napa cabbage or bok choy
2 cups snow peas, ends trimmed
1 cup shiitake or button mushrooms, sliced
2 cloves garlic, minced
2 teaspoons ground star anise*
¼ teaspoon ground coriander*
½ cup chicken broth
¼ cup rice wine vinegar
2 to 3 teaspoons reduced-sodium soy sauce
¼ cup cold water
2 tablespoons cornstarch
1 to 1½ teaspoons EQUAL® Measure™ or 3 to 4 packets EQUAL® sweetener or 2 to 3 tablespoons EQUAL® Spoonful™
4 cups hot cooked rice

Or, substitute 2 teaspoons five-spice powder for star anise and coriander; amounts of vinegar and soy sauce may need to be adjusted to taste.

• Heat oil in wok or large skillet. Stir-fry broccoli and onion 3 to 4 minutes. Add scallops, cabbage, snow peas, mushrooms, garlic, anise and coriander; stir-fry 2 to 3 minutes.

• Add chicken broth, vinegar and soy sauce; heat to boiling. Reduce heat and simmer, uncovered, until scallops are cooked and vegetables are tender, about 5 minutes. Heat to boiling.

• Mix cold water and cornstarch. Stir cornstarch mixture into boiling mixture; boil, stirring constantly, until thickened. Remove from heat; let stand 2 to 3 minutes. Stir in Equal®. Serve over rice.   *Makes 6 servings*

Nutritional Information per Serving (2 ounces scallops, ⅔ cup rice): *Calories: 330, Total Fat: 6 g, Cholesterol: 26 mg, Sodium: 276 mg*

Seafood Risotto

1 package (5.2 ounces) rice in creamy sauce (Risotto Milanese flavor)
1 package (14 to 16 ounces) frozen fully cooked shrimp
1 box (10 ounces) BIRDS EYE® frozen Mixed Vegetables
2 teaspoons grated Parmesan cheese

• In 4-quart saucepan, prepare rice according to package directions. Add frozen shrimp and vegetables during last 10 minutes.

• Sprinkle with cheese.   *Makes 4 servings*

Prep Time: 5 minutes

Cook Time: 15 minutes

Serving Suggestion: Serve with garlic bread and a tossed green salad.

Nutritional Information per Serving: *Calories: 303, Total Fat: 2 g, Cholesterol: 175 mg, Sodium: 866 mg*

Grilled Tuna Niçoise with Citrus Marinade

Citrus Marinade (recipe follows)
1 tuna steak (about 1 pound)
2 cups green beans, trimmed and halved
4 cups romaine lettuce leaves, washed and torn
8 small cooked red potatoes, quartered
1 cup chopped seeded tomato
4 cooked egg whites, chopped
¼ cup sliced red onion, halved
2 teaspoons chopped black olives

1. Prepare Citrus Marinade; combine with tuna in large resealable plastic food storage bag. Seal bag; turn to coat. Marinate in refrigerator 1 hour, turning occasionally.* Drain tuna; discard marinade.

2. To prevent sticking, spray grid with nonstick cooking spray. Prepare coals for grilling.

3. Place tuna on grid, 4 inches from hot coals. Grill 8 to 10 minutes or until tuna flakes easily when tested with fork, turning once. Or, place tuna on rack of broiler pan coated with nonstick cooking spray. Broil 4 inches from heat, 8 to 10 minutes or until tuna flakes easily when tested with fork. Slice tuna into ¼-inch-thick slices; set aside.

4. Place 2 cups water in large saucepan; bring to a boil over high heat. Add beans; cook 2 minutes. Drain; rinse with cold water and drain again.

5. Place lettuce on large serving platter. Arrange tuna, beans, potatoes, tomato, egg whites and onion on lettuce. Sprinkle servings with olives. Serve with low-calorie salad dressing, if desired.

Makes 4 servings

Marinate in refrigerator 1 hour for each inch of thickness.

Citrus Marinade

½ cup fresh lime juice
¼ cup vegetable oil
2 green onions, chopped
1 teaspoon dried tarragon leaves
¼ teaspoon garlic powder
¼ teaspoon black pepper

1. Blend all ingredients in small bowl.

Makes about ¾ cup

Nutritional Information per Serving: *Calories: 373, Total Fat: 7 g, Cholesterol: 48 mg, Sodium: 160 mg*

Crustless Crab Florentine Quiche

1 can (6 ounces) crabmeat, well-drained and flaked
½ package (10 ounces) frozen chopped spinach, thawed and well-drained
½ cup chopped onion
1 cup fat-free shredded Cheddar cheese
4 SAUDER® large egg whites
2 SAUDER® large eggs
1 can (12 ounces) evaporated low-fat milk
½ teaspoon salt-free herb and spice blend

Line bottom of quiche dish or 9-inch pie plate with crabmeat. Top with spinach, onion and cheese. Blend egg whites, eggs, milk and seasoning. Pour over crabmeat mixture. Bake at 350°F for 45 minutes. Allow to stand 10 minutes before serving.

Makes 4 to 6 servings

Nutritional Information per Serving: *Calories: 144, Total Fat: 5 g, Cholesterol: 10 mg, Sodium: 350 mg*

Pacific Rim Honey-Barbecued Fish

¼ cup honey
¼ cup chopped onion
2 tablespoons lime juice
2 tablespoons soy sauce
2 tablespoons hoisin sauce
2 cloves garlic, minced
1 jalapeño pepper, seeded and minced
1 teaspoon minced fresh ginger
4 swordfish steaks or other firm white
    fish (4 ounces each)

Combine all ingredients except swordfish in small bowl; mix well. Place fish in shallow baking dish; pour marinade over fish. Cover and refrigerate 1 hour. Remove fish from marinade. Grill over medium-hot coals or broil fish about 10 minutes per inch of thickness or until fish turns opaque and flakes easily when tested with fork.

Makes 4 servings

Nutritional Information per Serving: *Calories: 216, Total Fat: 5 g, Cholesterol: 44 mg, Sodium: 721 mg*

Favorite recipe from **National Honey Board**

Maryland Crab Cakes

1¼ pounds lump crabmeat, picked over
    and flaked
¾ cup plain dry bread crumbs, divided
1 cup (4 ounces) shredded ALPINE
    LACE® Reduced Fat Swiss Cheese
¼ cup plain low fat yogurt
⅓ cup finely chopped green onions
¼ cup minced fresh parsley
2 tablespoons fresh lemon juice
1 teaspoon minced garlic
½ teaspoon hot red pepper sauce
¼ cup egg substitute *or* 1 large egg,
    beaten
    Butter-flavor nonstick cooking spray
2 large lemons, thinly sliced

1. In a large bowl, lightly toss the crab with ¼ cup of the bread crumbs, the cheese, yogurt, green onions, parsley, lemon juice, garlic and hot pepper sauce. Gently stir in the egg substitute (or the whole egg).

2. Form the mixture into twelve 3-inch patties, using about ⅓ cup of crab mixture for each. Spray both sides of the patties with the cooking spray.

3. On wax paper, spread out the remaining ½ cup of bread crumbs. Coat each patty with the crumbs, pressing lightly, then refrigerate for 1 hour.

4. Preheat the oven to 400°F. Spray a baking sheet with the cooking spray. Place the crab cakes on the baking sheet and bake for 20 minutes or until golden brown and crispy, turning once halfway through. Serve immediately with the lemon slices.

Makes 6 servings
(2 crab cakes each)

Nutritional Information per Serving: *Calories: 215, Total Fat: 6 g, Cholesterol: 54 mg, Sodium: 935 mg*

Pacific Rim Honey-Barbecued Fish

Shrimp Étouffée

3 tablespoons vegetable oil
¼ cup all-purpose flour
1 cup chopped onion
1 cup chopped green bell pepper
½ cup chopped carrots
½ cup chopped celery
4 cloves garlic, minced
1 can (about 14 ounces) vegetable broth
1 bottle (8 ounces) clam juice
½ teaspoon salt
2½ pounds large shrimp, peeled and deveined
1 teaspoon red pepper flakes
1 teaspoon hot pepper sauce
4 cups hot cooked rice
½ cup chopped parsley

1. Heat oil in Dutch oven over medium heat. Add flour; cook and stir 10 to 15 minutes or until flour mixture is deep golden brown. Add onion, bell pepper, carrots, celery and garlic; cook and stir 5 minutes.

2. Stir in vegetable broth, clam juice and salt; bring to a boil. Simmer, uncovered, 10 minutes or until vegetables are tender. Stir in shrimp, red pepper flakes and pepper sauce; simmer 6 to 8 minutes or until shrimp are opaque.

3. Ladle into eight shallow bowls; top each with ½ cup rice. Sprinkle with parsley. Serve with additional pepper sauce, if desired.

Makes 8 servings

Nutritional Information per Serving: *Calories: 306, Total Fat: 7 g, Cholesterol: 219 mg, Sodium: 454 mg*

Hot Shrimp with Cool Salsa

¼ cup prepared salsa
4 tablespoons fresh lime juice, divided
1 teaspoon honey
1 clove garlic, minced
2 to 4 drops hot pepper sauce
1 pound large shrimp, peeled and deveined, with tails intact
1 cup finely diced honeydew melon
½ cup finely diced unpeeled cucumber
2 tablespoons minced parsley
1 green onion, finely chopped
1½ teaspoons sugar
1 teaspoon olive oil
¼ teaspoon salt

1. To prevent sticking, spray grid with nonstick cooking spray. Prepare coals for grilling.

2. To make marinade, combine prepared salsa, 2 tablespoons lime juice, honey, garlic and pepper sauce in small bowl. Thread shrimp onto skewers. Brush shrimp with marinade; set aside.

3. To make salsa, combine remaining 2 tablespoons lime juice, melon, cucumber, parsley, onion, sugar, oil and salt in medium bowl; mix well.

4. Grill shrimp over medium coals 4 to 5 minutes or until shrimp are opaque, turning once. Serve with salsa. *Makes 4 servings*

Nutritional Information per Serving: *Calories 132, Total Fat: 2 g, Cholesterol: 175 mg, Sodium: 398 mg*

Shrimp Étouffée

226

Shrimp in Tomatillo Sauce over Rice

1 teaspoon olive oil
¼ cup chopped onion
1 cup GUILTLESS GOURMET® Green
    Tomatillo Salsa
¾ cup white wine
    Juice of ½ lemon
12 ounces raw medium shrimp, peeled
    and deveined
4 cups hot cooked white rice
    Lemon peel strip (optional)

Heat oil in large nonstick skillet over medium-high heat until hot. Add onion; cook and stir until onion is translucent. Add salsa, wine and juice, stirring just until mixture begins to boil. Reduce heat to medium-low; simmer 10 minutes. Add shrimp; cook about 2 minutes or until shrimp turn pink and opaque, stirring occasionally. To serve, place 1 cup rice in each of 4 individual serving bowls. Pour shrimp mixture evenly over rice. Garnish with lemon peel, if desired.

Makes 4 servings

Nutritional Information per Serving: *Calories: 274, Total Fat: 2 g, Cholesterol: 130 mg, Sodium: 479 mg*

Shrimp and Pineapple Kabobs

8 ounces medium shrimp, peeled and
    deveined
½ cup pineapple juice
¼ teaspoon garlic powder
12 chunks canned pineapple
1 green bell pepper, cut into 1-inch
    pieces
¼ cup prepared chili sauce

1. Combine shrimp, juice and garlic powder in bowl; toss to coat. Marinate in refrigerator 30 minutes. Drain shrimp; discard marinade.

2. Alternately thread pineapple, pepper and shrimp onto 4 (10-inch) skewers. Brush with chili sauce. Grill, 4 inches from hot coals, 5 minutes or until shrimp are opaque, turning once and basting with chili sauce.

Makes 4 servings

Nutritional Information per Serving: *Calories: 100, Total Fat: trace, Cholesterol: 87 mg, Sodium: 302 mg*

Stir-Fry Shrimp and Snow Peas

¾ cup fat-free reduced-sodium chicken
    broth
1 tablespoon oyster sauce
1 teaspoon rice vinegar
1 tablespoon cornstarch
½ teaspoon sugar
2 teaspoons peanut oil
1 small red onion, cut into thin wedges
1 teaspoon minced fresh ginger
1 clove garlic, minced
½ pound medium shrimp, peeled and
    deveined
2 cups snow peas, cut diagonally into
    1-inch pieces
3 cups cooked rice

1. Blend chicken broth, oyster sauce and rice vinegar into cornstarch and sugar in small bowl until smooth.

2. Heat oil in wok or large nonstick skillet over medium heat until hot. Add onion, ginger and garlic; stir-fry 2 minutes. Add shrimp and snow peas. Stir-fry 3 minutes or until shrimp are opaque.

3. Stir chicken broth mixture and add to wok. Cook 1 minute or until sauce comes to a boil and thickens. Serve over rice.

Makes 4 servings

Nutritional Information per Serving: *Calories 287, Total Fat: 3 g, Cholesterol: 88 mg, Sodium: 251 mg*

Shrimp in Tomatillo Sauce over Rice

Pasta

Caribbean Shrimp & Pasta

- 6 ounces uncooked medium bow tie pasta
- 1 tablespoon ground allspice
- 1 tablespoon frozen orange juice concentrate, thawed
- 1 teaspoon ground thyme
- 1½ teaspoons vegetable oil, divided
- ¼ teaspoon minced Scotch bonnet pepper*
- 12 ounces medium shrimp, peeled and deveined
  Nonstick cooking spray
- ½ cup fat-free reduced-sodium chicken broth
- ⅓ cup finely chopped green onions, tops only
- 2 tablespoons lemon juice
- 1 tablespoon dark sesame oil
- 1 teaspoon Dijon mustard
- ¼ teaspoon salt
- 1 cup diced papaya
- ¾ cup diced mango

Scotch bonnet peppers can sting and irritate the skin; wear rubber gloves when handling peppers and do not touch eyes.

1. Cook pasta according to package directions, omitting salt. Drain; set aside.

2. Combine allspice, orange juice concentrate, thyme, 1 teaspoon vegetable oil and pepper in small bowl; add shrimp. Toss to coat. Spray large nonstick skillet with cooking spray. Heat over medium heat until hot. Add shrimp; cook and stir 3 to 5 minutes or until shrimp are opaque. Remove from heat.

3. Combine chicken broth, green onions, lemon juice, sesame oil, mustard, salt and remaining ½ teaspoon vegetable oil in large bowl. Add papaya and mango; toss to combine. Add pasta; toss again. Top with shrimp; serve immediately.

Makes 6 servings

Nutritional Information per Serving: *Calories: 217, Total Fat: 5 g, Cholesterol: 87 mg, Sodium: 208 mg*

Caribbean Shrimp & Pasta

Turkey & Pasta with Cilantro Pesto

1 pound turkey tenders, cut into strips
3 cloves garlic, minced
½ teaspoon ground cumin
¼ teaspoon ground red pepper
¼ teaspoon black pepper
2 tablespoons olive oil
1½ cups chopped seeded tomatoes
½ cup chopped fresh cilantro
¼ cup (1 ounce) grated Parmesan cheese
2 tablespoons orange juice
12 ounces dry linguine, cooked and kept warm

1. Combine turkey, garlic, cumin, red pepper and black pepper in medium bowl; toss to coat. Heat oil in large skillet over medium-high heat. Add turkey mixture; cook 4 to 6 minutes or until turkey is no longer pink in center.

2. Add tomatoes; cook 2 minutes. Stir in cilantro, cheese and orange juice; cook 1 minute.

3. Toss turkey mixture and linguine in large bowl. Serve immediately.

Makes 6 servings

Nutritional Information per Serving: *Calories: 365, Total Fat: 9 g, Cholesterol: 33 mg, Sodium: 112 mg*

Vegetable Manicotti

1 can HEALTHY CHOICE® Recipe Creations™ Cream of Celery with Sautéed Onion & Garlic Condensed Soup
¼ cup nonfat milk
2 tablespoons fat free shredded Parmesan cheese
½ teaspoon dried dill weed
3 medium zucchini, shredded (about 4 cups)
1 cup finely chopped red bell pepper
¾ cup fat free ricotta cheese
½ cup sliced green onions
½ teaspoon salt (optional)
⅛ teaspoon black pepper
Vegetable cooking spray
10 cooked manicotti shells

In medium bowl, combine soup, milk, Parmesan cheese and dill; mix well. Set aside. In another medium bowl, combine zucchini, bell pepper, ricotta cheese, green onions, salt, if desired, and black pepper; blend well.

In 13×9-inch baking dish sprayed with vegetable cooking spray, spread half the soup mixture. Fill manicotti shells with vegetable mixture; place filled shells over soup mixture. Pour remaining soup mixture over manicotti. Cover and bake at 350°F 30 to 35 minutes or until hot and bubbly.

Makes 5 servings

Nutritional Information per Serving: *Calories: 256, Total Fat: 2 g, Sodium: 330 mg*

Turkey & Pasta with Cilantro Pesto

Shrimp & Snow Peas with Fusilli

6 ounces uncooked fusilli
  Nonstick cooking spray
2 cloves garlic, finely chopped
¼ teaspoon red pepper flakes
12 ounces medium shrimp, peeled and deveined
2 cups snow peas
1 can (8 ounces) sliced water chestnuts, drained
⅓ cup sliced green onions
3 tablespoons lime juice
2 tablespoons chopped fresh cilantro
2 tablespoons olive oil
1 tablespoon reduced-sodium soy sauce
1½ teaspoons Mexican seasoning

1. Cook pasta according to package directions, omitting salt; drain. Set aside.

2. Spray large nonstick skillet with cooking spray; heat over medium heat until hot. Add garlic and red pepper flakes; stir-fry 1 minute. Add shrimp; stir-fry 5 minutes or until shrimp are opaque. Remove shrimp from skillet.

3. Add snow peas and 2 tablespoons water to skillet; cook, covered, 1 minute. Uncover; cook and stir 2 minutes or until snow peas are crisp-tender. Remove snow peas from skillet.

4. Combine pasta, shrimp, snow peas, water chestnuts and onions in large bowl. Blend lime juice, cilantro, oil, soy sauce and Mexican seasoning in small bowl. Drizzle over pasta mixture; toss to coat.

Makes 6 servings

Nutritional Information per Serving: *Calories: 228, Total Fat: 6 g, Cholesterol: 87 mg, Sodium: 202 mg*

Swiss Cheese Sauced Pasta Shells with Crumbled Bacon

1 cup frozen peas
10 ounces uncooked medium shell pasta
2½ cups skim milk
3 tablespoons all-purpose flour
2 teaspoons Dijon mustard
½ teaspoon salt
⅛ teaspoon black pepper
3 ounces sliced reduced-fat Swiss cheese
4 slices reduced-sodium bacon, cooked and crumbled
1 tablespoon grated Parmesan cheese

1. Preheat oven to 325°F. Spray 12×8-inch baking pan with nonstick cooking spray; set aside. Place peas in colander. Cook pasta according to package directions, omitting salt. Drain over peas in colander; set aside.

2. Meanwhile, whisk together milk, flour, mustard, salt and pepper in large skillet. Cook over medium heat, stirring constantly, 5 minutes or until thickened. Remove from heat; add Swiss cheese and whisk until smooth.

3. Place peas and pasta on bottom of prepared pan. Pour sauce evenly over pasta and peas; top with crumbled bacon. Bake 20 to 25 minutes. Remove from oven. Sprinkle with Parmesan cheese; let stand 5 minutes before serving.   *Makes 4 servings*

Nutritional Information per Serving: *Calories: 486, Total Fat: 9 g, Cholesterol: 23 mg, Sodium: 528 mg*

Shrimp & Snow Peas with Fusilli

Tuna Noodle Casserole

6 ounces uncooked noodles
1 tablespoon margarine
8 ounces fresh mushrooms, sliced
1 small onion, chopped
1 cup fat-free reduced-sodium chicken broth
1 cup skim milk
¼ cup all-purpose flour
1 can (12¼ ounces) tuna packed in water, drained
1 cup frozen peas, thawed
1 jar (2 ounces) chopped pimientos, drained
½ teaspoon dried thyme leaves
¼ teaspoon salt
⅛ teaspoon black pepper

1. Cook noodles according to package directions, omitting salt. Drain; cover. Set aside.

2. Melt margarine in large nonstick skillet over medium-high heat. Add mushrooms and onion; cook and stir 5 minutes or until onion is tender.

3. Using wire whisk, blend chicken broth, milk and flour in small bowl. Stir into mushroom mixture; bring to a boil. Cook and stir about 2 minutes or until thickened. Reduce heat to medium; stir in tuna, peas, pimientos, thyme and salt. Add noodles and pepper; mix thoroughly. *Casserole can be served at this point.*

4. Preheat oven to 350°F. Spray 2-quart casserole with nonstick cooking spray. Spread noodle mixture evenly in prepared casserole. Bake 30 minutes or until bubbly and heated through. Let stand 5 minutes before serving.   *Makes 6 servings*

Nutritional Information per Serving: *Calories: 254, Total Fat: 3 g, Cholesterol: 18 mg, Sodium: 585 mg*

Red Pepper & White Bean Pasta Sauce

12 ounces uncooked penne or ziti pasta
1 teaspoon olive oil
3 cloves garlic, chopped
1 jar (11.5 ounces) GUILTLESS GOURMET® Roasted Red Pepper Salsa
¾ cup canned cannellini beans (white kidney beans), rinsed well
½ cup low sodium chicken or vegetable broth, defatted
⅓ cup chopped fresh cilantro
¼ cup crumbled feta cheese
    Fresh thyme sprigs (optional)

Cook pasta according to package directions. Drain and keep warm.

Meanwhile, heat oil in medium nonstick skillet over medium-high heat until hot. Add garlic; cook and stir 30 seconds or until softened. *Do not brown.* Add salsa, beans, chicken broth and cilantro; bring just to a boil, stirring occasionally. (If mixture appears too thick, add water, 1 tablespoon at a time, until desired consistency.) To serve, place pasta in large serving bowl. Add salsa mixture; toss to coat well. Sprinkle with feta cheese. Garnish with thyme, if desired.
                    Makes 4 servings

Nutritional Information per Serving: *Calories: 399, Total Fat: 5 g, Cholesterol: 7 mg, Sodium: 452 mg*

Tuna Noodle Casserole

Sausage and Bow Tie Bash

1 can HEALTHY CHOICE® Recipe
  Creations™ Tomato with Garden
  Herbs Condensed Soup
¼ cup nonfat milk
  Vegetable cooking spray
½ cup *each* diced onion and green bell
  pepper
2 cloves garlic, minced
½ cup sliced mushrooms
½ teaspoon salt (optional)
1 (7-ounce package) HEALTHY
  CHOICE® Low Fat Smoked Sausage,
  cut into ⅛-inch slices
4 cups cooked bow tie pasta

In small bowl, combine soup and milk; mix
well. Set aside. In large nonstick skillet
sprayed with vegetable cooking spray, sauté
onion, pepper and garlic until tender. Add
mushrooms and salt; cook 2 to 3 minutes.
Add sausage and soup mixture; mix well.
Reduce heat; cover and simmer 2 minutes
longer. Add pasta and toss until coated with
sauce.　　　　　*Makes 6 servings*

Nutritional Information per Serving: *Calories: 440,
Total Fat: 3 g, Sodium: 410 mg*

Tuscany Cavatelli

16 ounces uncooked cavatelli pasta,
  penne or ziti
1½ cups diced seeded plum tomatoes
⅔ cup sliced pimiento-stuffed green
  olives
¼ cup capers, drained
2 tablespoons grated Parmesan cheese
2 tablespoons olive oil
2 tablespoons balsamic vinegar
½ teaspoon black pepper
2 cloves garlic, minced

1. Cook pasta according to package
directions, omitting salt. Drain; set aside.

2. Combine tomatoes, olives, capers, cheese,
oil, vinegar, pepper and garlic in medium
bowl. Stir in pasta until thoroughly coated.
Serve warm or at room temperature.
　　　　　Makes 5 servings

Nutritional Information per Serving: *Calories: 452,
Total Fat: 11 g, Cholesterol: 2 mg, Sodium: 777 mg*

Chicken Tetrazzini

  Vegetable cooking spray
2 cups sliced mushrooms
½ cup chopped onion
1 can HEALTHY CHOICE® Recipe
  Creations™ Cream of Roasted
  Chicken with Herbs Condensed
  Soup
½ cup nonfat milk
1½ tablespoons dry sherry
½ teaspoon salt (optional)
2 cups 1-inch cooked chicken cubes
⅓ cup fat free shredded Parmesan
  cheese, divided
¼ cup chopped fresh parsley
4 cups cooked spaghetti

In large saucepan sprayed with vegetable
cooking spray, sauté mushrooms and onion
until tender. Stir in soup, milk, sherry and
salt; heat through. Add chicken, ¼ cup
Parmesan cheese and parsley; blend well.
Add cooked spaghetti; toss to coat. Top with
remaining Parmesan cheese.
　　　　　Makes 4 servings

Nutritional Information per Serving: *Calories: 390,
Total Fat: 7 g, Sodium: 410 mg*

Sausage and Bow Tie Bash

Szechwan Beef Lo Mein

1 pound well-trimmed boneless beef top sirloin steak, 1 inch thick
4 cloves garlic, minced
2 teaspoons minced fresh ginger
¾ teaspoon red pepper flakes, divided
1 tablespoon vegetable oil
1 can (about 14 ounces) vegetable broth
1 cup water
2 tablespoons reduced-sodium soy sauce
1 package (8 ounces) frozen mixed vegetables for stir-fry
1 package (9 ounces) refrigerated angel hair pasta
¼ cup chopped cilantro (optional)

1. Cut steak crosswise into ⅛-inch strips; cut strips into 1½-inch pieces. Toss steak with garlic, ginger and ½ teaspoon red pepper flakes.

2. Heat oil in large nonstick skillet over medium-high heat. Add half of steak to skillet; cook and stir 3 minutes or until meat is barely pink in center. Remove from skillet; set aside. Repeat with remaining steak.

3. Add vegetable broth, water, soy sauce and remaining ¼ teaspoon red pepper flakes to skillet; bring to a boil over high heat. Add vegetables; return to a boil. Reduce heat to low; simmer, covered, 3 minutes or until vegetables are crisp-tender.

4. Uncover; stir in pasta. Return to a boil over high heat. Reduce heat to medium; simmer, uncovered, 2 minutes, separating pasta with two forks. Return steak and any accumulated juices to skillet; simmer 1 minute or until pasta is tender and steak is hot. Sprinkle with cilantro, if desired.

Makes 4 servings

Nutritional Information per Serving: *Calories: 408, Total Fat: 11 g, Cholesterol: 137 mg, Sodium: 386 mg*

Cheese Tortellini with Tuna

1 tuna steak* (about 6 ounces)
1 package (9 ounces) reduced-fat cheese tortellini
1 cup finely chopped red bell pepper
1 cup finely chopped green bell pepper
¼ cup finely chopped onion
¾ teaspoon fennel seeds, crushed
½ cup evaporated skimmed milk
2 teaspoons all-purpose flour
½ teaspoon dry mustard
½ teaspoon black pepper

Or, substitute 1 can (6 ounces) tuna packed in water, drained, for tuna steak.

1. Grill or broil tuna 4 inches from heat source until fish just begins to flake, about 7 to 9 minutes. Remove and discard skin. Cut tuna into chunks; set aside.

2. Cook pasta according to package directions, omitting salt. Drain; set aside.

3. Spray large nonstick skillet with nonstick cooking spray. Add bell peppers, onion and fennel seeds; cook over medium heat until crisp-tender.

4. Whisk together milk, flour, mustard and black pepper in small bowl until smooth; add to skillet. Cook until thickened, stirring constantly. Stir in tuna and pasta; reduce heat and simmer until heated through, about 3 minutes. Serve immediately.

Makes about 4 servings

Nutritional Information per Serving: *Calories: 180, Total Fat: 4 g, Cholesterol: 21 mg, Sodium: 160 mg*

Szechwan Beef Lo Mein

Linguine with Pesto-Marinara Clam Sauce

1 teaspoon vegetable oil
¼ cup chopped shallots
3 cloves garlic, finely chopped
2 cans (6 ounces each) minced clams, undrained
1⅓ cups Marinara Sauce (page 246)
2 tablespoons prepared pesto sauce
¼ teaspoon red pepper flakes
8 ounces uncooked linguine
¼ cup chopped fresh parsley

1. Heat oil in large nonstick saucepan over medium heat until hot. Add shallots and garlic. Cook, covered, 2 minutes.

2. Drain clams; reserve ½ cup juice. Add clams, reserved juice, Marinara Sauce, pesto and red pepper flakes to saucepan. Cook 10 minutes, stirring occasionally.

3. Prepare linguine according to package directions, omitting salt. Drain. Spoon sauce evenly over each serving; top with parsley.

Makes 4 servings

Nutritional Information per Serving: *Calories: 398, Total Fat: 6 g, Cholesterol: 58 mg, Sodium: 293 mg*

Fettuccine Alfredo

2 teaspoons margarine
3 cloves garlic, finely chopped
4½ teaspoons all-purpose flour
1½ cups skim milk
½ cup grated Parmesan cheese
3½ teaspoons Neufchâtel cheese
¼ teaspoon white pepper
4 ounces hot cooked fettuccine
¼ cup chopped fresh parsley

Melt margarine in medium saucepan. Add garlic. Cook and stir 1 minute. Stir in flour. Gradually stir in milk. Cook until sauce thickens, stirring constantly. Add cheeses and pepper; cook until melted. Serve on fettuccine; top with parsley.

Makes 4 servings

Nutritional Information per Serving: *Calories: 242, Total Fat: 9 g, Cholesterol: 18 mg, Sodium: 344 mg*

Spinach-Stuffed Shells

1 package (10 ounces) chopped frozen spinach, thawed and drained
1½ cups nonfat ricotta cheese
½ cup grated Parmesan cheese
½ cup cholesterol-free egg substitute
3 cloves garlic, finely chopped
1 teaspoon dried oregano leaves
½ teaspoon salt
½ teaspoon dried basil leaves
½ teaspoon dried marjoram leaves
¼ teaspoon black pepper
24 cooked large pasta shells
2 cans (14½ ounces each) crushed tomatoes, undrained
1 cup (4 ounces) shredded reduced-fat mozzarella cheese

1. Preheat oven to 350°F. Spray 13×9-inch baking pan with nonstick cooking spray.

2. Combine spinach, ricotta and Parmesan cheeses, egg substitute, garlic and seasonings in large bowl. Spoon into shells. Place shells in prepared pan. Top with tomatoes with liquid and mozzarella cheese. Bake 20 minutes or until cheese melts.

Makes 4 servings

Nutritional Information per Serving: *Calories: 456, Total Fat: 11 g, Cholesterol: 35 mg, Sodium: 803 mg*

Linguine with Pesto-Marinara Clam Sauce

Fresh Vegetable Lasagna

8 ounces uncooked lasagna noodles
1 package (10 ounces) frozen chopped
    spinach, thawed and squeezed dry
1 cup shredded carrots
½ cup sliced green onions
½ cup sliced red bell pepper
¼ cup chopped parsley
½ teaspoon black pepper
1½ cups 1% low-fat cottage cheese
1 cup buttermilk
½ cup plain nonfat yogurt
2 egg whites
1 cup sliced mushrooms
1 can (14 ounces) artichoke hearts,
    drained and chopped
2 cups (8 ounces) shredded part-skim
    mozzarella cheese
¼ cup grated Parmesan cheese

1. Cook pasta according to package directions, omitting salt. Drain. Rinse under cold water until cool; drain well. Set aside.

2. Preheat oven to 375°F. Combine spinach, carrots, green onions, bell pepper, parsley and black pepper in large bowl. Set aside.

3. Combine cottage cheese, buttermilk, yogurt and egg whites in food processor or blender; process until smooth.

4. Spray 13×9-inch baking pan with nonstick cooking spray. Arrange ⅓ of lasagna noodles on bottom of pan. Spread with half *each* of cottage cheese mixture, spinach mixture, mushrooms, artichokes and mozzarella. Repeat layers, ending with noodles. Sprinkle with Parmesan cheese.

5. Cover and bake 30 minutes. Remove cover; continue baking 20 minutes or until bubbling and heated through. Let stand 10 minutes before serving.   *Makes 8 servings*

Nutritional Information per Serving: *Calories: 250, Total Fat: 8 g, Cholesterol: 22 mg, Sodium: 508 mg*

Pasta Primavera

8 ounces uncooked linguine or
    medium pasta shells
1 tablespoon reduced-calorie
    margarine
2 green onions, diagonally sliced
1 clove garlic, minced
1 cup fresh mushroom slices
1 cup broccoli florets
2½ cups fresh snow peas
4 to 8 asparagus spears, cut into
    2-inch pieces
1 medium red bell pepper, cut into
    thin strips
1 small carrot, cut into thin rounds
    (optional)
½ cup evaporated skimmed milk
½ teaspoon dried tarragon leaves
½ teaspoon black pepper
⅓ cup grated Parmesan cheese

1. Cook pasta according to package directions, omitting salt. Drain and set aside.

2. Melt margarine in large nonstick skillet. Add green onions and garlic; cook over medium heat until softened. Add mushrooms and broccoli. Cover. Cook 3 minutes or until mushrooms are tender. Add snow peas, asparagus, bell pepper, carrot, if desired, milk, tarragon and black pepper. Cook and stir until vegetables are crisp-tender and lightly coated.

3. Add cheese and pasta; toss to coat evenly. Serve immediately.
    Makes 4 main-dish or 8 side-dish servings

Nutritional Information per Serving: *Calories: 329, Total Fat: 6 g, Cholesterol: 8 mg, Sodium: 243 mg*

Orange Ginger Seafood

8 ounces uncooked rigatoni
12 ounces firm, white-fleshed fish, fresh or frozen and thawed
    Salt and black pepper (optional)
    Nonstick cooking spray
1 cup orange juice, divided
2 cloves garlic, minced
2 teaspoons grated fresh ginger
2 to 3 teaspoons reduced-sodium soy sauce
1 teaspoon cornstarch
¾ cup finely chopped seeded fresh plum tomatoes
1 (11-ounce) can mandarin oranges, drained

1. Cook pasta according to package directions, omitting salt. Drain; set aside.

2. Season fish with salt and pepper, if desired. Spray large nonstick skillet with cooking spray. Heat over medium-high heat until hot. Add fish; cook 3 minutes each side or until fish begins to flake when tested with fork and is lightly browned. Remove; set aside and keep warm.

3. Heat 1 tablespoon orange juice in same skillet over medium-low heat, scraping browned bits from bottom of skillet. Add garlic and ginger; cook and stir 2 minutes. Reserving ¼ cup juice, add remaining juice and soy sauce to skillet. Bring to a boil over medium-high heat. Stir reserved ¼ cup juice into cornstarch in small bowl until smooth. Add cornstarch mixture to skillet; return to a boil. Stir constantly until slightly thickened. Stir in tomatoes; heat 1 minute. Remove from heat; stir in oranges.

4. Divide pasta among 4 plates; top with fish. Spoon sauce over fish. Garnish with fresh chives and orange peel, if desired.

Makes 4 servings

Nutritional Information per Serving: *Calories: 367, Total Fat: 2 g, Cholesterol: 45 mg, Sodium: 167 mg*

Pastitso

8 ounces uncooked elbow macaroni
½ cup cholesterol-free egg substitute
¼ teaspoon ground nutmeg
¾ pound lean ground lamb, beef or turkey
½ cup chopped onion
1 clove garlic, minced
1 can (8 ounces) tomato sauce
¾ teaspoon dried mint leaves
½ teaspoon dried oregano leaves
½ teaspoon black pepper
⅛ teaspoon ground cinnamon
2 teaspoons reduced-calorie margarine
3 tablespoons all-purpose flour
1½ cups skim milk
2 tablespoons grated Parmesan cheese

1. Cook pasta according to package directions, omitting salt. Drain and transfer to medium bowl; stir in egg substitute and nutmeg.

2. Lightly spray bottom of 9-inch square baking dish with nonstick cooking spray. Spread pasta mixture on bottom of baking dish. Set aside.

3. Preheat oven to 350°F. Cook ground lamb, onion and garlic in large nonstick skillet over medium heat until lamb is no longer pink. Stir in tomato sauce, mint, oregano, pepper and cinnamon. Reduce heat and simmer 10 minutes; spread over pasta.

4. Melt margarine in small nonstick saucepan. Add flour. Stir constantly for 1 minute. Whisk in milk. Cook, stirring constantly, until thickened, about 6 minutes; spread over meat mixture. Sprinkle with cheese. Bake 30 to 40 minutes or until set.

Makes 6 servings

Nutritional Information per Serving: *Calories: 280, Total Fat: 5 g, Cholesterol: 31 mg, Sodium: 366 mg*

Spicy Shrimp Puttanesca

8 ounces uncooked linguine, capellini or spaghetti
1 tablespoon olive oil
12 ounces medium shrimp, peeled and deveined
4 cloves garlic, minced
¾ teaspoon red pepper flakes
1 cup finely chopped onion
1 can (14½ ounces) no-salt-added stewed tomatoes, undrained
2 tablespoons tomato paste
2 tablespoons chopped pitted kalamata or black olives
1 tablespoon drained capers
¼ cup chopped fresh basil or parsley

1. Cook linguine according to package directions, omitting salt. Drain; set aside.

2. Meanwhile, heat oil in large nonstick skillet over medium-high heat. Add shrimp, garlic and red pepper flakes; cook and stir 3 to 4 minutes or until shrimp are opaque. Transfer shrimp mixture to bowl with slotted spoon; set aside.

3. Add onion to same skillet; cook over medium heat 5 minutes, stirring occasionally. Add tomatoes, tomato paste, olives and capers; simmer, uncovered, 5 minutes.

4. Return shrimp mixture to skillet; simmer 1 minute. Stir in basil; simmer 1 minute. Place linguine in large serving bowl; top with shrimp mixture.   *Makes 4 servings*

Nutritional Information per Serving: *Calories: 328, Total Fat: 8 g, Cholesterol: 131 mg, Sodium: 537 mg*

Spaghetti with Marinara Sauce

MARINARA SAUCE:
1 teaspoon olive oil
¾ cup chopped onion
3 cloves garlic, finely chopped
1 can (16 ounces) no-salt-added tomato sauce
1 can (6 ounces) tomato paste
2 bay leaves
1 teaspoon dried oregano leaves
1 teaspoon dried basil leaves
½ teaspoon dried marjoram leaves
½ teaspoon honey
¼ teaspoon black pepper

8 ounces uncooked spaghetti, cooked and drained

1. Heat oil in large saucepan. Add onion and garlic. Cook and stir 5 minutes or until onion is tender. Add 2 cups water, tomato sauce, tomato paste, bay leaves, oregano, basil, marjoram, honey and pepper. Bring to a boil, stirring occasionally. Reduce heat; simmer 1 hour, stirring occasionally.

2. Remove and discard bay leaves. Measure 2 cups sauce; reserve remaining sauce for another use. Spoon 2 cups sauce over pasta.
     Makes 4 servings

Nutritional Information per Serving: *Calories: 289, Total Fat: 2 g, Cholesterol: 0 mg, Sodium: 213 mg*

Spicy Shrimp Puttanesca

Country Kielbasa and Vegetables

Nonstick cooking spray
8 ounces turkey kielbasa sausage, cut into ⅛-inch rounds
1 cup chopped onion
¾ cup chopped green bell pepper
½ cup finely chopped celery
1 can (16 ounces) diced tomatoes, undrained
⅓ cup water
½ cup uncooked orzo pasta
½ teaspoon dried thyme leaves
2 teaspoons olive oil
Hot pepper sauce

1. Preheat oven to 350°F. Spray large nonstick skillet with cooking spray. Heat over high heat until hot. Add sausage; cook and stir 10 to 15 minutes or until sausage is brown. Add onion, bell pepper and celery; cook an additional 3 minutes.

2. Spoon into 1½-quart casserole. Add tomatoes, water, orzo and thyme; cover. Bake 1 hour, stirring after 30 minutes, or until heated through. Remove from heat. Add olive oil; stir to combine. Let stand, covered, 10 minutes before serving. Serve with hot pepper sauce.   *Makes 4 servings*

Nutritional Information per Serving: *Calories: 260, Total Fat: 7 g, Cholesterol: 38 mg, Sodium: 691 mg*

Celebration Pasta

2 cups fresh tortellini
1 bag (16 ounces) BIRDS EYE® frozen Farm Fresh Mixtures Broccoli, Corn & Red Peppers
1 tablespoon olive oil
1 teaspoon salt
1 teaspoon lemon juice
½ cup fresh or canned diced tomatoes

• In large saucepan, cook tortellini according to package directions; drain and return to saucepan.

• Cook vegetables according to package directions; drain and add to tortellini.

• In small bowl, combine oil, salt and lemon juice. Stir in tomatoes.

• Stir tomato mixture into pasta and vegetables; cook over medium heat 5 minutes or until heated through.
Makes 4 servings

Prep Time: 10 minutes

Cook Time: 10 minutes

Nutritional Information per Serving: *Calories: 246, Total Fat: 4 g, Cholesterol: 0 mg, Sodium: 671 mg*

Country Kielbasa and Vegetables

Vegetables with Spinach Fettuccine

6 sun-dried tomatoes (not packed in oil)
3 ounces uncooked spinach fettuccine
1 tablespoon olive oil
¼ cup chopped onion
¼ cup sliced red bell pepper
1 clove garlic, minced
½ cup sliced mushrooms
½ cup coarsely chopped fresh spinach
¼ teaspoon salt
¼ teaspoon ground nutmeg
⅛ teaspoon black pepper

1. Place sun-dried tomatoes in small bowl; pour boiling water over tomatoes to cover. Let stand 10 to 15 minutes or until tomatoes are tender. Drain tomatoes; discard liquid. Cut tomatoes into strips.

2. Cook pasta according to package directions, omitting salt. Drain; set aside.

3. Heat oil in large nonstick skillet over medium heat until hot. Add onion, bell pepper and garlic; cook and stir 3 minutes or until vegetables are crisp-tender. Add mushrooms and spinach; cook and stir 1 minute. Add sun-dried tomatoes, pasta, salt, nutmeg and black pepper; cook and stir 1 to 2 minutes or until heated through.

Makes 6 servings

Nutritional Information per Serving: *Calories: 82, Total Fat: 3 g, Cholesterol: 3 mg, Sodium: 101 mg*

Easy Tex-Mex Bake

8 ounces uncooked thin mostaccioli
1 pound ground turkey breast
1 package (10 ounces) frozen corn, thawed and drained
⅔ cup bottled medium or mild salsa
1 container (16 ounces) 1% low-fat cottage cheese
1 egg
1 tablespoon minced fresh cilantro
½ teaspoon white pepper
¼ teaspoon ground cumin
½ cup (2 ounces) shredded Monterey Jack cheese

1. Cook pasta according to package directions, omitting salt. Drain and rinse well; set aside.

2. Spray large nonstick skillet with nonstick cooking spray. Add turkey; cook until no longer pink, about 5 minutes. Stir in corn and salsa. Remove from heat.

3. Preheat oven to 350°F. Combine cottage cheese, egg, cilantro, white pepper and cumin in small bowl.

4. Spoon ½ turkey mixture onto bottom of 11½×7½-inch baking dish. Top with pasta. Spoon cottage cheese mixture over pasta. Top with remaining turkey mixture. Sprinkle Monterey Jack cheese over casserole.

5. Bake 25 to 30 minutes or until heated through. *Makes 6 servings*

Nutritional Information per Serving: *Calories: 365, Total Fat: 6 g, Cholesterol: 99 mg, Sodium: 800 mg*

Vegetables with Spinach Fettuccine

Broccoli Lasagna Bianca

1 (15- to 16-ounce) container fat-free
    ricotta cheese
1 cup EGG BEATERS® Healthy Real Egg
    Substitute
1 tablespoon minced basil *or*
    1 teaspoon dried basil leaves
½ cup chopped onion
1 clove garlic, minced
2 tablespoons FLEISCHMANN'S® 70%
    Corn Oil Spread
¼ cup all-purpose flour
2 cups skim milk
2 (10-ounce) packages frozen chopped
    broccoli, thawed and well drained
1 cup (4 ounces) shredded part-skim
    mozzarella cheese
9 lasagna noodles, cooked and drained
1 small tomato, chopped
2 tablespoons grated Parmesan cheese
    Fresh basil leaves, for garnish

In medium bowl, combine ricotta cheese,
Egg Beaters® and minced basil; set aside.

In large saucepan, over medium heat, sauté
onion and garlic in spread until tender-crisp.
Stir in flour; cook for 1 minute. Gradually stir
in milk; cook, stirring until mixture thickens
and begins to boil. Remove from heat; stir in
broccoli and mozzarella cheese.

In lightly greased 13×9×2-inch baking dish,
place 3 lasagna noodles; top with ⅓ each
ricotta and broccoli mixtures. Repeat layers
2 more times. Top with tomato; sprinkle
with Parmesan cheese. Bake at 350°F for 1
hour or until set. Let stand 10 minutes
before serving. Garnish with basil leaves.

Makes 8 servings

Prep Time: 20 minutes

Cook Time: 90 minutes

Nutritional Information per Serving: *Calories: 302,
Total Fat: 7 g, Cholesterol: 10 mg, Sodium: 291 mg*

Cajun Grilled Shrimp with Rotini and Roasted Red Pepper Sauce

10 ounces uncooked rotini pasta
2 jars (7 ounces each) roasted peppers
    packed in water, drained
2 cloves garlic
2 tablespoons olive oil
½ teaspoon salt
¼ cup chicken broth
⅛ teaspoon ground red pepper
    Nonstick cooking spray
12 ounces medium shrimp, peeled and
    deveined
1½ teaspoons chili powder
1½ teaspoons lemon pepper
¾ teaspoon paprika

1. Cook pasta according to package
directions, omitting salt. Drain; set aside.

2. Meanwhile, place roasted peppers, garlic,
oil, salt, chicken broth and ground red
pepper in food processor or blender; process
until smooth. Set aside.

3. Spray large nonstick skillet with cooking
spray. Heat over medium heat until hot. Add
shrimp, chili powder, lemon pepper and
paprika; cook and stir 8 minutes or until
shrimp are opaque. Add roasted pepper
mixture; heat thoroughly. *Do not boil.* Serve
over pasta.   *Makes 4 servings*

Nutritional Information per Serving: *Calories: 452,
Total Fat: 10 g, Cholesterol: 130 mg, Sodium: 468 mg*

Broccoli Lasagna Bianca

Lasagna Roll-Ups

Vegetable cooking spray
1 pound ground turkey breast or
    extra-lean ground beef
½ cup chopped onion
2 cloves garlic, minced
1 can HEALTHY CHOICE® Recipe
    Creations™ Tomato with Garden
    Herbs Condensed Soup
1 cup chopped zucchini
¾ cup water
1 (15-ounce) container fat free ricotta
    cheese
½ cup HEALTHY CHOICE® Fat Free
    Shredded Mozzarella Cheese
1 egg
4 cooked lasagna noodles

In large nonstick skillet sprayed with
vegetable cooking spray, cook turkey, onion
and garlic until turkey is no longer pink and
onion is tender. Add soup, zucchini and
water; simmer 5 minutes. Pour soup mixture
into shallow 2-quart baking dish.

In medium bowl, combine ricotta and
mozzarella cheeses and egg; mix well. Lay
lasagna noodles on flat surface; spread ½
cup cheese mixture on each noodle. Roll up
noodles, enclosing filling; place rolls seam
side down over soup mixture.

Cover and bake at 375°F 30 minutes;
uncover and continue baking 10 minutes
longer or until sauce is bubbly. Place lasagna
rolls on serving dish; spoon remaining sauce
over rolls. *Makes 4 servings*

Nutritional Information per Serving: *Calories: 404,
Total Fat: 6 g, Sodium: 558 mg*

Rush-Hour Lasagna

Nonstick cooking spray
8 ounces ground round
2 cups no-salt-added spaghetti sauce
1 can (4 ounces) sliced mushrooms,
    drained
4 cloves garlic, minced
2 tablespoons chopped fresh parsley
1½ teaspoons dried oregano
1½ teaspoons fennel seeds (optional)
6 uncooked lasagna noodles
½ cup nonfat cottage cheese
6 tablespoons grated fat-free
    Parmesan cheese
¾ cup (3 ounces) grated fat-free
    mozzarella cheese

1. Preheat oven to 350°F. Spray large
nonstick skillet with cooking spray. Heat over
high heat until hot. Brown beef in skillet
over medium-high heat 6 to 8 minutes or
until no longer pink, stirring to separate
beef; drain fat. Add spaghetti sauce,
mushrooms, garlic, parsley, oregano and
fennel seeds, if desired. Bring to a boil.
Reduce heat to low; simmer, uncovered,
8 minutes or until slightly thickened.

2. Spray 8-inch square baking pan with
nonstick cooking spray. Place 2 noodles on
bottom of pan. Spoon ⅓ sauce over
noodles, ¼ cup cottage cheese over sauce
and top with 2 tablespoons Parmesan
cheese. Repeat layers, ending with noodles.
Spread remaining sauce on top of noodles
and sprinkle with mozzarella cheese.

3. Cover; bake 30 minutes. Remove cover;
continue baking 10 minutes. Remove from
oven; top with remaining 2 tablespoons
Parmesan cheese. Let stand 10 minutes
before serving. *Makes 4 servings*

Nutritional Information per Serving: *Calories: 310,
Total Fat: 9 g, Cholesterol: 32 mg, Sodium: 460 mg*

Lasagna Roll-Ups

Spicy Mesquite Chicken Fettuccine

    8 ounces uncooked fettuccine
    1 tablespoon chili powder
    1 teaspoon ground cumin
    1 teaspoon paprika
    ¼ teaspoon ground red pepper
    2 teaspoons vegetable oil
    1 pound mesquite marinated chicken
        breasts, cut into bite-size pieces

1. Cook pasta according to package directions, omitting salt. Drain; set aside.

2. Combine chili powder, cumin, paprika and ground red pepper in small bowl; set aside.

3. Heat oil in large nonstick skillet over medium-high heat until hot. Add chili powder mixture; cook 30 seconds, stirring constantly. Add chicken; cook and stir 5 to 6 minutes or until no longer pink in center and lightly browned. Add pasta to skillet; stir. Cook 1 to 2 minutes or until heated through. Sprinkle with additional chili powder, if desired. Garnish with fresh cilantro and red bell pepper, if desired.

Makes 4 servings

Nutritional Information per Serving: *Calories: 520, Total Fat: 8 g, Cholesterol: 144 mg, Sodium: 699 mg*

Catalan Spinach and Pasta

    16 ounces uncooked rotelle pasta
     2 cups water
    20 ounces fresh spinach, stems removed
    ⅔ cup raisins, divided
     4 teaspoons balsamic vinegar
     2 teaspoons olive oil
    ½ teaspoon salt
    ¼ teaspoon black pepper
     2 cloves garlic, minced
     6 tablespoons pine nuts

1. Cook pasta according to package directions, omitting salt. Drain; set aside.

2. Bring water to a boil in large saucepan over high heat. Add spinach; cook, covered, 3 minutes or until spinach leaves start to wilt. Remove from heat; drain. Stir in 5 tablespoons raisins, vinegar, oil, salt, pepper and garlic. Place in food processor or blender; process until smooth. Add remaining raisins and pasta. Sprinkle with pine nuts. *Makes 6 servings*

Nutritional Information per Serving: *Calories: 442, Total Fat: 10 g, Cholesterol: 0 mg, Sodium: 256 mg*

Pasta Carbonara

     1 can HEALTHY CHOICE® Recipe
        Creations™ Cream of Roasted
        Garlic Condensed Soup
    ½ cup nonfat milk
        Vegetable cooking spray
     1 cup frozen peas and carrots, thawed
        and drained
     1 cup sliced mushrooms
    ½ cup chopped onion
     4 strips bacon, cooked until crisp and
        crumbled
    ½ teaspoon salt (optional)
     4 cups hot cooked pasta

In small bowl, combine soup and milk; mix well. Set aside. In large skillet sprayed with vegetable cooking spray, sauté peas and carrots, mushrooms and onion over medium-high heat until tender. Add bacon, soup mixture and salt; mix well. Reduce heat; cover and simmer 5 minutes or until heated through. Serve over hot pasta.

Makes 4 servings

Nutritional Information per Serving: *Calories: 310, Total Fat: 5 g, Sodium: 440 mg*

Spicy Mesquite Chicken Fettuccine

Pasta Picadillo

12 ounces uncooked medium shell pasta
    Nonstick cooking spray
 1 pound lean ground sirloin
⅔ cup finely chopped green bell
    pepper
½ cup finely chopped onion
 2 cloves garlic, minced
 1 (8-ounce) can tomato sauce
½ cup water
⅓ cup raisins
 3 tablespoons sliced pimiento-stuffed
    green olives
 2 tablespoons drained capers
 2 tablespoons vinegar
½ teaspoon black pepper
¼ teaspoon salt

1. Cook pasta according to package directions, omitting salt. Drain; set aside.

2. Spray large nonstick skillet with cooking spray. Add beef, bell pepper, onion and garlic. Brown beef mixture over medium-high heat 5 minutes or until no longer pink, stirring to separate beef; drain fat. Stir in tomato sauce, water, raisins, olives, capers, vinegar, pepper and salt. Reduce heat to medium-low; cook, covered, 15 minutes, stirring occasionally.

3. Add pasta to skillet; toss to coat. Cover and heat through, about 2 minutes.

Makes 6 servings

Nutritional Information per Serving: *Calories: 366, Total Fat: 5 g, Cholesterol: 43 mg, Sodium: 568 mg*

Alpine Fettuccine

½ pound white fettuccine, preferably
    fresh
½ pound green fettuccine, preferably
    fresh
1½ teaspoons extra virgin olive oil
 1 cup sliced fresh mushrooms
 1 cup chopped red bell pepper
½ cup skim milk
 6 ounces (1 carton) ALPINE LACE® Fat
    Free Cream Cheese with Garlic &
    Herbs

1. Cook the fettuccine according to package directions until al dente. Drain well and place in a large shallow pasta bowl. Toss with the oil and keep warm.

2. Meanwhile, spray a medium-size nonstick skillet with nonstick cooking spray. Add the mushrooms and bell pepper and sauté until soft. Toss with the fettuccine.

3. In a small saucepan, bring the milk to a boil over medium heat. Add the cream cheese and stir until melted. Toss with pasta and serve immediately.

*Makes 9 side-dish servings (1 cup each)
or 6 main-dish servings (1½ cups each)*

Nutritional Information per Serving (1 cup):
Calories: 228, Total Fat: 3 g, Cholesterol: 51 mg, Sodium: 138 mg

Pasta Picadillo

Side Dishes & Vegetables

Oriental Garden Toss

⅓ cup thinly sliced green onions
3 tablespoons reduced-sodium soy sauce
3 tablespoons water
1½ teaspoons roasted sesame oil
1 teaspoon EQUAL® Measure™ or
   3 packets EQUAL® sweetener or
   2 tablespoons EQUAL® Spoonful™
¼ teaspoon garlic powder
⅛ teaspoon crushed red pepper flakes
1 package (3 ounces) low-fat ramen noodle soup
2 cups fresh pea pods, halved crosswise
1 can (8¾ ounces) baby corn, drained and halved crosswise
1 cup fresh bean sprouts
1 cup sliced fresh mushrooms
1 red bell pepper, cut into bite-size strips
3 cups shredded Chinese cabbage
⅓ cup chopped lightly salted cashews (optional)

• Combine green onions, soy sauce, water, sesame oil, Equal®, garlic powder and red pepper flakes in screw-top jar; set aside.

• Break up ramen noodles (discard seasoning packet); combine with pea pods in large bowl. Pour boiling water over mixture to cover. Let stand 1 minute; drain.

• Combine noodles, pea pods, baby corn, bean sprouts, mushrooms and bell pepper in large bowl. Shake dressing and add to noodle mixture; toss to coat. Cover and chill 2 to 24 hours. Just before serving, add shredded cabbage; toss to combine. Sprinkle with cashews, if desired.

Makes 6 (1-cup) servings

Nutritional Information per Serving: *Calories: 124, Total Fat: 2 g, Cholesterol: 0 mg, Sodium: 605 mg*

Oriental Garden Toss

Hawaiian Stir-Fry

1 can (8 ounces) pineapple chunks in
    juice, undrained
2 teaspoons cornstarch
1 tablespoon vegetable oil
1 red bell pepper, cut into strips
1 teaspoon curry powder
8 ounces (about 3 cups) snow peas,
    ends trimmed
⅓ cup diagonally sliced green onions
2 teaspoons reduced-sodium soy sauce

1. Drain pineapple; reserve juice. Combine juice and cornstarch in small bowl; stir to blend. Set aside.

2. Heat large skillet or wok 1 minute over medium-high heat. Add oil, pepper and curry powder; stir-fry 1 minute. Add pineapple chunks; stir-fry 1 minute. Add snow peas; stir-fry 1 minute. Add pineapple juice mixture; bring sauce to a boil. Boil 1 minute to thicken sauce.

3. Stir in green onions and soy sauce.

Makes 6 servings

Nutritional Information per Serving: *Calories: 77, Total Fat: 3 g, Cholesterol: 0 mg, Sodium: 61 mg*

Cold Asparagus with Lemon-Mustard Dressing

12 spears fresh asparagus
2 tablespoons fat-free mayonnaise
1 tablespoon sweet brown mustard
1 tablespoon fresh lemon juice
1 teaspoon grated lemon peel, divided

1. Steam asparagus until crisp-tender and bright green; immediately drain. Run under cold running water until cool. Drain.

2. Combine mayonnaise, mustard and lemon juice in small bowl; blend well. Stir in ½ teaspoon lemon peel; set aside.

3. Divide asparagus between 2 plates. Spoon 2 tablespoons dressing over top of each serving; sprinkle each with ¼ teaspoon lemon peel.

Makes 2 servings

Nutritional Information per Serving: *Calories 39, Total Fat: 1 g, Cholesterol: 0 mg, Sodium: 294 mg*

Guiltless Zucchini

Nonstick cooking spray
4 medium zucchini, sliced
⅓ cup chopped onion
4 cloves garlic, minced
¼ teaspoon dried oregano leaves
½ cup GUILTLESS GOURMET® Medium
    Salsa
¼ cup (1 ounce) shredded low fat
    mozzarella cheese

Coat large nonstick skillet with cooking spray; heat over medium heat until hot. Add zucchini; cook and stir 5 minutes. Add onion, garlic and oregano; cook 5 minutes more or until zucchini and onion are lightly browned. Stir in salsa. Bring just to a boil. Reduce heat to low; simmer 5 minutes more or until zucchini is crisp-tender. Sprinkle cheese on top; cover and cook 1 to 2 minutes or until cheese melts. Serve hot.

Makes 4 servings

Nutritional Information per Serving: *Calories: 39, Total Fat: <1 g, Cholesterol: 2 mg, Sodium: 180 mg*

Hawaiian Stir-Fry

Broccoli & Cauliflower Stir-Fry

2 sun-dried tomatoes (not oil-packed)
4 teaspoons reduced-sodium soy sauce
1 tablespoon rice wine vinegar
1 teaspoon brown sugar
1 teaspoon dark sesame oil
1/8 teaspoon red pepper flakes
2 1/4 teaspoons vegetable oil
2 cups cauliflower florets
2 cups broccoli florets
1 clove garlic, finely chopped
1/3 cup thinly sliced red or green bell pepper

1. Place tomatoes in small bowl; cover with boiling water. Let stand 5 minutes. Drain; coarsely chop. Meanwhile, blend soy sauce, vinegar, sugar, sesame oil and red pepper flakes in small bowl.

2. Heat vegetable oil in wok or large nonstick skillet over medium-high heat until hot. Add cauliflower, broccoli and garlic; stir-fry 4 minutes. Add tomatoes and bell pepper; stir-fry 1 minute or until vegetables are crisp-tender. Add soy sauce mixture; cook and stir until heated through. Serve immediately.

Makes 2 servings

Nutritional Information per Serving: *Calories: 214, Total Fat: 8 g, Cholesterol: 0 mg, Sodium: 443 mg*

Broccoli with Creamy Lemon Sauce

2 tablespoons fat-free mayonnaise
4 1/2 teaspoons low-fat sour cream
1 tablespoon skim milk
1 to 1 1/2 teaspoons lemon juice
1/8 teaspoon ground turmeric
1 1/4 cups hot cooked broccoli florets

Combine all ingredients except broccoli in top of double boiler. Cook over simmering water 5 minutes or until heated through, stirring constantly. Serve over hot cooked broccoli.

Makes 2 servings

Nutritional Information per Serving: *Calories: 44, Total Fat: 1 g, Cholesterol: 4 mg, Sodium: 216 mg*

Carrot and Parsnip Purée

1 pound carrots, peeled
1 pound parsnips, peeled
1 cup chopped onion
1 cup vegetable broth
1 tablespoon margarine
1/8 teaspoon ground nutmeg

1. Cut carrots and parsnips crosswise into 1/2-inch pieces.

2. Combine carrots, parsnips, onion and vegetable broth in medium saucepan. Cover; bring to a boil over high heat. Reduce heat; simmer, covered, 20 to 22 minutes or until vegetables are very tender.

3. Drain vegetables, reserving broth. Combine vegetables, margarine, nutmeg and 1/4 cup reserved broth in food processor. Process until smooth. Serve immediately.

Makes 10 servings

Nutritional Information per Serving: *Calories: 78, Total Fat: 1 g, Cholesterol: 0 mg, Sodium: 56 mg*

Broccoli & Cauliflower Stir-Fry

Green Bean Casserole

Ranch-Style White Sauce (recipe
  follows)
Nonstick cooking spray
1 cup chopped onion
2 cloves garlic, minced
1½ cups sliced fresh mushrooms
1¼ pounds fresh green beans, cooked
  until crisp-tender
1 cup fresh bread crumbs
2 tablespoons minced parsley

1. Preheat oven to 350°F. Prepare Ranch-Style White Sauce. Set aside. Spray medium skillet with nonstick cooking spray; heat over medium-high heat. Add onion and garlic; cook 2 to 3 minutes or until tender. Remove half of onion mixture. Set aside.

2. Add mushrooms to skillet and cook about 5 minutes or until tender. Combine mushroom mixture, beans and sauce in 1½-quart casserole.

3. Spray medium skillet with nonstick cooking spray; heat over medium heat. Add bread crumbs to skillet; spray top of crumbs lightly with nonstick cooking spray. Cook 3 to 4 minutes or until crumbs are golden. Stir in reserved onion mixture and parsley. Sprinkle bread crumb mixture over casserole. Bake, uncovered, 20 to 30 minutes or until heated through.

Makes 6 servings

Ranch-Style White Sauce

1½ tablespoons margarine
3 tablespoons all-purpose flour
1½ cups skim milk
3 to 4 teaspoons ranch salad dressing
  mix
¼ to ½ teaspoon white pepper

1. Melt margarine in small saucepan over low heat. Stir in flour; cook 1 to 2 minutes, stirring constantly. Using wire whisk, stir in milk; bring to a boil. Cook, whisking constantly, 1 to 2 minutes or until thickened. Stir in dressing mix and pepper.

Makes 1½ cups

Nutritional Information per Serving: *Calories: 123, Total Fat: 3 g, Cholesterol: 1 mg, Sodium: 200 mg*

Vegetarian Broccoli Casserole

Vegetable cooking spray
½ cup *each* chopped onion and celery
⅓ cup chopped red bell pepper
1 can HEALTHY CHOICE® Recipe
  Creations™ Cream of Broccoli with
  Cheddar and Onion Condensed
  Soup
¼ cup fat free sour cream
1 (10-ounce) package frozen chopped
  broccoli, thawed and drained
2 cups cooked rice
1 tomato, cut into ¼-inch slices

In large skillet sprayed with vegetable cooking spray, sauté onion, celery and pepper until crisp-tender. Stir in soup and sour cream. In 1½-quart baking dish sprayed with vegetable cooking spray, layer broccoli and rice. Top rice with soup mixture, spreading evenly.

Cover and bake at 350°F 20 minutes. Top with tomato slices; bake, uncovered, 10 minutes.

Makes 6 servings

Nutritional Information per Serving: *Calories: 170, Total Fat: 2 g, Sodium: 230 mg*

Green Bean Casserole

Honey Glazed Carrots and Parsnips

½ pound carrots, peeled and cut into julienned strips
½ pound parsnips, peeled and cut into julienned strips
¼ cup chopped fresh parsley
2 tablespoons honey

1. Steam carrots and parsnips 3 to 4 minutes or until crisp-tender. Rinse under cold running water; drain and set aside.

2. Just before serving, combine carrots, parsnips, parsley and honey in large saucepan or skillet. Cook over medium heat just until heated through. Garnish with fresh Italian parsley, if desired. Serve immediately.
Makes 6 servings

Nutritional Information per Serving: *Calories: 69, Total Fat: trace, Cholesterol: 0 mg, Sodium: 19 mg*

Herbed Green Beans

1 pound fresh green beans, stem ends removed
1 teaspoon olive oil
2 tablespoons chopped fresh basil *or* 2 teaspoons dried basil leaves

1. Steam green beans 5 minutes or until crisp-tender. Rinse under cold running water; drain and set aside.

2. Just before serving, heat oil over medium-low heat in large nonstick skillet. Add basil; cook and stir 1 minute, then add green beans. Cook until heated through. Garnish with additional fresh basil, if desired. Serve immediately. *Makes 6 servings*

Nutritional Information per Serving: *Calories: 26, Total Fat: 1 g, Cholesterol: 0 mg, Sodium: 10 mg*

Hot Three-Bean Casserole

2 tablespoons olive oil
1 cup coarsely chopped onion
1 cup chopped celery
2 cloves garlic, minced
1 can (15 ounces) chick-peas, rinsed and drained
1 can (15 ounces) kidney beans, rinsed and drained
1 cup coarsely chopped tomato
1 can (8 ounces) tomato sauce
1 cup water
1 to 2 jalapeño peppers, minced*
1 tablespoon chili powder
2 teaspoons sugar
1½ teaspoons ground cumin
1 teaspoon salt
1 teaspoon dried oregano
¼ teaspoon black pepper
2½ cups (10 ounces) frozen cut green beans

Jalapeño peppers can sting and irritate the skin. Wear rubber gloves when handling peppers and do not touch eyes.

1. Heat oil in large skillet over medium heat until hot. Add onion, celery and garlic; cook and stir 5 minutes or until onion is translucent.

2. Add remaining ingredients except green beans. Bring to a boil; reduce heat to low. Simmer, uncovered, 20 minutes. Add green beans. Simmer, uncovered, 10 minutes or until green beans are just tender.
Makes 12 servings

Nutritional Information per Serving: *Calories 118, Total Fat: 3 g, Cholesterol: 0 mg, Sodium: 521 mg*

Top to bottom: Herbed Green Beans, Honey Glazed Carrots and Parsnips

Festive Stuffed Peppers

1 can HEALTHY CHOICE® Recipe
   Creations™ Tomato with Garden
   Herbs Condensed Soup, divided
¼ cup water
8 ounces extra-lean ground beef or
   turkey
1 cup cooked rice
½ cup frozen corn, thawed
¼ cup *each* sliced celery and chopped
   red bell pepper
½ teaspoon Italian seasoning
2 green, yellow or red bell peppers,
   cut in half lengthwise and seeds
   removed

In small bowl, mix ¼ cup soup and water.
Pour into 8×8-inch baking dish; set aside. In
large skillet, brown beef over medium-high
heat; drain well. In large bowl, combine
remaining soup with cooked beef, rice, corn,
celery, chopped pepper and Italian
seasoning; mix well.

Fill pepper halves equally with beef mixture.
Place stuffed peppers on top of soup
mixture in baking dish. Cover and bake at
350°F 35 to 40 minutes. Place peppers on
serving dish and spoon remaining sauce
from baking dish over peppers.

Makes 4 servings

Nutritional Information per Serving: *Calories: 260,*
Total Fat: 8 g, Sodium: 215 mg

Fresh Cranberry Relish

1 orange
1 package (12 ounces) fresh or thawed
   frozen cranberries
2 medium tart apples, unpeeled, cored
   and coarsely chopped
5¼ teaspoons EQUAL® Measure™ *or*
   18 packets EQUAL® sweetener *or*
   ¾ cup EQUAL® Spoonful™
⅛ teaspoon salt

• Grate rind from orange and reserve. Peel
orange; cut orange into large pieces.

• Place orange rind, orange pieces,
cranberries and apples in food processor;
process until finely chopped. Stir in Equal®
and salt. Refrigerate until ready to serve.

Makes 12 servings

Note: Amount of Equal® may vary
depending on the tartness of the apples and
cranberries.

Nutritional Information per Serving (⅔ cup):
Calories: 41, Total Fat: 0 g, Cholesterol: 0 mg, Sodium: 22 mg

Cranberry Gelatin Salad: Prepare 2
packages (0.3 ounces each) sugar-free
raspberry gelatin according to package
directions using 1½ cups boiling water and
1½ cups cold water; refrigerate until mixture
is consistency of unbeaten egg whites.
Prepare Fresh Cranberry Relish as directed
above; stir into gelatin mixture and spoon
into lightly greased 8-cup mold or casserole.
Refrigerate until set, about 4 hours. To
unmold, briefly dip mold into warm water
and loosen top edge of mold with tip of
sharp knife. Unmold onto serving plate lined
with salad greens.

Makes 12 (⅔-cup) servings

Nutritional Information per Serving (⅔ cup):
Calories: 46, Total Fat: 0 g, Cholesterol: 0 mg, Sodium: 60 mg

Festive Stuffed Peppers

Refrigerator Corn Relish

2 cups cut fresh corn (4 ears) *or*
    1 (10-ounce) package frozen corn
½ cup vinegar
⅓ cup cold water
1 tablespoon cornstarch
¼ cup chopped onion
¼ cup chopped celery
¼ cup chopped green or red bell
    pepper
2 tablespoons chopped pimientos
1 teaspoon ground turmeric
½ teaspoon salt
½ teaspoon dry mustard
1¾ teaspoons EQUAL® Measure™ *or*
    6 packets EQUAL® sweetener *or*
    ¼ cup EQUAL® Spoonful™

• Cook corn in boiling water until crisp-tender, 5 to 7 minutes; drain and set aside. Combine vinegar, water and cornstarch in large saucepan; stir until cornstarch is dissolved. Add corn, onion, celery, pepper, pimientos, turmeric, salt and mustard. Cook and stir until thickened and bubbly. Cook and stir 2 minutes more. Remove from heat; stir in Equal®. Cool. Cover and store in refrigerator up to 2 weeks. Serve with beef, pork or poultry. *Makes 2½ cups*

**Nutritional Information per Serving
(2 tablespoons):** *Calories: 22, Total Fat: 0 g,
Cholesterol: 0 mg, Sodium: 57 mg*

Quick Refrigerator Sweet Pickles

5 cups thinly sliced cucumbers
2 cloves garlic, halved
2 cups water
1 teaspoon mustard seed
1 teaspoon celery seed
1 teaspoon ground turmeric
2 cups sliced onions
1 cup julienne carrot strips
2 cups vinegar
3 tablespoons plus 1¾ teaspoons
    EQUAL® Measure™ *or 36 packets*
    EQUAL® sweetener *or 1½ cups*
    EQUAL® Spoonful™

• Place cucumbers and garlic in glass bowl. Combine water, mustard seed, celery seed and turmeric in medium saucepan. Bring to boiling. Add onion and carrots; cook 2 minutes. Add vinegar; bring just to boiling. Remove from heat; stir in Equal®. Pour over cucumbers and garlic. Cool. Cover and chill at least 24 hours before serving. Store in refrigerator up to 2 weeks.

Makes about 6 cups

Nutritional Information per Serving (¼ cup):
Calories: 8, Total Fat: 0 g, Cholesterol: 0 mg, Sodium: 3 mg

*Left to right: Refrigerator Corn Relish
and Quick Refrigerator Sweet Pickles*

Cranberry Sauce

**2 cups fresh or frozen cranberries
(8 ounces)**
⅔ cup water
**7¼ teaspoons EQUAL® Measure™ or
24 packets EQUAL® sweetener or
1 cup EQUAL® Spoonful™**

• Combine cranberries and water in medium saucepan. Bring just to boiling; reduce heat. Boil gently, uncovered, over medium heat 8 minutes, stirring occasionally. (Skins will pop.)

• Remove from heat; mash slightly. Stir in Equal®. Cover and chill. Serve chilled with beef, pork, ham or poultry.

Makes 1½ cups

**Nutritional Information per Serving
(2 tablespoons):** *Calories: 17, Total Fat: 0 g, Cholesterol: 0 mg, Sodium: 0 mg*

Orange-Cranberry Sauce: Reduce water to ⅓ cup and add ⅓ cup orange juice. Add 1 teaspoon finely grated orange peel and 1 orange, peeled, sectioned and chopped, when adding Equal®. *Makes 1⅔ cups*

Chunky Spiced Applesauce

**3½ pounds tart cooking apples (about
8 large), peeled and chopped**
½ cup water
**7¼ teaspoons EQUAL® Measure™ or
24 packets EQUAL® sweetener or
1 cup EQUAL® Spoonful™**
½ teaspoon ground cinnamon
¼ teaspoon ground nutmeg
1 to 2 dashes salt

• Combine apples and water in large saucepan; heat to boiling. Reduce heat and simmer, covered, until apples are tender, 20 to 25 minutes.

• Mash apples coarsely with fork; stir in Equal®, cinnamon, nutmeg and salt. Serve warm, or refrigerate and serve chilled.

Makes 10 (½-cup) servings

Note: Amount of Equal® may vary depending on the tartness of the apples.

Nutritional Information per Serving: *Calories: 104, Total Fat: 1 g, Cholesterol: 0 mg, Sodium: 14 mg*

Creamy Macaroni & Cheese

**1 can HEALTHY CHOICE® Recipe
Creations™ Cream of Celery with
Sautéed Onion & Garlic Condensed
Soup**
**2 cups HEALTHY CHOICE® Fat Free
Shredded Cheddar Cheese**
½ cup nonfat milk
**2 teaspoons *each* minced onion and
diced red or green bell pepper**
2 teaspoons horseradish
½ teaspoon salt (optional)
**4 cups cooked small elbow macaroni
Vegetable cooking spray**
3 slices fat free sharp Cheddar cheese

In large bowl, combine soup, shredded cheese, milk, onion, pepper, horseradish and salt; mix well. Add macaroni; mix well.

Place macaroni mixture in 2-quart baking dish sprayed with vegetable cooking spray. Top with cheese slices; cover and bake at 375°F 30 minutes or until hot and bubbly.

Makes 6 servings

Nutritional Information per Serving: *Calories: 247, Total Fat: 2 g, Sodium: 587 mg*

Baked Corn Timbales

6 sun-dried tomatoes (not packed in oil)
2 whole eggs
2 egg whites
2 cups frozen corn, thawed
¾ cup evaporated skimmed milk
1 teaspoon salt
1 teaspoon dry mustard
1 teaspoon hot pepper sauce

1. Preheat oven to 350°F. Spray 6 (6-ounce) ramekins or small ovenproof dishes with nonstick cooking spray.

2. To reconstitute sun-dried tomatoes, place in small bowl and cover with hot water. Let stand 15 minutes. Drain and finely chop.

3. Beat whole eggs and egg whites in medium bowl with wire whisk until frothy. Fold in tomatoes, corn, milk, salt, mustard and pepper sauce until well combined. Fill ramekins ¾ full with mixture.

4. Place ramekins in large roasting pan; pour hot water around ramekins to depth of about ½ inch. Bake 35 minutes or until set and lightly browned. Invert ramekins onto serving plate to release timbales. Serve immediately. *Makes 6 servings*

Nutritional Information per Serving: *Calories: 128, Total Fat: 2 g, Cholesterol: 72 mg, Sodium: 449 mg*

Wild & Brown Rice with Exotic Mushrooms

1⅔ cups packaged unseasoned wild & brown rice blend
¾ cup boiling water
½ ounce dried porcini or morel mushrooms
2 tablespoons margarine
8 ounces cremini or button mushrooms, sliced
2 cloves garlic, minced
2 tablespoons chopped fresh thyme *or* 2 teaspoons dried thyme leaves
1 teaspoon salt
¼ teaspoon black pepper
½ cup sliced green onions

1. Combine rice and 6 cups cold water in large saucepan; bring to a boil over high heat. Cover; simmer over low heat until rice is tender (check package for cooking time). Drain, but do not rinse.

2. Meanwhile, combine boiling water and porcini mushrooms in small bowl; let stand 30 minutes or until mushrooms are tender. Drain mushrooms, reserving liquid. Chop mushrooms; set aside.

3. Melt margarine in large, deep skillet over medium heat. Add cremini mushrooms and garlic; cook and stir 5 minutes. Sprinkle thyme, salt and pepper over mushrooms; cook and stir 1 minute or until mushrooms are tender.

4. Stir drained rice, porcini mushrooms and reserved mushroom liquid into skillet; cook and stir over medium-low heat 5 minutes or until hot. Stir in green onions.
Makes 8 servings

Nutritional Information per Serving: *Calories: 175, Total Fat: 4 g, Cholesterol: 0 mg, Sodium: 304 mg*

Spicy Chick-Peas & Couscous

1 can (about 14 ounces) vegetable broth
1 teaspoon ground coriander
½ teaspoon ground cardamom
½ teaspoon turmeric
½ teaspoon hot pepper sauce
¼ teaspoon salt
⅛ teaspoon ground cinnamon
1 cup julienned carrots
1 can (15 ounces) chick-peas, rinsed and drained
1 cup frozen peas
1 cup uncooked quick-cooking couscous
2 tablespoons chopped fresh mint or parsley

1. Combine vegetable broth, coriander, cardamom, turmeric, pepper sauce, salt and cinnamon in large saucepan; bring to a boil over high heat. Add carrots; reduce heat and simmer 5 minutes. Add chick-peas and peas; return to a simmer. Simmer, uncovered, 2 minutes.

2. Stir in couscous. Cover; remove from heat. Let stand 5 minutes or until liquid is absorbed. Sprinkle with mint.

Makes 6 servings

Nutritional Information per Serving: *Calories: 226, Total Fat: 2 g, Cholesterol: 0 mg, Sodium: 431 mg*

Green Pea & Rice Amandine

2 teaspoons reduced-calorie margarine
1 cup frozen baby green peas
¼ teaspoon ground cardamom
¼ teaspoon ground cinnamon
    Pinch ground cloves
    Pinch white pepper
¾ cup cooked white rice
2 teaspoons slivered almonds

Melt margarine in medium nonstick skillet over medium heat. Add peas, cardamom, cinnamon, cloves and pepper. Cook and stir 10 minutes or until peas are tender. Add rice. Cook until heated through, stirring occasionally. Sprinkle almonds evenly over servings. *Makes 4 servings*

Nutritional Information per Serving: *Calories: 100, Total Fat: 2 g, Cholesterol: 0 mg, Sodium: 57 mg*

Broccoli & Cheese Rice Pilaf

    Vegetable cooking spray
¼ cup *each* minced onion and diced red bell pepper
2 cups raw precooked long-grain rice
1⅓ cups water
1 can HEALTHY CHOICE® Recipe Creations™ Cream of Broccoli with Cheddar and Onion Condensed Soup
1 tablespoon minced fresh parsley
½ teaspoon salt (optional)

In medium saucepan sprayed with vegetable cooking spray, sauté onion and pepper until tender. Stir in rice. Add water, soup, parsley and salt; mix well. Bring to a boil; reduce heat. Cover and cook 10 minutes or until liquid is absorbed and rice is tender.

Makes 6 servings

Nutritional Information per Serving: *Calories: 170, Total Fat: 1 g, Sodium: 200 mg*

Spicy Chick-Peas & Couscous

Spicy Spanish Rice

1 teaspoon canola oil
1 cup uncooked white rice
1 medium onion, chopped
2 cups chicken stock or canned low
 sodium chicken broth, defatted
1 cup GUILTLESS GOURMET® Salsa
 (medium)
 Green chili pepper strips (optional)

Heat large skillet over medium-high heat until hot. Add oil; swirl to coat skillet. Add rice; cook and stir until lightly browned. Remove rice to small bowl. Add onion to same skillet; cook and stir until onion is translucent. Add stock and salsa to skillet; return rice to skillet. Bring to a boil. Reduce heat to low; cover and simmer until liquid is absorbed and rice is tender. Serve hot. Garnish with pepper, if desired.

Makes 4 servings

Nutritional Information per Serving: *Calories: 293, Total Fat: 2 g, Cholesterol: 0 mg, Sodium: 353 mg*

Athenian Rice with Feta Cheese

1 tablespoon olive oil
1 cup chopped red onion
1 red bell pepper, chopped
1 clove garlic, minced
3 cups cooked rice
1 can (4½ ounces) sliced black olives
½ cup sun-dried tomatoes, softened*
 and cut into julienned strips
1 tablespoon chopped fresh parsley
1½ teaspoons dried oregano leaves
½ cup crumbled feta cheese
1 tablespoon lemon juice
¼ teaspoon ground black pepper
 Fresh oregano for garnish

*To soften sun-dried tomatoes, place in ⅓ cup boiling water; stir to coat. Let stand 10 minutes; drain water.

Heat oil in large skillet over medium-high heat until hot. Add onion, bell pepper and garlic; cook and stir until onion is tender. Stir in rice, olives, tomatoes, parsley and oregano; heat thoroughly. Remove from heat; add cheese, lemon juice and black pepper. Stir until well blended. Garnish with fresh oregano. Serve immediately.

Makes 6 servings

Nutritional Information per Serving: *Calories: 204, Total Fat: 7 g, Cholesterol: 8 mg, Sodium: 612 mg*

Favorite recipe from **USA Rice Federation**

Rice Pilaf with Dried Cherries and Almonds

½ cup slivered almonds
2 tablespoons margarine
2 cups uncooked rice
½ cup chopped onion
1 can (about 14 ounces) vegetable
 broth
1½ cups water
½ cup dried cherries

1. To toast almonds, cook and stir in large nonstick skillet over medium heat until lightly browned. Remove from skillet; cool.

2. Melt margarine in skillet over low heat. Add rice and onion; cook and stir until rice is lightly browned. Add vegetable broth and water. Bring to a boil over high heat; reduce heat to low. Simmer, covered, 15 minutes.

3. Stir in almonds and cherries. Simmer 5 minutes or until liquid is absorbed and rice is tender.

Makes 12 servings

Nutritional Information per Serving: *Calories: 174, Total Fat: 5 g, Cholesterol: 0 mg, Sodium: 37 mg*

Spicy Spanish Rice

Spinach Parmesan Risotto

3⅔ cups fat-free reduced-sodium chicken broth
½ teaspoon white pepper
    Nonstick cooking spray
1 cup uncooked arborio rice
1½ cups chopped fresh spinach
½ cup frozen green peas
1 tablespoon minced fresh dill *or*
        1 teaspoon dried dill weed
½ cup grated Parmesan cheese
1 teaspoon grated lemon peel

1. Combine chicken broth and pepper in medium saucepan; cover. Bring to a simmer over medium-low heat; maintain simmer by adjusting heat.

2. Spray large saucepan with cooking spray; heat over medium-low heat. Add rice; cook and stir 1 minute. Stir in ⅔ cup hot chicken broth; cook, stirring constantly until chicken broth is absorbed.

3. Stir remaining hot chicken broth into rice mixture, ½ cup at a time, stirring constantly until all chicken broth is absorbed before adding next ½ cup. When adding last ½ cup chicken broth, stir in spinach, peas and dill. Cook, stirring gently until all chicken broth is absorbed and rice is just tender but still firm to the bite. (Total cooking time for chicken broth absorption is 35 to 40 minutes.)

4. Remove saucepan from heat; stir in cheese and lemon peel.   *Makes 6 servings*

Nutritional Information per Serving: *Calories: 179, Total Fat: 3 g, Cholesterol: 7 mg, Sodium: 198 mg*

Garden-Style Risotto

1 can (14½ ounces) low-sodium chicken broth
1¾ cups water
2 cloves garlic, finely chopped
1 teaspoon dried basil leaves
½ teaspoon dried thyme leaves
1 cup uncooked arborio rice
    Vegetable cooking spray
2 cups packed DOLE® Fresh Spinach, torn
1 cup DOLE® Shredded Carrots
3 tablespoons grated Parmesan cheese

• **Combine** chicken broth, water, garlic, basil and thyme in large saucepan. Bring to boil.

• **Place** rice in large nonstick saucepan sprayed with vegetable cooking spray. Cook and stir over medium heat 2 minutes or until rice is browned.

• **Pour** 1 cup boiling broth mixture into rice; cook, stirring constantly, until broth is almost absorbed (there should be some broth left).

• **Add** enough remaining broth mixture to barely cover rice; continue cooking, stirring constantly, until broth is almost absorbed. Repeat adding broth and cooking, stirring constantly, until broth is almost absorbed, about 15 minutes, adding spinach and carrots with the last addition of broth.

• **Cook** 3 to 5 more minutes or until liquid is almost absorbed and rice and vegetables are tender, stirring constantly. (*Do not overcook. Risotto will be saucy and have a creamy texture.*) Stir in Parmesan cheese. Serve warm. Garnish, if desired.

Makes 6 servings

Prep Time: 5 minutes

Cook Time: 25 minutes

Nutritional Information per Serving: *Calories: 170, Total Fat: 2 g, Cholesterol: 4 mg, Sodium: 155 mg*

Spinach Parmesan Risotto

Potatoes au Gratin

1 pound baking potatoes
4 teaspoons reduced-calorie margarine
4 teaspoons all-purpose flour
1¼ cups skim milk
¼ teaspoon ground nutmeg
¼ teaspoon paprika
Pinch white pepper
½ cup thinly sliced red onion, divided
⅓ cup whole wheat bread crumbs
1 tablespoon finely chopped red onion
1 tablespoon grated Parmesan cheese

1. Spray 4- or 6-cup casserole with nonstick cooking spray; set aside.

2. Place potatoes in large saucepan; add water to cover. Bring to a boil over high heat. Boil 12 minutes or until potatoes are tender. Drain; let potatoes stand 10 minutes or until cool enough to handle.

3. Melt margarine in small saucepan over medium heat. Add flour. Cook and stir 3 minutes or until small clumps form. Gradually whisk in milk. Cook 8 minutes or until sauce thickens, stirring constantly. Remove saucepan from heat. Stir in nutmeg, paprika and pepper.

4. Preheat oven to 350°F. Cut potatoes into thin slices. Arrange half of potato slices in prepared casserole. Sprinkle with half of onion slices. Repeat layers. Spoon sauce over potato mixture. Combine bread crumbs, finely chopped red onion and cheese in small bowl. Sprinkle mixture evenly over sauce.

5. Bake 20 minutes. Let stand 5 minutes before serving. *Makes 4 servings*

Nutritional Information per Serving: *Calories: 178, Total Fat: 3 g, Cholesterol: 2 mg, Sodium: 144 mg*

Potato-Swiss Galette

2 tablespoons butter substitute
1 pound yellow onions, sliced ¼ inch thick (2 cups)
1 teaspoon minced garlic
2 pounds unpeeled small red-skinned potatoes, sliced ¼ inch thick (4 cups)
Nonstick cooking spray
½ teaspoon salt
¼ teaspoon freshly ground black pepper
1 cup (4 ounces) shredded ALPINE LACE® Reduced Fat Swiss Cheese
¼ cup minced fresh parsley
½ teaspoon snipped fresh rosemary leaves *or* ¼ teaspoon dried rosemary

1. In large nonstick skillet, melt butter over medium-high heat. Add onions and garlic; sauté for 5 minutes or until softened. Spray both sides of potatoes with cooking spray; sprinkle with salt and pepper. Add potatoes to skillet with onion mixture. Sauté for 5 minutes or until golden brown on both sides. Cover; cook, stirring occasionally, for 10 minutes or until potatoes are tender.

2. In small bowl, toss the cheese with parsley and rosemary. Sprinkle over potatoes and toss gently just until cheese has melted.

Makes 6 servings

Nutritional Information per Serving: *Calories: 243, Total Fat: 8 g, Cholesterol: 13 mg*

Potatoes au Gratin

Broccoli and Cheese Topped Potatoes

4 large baking potatoes (6 to 8 ounces each)
2 cups broccoli florets
1 cup skim milk
½ cup nonfat cottage cheese
1 teaspoon dry mustard
½ teaspoon red pepper flakes
1 cup (4 ounces) shredded reduced-fat sharp Cheddar cheese, divided
1 cup (4 ounces) shredded part-skim mozzarella cheese
2 tablespoons all-purpose flour

1. Pierce potatoes several times with fork. Place in microwave oven on paper towel. Microwave at HIGH 15 minutes or just until softened. Wrap in paper towels; let stand 5 minutes.

2. Bring water to a boil in medium saucepan over medium heat. Add broccoli. Cook 5 minutes or until broccoli is crisp-tender. Drain and discard water. Add milk, cottage cheese, mustard and red pepper flakes to broccoli in saucepan. Bring to a boil. Reduce heat to medium-low; remove from heat.

3. Combine ¾ cup Cheddar cheese, mozzarella cheese and flour in medium bowl. Toss to coat cheese with flour; add to broccoli mixture. Cook and stir over medium-low heat until cheese is melted and mixture is thickened.

4. Cut potatoes open. Divide broccoli mixture evenly among potatoes. Sprinkle with remaining ¼ cup Cheddar cheese.

Makes 4 servings

Nutritional Information per Serving: *Calories: 381, Total Fat: 9 g, Cholesterol: 33 mg, Sodium: 647 mg*

Spirited Sweet Potato Casserole

2½ pounds sweet potatoes
2 tablespoons reduced-calorie margarine
⅓ cup 1% low-fat or skim milk
¼ cup packed brown sugar
2 tablespoons bourbon or apple juice
1 teaspoon ground cinnamon
1 teaspoon vanilla
2 egg whites
½ teaspoon salt
⅓ cup chopped pecans

1. Preheat oven to 375°F. Bake potatoes 50 to 60 minutes or until very tender. Cool 10 minutes; leave oven on. Scoop pulp from warm potatoes into large bowl; discard potato skins. Add margarine to bowl; mash with potato masher until potatoes are fairly smooth and margarine has melted. Stir in milk, brown sugar, bourbon, cinnamon and vanilla; mix well.

2. Beat egg whites with electric mixer at high speed until soft peaks form. Add salt; beat until stiff peaks form. Fold egg whites into sweet potato mixture.

3. Spray 1½-quart soufflé dish with nonstick cooking spray. Spoon sweet potato mixture into dish; top with pecans.

4. Bake 30 to 35 minutes or until casserole is puffed and pecans are toasted. Serve immediately. *Makes 8 servings*

Nutritional Information per Serving: *Calories: 203, Total Fat: 5 g, Cholesterol: trace, Sodium: 202 mg*

Broccoli and Cheese Topped Potatoes

Roast Cajun Potatoes

1 pound russet potatoes
2 tablespoons finely chopped parsley
2 teaspoons canola oil
½ teaspoon garlic powder
½ teaspoon onion powder
½ teaspoon ground red pepper
½ teaspoon dried thyme leaves
¼ teaspoon black pepper

1. Preheat oven to 400°F. Peel potatoes; cut each potato lengthwise into 8 wedges. Place on ungreased jelly-roll pan.

2. Toss potatoes with parsley, oil, garlic powder, onion powder, ground red pepper, thyme and black pepper until evenly coated.

3. Bake 50 minutes, turning wedges halfway through cooking time. Serve immediately.

Makes 4 servings

Nutritional Information per Serving: *Calories: 120, Total Fat: 2 g, Cholesterol: 0 mg, Sodium: 7 mg*

Country-Style Mashed Potatoes

4 pounds Yukon gold or Idaho potatoes, unpeeled and cut into 1-inch pieces
6 large cloves garlic, peeled
½ cup nonfat sour cream
½ cup skim milk, warmed
2 tablespoons margarine
2 tablespoons finely chopped fresh rosemary *or* 1 teaspoon dried rosemary
2 tablespoons finely chopped fresh thyme *or* ½ teaspoon dried thyme leaves
2 tablespoons finely chopped parsley

1. Place potatoes and garlic in medium saucepan; cover with water. Bring to a boil. Reduce heat and simmer, covered, about 15 minutes or until potatoes are fork-tender. Drain well.

2. Place potatoes and garlic in large bowl. Beat with electric mixer just until mashed. Beat in sour cream, milk and margarine until almost smooth. Mix in rosemary, thyme and parsley. *Makes 8 servings*

Nutritional Information per Serving: *Calories: 191, Total Fat: 2 g, Cholesterol: 0 mg, Sodium: 38 mg*

Sweet Potato Puffs

2 pounds sweet potatoes
⅓ cup orange juice
1 egg, beaten
1 tablespoon grated orange peel
½ teaspoon ground nutmeg
¼ cup chopped pecans

1. Peel and cut sweet potatoes into 1-inch pieces. Place potatoes in medium saucepan. Add enough water to cover; bring to a boil over medium-high heat. Cook 10 to 15 minutes or until tender. Drain potatoes and place in large bowl; mash until smooth. Add orange juice, egg, orange peel and nutmeg; mix well.

2. Preheat oven to 375°F. Spray baking sheet with nonstick cooking spray. Spoon potato mixture into 10 mounds on prepared baking sheet. Sprinkle pecans on tops of mounds.

3. Bake 30 minutes or until centers are hot.

Makes 10 servings

Nutritional Information per Serving: *Calories: 105, Total Fat: 3 g, Cholesterol: 21 mg, Sodium: 15 mg*

Roast Cajun Potatoes

Potato-Zucchini Pancakes with Warm Corn Salsa

Warm Corn Salsa (recipe follows)
2 cups frozen hash brown potatoes, thawed
1½ cups shredded zucchini, drained
½ cup cholesterol-free egg substitute
¼ cup all-purpose flour
2 tablespoons chopped onion
2 tablespoons chopped green bell pepper
¼ teaspoon salt
⅛ teaspoon black pepper
Nonstick cooking spray

1. Prepare Warm Corn Salsa. Keep warm.

2. Combine potatoes, zucchini, egg substitute, flour, onion, bell pepper, salt and black pepper in medium bowl until well blended.

3. Spray large nonstick skillet with cooking spray; heat over medium-high heat until hot. Drop potato mixture by ¼ cupfuls into skillet. Cook pancakes, four or six at a time, about 3 minutes on each side or until golden brown. Place 2 pancakes onto serving plate; top with ½ cup Warm Corn Salsa. *Makes 6 servings*

Warm Corn Salsa

Nonstick cooking spray
2 tablespoons chopped onion
2 tablespoons finely chopped green bell pepper
1 package (9 ounces) frozen corn, thawed
1 cup chunky salsa
2 teaspoons chopped cilantro

1. Spray small nonstick skillet with cooking spray; heat over medium heat until hot. Add onion and bell pepper. Cook and stir

3 minutes or until crisp-tender. Add corn, salsa and cilantro. Reduce heat to medium-low. Cook 5 minutes or until heated through. *Makes 3 cups*

Nutritional Information per Serving: *Calories: 110, Total Fat: trace, Cholesterol: 0 mg, Sodium: 437 mg*

Apple-Potato Pancakes

1¼ cups unpeeled, finely chopped apples
1 cup peeled, grated potatoes
½ cup MOTT'S® Natural Apple Sauce
½ cup all-purpose flour
2 egg whites
1 teaspoon salt
Additional MOTT'S® Natural Apple Sauce or apple slices (optional)

1. Preheat oven to 475°F. Spray cookie sheet with nonstick cooking spray.

2. In medium bowl, combine apples, potatoes, ½ cup apple sauce, flour, egg whites and salt.

3. Spray large nonstick skillet with nonstick cooking spray; heat over medium heat until hot. Drop rounded tablespoonfuls of batter 2 inches apart into skillet. Cook 2 to 3 minutes on each side or until lightly browned. Place pancakes on prepared cookie sheet.

4. Bake 10 to 15 minutes or until crisp. Serve with additional apple sauce or apple slices, if desired. Refrigerate leftovers. *Makes 12 servings*

Nutritional Information per Serving (1 pancake): *Calories: 60, Total Fat: 0 g, Cholesterol: 0 mg, Sodium: 190 mg*

Potato-Zucchini Pancakes with Warm Corn Salsa

Mushroom Ragoût with Polenta

1 package (about ½ ounce) dried porcini mushrooms
½ cup boiling water
1 can (about 14 ounces) vegetable broth
½ cup yellow cornmeal
1 tablespoon olive oil
⅓ cup sliced shallots or chopped sweet onion
1 package (4 ounces) sliced mixed fresh exotic mushrooms or sliced cremini mushrooms
4 cloves garlic, minced
1 can (14½ ounces) Italian-style diced tomatoes, undrained
¼ teaspoon red pepper flakes
¼ cup chopped fresh basil or parsley
½ cup grated fat-free Parmesan cheese

1. Soak porcini mushrooms in boiling water 10 minutes.

2. Meanwhile, whisk together vegetable broth and cornmeal in large microwavable bowl. Cover with waxed paper; microwave at HIGH 5 minutes. Whisk well; cook at HIGH 3 to 4 minutes or until polenta is very thick. Whisk again; cover. Set aside.

3. Heat oil in large nonstick skillet over medium-high heat. Add shallots; cook and stir 3 minutes. Add fresh mushrooms and garlic; cook and stir 3 to 4 minutes. Add tomatoes and red pepper flakes.

4. Drain porcini mushrooms; add liquid to skillet. If mushrooms are large, cut into ½-inch pieces; add to skillet. Bring to a boil over high heat. Reduce heat to medium; simmer, uncovered, 5 minutes or until slightly thickened. Stir in basil.

5. Spoon polenta onto 4 plates; top with mushroom mixture. Sprinkle with cheese.

Makes 4 servings

Nutritional Information per Serving: *Calories: 184, Total Fat: 5 g, Cholesterol: 0 mg, Sodium: 572 mg*

Italian Bread Sticks

1 cup (4 ounces) shredded ALPINE LACE® Fat Free Pasteurized Process Skim Milk Cheese Product—For Parmesan Lovers
1 teaspoon fresh rosemary leaves *or* ½ teaspoon dried rosemary
¼ cup sesame seeds
1 pound frozen bread dough, thawed
¼ cup egg substitute *or* 1 large egg
1 tablespoon water
2 tablespoons kosher salt (optional)

1. Preheat the oven to 425°F. Spray 2 baking sheets with nonstick cooking spray.

2. In a food processor or blender, process the cheese and rosemary leaves for 15 seconds or just until finely chopped. Transfer to a small bowl and stir in the sesame seeds. Spread out on a plate.

3. On a lightly floured surface, cut the dough into 12 equal pieces. Roll each piece into a rope, about 8 inches long and ½ inch thick. Place on a baking sheet about 3 inches apart.

4. In a small cup, whisk the egg substitute (or the whole egg) with the water. Brush the tops and sides of bread sticks with this mixture. Twist each stick 3 times. Generously sprinkle with the cheese mixture, plus some of the salt, if you wish. Bake for 12 minutes or until golden brown.

Makes 12 bread sticks

Nutritional Information per Serving (8-inch bread stick): *Calories: 131, Total Fat: 3 g, Cholesterol: 6 mg*

Mushroom Ragoût with Polenta

Apple Stuffing

1 cup finely chopped onion
½ cup finely chopped celery
½ cup unpeeled, finely chopped apple
1½ cups MOTT'S® Natural Apple Sauce
1 (8-ounce) package stuffing mix
    (original or cornbread)
1 cup defatted* chicken broth
1½ teaspoons dried thyme leaves
1 teaspoon ground sage
½ teaspoon salt
½ teaspoon black pepper

To defat chicken broth, chill canned broth thoroughly. Use can opener to punch two holes in top of can. Quickly pour out the contents of the can into bowl. Most of the fat will remain in the can and the remaining broth is "defatted."

1. Spray medium nonstick skillet with nonstick cooking spray. Heat over medium heat until hot. Add onion and celery; cook and stir about 5 minutes or until transparent. Add apple; cook and stir about 3 minutes or until golden. Transfer to large bowl. Stir in remaining ingredients.

2. Loosely stuff chicken or turkey just before roasting or place stuffing in greased 8-inch square baking pan. Cover; bake in preheated 350°F oven 20 to 25 minutes or until hot. Refrigerate leftovers.   *Makes 8 servings*

Note: Cooked stuffing can also be used to fill centers of cooked acorn squash.

Nutritional Information per Serving: *Calories: 150, Total Fat: 2 g, Cholesterol: 0 mg, Sodium: 620 mg*

Tex-Mex Corn Bread

1½ cups all-purpose flour
¾ cup yellow cornmeal
2 tablespoons sugar
1 tablespoon baking powder
1 teaspoon baking soda
¾ teaspoon salt
1⅓ cups low fat buttermilk
3 tablespoons unsalted butter, melted
½ cup finely chopped red bell pepper
¼ cup minced green onions
1 cup fresh corn kernels or frozen
    corn, thawed
¾ cup (3 ounces) shredded ALPINE
    LACE® American Flavor Pasteurized
    Process Cheese Product with
    Jalapeño Peppers

1. Preheat the oven to 425°F. Spray a deep ovenproof 10-inch skillet (preferably cast iron) with nonstick cooking spray and place in the oven on the middle rack to heat.

2. In a large bowl, stir together the flour, cornmeal, sugar, baking powder, baking soda and salt. In a medium-size bowl, whisk together the buttermilk and butter. Stir in the bell pepper and green onions.

3. Using a wooden spoon, make a hole in the center of the flour mixture, then pour in the buttermilk mixture all at once. Stir just until the flour disappears. (Avoid overmixing!) Fold in the corn and cheese. Spoon the batter into the hot skillet.

4. Bake the bread for 25 minutes or until golden brown and a toothpick inserted in the center comes out with moist crumbs. Serve immediately, straight from the skillet.
          Makes 12 servings

Nutritional Information per Serving: *Calories: 164, Total Fat: 5 g, Cholesterol: 14 mg, Sodium: 382 mg*

Roasted Pepper Focaccia

1 medium green bell pepper
1 medium yellow bell pepper
2 tablespoons yellow cornmeal
2 tablespoons olive oil, divided
1 cup thin yellow onion rings
1 tablespoon minced garlic
1 pound frozen bread dough, thawed
1 teaspoon freshly ground black
  pepper
2 teaspoons finely chopped fresh
  rosemary leaves
1 cup (4 ounces) shredded ALPINE
  LACE® Reduced Fat Mozzarella
  Cheese

1. Preheat the broiler. Place the bell peppers on a baking sheet. Broil 3 inches from heat for 7 minutes or until blackened, turning frequently. Transfer to a paper bag, close tightly and let stand 15 minutes or until peppers are soft. Scrape off outside skins; seed and cut the peppers into thin strips. (You will have about 1½ cups.)

2. Preheat the oven to 425°F and spray a 15-inch pizza pan with nonstick cooking spray and sprinkle with the cornmeal. Spray a medium-size skillet with the cooking spray.

3. In the skillet, heat 1 tablespoon of the oil over medium-high heat. Add the onion and garlic and sauté for 5 minutes; keep warm.

4. Gently press the bread dough onto the bottom and up the sides of the pan. Brush the dough with the remaining tablespoon of oil; sprinkle with the black pepper. Using your fingertips, dimple the dough all over, pressing in the pepper at the same time. Sprinkle with the rosemary.

5. Top the dough with the onion mixture and the bell peppers. Sprinkle with the mozzarella. Bake, uncovered, for 12 to 15 minutes or until the cheese melts and the focaccia is golden brown.

Makes 8 servings

Nutritional Information per Serving: *Calories: 238, Total Fat: 7 g, Cholesterol: 5 mg*

Apple Sauce Irish Soda Bread

3 cups all-purpose flour
1 tablespoon sugar
2 teaspoons baking soda
1 teaspoon salt
1 cup low-fat buttermilk
½ cup MOTT'S® Natural Apple Sauce
2 tablespoons margarine, melted
½ cup raisins
2 tablespoons skim milk

1. Preheat oven to 375°F. Spray 8-inch round baking pan with nonstick cooking spray.

2. In large bowl, combine flour, sugar, baking soda and salt.

3. In small bowl, combine buttermilk, apple sauce and margarine.

4. Add apple sauce mixture to flour mixture; stir until mixture forms a ball.

5. Turn out dough onto well-floured surface; knead raisins into dough. Pat into 7-inch round.

6. Place dough in prepared pan. Cut cross in top of dough, ¼ inch deep, with tip of sharp knife. Brush top of dough with milk.

7. Bake 35 minutes or until toothpick inserted in center comes out clean. Cool in pan 10 minutes. Invert onto wire rack; turn right side up. Cool completely. Cut into 16 wedges.

Makes 16 servings

Nutritional Information per Serving: *Calories: 130, Total Fat: 2 g, Cholesterol: 0 mg, Sodium: 270 mg*

Stacked Burrito Pie

½ cup GUILTLESS GOURMET® Mild
  Black Bean Dip
2 teaspoons water
5 low fat flour tortillas (6 inches each)
½ cup nonfat sour cream or plain
  yogurt
½ cup GUILTLESS GOURMET® Roasted
  Red Pepper Salsa
1¼ cups (5 ounces) shredded low fat
  Monterey Jack cheese
4 cups shredded iceberg or romaine
  lettuce
½ cup GUILTLESS GOURMET® Salsa
  (medium)
  Lime slices and chili pepper
  (optional)

Preheat oven to 350°F. Combine bean dip
and 2 teaspoons water in small bowl; mix
well. Line 7½-inch springform pan with 1
tortilla. Spread 2 tablespoons bean dip
mixture over tortilla, then spread with 2
tablespoons sour cream and 2 tablespoons
red pepper salsa. Sprinkle with ¼ cup
cheese. Repeat layers 3 more times. Place
remaining tortilla on top and sprinkle with
remaining ¼ cup cheese.

Bake 40 minutes or until heated through.
(Place sheet of foil under springform pan to
catch any juices that may seep through the
bottom.) Cool slightly before unmolding.
To serve, cut into 4 quarters. Place 1 cup
lettuce on 4 serving plates. Top each serving
with 1 quarter burrito pie and 2 tablespoons
salsa. Garnish with lime slices and pepper, if
desired. *Makes 4 servings*

Nutritional Information per Serving (1 quarter):
*Calories: 302, Total Fat: 7 g, Cholesterol: 12 mg,
Sodium: 650 mg*

Iowa Corn Pudding

½ cup egg substitute *or* 2 large eggs
2 large egg whites
3 tablespoons all-purpose flour
1 tablespoon sugar
½ teaspoon freshly ground black
  pepper
1 can (16½ ounces) cream-style corn
2 cups fresh corn kernels or frozen
  corn, thawed and drained
1 cup (4 ounces) shredded ALPINE
  LACE® American Flavor Pasteurized
  Process Cheese Product
½ cup finely chopped red bell pepper
⅓ cup 2% low fat milk
1 tablespoon unsalted butter
  substitute
¼ teaspoon paprika
  Sprigs of fresh parsley

1. Preheat the oven to 350°F. Spray an
8-inch round baking dish with nonstick
cooking spray. (A deep-dish pie plate works
well.) Place in the oven to heat.

2. Meanwhile, in a large bowl, using an
electric mixer set on high, beat the egg
substitute (or the whole eggs) and egg
whites with the flour, sugar and black
pepper until smooth. Stir in the creamed
corn, corn kernels, cheese, bell pepper and
milk. Pour into the hot baking dish.

3. Dot with the butter and sprinkle with the
paprika. Bake, uncovered, for 55 minutes or
until set. Let stand for 15 minutes before
serving. Garnish with the parsley.
Makes 6 servings

Nutritional Information per Serving: *Calories: 226,
Total Fat: 6 g, Cholesterol: 17 mg, Sodium: 556 mg*

Stacked Burrito Pie

Cookies & Brownies

Hershey's 50% Reduced Fat Oatmeal Chip Cookies

¾ cup (1½ sticks) 56-60% vegetable oil spread, softened
¾ cup granulated sugar
¾ cup packed light brown sugar
2 eggs
1 teaspoon vanilla extract
1¼ cups all-purpose flour
1 teaspoon baking soda
½ to ¾ teaspoon ground cinnamon
½ teaspoon salt
2¾ cups quick-cooking rolled oats
2 cups (12-ounce package) HERSHEY'S Reduced Fat Semi-Sweet Baking Chips
1 cup raisins

1. Heat oven to 375°F.

2. In large bowl, beat vegetable oil spread, granulated sugar and brown sugar with electric mixer until well mixed. Add eggs and vanilla; beat until creamy. Stir together flour, baking soda, cinnamon and salt; gradually add to sugar mixture, mixing well. Stir in oats, chips and raisins. Drop by teaspoons onto *ungreased* cookie sheet.

3. Bake 8 to 10 minutes or until golden brown. Cool slightly; remove from cookie sheet to wire rack. Cool completely.

Makes 4 dozen cookies

Nutritional Information per Serving (1 cookie):
Calories: 110, Total Fat: 4 g, Cholesterol: 10 mg, Sodium: 70 mg

Hershey's 50% Reduced Fat Oatmeal Chip Cookies

Mocha Crinkles

1¾ cups all-purpose flour
¾ cup unsweetened cocoa powder
2 teaspoons instant espresso or coffee granules
1 teaspoon baking soda
¼ teaspoon salt
⅛ teaspoon ground black pepper
1⅓ cups packed light brown sugar
½ cup vegetable oil
¼ cup low-fat sour cream
1 egg
1 teaspoon vanilla
½ cup powdered sugar

1. Mix flour, cocoa, espresso, baking soda, salt and pepper in medium bowl; set aside.

2. Beat brown sugar and oil in another medium bowl with electric mixer at medium speed until well blended. Beat in sour cream, egg and vanilla.

3. Beat in flour mixture until soft dough forms. Form dough into disc; cover. Refrigerate dough until firm, 3 to 4 hours.

4. Preheat oven to 350°F. Place powdered sugar in shallow bowl. Cut dough into 1-inch pieces; roll into balls. Coat with powdered sugar. Place on ungreased cookie sheets.

5. Bake 10 to 12 minutes or until tops of cookies are firm to the touch. Do not overbake. Cool cookies completely on wire racks.
*Makes 6 dozen cookies
(1 cookie per serving)*

Nutritional Information per Serving: *Calories: 44, Total Fat: 1 g, Cholesterol: 3 mg, Sodium: 28 mg*

Cream Cheese and Jelly Cookies

1 package (8 ounces) reduced-fat cream cheese, softened
¾ cup margarine, softened
2½ teaspoons EQUAL® Measure™ *or*
    8 packets EQUAL® sweetener *or*
    ⅓ cup EQUAL® Spoonful™
2 cups all-purpose flour
¼ teaspoon salt
¼ cup black cherry or seedless raspberry spreadable fruit

• Beat cream cheese, margarine and Equal® in medium bowl until fluffy; mix in flour and salt to form a soft dough. Cover and refrigerate until dough is firm, about 3 hours.

• Roll dough on lightly floured surface into circle ⅛ inch thick; cut into rounds with 3-inch cutter. Place rounded ¼ teaspoon spreadable fruit in center of each round; fold rounds into halves and crimp edges firmly with tines of fork. Pierce tops of cookies with tip of sharp knife. Bake cookies on greased cookie sheets in preheated 350°F oven until lightly browned, about 10 minutes. Cool on wire racks.
Makes about 3 dozen

Nutritional Information per Serving (1 cookie):
Calories: 80, Total Fat: 5 g, Cholesterol: 4 mg, Sodium: 78 mg

Mocha Crinkles

Low Fat Molasses Jumbles

½ cup Prune Purée (page 83) or
    prepared prune butter
½ cup sugar
½ cup molasses
1 egg
2 cups all-purpose flour
2 teaspoons ground cinnamon
1 teaspoon ground ginger
½ teaspoon baking soda
½ teaspoon salt
    Additional sugar

Preheat oven to 350°F. Coat baking sheets with vegetable cooking spray. In large bowl, mix prune purée, sugar and molasses until well blended. Add egg; mix well. Combine remaining ingredients except sugar; stir into prune purée mixture just until blended. Roll heaping tablespoonfuls of dough in additional sugar. Place on baking sheets, spacing 2 inches apart. With fork, flatten dough in crisscross fashion until ½ inch thick. Bake in center of oven about 12 to 13 minutes or until set and bottoms are lightly browned. Remove from baking sheets to wire racks to cool completely.

Makes 30 (2½-inch) cookies

Tip: For easy cleanup, measure molasses in a cup that has been lightly sprayed with vegetable cooking spray.

Nutritional Information per Serving (1 cookie):
Calories: 68, Total Fat: 1 g, Cholesterol: 7 mg, Sodium: 57 mg

Favorite recipe from **California Prune Board**

Soft Apple Cider Cookies

1 cup firmly packed light brown sugar
½ cup FLEISCHMANN'S® 70% Corn Oil
    Spread, softened
½ cup apple cider
½ cup EGG BEATERS® Healthy Real Egg
    Substitute
2¼ cups all-purpose flour
1½ teaspoons ground cinnamon
1 teaspoon baking soda
¼ teaspoon salt
2 medium apples, peeled and diced
    (about 1½ cups)
¾ cup almonds, chopped
    Cider Glaze (recipe follows)

In large bowl, with electric mixer at medium speed, beat sugar and corn oil spread until creamy. Add cider and Egg Beaters®; beat until smooth. With electric mixer at low speed, gradually blend in flour, cinnamon, baking soda and salt. Stir in apples and almonds.

Drop dough by tablespoonfuls, 2 inches apart, onto greased baking sheets. Bake at 375°F for 10 to 12 minutes or until golden brown. Remove from sheets; cool on wire racks. Drizzle with Cider Glaze.

Makes 4 dozen cookies

Prep Time: 30 minutes

Cook Time: 12 minutes

Cider Glaze: In small bowl, combine 1 cup powdered sugar and 2 tablespoons apple cider until smooth.

Nutritional Information per Serving: *Calories: 80, Total Fat: 3 g, Cholesterol: 0 mg, Sodium: 50 mg*

Low Fat Molasses Jumbles

Chocolate Chip Cookies

1½ cups packed light brown sugar
8 tablespoons margarine, softened
2 egg whites
1 teaspoon vanilla
2½ cups all-purpose flour
1½ teaspoons baking soda
½ teaspoon salt
⅓ cup skim milk
¾ cup (4 ounces) semisweet chocolate chips
½ cup chopped pecans or walnuts (optional)

1. Preheat oven to 350°F. Spray cookie sheets with nonstick cooking spray.

2. Beat brown sugar and margarine in large bowl until fluffy. Beat in egg whites and vanilla.

3. Combine flour, baking soda and salt in medium bowl. Add flour mixture to margarine mixture alternately with milk, ending with flour mixture. Stir in chocolate chips and pecans, if desired.

4. Drop dough by slightly rounded tablespoonfuls onto prepared cookie sheets. Bake about 10 minutes or until lightly browned. Cool on wire racks.

Makes about 6 dozen cookies

Nutritional Information per Serving (1 cookie):
Calories: 56, Total Fat: 2 g, Cholesterol: 0 mg, Sodium: 61 mg

Pumpkin Harvest Bars

1¾ cups all-purpose flour
2 teaspoons baking powder
1 teaspoon grated orange peel
1 teaspoon ground cinnamon
½ teaspoon salt
½ teaspoon ground nutmeg
¼ teaspoon ground ginger
¼ teaspoon ground cloves
¾ cup sugar
½ cup MOTT'S® Natural Apple Sauce
½ cup solid-pack pumpkin
1 whole egg
1 egg white
2 tablespoons vegetable oil
½ cup raisins

1. Preheat oven to 350°F. Spray 13×9-inch baking pan with nonstick cooking spray.

2. In small bowl, combine flour, baking powder, orange peel, cinnamon, salt, nutmeg, ginger and cloves.

3. In large bowl, combine sugar, apple sauce, pumpkin, whole egg, egg white and oil.

4. Add flour mixture to apple sauce mixture; stir until well blended. Stir in raisins. Spread batter into prepared pan.

5. Bake 25 to 30 minutes or until toothpick inserted in center comes out clean. Cool on wire rack 15 minutes; cut into 16 bars.

Makes 16 servings

Nutritional Information per Serving: *Calories: 130, Total Fat: 2 g, Cholesterol: 15 mg, Sodium: 110 mg*

Chocolate Chip Cookies

Fabulous Fruit Bars

1½ cups all-purpose flour, divided
1½ cups sugar, divided
½ cup MOTT'S® Apple Sauce, divided
½ teaspoon baking powder
2 tablespoons margarine
½ cup peeled, chopped apple
½ cup chopped dried apricots
½ cup chopped cranberries
1 whole egg
1 egg white
1 teaspoon lemon juice
½ teaspoon vanilla extract
1 teaspoon ground cinnamon

1. Preheat oven to 350°F. Spray 13×9-inch baking pan with nonstick cooking spray.

2. In medium bowl, combine 1¼ cups flour, ½ cup sugar, ⅓ cup apple sauce and baking powder. Cut in margarine with pastry blender or fork until mixture resembles coarse crumbs.

3. In large bowl, combine apple, apricots, cranberries, remaining apple sauce, whole egg, egg white, lemon juice and vanilla.

4. In small bowl, combine remaining 1 cup sugar, ¼ cup flour and cinnamon. Add to fruit mixture, stirring just until mixed.

5. Press half of crumb mixture evenly onto bottom of prepared pan. Top with fruit mixture. Sprinkle with remaining crumb mixture.

6. Bake 40 minutes or until lightly browned. Broil, 4 inches from heat, 1 to 2 minutes or until golden brown. Cool on wire rack 15 minutes; cut into 16 bars.

Makes 16 servings

Nutritional Information per Serving: *Calories: 150, Total Fat: 2 g, Cholesterol: 15 mg, Sodium: 35 mg*

Chewy Coconut Bars

2 eggs
7¼ teaspoons EQUAL® Measure™ *or*
24 packets EQUAL® sweetener *or*
1 cup EQUAL® Spoonful™
¼ teaspoon maple flavoring
½ cup margarine, melted
1 teaspoon vanilla
½ cup all-purpose flour
1 teaspoon baking powder
¼ teaspoon salt
1 cup unsweetened coconut,* finely chopped
½ cup chopped walnuts (optional)
½ cup raisins

Unsweetened coconut can be purchased in health food stores. Or, substitute sweetened coconut and decrease amount of EQUAL® to 5¼ teaspoons EQUAL® Measure™ or 18 packets EQUAL® sweetener or ¾ cup EQUAL® Spoonful™.

• Beat eggs, Equal® and maple flavoring in medium bowl; mix in margarine and vanilla. Combine flour, baking powder and salt in small bowl; stir into egg mixture. Mix in coconut, walnuts and raisins. Spread batter evenly in greased 8-inch square baking pan.

• Bake in preheated 350°F oven until browned and toothpick inserted in center comes out clean, about 20 minutes. Cool in pan on wire rack; cut into squares.

Makes 16 bars

Nutritional Information per Serving (1 bar):
Calories: 126, Total Fat: 9 g, Cholesterol: 27 mg, Sodium: 141 mg

Fabulous Fruit Bars

Raspberry-Almond Bars

2 cups all-purpose flour
3½ teaspoons EQUAL® Measure™ *or*
    12 packets EQUAL® sweetener *or*
    ½ cup EQUAL® Spoonful™
⅛ teaspoon salt
8 tablespoons cold margarine, cut into
    pieces
1 egg
1 tablespoon skim milk or water
2 teaspoons grated lemon peel
⅔ cup seedless raspberry spreadable
    fruit
1 teaspoon cornstarch
½ cup chopped toasted almonds,
    walnuts or pecans

• Combine flour, Equal® and salt in medium bowl; cut in margarine with pastry blender until mixture resembles coarse crumbs. Mix in egg, milk and lemon peel. (Mixture will be crumbly.)

• Press mixture evenly onto bottom of greased 11×7-inch baking dish. Bake in preheated 400°F oven until edges of crust are browned, about 15 minutes. Cool on wire rack.

• Mix spreadable fruit and cornstarch in small saucepan; heat to boiling. Boil until thickened, stirring constantly, 1 minute; cool slightly. Spread mixture evenly over cooled crust; sprinkle with almonds. Bake in preheated 400°F oven until spreadable fruit is thick and bubbly, about 15 minutes. Cool on wire rack; cut into squares.

Makes 2 dozen bars

Nutritional Information per Serving (1 bar):
Calories: 116, Total Fat: 6 g, Cholesterol: 9 mg, Sodium: 59 mg

Date Cake Squares

1¼ cups water
1 cup chopped dates
¾ cup chopped pitted prunes
½ cup dark raisins
8 tablespoons margarine, cut into
    pieces
2 eggs
1 teaspoon vanilla
1 cup all-purpose flour
5½ teaspoons EQUAL® Measure™ *or*
    18 packets EQUAL® sweetener *or*
    ¾ cup EQUAL® Spoonful™
1 teaspoon baking soda
½ teaspoon ground cinnamon
¼ teaspoon ground nutmeg
¼ teaspoon salt
¼ cup chopped walnuts

• Combine water, dates, prunes and raisins in medium saucepan; heat to boiling. Reduce heat and simmer, uncovered, until fruit is tender and water is absorbed, about 10 minutes. Remove from heat and add margarine, stirring until melted; cool to room temperature.

• Mix eggs and vanilla into fruit mixture; mix in combined flour, Equal®, baking soda, cinnamon, nutmeg and salt. Spread batter evenly in greased 11×7×2-inch baking dish; sprinkle with walnuts.

• Bake in preheated 350°F oven until cake springs back when touched lightly, 30 to 35 minutes. Cool on wire rack; cut into squares.

Makes 2 dozen squares

Nutritional Information per Serving (1 square):
Calories: 117, Total Fat: 5 g, Cholesterol: 18 mg, Sodium: 126 mg

Raspberry-Almond Bars

Brownies

½ cup boiling water
½ cup unsweetened cocoa powder
1¼ cups all-purpose flour
¾ cup granulated sugar
¾ cup packed light brown sugar
1 teaspoon baking powder
¼ teaspoon salt
4 egg whites, lightly beaten
⅓ cup vegetable oil
1½ teaspoons vanilla
½ cup chopped unsalted mixed nuts (optional)

1. Preheat oven to 350°F.

2. Spray 13×9-inch baking pan with nonstick cooking spray. Combine boiling water and cocoa in large bowl. Mix until completely dissolved. Add flour, granulated sugar, brown sugar, baking powder, salt, egg whites, oil and vanilla; mix well. Fold in chopped nuts.

3. Pour mixture into prepared pan. Bake 25 minutes or until brownies spring back when lightly touched. *Do not overbake.* Cool in pan on wire rack; cut into squares.

Makes 32 brownies

Nutritional Information per Serving: *Calories: 81, Total Fat: 2 g, Cholesterol: 0 mg, Sodium: 37 mg*

Granola Bites

2 cups cornflakes cereal
⅔ cup uncooked quick-cooking oats
½ cup chopped pitted dates or raisins
¼ cup 100% bran cereal
½ cup reduced-fat crunchy peanut butter
4 egg whites *or* ½ cup real liquid egg product
5 teaspoons EQUAL® Measure™ *or* 16 packets EQUAL® sweetener *or* ⅔ cup EQUAL® Spoonful™
2 teaspoons vanilla

• Combine cornflakes, oats, dates and bran cereal in large bowl. Mix peanut butter, egg whites, Equal® and vanilla in small bowl until smooth; pour over cereal mixture and stir until all ingredients are coated.

• Shape mixture into 1-inch mounds; place on lightly greased cookie sheets. Bake in preheated 350°F oven until cookies are set and browned, 8 to 10 minutes. Cool on wire racks.

Makes about 2 dozen

Nutritional Information per Serving (1 cookie): *Calories: 67, Total Fat: 3 g, Cholesterol: 0 mg, Sodium: 61 mg*

Brownies

Chocolate Espresso Brownies

4 squares (1 ounce each) unsweetened
   chocolate
1 cup sugar
¼ cup Prune Purée (page 83) or
   prepared prune butter
3 egg whites
1 to 2 tablespoons instant espresso
   coffee powder
1 teaspoon baking powder
1 teaspoon salt
1 teaspoon vanilla
½ cup all-purpose flour
   Powdered sugar (optional)

Preheat oven to 350°F. Coat 8-inch square
baking pan with vegetable cooking spray. In
small heavy saucepan, melt chocolate over
very low heat, stirring until melted and
smooth. Remove from heat; cool. In mixer
bowl, beat chocolate and remaining
ingredients except flour and powdered
sugar at medium speed until well blended;
mix in flour. Spread batter evenly in
prepared pan. Bake in center of oven about
30 minutes or until toothpick inserted into
center comes out clean. Cool completely in
pan on wire rack. Dust with powdered
sugar. Cut into 1⅓-inch squares.

Makes 36 brownies

Nutritional Information per Serving (1 brownie):
*Calories: 97, Total Fat: 3 g, Cholesterol: 0 mg,
Sodium: 142 mg*

Favorite recipe from **California Prune Board**

No-Guilt Chocolate Brownies

1 cup semisweet chocolate chips
¼ cup packed brown sugar
2 tablespoons granulated sugar
½ teaspoon baking powder
¼ teaspoon salt
½ cup cholesterol-free egg substitute
1 jar (2½ ounces) first-stage baby food
   prunes
1 teaspoon vanilla
1 cup uncooked rolled oats
⅓ cup nonfat dry milk solids
¼ cup wheat germ
2 teaspoons powdered sugar

1. Preheat oven to 350°F. Spray 8-inch
square baking pan with nonstick cooking
spray; set aside. Melt chips in top of double
boiler over simmering water.

2. Combine brown and granulated sugars,
baking powder and salt in large bowl with
electric mixer. Add egg substitute, prunes
and vanilla. Beat at medium speed until well
blended. Stir in oats, milk solids, wheat
germ and chocolate.

3. Pour batter into prepared pan. Bake 30
minutes or until toothpick inserted in center
comes out clean. Cool completely. Cut into
2-inch squares. Dust with powdered sugar
before serving. *Makes 16 servings*

Nutritional Information per Serving: *Calories: 124,
Total Fat: 5 g, Cholesterol: trace, Sodium: 65 mg*

Chocolate Espresso Brownies

Cakes & Pies

Rich Chocolate Cheesecake

1¼ cups graham cracker crumbs
4 tablespoons margarine, melted
1 teaspoon EQUAL® Measure™ *or*
 3 packets EQUAL® sweetener™ *or*
 2 tablespoons EQUAL® Spoonful™
2 packages (8 ounces each) reduced-
 fat cream cheese, softened
1 package (8 ounces) fat-free cream
 cheese, softened
5½ teaspoons EQUAL® Measure™ *or*
 18 packets EQUAL® sweetener *or*
 ¾ cup EQUAL® Spoonful™
2 eggs
2 egg whites
2 tablespoons cornstarch
1 cup reduced-fat sour cream
⅓ cup European or Dutch-process
 cocoa
1 teaspoon vanilla
 Fresh mint sprigs, raspberries, nonfat
 whipped topping and orange peel
 (optional)

• Mix graham cracker crumbs, margarine and 1 teaspoon Equal® Measure™ *or* 3 packets Equal® sweetener *or* 2 tablespoons Equal® Spoonful™ in bottom of 9-inch springform pan. Pat mixture evenly on bottom and ½ inch up side of pan.

• Beat cream cheese and 5½ teaspoons Equal® Measure™ *or* 18 packets Equal® sweetener *or* ¾ cup Equal® Spoonful™ in large bowl until fluffy; beat in eggs, egg whites and cornstarch. Mix in sour cream, cocoa and vanilla until well blended. Pour mixture into crust.

• Place cheesecake in roasting pan on oven rack; add 1 inch hot water to roasting pan. Bake cheesecake in preheated 300°F oven just until set in the center, 45 to 50 minutes. Remove cheesecake from roasting pan; return cheesecake to oven. Turn oven off and let cheesecake cool 3 hours in oven with door ajar. Refrigerate 8 hours or overnight. Remove side of pan; place cheesecake on serving plate. Garnish, if desired.

Makes 16 servings

Nutritional Information per Serving: *Calories: 189, Total Fat: 11 g, Cholesterol: 51 mg, Sodium: 280 mg*

Rich Chocolate Cheesecake

Chocolate Cheesecake

24 chocolate wafers, finely crushed
2 to 3 tablespoons water
1 cup nonfat cottage cheese
½ cup EGG BEATERS® Healthy Real Egg
    Substitute
12 ounces light cream cheese
    (Neufchâtel), softened
1 cup granulated sugar
½ cup unsweetened cocoa
¼ cup all-purpose flour
1 teaspoon vanilla extract
¾ cup powdered sugar
¾ cup nonfat sour cream
    Lavender flowers, for garnish

In small bowl, toss chocolate wafer crumbs with water, 1 tablespoon at a time, until crumbs are moistened. Press onto bottom of 8-inch springform pan; set aside.

In electric blender container or food processor, blend cottage cheese and Egg Beaters® until smooth, scraping down sides of container as necessary. In large bowl, with electric mixer at medium speed, beat cream cheese and granulated sugar until smooth. Add cottage cheese mixture, cocoa, flour and vanilla; beat until well blended and smooth. Pour batter into prepared crust.

Bake at 300°F for 60 to 65 minutes or until puffed and set. Cool in pan on wire rack 15 minutes. Carefully run metal spatula around edge of cheesecake to loosen. Cover; chill at least 4 hours. In small bowl, combine powdered sugar and sour cream. Serve with cheesecake. Garnish with lavender.

Makes 12 servings

Prep Time: 30 minutes

Cook Time: 65 minutes

Nutritional Information per Serving: *Calories: 263, Total Fat: 9 g, Cholesterol: 23 mg, Sodium: 308 mg*

Orange Chiffon Cheesecake

2 cups graham cracker crumbs
8 tablespoons light margarine, melted
1 teaspoon EQUAL® Measure™ *or*
    3 packets EQUAL® sweetener *or*
    2 tablespoons EQUAL® Spoonful™
1 cup orange juice
1 envelope (¼ ounce) unflavored
    gelatin
12 ounces reduced-fat cream cheese,
    softened
1 cup part-skim ricotta cheese
3½ teaspoons EQUAL® Measure™ *or*
    12 packets EQUAL® sweetener *or*
    ½ cup EQUAL® Spoonful™
2 cups light whipped topping
2 medium oranges, peeled, seeded and
    chopped

• Spray 9-inch springform pan with nonstick cooking spray. Mix graham cracker crumbs, margarine and 1 teaspoon Equal® Measure™ *or* 3 packets Equal® sweetener *or* 2 tablespoons Equal® Spoonful™. Pat mixture evenly on bottom and halfway up side of pan. Bake in preheated 350°F oven 8 to 10 minutes or until set. Cool.

• Pour orange juice into small saucepan. Sprinkle gelatin over orange juice and let soften 1 minute. Heat, stirring constantly, until gelatin dissolves, about 3 minutes. Blend cream cheese and ricotta cheese in large bowl until smooth; stir in 3½ teaspoons Equal® Measure™ *or* 12 packets Equal® sweetener *or* ½ cup Equal® Spoonful™. Add gelatin mixture to cheese mixture; blend until smooth. Fold whipped topping into cheese mixture. Stir in chopped oranges. Spoon into prepared crust and spread evenly.

• Chill 6 hours or overnight. Remove side of pan; place cheesecake on serving plate.

Makes 16 servings

Nutritional Information per Serving: *Calories: 204, Total Fat: 11 g, Cholesterol: 17 mg, Sodium: 209 mg*

New York Cheesecake

1¼ cups vanilla wafer crumbs
4 tablespoons margarine, melted
1 teaspoon EQUAL® Measure™ *or*
   3 packets EQUAL® sweetener *or*
   2 tablespoons EQUAL® Spoonful™
2 packages (8 ounces each) reduced-
   fat cream cheese, softened
1 package (8 ounces) fat-free cream
   cheese, softened
5½ teaspoons EQUAL® Measure™ *or*
   18 packets EQUAL® sweetener *or*
   ¾ cup EQUAL® Spoonful™
2 eggs
2 egg whites
2 tablespoons cornstarch
1 cup reduced-fat sour cream
1 teaspoon vanilla
1 pint strawberries, sliced (optional)
   Strawberry Sauce (recipe follows)

• Mix vanilla wafer crumbs, margarine and 1 teaspoon Equal® Measure™ *or* 3 packets Equal® sweetener *or* 2 tablespoons Equal® Spoonful™ in bottom of 9-inch springform pan. Reserve 1 tablespoon of crumb mixture. Pat remaining mixture evenly on bottom and ½ inch up side of pan. Bake in preheated 350°F oven until crust is lightly browned, about 8 minutes. Cool on wire rack.

• Beat cream cheese and 5½ teaspoons Equal® Measure™ *or* 18 packets Equal® sweetener *or* ¾ cup Equal® Spoonful™ in large bowl until fluffy; beat in eggs, egg whites and cornstarch. Mix in sour cream and vanilla until well blended. Pour mixture into crust.

• Place cheesecake in roasting pan on oven rack; add 1 inch hot water to roasting pan. Bake in preheated 300°F oven just until set in the center, 45 to 60 minutes. Remove cheesecake from roasting pan, sprinkle with reserved crumb mixture and return to oven. Turn oven off and let cheesecake cool 3 hours in oven with door ajar. Refrigerate 8 hours or overnight.

• Remove side of pan; place cheesecake on serving plate. Serve with strawberries and Strawberry Sauce. *Makes 16 servings*

Nutritional Information per Serving: *Calories: 187, Total Fat: 12 g, Cholesterol: 56 mg, Sodium: 253 mg*

Strawberry Sauce

1 package (16 ounces) frozen
   unsweetened strawberries, thawed
1 tablespoon lemon juice
1¾ teaspoons EQUAL® Measure™ *or*
   6 packets EQUAL® sweetener *or*
   ¼ cup EQUAL® Spoonful™

• Process strawberries in food processor or blender until smooth. Stir in lemon juice and Equal®; refrigerate until serving time.
Makes about 2 cups

Nutritional Information per Serving (2 tablespoons): *Calories: 12, Total Fat: 0 g, Cholesterol: 0 mg, Sodium: 1 mg*

Turtle Cheesecake

6 tablespoons reduced-calorie margarine
1½ cups graham cracker crumbs
2 envelopes unflavored gelatin
2 packages (8 ounces each) fat-free cream cheese
2 cups 1% low-fat cottage cheese
1 cup sugar
1½ teaspoons vanilla
1 container (8 ounces) thawed reduced-fat nondairy whipped topping
¼ cup prepared fat-free caramel topping
¼ cup prepared fat-free hot fudge topping
¼ cup chopped pecans

1. Preheat oven to 350°F. Spray bottom and side of 9-inch springform pan with nonstick cooking spray. Melt margarine in small saucepan over medium heat. Stir in graham cracker crumbs. Press crumb mixture firmly onto bottom and side of prepared pan. Bake 10 minutes. Cool.

2. Place ½ cup cold water in small saucepan; sprinkle gelatin over water. Let stand 3 minutes to soften. Heat gelatin mixture over low heat until completely dissolved, stirring constantly.

3. Combine cream cheese, cottage cheese, sugar and vanilla in food processor or blender; process until smooth. Add gelatin mixture; process until well blended. Fold in whipped topping. Pour into prepared crust. Refrigerate 4 hours or until set.

4. Loosen cake from side of pan. Remove side of pan from cake. Drizzle caramel and hot fudge toppings over cake. Sprinkle pecans evenly over top of cake before serving.   *Makes 16 servings*

Nutritional Information per Serving: *Calories: 231, Total Fat: 7 g, Cholesterol: 1 mg, Sodium: 419 mg*

Luscious Chocolate Cheesecake

2 cups (16 ounces) nonfat cottage cheese
¾ cup frozen egg substitute, thawed
⅔ cup sugar
4 ounces (½ of 8-ounce package) Neufchâtel cheese (light cream cheese), softened
⅓ cup HERSHEY'S Cocoa or HERSHEY'S European Style Cocoa
½ teaspoon vanilla extract
Yogurt Topping (recipe follows)
Sliced strawberries or mandarin orange segments (optional)

Heat oven to 300°F. Spray 9-inch springform pan with vegetable cooking spray. In food processor, place cottage cheese, egg substitute, sugar, Neufchâtel cheese, cocoa and vanilla; process until smooth. Pour into prepared pan.

Bake 35 minutes or until edge is set. Meanwhile, prepare Yogurt Topping. Carefully spread topping over top of warm cheesecake. Return cheesecake to oven; bake 5 minutes. With knife, loosen cheesecake from side of pan. Cool completely in pan on wire rack. Cover; refrigerate until chilled. Just before serving, remove side of pan. Serve with strawberries or oranges, if desired. Garnish as desired. Cover; refrigerate leftover cheesecake.
Makes 9 servings

Yogurt Topping: In small bowl, stir together ⅔ cup plain nonfat yogurt and 2 tablespoons sugar until well blended.

Nutritional Information per Serving: *Calories: 170, Total Fat: 5 g, Cholesterol: 10 mg, Sodium: 290 mg*

Turtle Cheesecake

Mocha Marble Pound Cake

2 cups all-purpose flour
2 teaspoons baking powder
1 teaspoon baking soda
½ teaspoon salt
1 cup sugar
¼ cup FLEISCHMANN'S® 70% Corn Oil Spread, softened
1 teaspoon vanilla extract
½ cup EGG BEATERS® Healthy Real Egg Substitute
1 (8-ounce) container low fat coffee yogurt
¼ cup unsweetened cocoa
   Mocha Yogurt Glaze (recipe follows)

In small bowl, combine flour, baking powder, baking soda and salt; set aside.

In large bowl, with electric mixer at medium speed, beat sugar, corn oil spread and vanilla until creamy. Add Egg Beaters®; beat until smooth. With mixer at low speed, add yogurt alternately with flour mixture, beating well after each addition. Remove half of batter to medium bowl. Add cocoa to batter remaining in large bowl; beat until blended. Alternately spoon coffee and chocolate batters into greased 9×5×3-inch loaf pan. With knife, cut through batters to create marbled effect.

Bake at 325°F for 60 to 65 minutes or until toothpick inserted in center comes out clean. Cool in pan on wire rack for 10 minutes. Remove from pan; cool completely on wire rack. Frost with Mocha Yogurt Glaze. *Makes 16 servings*

Mocha Yogurt Glaze: In small bowl, combine ½ cup powdered sugar, 1 tablespoon unsweetened cocoa and 1 tablespoon low fat coffee yogurt until smooth; add more yogurt if necessary to make spreading consistency.

Nutritional Information per Serving: *Calories: 159, Total Fat: 3 g, Cholesterol: 1 mg, Sodium: 215 mg*

Marbled Angel Cake

1 package (about 15 ounces) angel food cake mix
¼ cup HERSHEY₅S Cocoa
   Chocolate Glaze (recipe follows)

Place oven rack in lowest position. Heat oven to 375°F. Prepare cake batter as directed on package. Transfer 4 cups batter to medium bowl; gradually fold in cocoa until well blended, being careful not to deflate batter. Alternately pour vanilla and chocolate batters into ungreased 10-inch tube pan. With knife or metal spatula, cut through batters for marble effect.

Bake 30 to 35 minutes or until top crust is firm and looks very dry. *Do not underbake.* Invert pan on heatproof funnel or bottle; cool completely, at least 1½ hours. Carefully run knife along side of pan to loosen cake; remove from pan. Place on serving plate; drizzle with Chocolate Glaze. Let stand until set. Store, covered, at room temperature. *Makes 16 servings*

Chocolate Glaze: In small saucepan, combine ⅓ cup sugar and ¼ cup water. Cook over medium heat, stirring constantly, until mixture comes to a boil. Stir until sugar dissolves; remove from heat. Immediately add 1 cup HERSHEY₅S MINI CHIPS Semi-Sweet Chocolate; stir until chips are melted and mixture is smooth. Cool to desired consistency; use immediately.

Nutritional Information per Serving: *Calories: 180, Total Fat: 4 g, Cholesterol: 0 mg, Sodium: 200 mg*

Low Fat Devil's Chocolate Fudge Cake

CAKE:

1 cup water
½ cup Prune Purée (page 83) or prepared prune butter
3 egg whites
1½ teaspoons vanilla
1 cup plus 2 tablespoons all-purpose flour
1 cup plus 2 tablespoons granulated sugar
¾ cup unsweetened cocoa powder
1½ teaspoons baking powder
¼ teaspoon baking soda
¼ teaspoon salt

ICING:

2½ cups powdered sugar
¼ cup unsweetened cocoa powder
¼ cup 1% low-fat milk
Fresh raspberries and mint sprig, for garnish

Preheat oven to 350°F. Coat 9-inch square baking pan with vegetable cooking spray. To make cake, in mixer bowl, beat water, prune purée, egg whites and vanilla until well blended. Add flour, granulated sugar, ¾ cup cocoa, baking powder, baking soda and salt; mix well. Spread batter evenly in prepared pan. Bake in center of oven about 30 minutes or until toothpick inserted into center comes out clean. Cool completely in pan on wire rack.

To make icing, in small mixer bowl, beat powdered sugar, ¼ cup cocoa and milk until smooth. Spread on cake. Garnish with raspberries and mint. Cut cake into 3-inch squares.   *Makes 9 servings*

Nutritional Information per Serving: *Calories: 345, Total Fat: 2 g, Cholesterol: 1 mg, Sodium: 161 mg*

Favorite recipe from **California Prune Board**

Pineapple Upside-Down Cake

1 (8-ounce) can crushed pineapple in juice, undrained
2 tablespoons margarine, melted, divided
½ cup firmly packed light brown sugar
6 whole maraschino cherries
1½ cups all-purpose flour
2 tablespoons baking powder
¼ teaspoon salt
1 cup granulated sugar
½ cup MOTT'S® Natural Apple Sauce
1 whole egg
3 egg whites, beaten until stiff

1. Preheat oven to 375°F. Drain pineapple; reserve juice. Spray sides of 8-inch square baking pan with nonstick cooking spray.

2. Spread 1 tablespoon melted margarine evenly on bottom of prepared pan. Sprinkle with brown sugar; top with pineapple. Slice cherries in half. Arrange cherries, cut side up, so that when cake is cut, each piece will have cherry half in center.

3. In small bowl, combine flour, baking powder and salt.

4. In large bowl, combine granulated sugar, apple sauce, whole egg, remaining 1 tablespoon melted margarine and reserved pineapple juice.

5. Add flour mixture to apple sauce mixture; stir until well blended. Fold in egg whites. Gently pour batter over fruit, spreading evenly.

6. Bake 35 to 40 minutes or until lightly browned. Cool on wire rack 10 minutes. Invert cake onto serving plate. Serve warm or cool completely. Cut into 12 pieces.
          Makes 12 servings

Nutritional Information per Serving: *Calories: 200, Total Fat: 3 g, Cholesterol: 20 mg, Sodium: 240 mg*

Brownie Cake Delight

1 package reduced-fat fudge brownie mix
⅓ cup strawberry all-fruit spread
2 cups thawed reduced-fat nondairy whipped topping
¼ teaspoon almond extract
2 cups strawberries, stems removed and cut into halves
¼ cup chocolate sauce

1. Prepare brownies according to package directions, substituting 11×7-inch baking pan. Cool completely in pan.

2. Whisk fruit spread in small bowl until smooth.

3. Combine whipped topping and almond extract in medium bowl.

4. Cut brownie crosswise in half. Place half of brownie, flat-side down, on serving dish. Spread with fruit spread and 1 cup whipped topping. Place second half of brownie, flat-side down, over bottom layer. Spread with remaining whipped topping. Arrange strawberries on whipped topping. Drizzle chocolate sauce onto cake before serving. Garnish with fresh mint, if desired.

Makes 16 servings

Nutritional Information per Serving: *Calories: 193, Total Fat: 3 g, Cholesterol: trace, Sodium: 140 mg*

Light & Luscious Chocolate Cake with Raspberry Sauce

2 cups all-purpose flour
1⅓ cups skim milk
1 cup sugar
1 cup EGG BEATERS® Healthy Real Egg Substitute
⅔ cup unsweetened cocoa
⅔ cup FLEISCHMANN'S® 70% Corn Oil Spread, softened
1½ teaspoons baking powder
1½ teaspoons vanilla extract
½ teaspoon baking soda
Raspberry Sauce (recipe follows)
Fresh raspberries and fresh mint sprigs, for garnish

In large bowl, with electric mixer at medium speed, combine flour, milk, sugar, Egg Beaters®, cocoa, corn oil spread, baking powder, vanilla and baking soda just until blended. Beat at high speed for 3 minutes. Spread batter into lightly greased 13×9×2-inch baking pan. Bake at 350°F for 30 to 35 minutes or until toothpick inserted in center comes out clean. Cool in pan on wire rack. Cut into 16 (3×2-inch) pieces. Serve topped with Raspberry Sauce. Garnish with raspberries and mint. *Makes 16 servings*

Prep Time: 20 minutes

Cook Time: 35 minutes

Raspberry Sauce: In electric blender container, purée 2 cups thawed frozen raspberries in syrup; strain. Stir in 2 tablespoons sugar and 1 tablespoon cornstarch. In small saucepan, cook raspberry mixture until thickened and boiling. Cover; chill.

Nutritional Information per Serving (1 piece cake, 2 tablespoons sauce): *Calories: 238, Total Fat: 8 g, Cholesterol: 0 mg, Sodium: 161 mg*

Brownie Cake Delight

Pineapple Upside-Down Cake

1 can (14 ounces) unsweetened
    crushed pineapple in juice,
    undrained
¼ cup pecan pieces (optional)
2 tablespoons lemon juice, divided
1¾ teaspoons EQUAL® Measure™ or
    6 packets EQUAL® sweetener or
    ¼ cup EQUAL® Spoonful™
1 teaspoon cornstarch
4 tablespoons margarine, at room
    temperature
3½ teaspoons EQUAL® Measure™ or
    12 packets EQUAL® sweetener or
    ½ cup EQUAL® Spoonful™
1 egg
1 cup cake flour
1½ teaspoons baking powder
½ teaspoon baking soda
¼ teaspoon ground cinnamon
¼ teaspoon ground nutmeg
⅛ teaspoon ground ginger
⅓ cup buttermilk

• Drain pineapple, reserving ¼ cup juice.
Mix pineapple, pecans, 1 tablespoon lemon
juice, 1¾ teaspoons Equal® Measure™ or 6
packets Equal® sweetener or ¼ cup Equal®
Spoonful™ and cornstarch in bottom of
8-inch square or 9-inch round cake pan;
spread mixture evenly in pan.

• Beat margarine and 3½ teaspoons Equal®
Measure™ or 12 packets Equal® sweetener or
½ cup Equal® Spoonful™ in medium bowl
until fluffy; beat in egg. Combine flour,
baking powder, baking soda and spices in
small bowl. Add to margarine mixture
alternately with buttermilk, ¼ cup reserved
pineapple juice and remaining 1 tablespoon
lemon juice, beginning and ending with dry
ingredients. Spread batter over pineapple
mixture in cake pan.

• Bake in preheated 350°F oven until
browned and toothpick inserted in center
comes out clean, about 25 minutes. Invert
cake immediately onto serving plate. Serve
warm or at room temperature.

Makes 8 servings

Note: If desired, maraschino cherry halves
may be placed on bottom of cake pan with
pineapple mixture.

Nutritional Information per Serving: *Calories: 156,
Total Fat: 7 g, Cholesterol: 27 mg, Sodium: 257 mg*

Blueberry Angel Food Cake Rolls

1 package DUNCAN HINES® Angel
    Food Cake Mix
    Confectioners sugar
1 can (21 ounces) blueberry pie filling
¼ cup confectioners sugar
    Mint leaves, for garnish (optional)

1. Preheat oven to 350°F. Line two
15½×10½×1-inch jelly-roll pans with
aluminum foil.

2. Prepare cake following package directions.
Divide into pans. Spread evenly. Cut
through batter with knife or spatula to
remove large air bubbles. Bake at 350°F for
15 minutes or until set. Invert cakes at once
onto clean, lint-free dish towels dusted with
confectioners sugar. Remove foil carefully.
Roll up each cake with towel jelly-roll
fashion, starting at short end. Cool
completely.

3. Unroll cakes. Spread about 1 cup
blueberry pie filling to within 1 inch of
edges on each cake. Reroll and place seam
side down on serving plate. Dust with ¼
cup confectioners sugar. Garnish with mint
leaves, if desired.

Makes 2 cakes (8 servings each)

Nutritional Information per Serving: *Calories: 143,
Total Fat: 0 g, Cholesterol: 0 mg, Sodium: 77 mg*

Pineapple Upside-Down Cake

Easy Carrot Cake

½ cup Prune Purée (recipe follows)
2 cups all-purpose flour
2 teaspoons ground cinnamon
1½ teaspoons baking soda
½ teaspoon salt
4 cups shredded DOLE® Carrots
2 cups sugar
½ cup DOLE® Pineapple Juice
2 eggs
2 teaspoons vanilla extract
Vegetable cooking spray

• **Prepare** Prune Purée; set aside.

• **Combine** flour, cinnamon, baking soda and salt in medium bowl; set aside.

• **Beat** together Prune Purée, carrots, sugar, juice, eggs and vanilla in large bowl until blended. Add flour mixture; stir until well blended.

• **Spread** batter into 13×9-inch baking dish sprayed with vegetable cooking spray.

• **Bake** at 375°F 30 to 35 minutes or until toothpick inserted in center comes out clean. Cool completely in dish on wire rack. Dust with powdered sugar and garnish with carrot curls, if desired.   *Makes 12 servings*

Prep Time: 15 minutes

Bake Time: 35 minutes

Prune Purée: Combine 1⅓ cups DOLE® Pitted Prunes, halved, and ½ cup hot water in food processor or blender container. Process until prunes are finely chopped, stopping to scrape down side occasionally. (Purée can be refrigerated in airtight container for up to 1 week.)

Nutritional Information per Serving: *Calories: 240, Total Fat: 1 g, Cholesterol: 32 mg, Sodium: 244 mg*

Spice Cake with Fresh Peach Sauce

CAKE:

1 package DUNCAN HINES® Moist Deluxe Spice Cake Mix
3 egg whites
1¼ cups water
⅓ cup CRISCO® Oil or CRISCO® PURITAN® Canola Oil

SAUCE:

6 cups sliced fresh peaches
1 cup water
⅓ cup sugar
⅛ teaspoon ground cinnamon

1. Preheat oven to 350°F. Grease and flour 10-inch bundt or tube pan.

2. For Cake, place cake mix, egg whites, water and oil in large bowl. Beat at low speed with electric mixer until blended. Beat at medium speed 2 minutes. Bake at 350°F for 42 to 47 minutes or until toothpick inserted in center comes out clean. Cool in pan 25 minutes. Invert onto serving plate. Cool completely. Dust with confectioners sugar, if desired.

2. For Sauce, combine peaches and water in large saucepan. Cook over medium heat 5 minutes. Reduce heat to low. Cover and simmer 10 minutes. Cool. Reserve ½ cup peach slices. Combine remaining peaches with any cooking liquid, sugar and cinnamon in blender or food processor. Process until smooth. Stir in reserved peach slices. To serve, spoon peach sauce over cake slices.   *Makes 12 to 16 servings*

Tip: Fresh peach sauce can be served either warm or chilled.

Note: Use ¾ cup egg substitute in place of egg whites, if desired.

Nutritional Information per Serving: *Calories: 299, Total Fat: 10 g, Cholesterol: 0 mg, Sodium: 294 mg*

Blueberry Lattice Pie

6 cups fresh blueberries *or* 2 packages
(16 ounces each) frozen
unsweetened blueberries
3 tablespoons lemon juice
6 tablespoons cornstarch
8 teaspoons EQUAL® Measure™ *or*
27 packets EQUAL® sweetener *or*
1 cup plus 2 tablespoons EQUAL®
Spoonful™
Reduced-Fat Pie Pastry (recipe
follows), 2 recipes for double crust
or favorite pastry for double crust
9-inch pie

• Toss blueberries and lemon juice in large
bowl. Sprinkle with combined cornstarch
and Equal® and toss to coat. Let stand 30
minutes.

• Roll half of pastry on lightly floured surface
into circle 1 inch larger than inverted 9-inch
pie pan. Ease pastry into pan; trim within 1
inch of edge of pan. Roll remaining pastry
to ⅛-inch thickness; cut into 10 to 12 strips,
½ inch wide.

• Pour blueberry mixture into pastry. Arrange
pastry strips over filling and weave into
lattice design. Trim ends of lattice strips; fold
edge of lower crust over ends of lattice
strips. Seal and flute edge.

• Bake in preheated 425°F oven until crust is
browned and filling is bubbly, about 1 hour.
Cover edge of crust with aluminum foil if
browning too quickly. Cool on wire rack;
refrigerate leftovers.   *Makes 8 servings*

Nutritional Information per Serving: *Calories: 345,
Total Fat: 12 g, Cholesterol: 0 mg, Sodium: 143 mg*

Reduced-Fat Pie Pastry

1¼ cups all-purpose flour
1 teaspoon EQUAL® Measure™ *or*
3 packets EQUAL® sweetener *or*
2 tablespoons EQUAL® Spoonful™
¼ teaspoon salt
4 tablespoons cold margarine, cut into
pieces
5 to 5½ tablespoons ice water

• Combine flour, Equal® and salt in medium
bowl; cut in margarine with pastry blender
until mixture resembles coarse crumbs. Mix
in water, 1 tablespoon at a time, stirring
lightly with fork after each addition until
dough is formed. Wrap and refrigerate until
ready to use.

• For prebaked crust, roll pastry on lightly
floured surface into circle 1 inch larger than
inverted 9-inch pie pan. Ease pastry into
pan; trim and flute edge. Pierce bottom and
side of pastry with fork. Bake in preheated
425°F oven until pastry is browned, 10 to 15
minutes. Cool on wire rack.
          Makes pastry for 9-inch pie (8 servings)

Tip: Double recipe for double crust or lattice
pies.

Nutritional Information per Serving: *Calories: 123,
Total Fat: 6 g, Cholesterol: 0 mg, Sodium: 134 mg*

Chocolate Cream Pie

Reduced-Fat Pie Pastry (page 325) or favorite pastry for 9-inch pie
⅓ cup cornstarch
¼ to ⅓ cup European or Dutch-process cocoa
10¾ teaspoons EQUAL® Measure™ or
    36 packets EQUAL® sweetener or
    1½ cups EQUAL® Spoonful™
⅛ teaspoon salt
3 cups skim milk
2 eggs
2 egg whites
1 teaspoon vanilla
8 tablespoons thawed frozen light whipped topping
Chocolate leaves (optional)

• Roll pastry on lightly floured surface into circle 1 inch larger than inverted 9-inch pie pan. Ease pastry into pan; trim and flute edge. Pierce bottom and side of pastry with fork. Bake in preheated 425°F oven until crust is browned, 10 to 15 minutes. Cool on wire rack.

• Combine cornstarch, cocoa, Equal® and salt in medium saucepan; stir in milk. Heat to boiling over medium-high heat, whisking constantly. Boil until thickened, about 1 minute.

• Beat eggs and egg whites in small bowl; whisk about 1 cup chocolate mixture into eggs. Whisk egg mixture into chocolate mixture in saucepan. Cook over very low heat, whisking constantly, 30 to 60 seconds. Remove from heat; stir in vanilla.

• Spread hot filling in baked crust; refrigerate until chilled and set, about 6 hours. Cut into wedges and place on serving plates; garnish each serving with dollop of whipped topping and chocolate leaves, if desired.

Makes 8 servings

Nutritional Information per Serving: *Calories: 234, Total Fat: 8 g, Cholesterol: 55 mg, Sodium: 245 mg*

Double Chocolate Mousse Pie

1¼ cups chocolate graham cracker crumbs
3 tablespoons sugar
¼ cup Prune Purée (page 83) or prepared prune butter
3 cups nonfat milk
2 packages (3.4 ounces each) instant chocolate pudding mix
1½ cups low-fat nondairy whipped topping, divided
Chocolate curls, for garnish (optional)

Preheat oven to 375°F. Coat 9-inch pie plate with vegetable cooking spray. In large bowl, combine crumbs and sugar. Cut in prune purée with pastry blender until mixture resembles coarse crumbs. Press evenly onto bottom and side of prepared pie plate. Bake in center of oven 15 minutes. Cool completely on wire rack.

Meanwhile, in large bowl, combine milk and pudding mixes; whisk 2 minutes. Fold in 1 cup whipped topping. Spoon into prepared crust. Chill at least 2 hours. Pipe remaining whipped topping along edge. Garnish with chocolate curls, if desired. Cut into wedges.

Makes 8 servings

Nutritional Information per Serving: *Calories: 240, Total Fat: 4 g, Cholesterol: 5 mg, Sodium: 410 mg*

Favorite recipe from **California Prune Board**

Chocolate Cream Pie

Mile-High Apple Pie

Reduced-Fat Pie Pastry (2 recipes for
    double crust, page 325) or favorite
    pastry for double crust 9-inch pie
3 tablespoons cornstarch
7¼ teaspoons EQUAL® Measure™ or
    24 packets EQUAL® sweetener or
    1 cup EQUAL® Spoonful™
¾ teaspoon ground cinnamon
¼ teaspoon salt
¼ teaspoon ground nutmeg
8 cups sliced cored peeled Granny
    Smith or other baking apples
    (about 8 medium)

• Roll half the pastry on floured surface into circle 1 inch larger than inverted 9-inch pie pan. Ease pastry into pan.

• Combine cornstarch, Equal®, cinnamon, salt and nutmeg; sprinkle over apples in large bowl and toss. Arrange apple mixture in pie crust.

• Roll remaining pastry into circle large enough to fit top of pie. Cut out hearts from pastry with cookie cutters. Place remaining pastry on pie; seal edges, trim and flute. Press heart cut-outs on pastry. Bake in preheated 425°F oven until pastry is golden and apples are tender, 40 to 50 minutes. Cool on wire rack.   *Makes 8 servings*

Nutritional Information per Serving: *Calories: 334, Total Fat: 12 g, Cholesterol: 0 mg, Sodium: 335 mg*

Key Lime Pie

1 cup graham cracker crumbs
3 tablespoons melted margarine
1 teaspoon EQUAL® Measure™ or
    3 packets EQUAL® sweetener or
    2 tablespoons EQUAL® Spoonful™
1 envelope (¼ ounce) unflavored
    gelatin
1¾ cups skim milk, divided
1 package (8 ounces) reduced-fat
    cream cheese, softened
⅓ to ½ cup fresh lime juice
3½ teaspoons EQUAL® Measure™ or
    12 packets EQUAL® sweetener or
    ½ cup EQUAL® Spoonful™
Lime slices, raspberries and fresh
    mint sprigs, for garnish (optional)

• Combine graham cracker crumbs, margarine and 1 teaspoon Equal® Measure™ or 3 packets Equal® sweetener or 2 tablespoons Equal® Spoonful™ in bottom of 7-inch springform pan; pat evenly on bottom and ½ inch up side of pan.

• Sprinkle gelatin over ½ cup milk in small saucepan; let stand 2 to 3 minutes. Cook over low heat, stirring constantly, until gelatin is dissolved. Beat cream cheese in small bowl until fluffy; beat in remaining 1¼ cups milk and gelatin mixture. Mix in lime juice and 3½ teaspoons Equal® Measure™ or 12 packets Equal® sweetener or ½ cup Equal® Spoonful™. Refrigerate pie until set, about 2 hours.

• To serve, loosen side of pie from pan with small spatula and remove side of pan. Place pie on serving plate; garnish with lime slices, raspberries and mint, if desired.
    Makes 8 servings

Nutritional Information per Serving: *Calories: 150, Total Fat: 10 g, Cholesterol: 16 mg, Sodium: 231 mg*

Mile-High Apple Pie

Strawberry Margarita Pie

3 tablespoons margarine
2 tablespoons honey
1½ cups crushed pretzels
3 cups low-fat sugar-free strawberry
    frozen yogurt, softened
1½ cups thawed reduced-fat nondairy
    whipped topping
2 teaspoons grated lime peel, divided
1 package (16 ounces) strawberries in
    syrup, thawed
1 tablespoon lime juice
1 tablespoon tequila (optional)

1. Combine margarine and honey in medium microwavable bowl. Microwave on HIGH 30 seconds or until smooth when stirred. Add pretzels; stir until evenly coated. Press onto bottom and side of 9-inch pie plate; freeze 30 minutes or until firm.

2. Combine frozen yogurt, whipped topping and 1 teaspoon lime peel in medium bowl; fold with rubber spatula. Spoon into crust. Freeze 2 hours or until firm.

3. Combine strawberries, lime juice and remaining 1 teaspoon lime peel in small bowl; stir to blend.

4. Cut pie into 8 slices; serve with strawberry mixture. Add tequila to strawberry mixture just before serving, if desired.

Makes 8 servings

Nutritional Information per Serving: *Calories: 306, Total Fat: 8 g, Cholesterol: 19 mg, Sodium: 390 mg*

Rhubarb-Strawberry Pie

Reduced-Fat Pie Pastry (page 325)
    or favorite pastry for 9-inch pie
3 cups 1-inch rhubarb pieces *or*
    1 package (16 ounces) frozen
    unsweetened rhubarb, thawed,
    undrained
¾ cup water
¼ cup all-purpose flour
3 tablespoons cornstarch
2 tablespoons lemon juice
3 cups sliced strawberries
12¼ teaspoons EQUAL® Measure™ *or*
    40 packets EQUAL® sweetener *or*
    1⅔ cups EQUAL® Spoonful™
¼ teaspoon ground nutmeg

• Roll pastry on lightly floured surface into circle 1 inch larger than inverted 9-inch pie pan. Ease pastry into pan; trim and flute edge. Pierce bottom and side of pastry with fork. Bake in preheated 425°F oven until pastry is browned, 10 to 15 minutes. Cool on wire rack.

• Cook rhubarb in large covered saucepan over medium heat until rhubarb releases liquid, about 5 minutes. Combine water, flour, cornstarch and lemon juice; stir into rhubarb and heat to boiling. Reduce heat and simmer, uncovered, until mixture is thickened and rhubarb is almost tender, 3 to 5 minutes, stirring frequently. Stir in strawberries and cook 2 to 3 minutes longer.

• Stir Equal® and nutmeg into fruit mixture; spoon into baked crust, spreading evenly. Bake in 350°F oven until bubbly, about 40 minutes. Cover edge of crust with aluminum foil if browning too quickly. Cool briefly on wire rack; serve warm.   *Makes 8 servings*

Nutritional Information per Serving: *Calories: 199, Total Fat: 6 g, Cholesterol: 0 mg, Sodium: 138 mg*

Strawberry Margarita Pie

Cherry Lattice Pie

2 packages (16 ounces each) frozen
    no-sugar-added pitted cherries
12¾ teaspoons EQUAL® Measure™ *or*
    42 packets EQUAL® sweetener *or*
    1¾ cup EQUAL® Spoonful™
4 teaspoons all-purpose flour
4 teaspoons cornstarch
¼ teaspoon ground nutmeg
5 to 7 drops red food color
    Reduced-Fat Pie Pastry (2 recipes for
    double crust, page 325) or favorite
    pastry for double crust 9-inch pie

• Thaw cherries completely in strainer set in bowl; reserve ¾ cup cherry juice. Mix Equal®, flour, cornstarch and nutmeg in small saucepan; stir in cherry juice and heat to boiling. Boil, stirring constantly, 1 minute. Remove from heat and stir in cherries; stir in food color.

• Roll half of pastry on floured surface into circle 1 inch larger than inverted 9-inch pie pan; ease pastry into pan. Pour cherry mixture into pastry. Roll remaining pastry on floured surface to ⅛-inch thickness; cut into 10 to 12 strips, ½ inch wide. Arrange pastry strips over filling and weave into lattice design. Trim ends of lattice strips; fold edge of lower crust over ends of lattice strips. Seal and flute edge.

• Bake in preheated 425°F oven until pastry is browned, 35 to 40 minutes. Cool on wire rack.   *Makes 8 servings*

Nutritional Information per Serving: *Calories: 330, Total Fat: 12 g, Cholesterol: 0 mg, Sodium: 269 mg*

Apple-Raisin Sour Cream Pie

1½ cups graham cracker crumbs
⅓ cup margarine, melted
1¾ teaspoons EQUAL® Measure™ *or*
    6 packets EQUAL® sweetener *or*
    ¼ cup EQUAL® Spoonful™
4 cups sliced cored peeled Granny
    Smith or other baking apples
    (4 to 6 medium)
2 teaspoons lemon juice
¼ cup dark raisins
½ cup reduced-fat sour cream
1 egg white, beaten
3½ teaspoons EQUAL® Measure™ *or*
    12 packets EQUAL® sweetener *or*
    ½ cup EQUAL® Spoonful™
1 tablespoon all-purpose flour
¼ teaspoon ground cinnamon
⅛ teaspoon ground nutmeg

• Mix graham cracker crumbs, margarine and 1¾ teaspoons Equal® Measure™ *or* 6 packets Equal® sweetener *or* ¼ cup Equal® Spoonful™ in bottom of 9-inch springform pan. Reserve ¼ cup mixture; press remaining mixture firmly on bottom and 1 inch up side of pan. Bake in preheated 350°F oven until lightly browned, 5 to 8 minutes. Cool on wire rack.

• Toss apples with lemon juice in large bowl; add raisins. Combine sour cream and remaining ingredients; spoon mixture over apples, mixing until apples are coated.

• Spoon apple mixture into crust; sprinkle with reserved ¼ cup crumb mixture.

• Bake pie in 350°F oven until apples are tender, about 55 minutes. Cool on wire rack. Remove side of pan; place pie on serving plate.   *Makes 8 servings*

Nutritional Information per Serving: *Calories: 245, Total Fat: 12 g, Cholesterol: 6 mg, Sodium: 239 mg*

Cherry Lattice Pie

Spiced Pumpkin Pie

Reduced-Fat Pie Pastry (page 325)
  or favorite pastry for 9-inch pie
1 can (16 ounces) pumpkin
1 can (12 ounces) evaporated skimmed
  milk
3 eggs
5½ teaspoons EQUAL® Measure™ *or*
    18 packets EQUAL® sweetener *or*
    ¾ cup EQUAL® Spoonful™
1 teaspoon ground cinnamon
½ teaspoon ground ginger
¼ teaspoon salt
¼ teaspoon ground nutmeg
⅛ teaspoon ground cloves

• Roll pastry on floured surface into circle 1 inch larger than inverted 9-inch pie pan. Ease into pan; trim and flute edge.

• Beat pumpkin, evaporated milk and eggs in medium bowl; beat in remaining ingredients. Pour into pastry shell. Bake in preheated 425°F oven 15 minutes; *reduce heat to 350°F* and bake until knife inserted near center comes out clean, about 40 minutes. Cool on wire rack.

Makes 8 servings

Nutritional Information per Serving: *Calories: 219, Total Fat: 8 g, Cholesterol: 81 mg, Sodium: 282 mg*

Maple Pumpkin Pie

1⅓ cups all-purpose flour
 ⅓ cup plus 1 tablespoon sugar, divided
 ¾ teaspoon salt, divided
 2 tablespoons vegetable shortening
 2 tablespoons margarine
 4 to 5 tablespoons ice water
 1 can (15 ounces) solid-pack pumpkin
 2 egg whites
 1 cup evaporated skimmed milk
 ⅓ cup maple syrup
 1 teaspoon ground cinnamon
 ½ teaspoon ground ginger
   Thawed reduced-fat whipped
     topping (optional)

1. Combine flour, 1 tablespoon sugar and ¼ teaspoon salt in medium bowl. Cut in shortening and margarine with pastry blender or two knives until mixture forms coarse crumbs. Mix in ice water, 1 tablespoon at a time, until mixture comes together and forms a soft dough. Wrap in plastic wrap. Refrigerate 30 minutes.

2. Preheat oven to 425°F. Roll out pastry on floured surface to ⅛-inch thickness. Cut into 12-inch circle. Ease pastry into 9-inch pie plate; turn edge under and flute edge.

3. Combine pumpkin, remaining ⅓ cup sugar, egg whites, milk, syrup, cinnamon, ginger and remaining ½ teaspoon salt in large bowl; mix well. Pour into unbaked pie shell. Bake 15 minutes; *reduce oven temperature to 350°F.* Continue baking 45 to 50 minutes or until center is set. Transfer to wire cooling rack; let stand at least 30 minutes before serving. Serve warm, at room temperature or chilled with whipped topping, if desired.   *Makes 10 servings*

Nutritional Information per Serving: *Calories 198, Total Fat: 5 g, Cholesterol: 1 mg, Sodium: 231 mg*

Banana Cream Pie

Reduced-Fat Pie Pastry (page 325)
 or favorite pastry for 9-inch pie
⅓ cup cornstarch
3½ teaspoons EQUAL® Measure™ *or*
 12 packets EQUAL® sweetener *or*
 ½ cup EQUAL® Spoonful™
⅛ teaspoon salt
2½ cups skim milk
2 egg yolks
1 teaspoon vanilla
2 bananas, sliced
3 egg whites
¼ teaspoon cream of tartar
3½ teaspoons EQUAL® Measure™ *or*
 12 packets EQUAL® sweetener*

EQUAL® Spoonful™ cannot be used in meringue recipes.

• Roll pastry on lightly floured surface into circle 1 inch larger than inverted 9-inch pie pan. Ease pastry into pan; trim and flute edge. Pierce bottom and side of pastry with fork. Bake in preheated 425°F oven until crust is browned, 10 to 15 minutes. Cool on wire rack.

• Combine cornstarch, 3½ teaspoons Equal® Measure™ *or* 12 packets Equal® sweetener *or* ½ cup Equal® Spoonful™ and salt in medium saucepan; stir in milk. Heat to boiling over medium-high heat, whisking constantly. Boil until thickened, about 1 minute, whisking constantly.

• Beat egg yolks and vanilla in small bowl; whisk about 1 cup hot custard mixture into eggs. Whisk egg mixture back into custard mixture in saucepan. Cook over very low heat, whisking constantly, 30 to 60 seconds. Arrange bananas on bottom of baked crust; pour custard mixture over bananas, spreading evenly.

• Beat egg whites in medium bowl with electric mixer until foamy; add cream of tartar and beat to soft peaks. Gradually beat in 3½ teaspoons Equal® Measure™ *or* 12 packets Equal® sweetener, beating until stiff peaks form. Spread meringue over hot custard mixture, carefully sealing to edge of crust. Bake in preheated 425°F oven until meringue is browned, about 2 minutes. Cool on wire rack 30 minutes; refrigerate until set and chilled, about 6 hours. Cut just before serving. *Makes 8 servings*

Nutritional Information per Serving: *Calories: 230, Total Fat: 7 g, Cholesterol: 55 mg, Sodium: 230 mg*

Coconut Custard Pie

Reduced-Fat Pie Pastry (page 325)
 or favorite pastry for 9-inch pie
4 eggs
¼ teaspoon salt
2 cups skim milk
½ cup flaked coconut
5½ teaspoons EQUAL® Measure™ *or*
 18 packets EQUAL® sweetener *or*
 ¾ cup EQUAL® Spoonful™
2 teaspoons coconut extract

• Roll pastry on floured surface into circle 1 inch larger than inverted 9-inch pie pan. Ease into pan; trim and flute edge.

• Beat eggs and salt in large bowl until thick and lemon-colored, about 5 minutes. Mix in milk and remaining ingredients. Pour mixture into pastry shell.

• Bake pie in preheated 425°F oven 15 minutes. *Reduce temperature to 350°F* and bake until sharp knife inserted halfway between center and edge of pie comes out clean, 20 to 25 minutes. Cool on wire rack. Serve at room temperature, or refrigerate and serve chilled. *Makes 8 servings*

Nutritional Information per Serving: *Calories: 213, Total Fat: 10 g, Cholesterol: 107 mg, Sodium: 275 mg*

Mom's Lemon Meringue Pie

Reduced-Fat Pie Pastry (page 325)
　　or favorite pastry for 9-inch pie
2¼ cups water
½ cup lemon juice
10¾ teaspoons EQUAL® Measure™ or
　　36 packets EQUAL® sweetener or
　　1½ cups EQUAL® Spoonful™
⅓ cup plus 2 tablespoons cornstarch
2 eggs
2 egg whites
2 tablespoons margarine
1 to 2 drops yellow food color
　　(optional)
3 egg whites
¼ teaspoon cream of tartar
3½ teaspoons EQUAL® Measure™ or
　　12 packets EQUAL® sweetener*

*EQUAL® Spoonful™ cannot be used in meringue recipes.

• Roll pastry on lightly floured surface into circle 1 inch larger than inverted 9-inch pie pan. Ease pastry into pan; trim and flute edge. Pierce bottom and side of pastry with fork. Bake in preheated 425°F oven until pastry is browned, 10 to 15 minutes. Cool on wire rack.

• Mix water, lemon juice, 10¾ teaspoons Equal® Measure™ or 36 packets Equal® sweetener or 1½ cups Equal® Spoonful™ and cornstarch in medium saucepan. Heat to boiling over medium-high heat, stirring constantly; boil and stir 1 minute. Beat eggs and 2 egg whites in small bowl; stir in about half of hot cornstarch mixture. Stir egg mixture back into remaining cornstarch mixture in saucepan; cook and stir over low heat 1 minute. Remove from heat; add margarine, stirring until melted. Stir in food color, if desired. Pour mixture into baked pie shell.

• Beat 3 egg whites in medium bowl with electric mixer until foamy; add cream of tartar and beat to soft peaks. Gradually beat in 3½ teaspoons Equal® Measure™ or 12 packets Equal® sweetener, beating until stiff peaks form. Spread meringue over hot lemon filling, carefully sealing to edge of crust to prevent shrinking or weeping.

• Bake pie in preheated 425°F oven until meringue is browned, about 5 minutes. Cool completely on wire rack before cutting.

Makes 8 servings

Nutritional Information per Serving: *Calories: 233, Total Fat: 10 g, Cholesterol: 53 mg, Sodium: 223 mg*

Honey Pumpkin Pie

1 can (16 ounces) solid-pack pumpkin
1 cup evaporated low-fat milk
¾ cup honey
3 eggs, slightly beaten
2 tablespoons all-purpose flour
1 teaspoon ground cinnamon
½ teaspoon ground ginger
½ teaspoon rum extract
　　Pastry for single 9-inch pie crust

Combine all ingredients except pastry in large bowl; beat until well blended. Pour into pastry-lined 9-inch pie plate. Bake at 400°F 45 minutes or until knife inserted near center comes out clean.

Makes 8 servings

Nutritional Information per Serving: *Calories: 284, Total Fat: 9 g, Cholesterol: 82 mg, Sodium: 209 mg*

Favorite recipe from **National Honey Board**

Mom's Lemon Meringue Pie

Summer Fruit Tart

1¼ cups all-purpose flour
¼ teaspoon salt
⅓ cup shortening
3 to 4 tablespoons cold water
¼ cup plain nonfat yogurt
¼ cup reduced-fat dairy sour cream
½ teaspoon EQUAL® Measure™ or
    2 packets EQUAL® sweetener or
    4 teaspoons EQUAL® Spoonful™
¼ teaspoon almond extract
4 cups assorted fresh fruit
¾ cup pineapple juice
1 tablespoon lemon juice
2 teaspoons cornstarch
1 teaspoon EQUAL® Measure™ or
    3 packets EQUAL® sweetener or
    2 tablespoons EQUAL® Spoonful™

• Combine flour and salt; cut in shortening. Sprinkle water over mixture; toss with fork until moistened. Form into a ball.

• Roll pastry on lightly floured surface into 10- or 11-inch circle and place in 9- or 10-inch tart pan with removable bottom. Press pastry up side; trim excess. Prick with fork. Line with foil. Bake in preheated 450°F oven 8 minutes. Remove foil; bake until golden, 5 to 6 minutes. Cool on wire rack.

• Combine yogurt, sour cream, ½ teaspoon Equal® Measure™ or 2 packets Equal® sweetener or 4 teaspoons Equal® Spoonful™ and almond extract. Spread over cooled crust. Arrange fruit on top.

• Combine pineapple juice, lemon juice and cornstarch in small saucepan. Cook and stir until thickened and bubbly. Cook and stir 2 minutes more. Remove from heat; stir in 1 teaspoon Equal® Measure™ or 3 packets Equal® sweetener or 2 tablespoons Equal® Spoonful™. Cool. Spoon over fruit; cover and chill. *Makes 10 servings*

Nutritional Information per Serving: *Calories: 166, Total Fat: 8 g, Cholesterol: 1 mg, Sodium: 65 mg*

Nectarine and Berry Pie

Reduced-Fat Pie Pastry (page 325)
    or favorite pastry for 9-inch pie
5 cups sliced nectarines (about
    5 medium)
1 cup raspberries or sliced strawberries
1 cup fresh or frozen blueberries,
    partially thawed
2 teaspoons lemon juice
3 tablespoons cornstarch
7¼ teaspoons EQUAL® Measure™ or
    24 packets EQUAL® sweetener or
    1 cup EQUAL® Spoonful™
1 teaspoon grated lemon peel
¼ teaspoon ground allspice

• Roll pastry on floured surface into 12-inch circle; transfer to ungreased cookie sheet.

• Toss nectarines and berries with lemon juice in large bowl; sprinkle fruit with combined cornstarch, Equal®, lemon peel and allspice and toss to coat. Arrange fruit over pastry, leaving 2-inch border around edge of pastry. Bring edge of pastry toward center, overlapping as necessary. Bake pie in preheated 425°F oven until pastry is golden and fruit is tender, 35 to 40 minutes. Cool on wire rack. *Makes 8 servings*

Nutritional Information per Serving: *Calories: 216, Total Fat: 7 g, Cholesterol: 0 mg, Sodium: 138 mg*

Summer Fruit Tart

Key Lime Tarts

¾ cup skim milk
6 tablespoons fresh lime juice
2 tablespoons cornstarch
½ cup cholesterol-free egg substitute
½ cup reduced-fat sour cream
12 packages artificial sweetener or
     equivalent of ½ cup sugar
4 sheets phyllo dough*
    Butter-flavored nonstick cooking
     spray
¾ cup thawed fat-free nondairy
     whipped topping

Cover with damp kitchen towel to prevent dough from drying out.

1. Whisk together milk, lime juice and cornstarch in medium saucepan. Cook over medium heat 2 to 3 minutes, stirring constantly until thick. Remove from heat.

2. Add egg substitute; whisk constantly for 30 seconds to allow egg substitute to cook. Stir in sour cream and artificial sweetener; cover and refrigerate until cool.

3. Preheat oven to 350°F. Spray 8 (2½-inch) muffin cups with cooking spray; set aside.

4. Place 1 sheet of phyllo dough on cutting board; spray with cooking spray. Top with second sheet of phyllo dough; spray with cooking spray. Top with third sheet of phyllo dough; spray with cooking spray. Top with last sheet; spray with cooking spray.

5. Cut stack of phyllo dough into 8 squares. Gently fit each stacked square into prepared muffin cups; press firmly against bottom and side. Bake 8 to 10 minutes or until golden brown. Carefully remove from muffin cups; cool on wire rack.

6. Divide lime mixture evenly among phyllo cups; top with whipped topping. Garnish with fresh raspberries and lime slices, if desired. *Makes 8 servings*

Nutritional Information per Serving: *Calories: 82, Total Fat: 1 g, Cholesterol: 5 mg, Sodium: 88 mg*

Country Peach Tart

Reduced-Fat Pie Pastry (page 325)
    or favorite pastry for 9-inch pie
1 tablespoon all-purpose flour
2½ teaspoons EQUAL® Measure™ *or*
    8 packets EQUAL® sweetener *or*
    ⅓ cup EQUAL® Spoonful™
4 cups sliced pitted peeled fresh
    peaches (about 4 medium) or
    frozen peaches, thawed
Ground nutmeg

• Roll pastry on floured surface into 12-inch circle; transfer to ungreased cookie sheet. Combine flour and Equal®; sprinkle over peaches. Toss to coat. Arrange peaches over pastry, leaving 2-inch border around edge. Sprinkle lightly with nutmeg. Bring pastry edge toward center, overlapping as necessary. Bake tart in preheated 425°F oven until crust is browned and fruit is tender, 25 to 30 minutes. *Makes 8 servings*

Nutritional Information per Serving: *Calories: 168, Total Fat: 6 g, Cholesterol: 0 mg, Sodium: 134 mg*

Key Lime Tarts

More Desserts

Lemon Raspberry Tiramisu

2 packages (8 ounces each) fat-free
    cream cheese, softened
6 packages artificial sweetener or
    equivalent of ¼ cup sugar
1 teaspoon vanilla
⅓ cup water
1 package (0.3 ounce) sugar-free
    lemon-flavored gelatin
2 cups thawed fat-free nondairy
    whipped topping
½ cup all-fruit red raspberry preserves
¼ cup water
2 tablespoons marsala wine
2 packages (3 ounces each) ladyfingers
1 pint fresh raspberries or frozen
    unsweetened raspberries, thawed

1. Combine cream cheese, artificial
sweetener and vanilla in large bowl. Beat
with electric mixer at high speed until
smooth; set aside.

2. Combine water and gelatin in small
microwavable bowl; microwave at HIGH 30
seconds to 1 minute or until water is boiling
and gelatin is dissolved. Cool slightly.

3. Add gelatin mixture to cheese mixture;
beat 1 minute. Add whipped topping; beat
1 minute more, scraping side of bowl. Set
aside.

4. Whisk together preserves, water and
marsala in small bowl until well blended.
Reserve 2 tablespoons preserves mixture; set
aside. Spread ⅓ cup preserves mixture
evenly over bottom of 11×7-inch glass
baking dish.

5. Split ladyfingers in half; place half on
bottom of baking dish. Spread ½ of cheese
mixture evenly over ladyfingers; sprinkle 1
cup raspberries evenly over cheese mixture.
Top with remaining ladyfingers; spread
remaining preserves mixture over
ladyfingers. Top with remaining cheese
mixture. Cover; refrigerate at least 2 hours.
Sprinkle with remaining raspberries and
drizzle with reserved 2 tablespoons preserves
mixture before serving.

Makes 12 servings

Nutritional Information per Serving: *Calories: 158,
Total Fat: 1 g, Cholesterol: 52 mg, Sodium: 272 mg*

Lemon Raspberry Tiramisu

Sherry-Poached Peaches with Gingered Fruit and Custard Sauce

4 large ripe peaches, peeled, pitted and halved *or* 2 cans (16 ounces each) peach halves packed in juice, drained
⅓ cup dry sherry
1 cup assorted chopped mixed dried or fresh fruit (such as apples, golden raisins, prunes, peaches, apricots, pineapple, raisins and cranberries)
¼ cup water
½ teaspoon fresh minced ginger *or* ¼ teaspoon ground ginger
½ teaspoon grated orange peel
¼ cup all-fruit apricot preserves
1 cup skim milk
½ vanilla bean*
1 egg yolk
3 packages artificial sweetener or equivalent of 2 tablespoons sugar
2½ teaspoons cornstarch

1½ teaspoons vanilla extract may be substituted for vanilla bean. Stir into cooked custard before serving.

1. Combine peaches and sherry in medium saucepan. Simmer, covered, over low heat for 8 to 15 minutes, stirring often, until peaches are tender. (Cooking time will vary based on ripeness of fruit.) Remove peaches from sherry; cool to room temperature.

2. Combine dried fruit, water, ginger and orange peel in medium microwavable bowl. Cover; microwave at HIGH 2 to 3 minutes or until fruit is soft. Stir in preserves; cool to room temperature.

3. Pour milk into small saucepan. Cut vanilla bean in half lengthwise; scrape seeds into saucepan. Add bean halves to saucepan. Heat over medium heat just until milk begins to boil; remove from heat. Remove bean halves from milk; discard.

4. Combine egg yolk, artificial sweetener and cornstarch in medium bowl. Beat mixture with wire whisk until thick and lemon colored. Continue whisking mixture while very slowly pouring in hot milk mixture.

5. Slowly pour egg mixture back into saucepan. Cook over medium-low heat, stirring constantly until mixture thickens and coats metal spoon. *Do not boil.* Remove from heat.

6. Divide peach halves and fruit mixture among 4 plates. Top each serving with 2 tablespoons custard sauce.

Makes 4 servings

Nutritional Information per Serving: *Calories: 290, Total Fat: 1 g, Cholesterol: 54 mg, Sodium: 102*

Dreamy Orange Cheesecake Dip

1 package (8 ounces) Neufchâtel cheese, softened
½ cup orange marmalade
½ teaspoon vanilla
2 cups whole strawberries
2 cups cantaloupe chunks
2 cups apple slices

1. Combine cheese, marmalade and vanilla in small bowl; mix well. Serve with fruit dippers. *Makes 12 servings*

Nutritional Information per Serving (2 tablespoons dip, ½ cup fruit): *Calories: 102, Total Fat: 4 g, Cholesterol: 7 mg, Sodium: 111 mg*

Sherry-Poached Peaches with Gingered Fruit and Custard Sauce

Fruit Baked Apples

3½ teaspoons EQUAL® Measure™ *or*
    12 packets EQUAL® sweetener *or*
    ½ cup EQUAL® Spoonful™
1 tablespoon cornstarch
  Pinch ground cinnamon
  Pinch ground nutmeg
2 cups apple cider or juice
1 package (6 ounces) dried mixed fruit,
  chopped
1 tablespoon margarine
8 tart baking apples

• Combine Equal®, cornstarch, cinnamon and nutmeg in medium saucepan; stir in cider. Add dried fruit; heat to boiling. Reduce heat and simmer, uncovered, until fruit is tender and cider mixture is reduced to about 1 cup, 10 to 15 minutes. Add margarine and stir until melted.

• Remove cores from apples, cutting to, but not through, bottoms. Peel 1 inch around tops. Place apples in greased baking pan. Fill centers with fruit; spoon remaining cider mixture over apples.

• Bake, uncovered, in preheated 350°F oven until fork-tender, about 45 minutes.

Makes 8 servings

Nutritional Information per Serving: *Calories: 176, Total Fat: 2 g, Cholesterol: 0 mg, Sodium: 22 mg*

Cheese-Filled Poached Pears

1½ quarts cranberry-raspberry juice
  cocktail
2 ripe Bartlett pears with stems,
  peeled
2 tablespoons Neufchâtel cheese
2 teaspoons crumbled Gorgonzola
  cheese
1 tablespoon chopped walnuts

1. Bring juice to a boil in medium saucepan over high heat. Add pears; reduce heat to medium-low. Simmer 15 minutes or until pears are tender, turning occasionally. Remove pears from saucepan; discard liquid. Let stand 10 minutes or until cool enough to handle.

2. Combine cheeses in small bowl until well blended. Cut thin slice off bottom of each pear so that pears stand evenly. Cut pears lengthwise in half, leaving stems intact. Scoop out seeds and membranes to form small hole in each pear half. Fill holes with cheese mixture; press halves together. Place nuts in large bowl; roll pears in nuts to coat. Cover; refrigerate until ready to serve.

Makes 2 servings

Nutritional Information per Serving: *Calories: 240, Total Fat: 7 g, Cholesterol: 13 mg, Sodium: 98 mg*

Honey-Caramelized Bananas and Oranges

2 large bananas
1 orange, peeled and sliced
¼ cup honey
2 tablespoons chopped walnuts
3 tablespoons brandy (optional)

Peel and cut bananas in half lengthwise; place in small flameproof dish with orange slices. Drizzle with honey; sprinkle with walnuts. On top rack of preheated broiler, broil fruit about 5 minutes or until heated but not burnt. Remove from broiler. If desired, pour brandy over top and flame.

Makes 2 servings

Nutritional Information per Serving: *Calories: 362, Total Fat: 4 g, Cholesterol: 0 mg, Sodium: 3 mg*

Favorite recipe from **National Honey Board**

Fruit Baked Apples

Triple Fruit Trifle

2 ripe pears, peeled, cored and
    coarsely chopped
2 ripe bananas, thinly sliced
2 cups fresh or thawed frozen
    raspberries
1 tablespoon lemon juice
¼ cup reduced-calorie margarine
1 cup graham cracker crumbs
1 can (12 ounces) evaporated skimmed
    milk, divided
⅓ cup sugar
¼ cup cornstarch
⅓ cup cholesterol-free egg substitute
2 tablespoons nonfat sour cream
1½ teaspoons vanilla
3 tablespoons apricot all-fruit spread

1. Combine pears, bananas, raspberries and lemon juice in large bowl.

2. Melt margarine in small saucepan over medium heat. Stir in graham cracker crumbs until well blended. Remove saucepan from heat; set aside.

3. Blend ¼ cup milk, sugar and cornstarch in another small saucepan. Whisk in remaining milk. Bring to a boil over medium heat, stirring constantly. Boil 1 minute or until mixture thickens, stirring constantly. Reduce heat to medium-low.

4. Blend ⅓ cup hot milk mixture and egg substitute in small bowl. Add to milk mixture. Cook 2 minutes, stirring constantly. Remove saucepan from heat. Let stand 10 minutes, stirring frequently. Stir in sour cream and vanilla; blend well.

5. Spoon half of milk mixture into trifle dish or medium straight-sided glass serving bowl. Layer half of fruit mixture and ½ cup graham cracker crumb mixture over milk mixture. Repeat layers, ending with graham cracker crumb mixture. Blend fruit spread and 1 teaspoon water until smooth. Drizzle over trifle. Garnish with additional fresh fruit, if desired. *Makes 12 servings*

Nutritional Information per Serving: *Calories: 181, Total Fat: 3 g, Cholesterol: 1 mg, Sodium: 151 mg*

Fresh Fruit Trifle

2 cups skim milk
2 tablespoons cornstarch
⅓ cup sugar
4 egg whites, lightly beaten
2 teaspoons vegetable oil
1½ teaspoons vanilla
6 tablespoons sherry or apple juice,
    divided
4 cups cubed angel food cake
6 cups diced assorted fruit (apricots,
    peaches, nectarines, plums and
    berries)

1. Combine milk and cornstarch in medium saucepan; stir until cornstarch is dissolved. Add sugar, egg whites and oil; mix well. Bring to a boil over medium-low heat, stirring constantly with wire whisk; boil until thickened. Remove from heat. Cool. Add vanilla and 2 tablespoons sherry.

2. Place one-third cake pieces on bottom of 2-quart glass bowl or trifle dish. Sprinkle with one-third remaining sherry. Spoon ⅔ cup custard over cake. Spoon one-third fruit over custard. Repeat process twice, ending with fruit. Serve immediately.

Makes 12 servings

Nutritional Information per Serving: *Calories: 133, Total Fat: 1 g, Cholesterol: 1 mg, Sodium: 111 mg*

Triple Fruit Trifle

Caramelized Peaches & Cream

2 pounds (about 8 medium) sliced
    peeled peaches, or thawed and
    well-drained unsweetened frozen
    peaches
2 tablespoons bourbon
¾ cup reduced-fat sour cream
½ teaspoon ground cinnamon
¼ teaspoon ground nutmeg
¾ cup packed light brown sugar
8 slices (1½ ounces each) angel food
    cake, cut into cubes

1. Toss peaches with bourbon in shallow ovenproof 1½-quart casserole or 11×7-inch glass baking dish. Press down into even layer.

2. Combine sour cream, cinnamon and nutmeg in small bowl; mix well. Spoon mixture evenly over peaches. (Mixture may be covered and refrigerated up to 2 hours before cooking time.)

3. Preheat broiler. Sprinkle brown sugar evenly over sour cream mixture to cover. Broil 4 to 5 inches from heat, 3 to 5 minutes or until brown sugar is melted and bubbly. (Watch closely after 3 minutes so that sugar does not burn.)

4. Spoon immediately over angel food cake.

Makes 10 servings

Nutritional Information per Serving: *Calories: 215, Total Fat: 1 g, Cholesterol: 6 mg, Sodium: 272 mg*

Spiced Grilled Bananas

3 large ripe firm bananas
¼ cup golden raisins
3 tablespoons packed brown sugar
½ teaspoon ground cinnamon
¼ teaspoon ground cardamom
¼ teaspoon ground nutmeg
2 tablespoons margarine, cut into
    8 pieces
1 tablespoon fresh lime juice
    Vanilla low-fat frozen yogurt
    (optional)
    Additional fresh lime juice (optional)

1. Spray grill-proof 9-inch pie plate with nonstick cooking spray. Prepare coals for grilling. Cut bananas diagonally into ½-inch-thick slices. Arrange, overlapping, in prepared pie plate. Sprinkle with raisins.

2. Combine sugar, cinnamon, cardamom and nutmeg in small bowl; sprinkle over bananas and raisins and dot with margarine. Cover pie plate tightly with foil. Place on grid and grill on covered grill over low coals 10 to 15 minutes or until bananas are hot and tender. Carefully remove foil and sprinkle with 1 tablespoon lime juice. Serve over low-fat frozen yogurt and sprinkle with additional lime juice, if desired.

Makes 4 servings

Nutritional Information per Serving: *Calories: 202, Total Fat: 6 g, Cholesterol: 0 mg, Sodium: 72 mg*

Caramelized Peaches & Cream

Apple-Cherry Crisp

1 pound Granny Smith apples, peeled, cored and sliced ¼ inch thick
1 can (16 ounces) tart pie cherries packed in water, drained
1 can (16 ounces) dark sweet pitted cherries in heavy syrup, drained
2 teaspoons vanilla
1 teaspoon ground cinnamon
1 cup fruit juice-sweetened granola without raisins*
⅓ cup sliced almonds
1 quart fat-free vanilla ice cream or frozen yogurt

Available in the health food section of supermarkets.

1. Preheat oven to 350°F. Spray 11×7-inch glass baking dish with nonstick cooking spray; set aside.

2. Combine apples, cherries, vanilla and cinnamon in large bowl; stir until well blended. Spoon into prepared baking dish. Cover with foil; bake 30 minutes.

3. Remove from oven; stir to distribute juices. Sprinkle granola and almonds evenly over fruit. Bake, uncovered, 15 minutes more or until juice is bubbling and almonds are golden; serve warm or at room temperature topped with ice cream.　*Makes 8 servings*

Nutritional Information per Serving: *Calories: 296, Total Fat: 5 g, Cholesterol: 0 mg, Sodium: 100 mg*

Cherry Cobbler

1 cup all-purpose flour
¾ cup sugar, divided
2 tablespoons instant nonfat dry milk powder
2 teaspoons baking powder
¼ teaspoon baking soda
¼ teaspoon salt
2 tablespoons vegetable oil
7 tablespoons buttermilk
2 tablespoons cornstarch
½ cup water
1 package (16 ounces) frozen unsweetened cherries, thawed and drained
½ teaspoon vanilla
　Nonfat frozen yogurt (optional)

1. Preheat oven to 400°F. Combine flour, ¼ cup sugar, milk powder, baking powder, baking soda and salt in medium bowl. Stir in oil until mixture becomes crumbly. Add buttermilk; stir until moistened. Set aside.

2. Combine cornstarch, remaining ½ cup sugar and water in medium saucepan. Stir until cornstarch is dissolved. Cook over medium heat, stirring constantly until thickened. Add cherries and vanilla; stir until cherries are completely coated. Pour into 8-inch square baking pan; spoon biscuit mixture over cherries.

3. Bake 25 minutes or until topping is golden brown. Serve warm with nonfat frozen yogurt, if desired.　*Makes 8 servings*

Nutritional Information per Serving: *Calories: 204, Total Fat: 4 g, Cholesterol: 1 mg, Sodium: 209 mg*

Apple-Cherry Crisp

Grandma's Apple Crisp

¾ cup apple juice
3½ teaspoons EQUAL® Measure™ *or*
    12 packets EQUAL® sweetener *or*
    ½ cup EQUAL® Spoonful™
1 tablespoon cornstarch
1 teaspoon grated lemon peel
4 cups sliced peeled apples
    Crispy Topping (recipe follows)

• Combine apple juice, Equal®, cornstarch and lemon peel in medium saucepan; add apples and heat to boiling. Reduce heat and simmer, uncovered, until juice is thickened and apples begin to lose their crispness, about 5 minutes.

• Arrange apples in 8-inch square baking pan; sprinkle Crispy Topping over apples. Bake in preheated 400°F oven until topping is browned and apples are tender, about 25 minutes. Serve warm.   *Makes 6 servings*

Crispy Topping

¼ cup all-purpose flour
2½ teaspoons EQUAL® Measure™ *or*
    8 packets EQUAL® sweetener *or*
    ⅓ cup EQUAL® Spoonful™
1 teaspoon ground cinnamon
½ teaspoon ground nutmeg
3 dashes ground allspice
4 tablespoons cold margarine, cut into
    pieces
¼ cup uncooked quick-cooking oats
¼ cup unsweetened flaked coconut*

*Unsweetened coconut can be purchased in health food stores.

• Combine flour, Equal® and spices in small bowl; cut in margarine with pastry blender until mixture resembles coarse crumbs. Stir in oats and coconut.

Nutritional Information per Serving: *Calories: 196, Total Fat: 10 g, Cholesterol: 0 mg, Sodium: 91 mg*

Baked Apple Crisp

8 cups unpeeled, thinly sliced apples
    (about 8 medium)
2 tablespoons granulated sugar
1½ tablespoons lemon juice
4 teaspoons ground cinnamon, divided
1½ cups MOTT'S® Natural Apple Sauce
1 cup uncooked rolled oats
½ cup firmly packed light brown sugar
⅓ cup all-purpose flour
⅓ cup evaporated skimmed milk
¼ cup nonfat dry milk powder
1 cup nonfat vanilla yogurt

1. Preheat oven to 350°F. Spray 2-quart casserole with nonstick cooking spray.

2. In large bowl, toss apple slices with granulated sugar, lemon juice and 2 teaspoons cinnamon. Spoon into prepared dish. Spread apple sauce evenly over apple mixture.

3. In medium bowl, combine oats, brown sugar, flour, evaporated milk, dry milk powder and remaining 2 teaspoons cinnamon. Spread over apple sauce.

4. Bake 35 to 40 minutes or until lightly browned and bubbly. Cool slightly; serve warm. Top each serving with dollop of yogurt.   *Makes 12 servings*

Nutritional Information per Serving: *Calories: 185, Total Fat: 2 g, Cholesterol: 0 mg, Sodium: 35 mg*

Grandma's Apple Crisp

Fresh Plum Cobbler

½ cup water
5½ teaspoons EQUAL® Measure™ *or*
    18 packets EQUAL® sweetener *or*
    ¾ cup EQUAL® Spoonful™
1½ tablespoons cornstarch
1 teaspoon lemon juice
4 cups sliced pitted plums
¼ teaspoon ground nutmeg
¼ teaspoon ground allspice, divided
1 cup all-purpose flour
1¾ teaspoons EQUAL® Measure™ *or*
    6 packets EQUAL® sweetener *or*
    ¼ cup EQUAL® Spoonful™
1½ teaspoons baking powder
½ teaspoon salt
3 tablespoons cold margarine, cut into
    pieces
½ cup skim milk

• Combine water, 5½ teaspoons Equal® Measure™ *or* 18 packets Equal® sweetener *or* ¾ cup Equal® Spoonful™, cornstarch and lemon juice in large saucepan; add plums and heat to boiling. Boil, stirring constantly, until thickened, about 1 minute. Stir in nutmeg and ⅛ teaspoon allspice. Pour mixture into *ungreased* 1½-quart casserole.

• Combine flour, 1¾ teaspoons Equal® Measure™ *or* 6 packets Equal® sweetener *or* ¼ cup Equal® Spoonful™, baking powder, salt and remaining ⅛ teaspoon allspice in medium bowl; cut in margarine with pastry blender until mixture resembles coarse crumbs. Stir in milk, forming dough. Spoon dough into 6 mounds on fruit.

• Bake cobbler, uncovered, in preheated 400°F oven until topping is golden brown, about 25 minutes. Serve warm.

Makes 6 servings

Nutritional Information per Serving: *Calories: 195, Total Fat: 6 g, Cholesterol: 0 mg, Sodium: 378 mg*

Fresh & Fruity Cobbler

Biscuit Topping (recipe follows)
5 teaspoons sugar, divided
1 teaspoon cornstarch
½ cup fresh blueberries
½ cup peeled nectarine slices
½ cup strawberries, halved

1. Preheat oven to 350°F. Prepare Biscuit Topping.

2. Blend ¼ cup water, 3 teaspoons sugar and cornstarch in small saucepan. Cook over medium heat 5 minutes or until mixture thickens, stirring constantly. Remove saucepan from heat; let stand 5 minutes.

3. Add blueberries, nectarine and strawberries to sugar mixture; toss to coat. Spoon fruit mixture into 2-cup casserole; sprinkle with remaining 2 teaspoons sugar. Drop tablespoonfuls topping around edge of casserole.

4. Bake 20 minutes or until topping is browned. *Makes 2 servings*

Biscuit Topping

⅓ cup all-purpose flour
1 tablespoon sugar
¼ teaspoon baking powder
⅛ teaspoon baking soda
1 tablespoon plus 1 teaspoon
    reduced-calorie margarine
3 tablespoons nonfat sour cream
2 teaspoons cholesterol-free egg
    substitute
¼ teaspoon vanilla

Combine flour, sugar, baking powder and baking soda in medium bowl. Cut in margarine with pastry blender until mixture resembles coarse crumbs. Blend remaining ingredients in small bowl. Stir into flour mixture just until dry ingredients are moistened.

Nutritional Information per Serving: *Calories: 244, Total Fat: 4 g, Cholesterol: 0 mg, Sodium: 231 mg*

Smucker's® Peachy Pear Crumble

½ cup SMUCKER'S® Peach Preserves
¼ cup lemon juice
¼ teaspoon ground ginger
6 pears, peeled, cored and sliced
¼ cup all-purpose flour
¼ cup oatmeal
⅛ teaspoon salt
¼ teaspoon ground cinnamon
1 tablespoon margarine
1 tablespoon brown sugar
2 tablespoon milk
6 teaspoons low-fat frozen yogurt or non-fat sour cream (optional)

Preheat oven to 375°F. Place Smucker's® Peach Preserves, lemon juice and ginger in saucepan over medium high heat. Simmer until preserves are liquefied. Add pear slices and simmer 5 minutes.

While pears are simmering, combine flour, oatmeal, brown sugar and cinnamon in small bowl. Blend in margarine until mixture resembles rough meal. Add milk and loosely combine until just blended.

Pour pear mixture into 8-inch square baking pan. Sprinkle crumble topping evenly over surface of pear mixture. Place pan in pre-heated oven and bake 25 to 30 minutes or until top is lightly browned and bubbling.

Serve warm plain or with several tablespoons low-fat frozen yogurt, if desired.

Makes 6 servings

Note: If time is of the essence, substitute pear halves packaged in light syrup for the fresh pears in this recipe. Bake 15 minutes rather than 25 to 30. Top the pear mixture with a few tablespoons of your favorite granola for a speedy topping.

Nutritional Information per Serving: *Calories: 197, Total Fat: 3 g, Cholesterol: <1 mg, Sodium: 84 mg*

Tropical Bread Pudding with Piña Colada Sauce

BREAD PUDDING:
6 cups cubed day-old French bread
1 cup skim milk
1 cup frozen orange-pineapple-banana juice concentrate, thawed
½ cup cholesterol-free egg substitute
2 teaspoons vanilla
½ teaspoon butter-flavored extract
1 can (8 ounces) crushed pineapple in juice, undrained
½ cup golden raisins

PIÑA COLADA SAUCE:
¾ cup all-fruit pineapple preserves
⅓ cup shredded unsweetened coconut, toasted
1 teaspoon rum *or* ⅛ teaspoon rum extract

1. To prepare bread pudding, preheat oven to 350°F. Spray 11×7-inch glass baking dish with nonstick cooking spray. Place cubed bread in large bowl; set aside.

2. Combine milk, juice concentrate, egg substitute, vanilla and butter-flavored extract in another large bowl; mix until smooth. Drain pineapple; reserve juice. Add milk mixture, pineapple and raisins to bread; gently mix with large spoon. Spoon bread mixture evenly into prepared baking dish and flatten slightly; bake, uncovered, 40 minutes. Cool slightly.

3. To prepare Piña Colada Sauce, add water to reserved pineapple juice to equal ¼ cup. Combine juice, preserves, coconut and rum in microwavable bowl. Microwave at HIGH 2 to 3 minutes or until sauce is hot and bubbling; cool to room temperature.

4. Divide pudding among 8 plates; top each serving with 2 tablespoons Piña Colada Sauce. *Makes 8 servings*

Nutritional Information per Serving: *Calories: 280, Total Fat: 2 g, Cholesterol: 1 mg, Sodium: 178 mg*

Maple Caramel Bread Pudding

8 slices cinnamon raisin bread
2 whole eggs
1 egg white
⅓ cup sugar
1½ cups 2% low-fat milk
½ cup maple syrup
½ teaspoon ground cinnamon
¼ teaspoon salt
¼ teaspoon ground nutmeg
6 tablespoons fat-free caramel ice
cream topping

1. Preheat oven to 350°F. Spray 8×8-inch baking dish with nonstick cooking spray. Cut bread into ¾-inch cubes; arrange in prepared dish.

2. Beat whole eggs, egg white and sugar in medium bowl. Beat in milk, syrup, cinnamon, salt and nutmeg; pour evenly over bread. Toss bread gently to coat.

3. Bake 45 minutes or until center is set. Transfer dish to wire cooling rack; let stand 20 minutes before serving. Serve warm with caramel topping.   *Makes 8 servings*

Nutritional Information per Serving: *Calories: 235, Total Fat: 3 g, Cholesterol: 57 mg, Sodium: 228 mg*

Blueberry Bread Pudding with Caramel Sauce

8 slices white bread, cubed
1 cup fresh or frozen blueberries
2 cups skim milk
1 cup EGG BEATERS® Healthy Real Egg
Substitute
⅔ cup sugar
1 teaspoon vanilla extract
¼ teaspoon ground cinnamon
Caramel Sauce (recipe follows)

Place bread cubes on bottom of lightly greased 8×8×2-inch baking pan. Sprinkle with blueberries; set aside.

In large bowl, combine milk, Egg Beaters®, sugar, vanilla and cinnamon; pour over bread mixture. Set pan in larger pan filled with 1-inch depth hot water. Bake at 350°F for 1 hour or until knife inserted in center comes out clean. Serve warm with Caramel Sauce.   *Makes 9 servings*

Prep Time: 20 minutes

Cook Time: 1 hour

Caramel Sauce: In small saucepan, over low heat, heat ¼ cup skim milk and 14 vanilla caramels until caramels are melted, stirring frequently.

Nutritional Information per Serving: *Calories: 210, Total Fat: 2 g, Cholesterol: 2 mg, Sodium: 227 mg*

Creamy Tapioca Pudding

2 cups skim milk
3 tablespoons quick-cooking tapioca
1 egg
⅛ teaspoon salt
3½ teaspoons EQUAL® Measure™ *or*
12 packets EQUAL® sweetener *or*
½ cup EQUAL® Spoonful™
1 to 2 teaspoons vanilla
Ground cinnamon and nutmeg

• Combine milk, tapioca, egg and salt in medium saucepan. Let stand 5 minutes. Cook over medium-high heat, stirring constantly, until boiling. Remove from heat; stir in Equal® and vanilla.

• Spoon mixture into serving dishes; sprinkle lightly with cinnamon and nutmeg. Serve warm, or refrigerate and serve chilled.
           Makes 4 (⅔-cup) servings

Nutritional Information per Serving: *Calories: 101, Total Fat: 1 g, Cholesterol: 55 mg, Sodium: 146 mg*

Maple Caramel Bread Pudding

Rice Pudding

1¼ cups water, divided
½ cup uncooked long-grain rice
2 cups evaporated skimmed milk
½ cup granulated sugar
½ cup raisins
½ cup MOTT'S® Natural Apple Sauce
3 tablespoons cornstarch
1 teaspoon vanilla extract
   Brown sugar or nutmeg (optional)
   Fresh raspberries (optional)
   Orange peel strips (optional)

1. In medium saucepan, bring 1 cup water to a boil. Add rice. Reduce heat to low and simmer, covered, 20 minutes or until rice is tender and water is absorbed.

2. Add milk, granulated sugar, raisins and apple sauce. Bring to a boil. Reduce heat to low and simmer for 3 minutes, stirring occasionally.

3. Combine cornstarch and remaining ¼ cup water in small bowl. Stir into rice mixture. Simmer about 20 minutes or until mixture thickens, stirring occasionally. Remove from heat; stir in vanilla. Cool 15 to 20 minutes before serving. Sprinkle each serving with brown sugar or nutmeg and garnish with raspberries and orange peel, if desired. Refrigerate leftovers.   *Makes 8 servings*

Nutritional Information per Serving: *Calories: 190, Total Fat: 1 g, Cholesterol: 2 mg, Sodium: 75 mg*

Creamy Rice Pudding

2 cups water
1 cinnamon stick, broken into pieces
1 cup converted rice
4 cups skim milk
¼ teaspoon salt
7¼ teaspoons EQUAL® Measure™ *or*
   24 packets EQUAL® sweetener *or*
   1 cup EQUAL® Spoonful™
3 egg yolks
2 egg whites
1 teaspoon vanilla
¼ cup raisins
   Ground cinnamon and nutmeg

• Heat water and cinnamon stick to boiling in large saucepan; stir in rice. Reduce heat and simmer, covered, until rice is tender and water is absorbed, 20 to 25 minutes. Discard cinnamon stick.

• Stir in milk and salt; heat to boiling. Reduce heat and simmer, covered, until mixture starts to thicken, about 15 to 20 minutes, stirring frequently. (Milk will not be absorbed and pudding will thicken when it cools.) Remove from heat and cool 1 to 2 minutes; stir in Equal®.

• Beat egg yolks, egg whites and vanilla in small bowl until blended. Stir about ½ cup rice mixture into egg mixture; stir back into saucepan. Cook over low heat, stirring constantly, 1 to 2 minutes. Stir in raisins.

• Spoon pudding into serving bowl; sprinkle with cinnamon and nutmeg. Serve warm or at room temperature.

Makes 6 (⅔-cup) servings

Nutritional Information per Serving: *Calories: 244, Total Fat: 3 g, Cholesterol: 109 mg, Sodium: 200 mg*

Rice Pudding

Tropical Fruit Cream Parfaits

1 cup 2% low-fat milk
1 package (4-serving size) sugar-free
    vanilla instant pudding mix
½ cup mango nectar
    Cinnamon-Ginger Tortilla Sticks
    (recipe follows)
1 large orange, peeled, chopped

1. Pour milk into medium bowl. Add pudding mix; stir with wire whisk 1 minute or until smooth and thickened. Stir in mango nectar; chill.

2. Prepare Cinnamon-Ginger Tortilla Sticks. Reserve 10 sticks; divide remaining sticks equally in 5 parfait dishes or small glasses. Top each with pudding mixture, orange and two reserved tortilla sticks.

Makes 5 servings

Cinnamon-Ginger Tortilla Sticks

3 tablespoons brown sugar
2 tablespoons margarine
½ teaspoon ground ginger
½ teaspoon ground cinnamon
4 (6-inch) flour tortillas, cut into
    ½-inch strips

1. Preheat oven to 375°F. Combine sugar, margarine, ginger and cinnamon in small microwavable bowl. Microwave at HIGH 1 minute or until smooth when stirred.

2. Twist tortillas into spirals and arrange on baking sheet sprayed with nonstick cooking spray. Brush each with brown sugar mixture. Bake 10 to 12 minutes or until edges are lightly browned; cool.   *Makes 5 servings*

Nutritional Information per Serving: *Calories: 277, Total Fat: 7 g, Cholesterol: 16 mg, Sodium: 357 mg*

Shamrock Parfaits

1 envelope unflavored gelatin
½ cup cold water
¾ cup sugar
½ cup HERSHEY¡S Cocoa
1¼ cups evaporated skim milk
1 teaspoon vanilla extract
2 cups frozen light non-dairy whipped
    topping, thawed, divided
⅛ teaspoon mint extract
6 to 7 drops green food color

In medium saucepan, sprinkle gelatin over water; let stand 2 minutes to soften. Cook over low heat, stirring constantly, until gelatin is completely dissolved, about 3 minutes. In small bowl, stir together sugar and cocoa; add gradually to gelatin mixture, stirring with whisk until well blended. Continue to cook over low heat, stirring constantly, until sugar is dissolved, about 3 minutes. Remove from heat. Stir in evaporated milk and vanilla. Pour mixture into large bowl. Refrigerate, stirring occasionally, until mixture mounds slightly when dropped from spoon, about 20 minutes.

Fold ½ cup whipped topping into chocolate mixture. Divide about half of mixture evenly among 8 parfait or wine glasses. Stir extract and food color into remaining 1½ cups topping; divide evenly among glasses. Spoon remaining chocolate mixture over topping in each glass. Garnish as desired. Serve immediately or cover and refrigerate until serving time.   *Makes 8 servings*

Nutritional Information per Serving: *Calories: 160, Total Fat: 3 g, Cholesterol: 0 mg, Sodium: 50 mg*

Tropical Fruit Cream Parfait

362

Fudgey Chocolate Cupcakes

¾ cup water
½ cup (1 stick) 56-60% corn oil spread,
    melted
2 egg whites, slightly beaten
1 teaspoon vanilla extract
2¼ cups HERSHEY'S Basic Cocoa Baking
    Mix (recipe follows)
2 teaspoons powdered sugar
2 teaspoons HERSHEY'S Cocoa
    (optional)

Heat oven to 350°F. Line 16 muffin cups (2½ inches in diameter) with foil or paper bake cups. In large mixer bowl, stir together water, corn oil spread, egg whites and vanilla. Add Basic Cocoa Baking Mix; beat on low speed of electric mixer until blended. Fill muffin cups ⅔ full with batter.

Bake 20 to 25 minutes or until wooden pick inserted in centers comes out clean. Remove from pans to wire racks. Cool completely. Sift powdered sugar over tops of cupcakes. If desired, partially cover part of each cupcake with paper cutout. Sift cocoa over exposed powdered sugar. Carefully lift off cutout. Store, covered, at room temperature.

Makes 16 cupcakes

Hershey's Basic Cocoa Baking Mix

4½ cups all-purpose flour
2¾ cups sugar
1¾ cups HERSHEY'S Cocoa
1 tablespoon plus ½ teaspoon baking
    powder
1¾ teaspoons salt
1¼ teaspoons baking soda

In large bowl, stir together all ingredients. Store in airtight container in cool, dry place for up to 1 month. Stir before using.

Makes 8 cups mix

Nutritional Information per Serving (1 cupcake): *Calories: 120, Total Fat: 5 g, Cholesterol: 0 mg, Sodium: 200 mg*

Chocolate Peanut Butter Fondue

⅓ cup unsweetened cocoa powder
⅓ cup sugar
⅓ cup 1% low-fat milk
3 tablespoons light corn syrup
2 tablespoons reduced-fat peanut
    butter
½ teaspoon vanilla
2 medium bananas, cut into 1-inch
    pieces
16 large strawberries
2 medium apples, cored and sliced

1. Mix cocoa, sugar, milk, corn syrup and peanut butter in medium saucepan. Cook over medium heat, stirring constantly, until hot. Remove from heat; stir in vanilla.

2. Pour fondue into medium serving bowl; serve warm or at room temperature with fruit dippers. *Makes 8 servings*

Nutritional Information per Serving: *Calories: 242, Total Fat: 4 g, Cholesterol: 14 mg, Sodium: 30 mg*

Fudgey Chocolate Cupcakes

Fudge Brownie Sundaes

1 cup all-purpose flour
¾ cup granulated sugar
½ cup unsweetened cocoa powder, divided
2 teaspoons baking powder
½ teaspoon salt
½ cup skim milk
¼ cup MOTT'S® Natural Apple Sauce
1 teaspoon vanilla extract
1¾ cups hot water
¾ cup packed light brown sugar
½ gallon frozen nonfat vanilla yogurt
 Maraschino cherries (optional)

1. Preheat oven to 350°F. Spray 8-inch square baking pan with nonstick cooking spray.

2. In large bowl, combine flour, granulated sugar, ¼ cup cocoa, baking powder and salt. Add milk, apple sauce and vanilla; stir until well blended. Pour batter into prepared pan.

3. In medium bowl, combine hot water, brown sugar and remaining ¼ cup cocoa. Pour over batter. *Do not stir.*

4. Bake 40 minutes or until center is almost set. Cool completely on wire rack. Cut into 12 bars. Top each bar with ½-cup scoop of frozen yogurt; spoon sauce from bottom of pan over yogurt. Garnish with cherry, if desired. *Makes 12 servings*

Nutritional Information per Serving: *Calories: 300, Total Fat: 3 g, Cholesterol: 5 mg, Sodium: 200 mg*

Baked Vanilla Custard

1 quart skim milk
6 eggs
6¼ teaspoons EQUAL® Measure™ *or*
 21 packets EQUAL® sweetener *or*
 ¾ cup plus 2 tablespoons EQUAL® Spoonful™
2 teaspoons vanilla
¼ teaspoon salt
 Ground nutmeg

• Heat milk just to boiling in medium saucepan; let cool 5 minutes.

• Beat eggs, Equal®, vanilla and salt in large bowl until smooth; gradually beat in hot milk. Pour mixture into 10 custard cups or 1½-quart glass casserole; sprinkle generously with nutmeg. Place custard cups or casserole in roasting pan; add 1 inch hot water to roasting pan.

• Bake, uncovered, in preheated 325°F oven until sharp knife inserted halfway between center and edge of custard comes out clean, 45 to 60 minutes. Remove custard dishes from roasting pan; cool on wire rack. Refrigerate until chilled.

Makes 10 (½-cup) servings

Nutritional Information per Serving: *Calories: 90, Total Fat: 3 g, Cholesterol: 129 mg, Sodium: 142 mg*

Fudge Brownie Sundae

Caribbean Freeze

⅔ cup sugar
3 tablespoons HERSHEY'S Cocoa
1¾ cups water
3 tablespoons frozen pineapple juice concentrate, thawed
1 tablespoon golden rum or
½ teaspoon rum extract

In medium saucepan, stir together sugar and cocoa; stir in water. Cook over medium heat, stirring occasionally, until mixture comes to a boil. Reduce heat; simmer 3 minutes, stirring occasionally. Cool completely. Stir concentrate and rum into chocolate mixture. Cover; refrigerate until cold, about 6 hours. Pour into 1-quart ice cream freezer container. Freeze according to manufacturer's directions. Garnish as desired.   *Makes 6 servings*

Nutritional Information per Serving: *Calories: 110, Total Fat: 0 g, Cholesterol: 0 mg, Sodium: 0 mg*

Mocha Sauce

1 cup skim milk
4 teaspoons unsweetened cocoa
2 teaspoons cornstarch
1 teaspoon instant coffee crystals
1 teaspoon vanilla
1¼ teaspoons EQUAL® Measure™ or
     4 packets EQUAL® sweetener or
     3 tablespoons EQUAL® Spoonful™

• Combine milk, cocoa, cornstarch and coffee crystals in small saucepan. Cook and stir until thickened and bubbly. Cook and stir 2 minutes more. Remove from heat; stir in vanilla and Equal®. Cool. Cover and chill.
                    Makes about 1 cup

Nutritional Information per Serving (1 tablespoon): *Calories: 10, Total Fat: 0 g, Cholesterol: 0 mg, Sodium: 8 mg*

French Vanilla Freeze

10¾ teaspoons EQUAL® Measure™ or
     36 packets EQUAL® sweetener or
     1½ cups EQUAL® Spoonful™
2 tablespoons cornstarch
1 piece vanilla bean (2 inches)
⅛ teaspoon salt
2 cups skim milk
2 tablespoons margarine
1 cup real liquid egg product
1 teaspoon vanilla

• Combine Equal®, cornstarch, vanilla bean and salt in medium saucepan; stir in milk and margarine. Heat to boiling over medium-high heat, whisking constantly. Boil until thickened, whisking constantly, about 1 minute.

• Whisk about 1 cup milk mixture into egg product in small bowl; whisk egg mixture back into milk mixture in saucepan. Cook over very low heat, whisking constantly, 30 to 60 seconds. Remove from heat and stir in vanilla. Let cool; remove vanilla bean. Refrigerate until chilled, about 1 hour.

• Freeze mixture in ice cream maker according to manufacturer's directions. Pack into freezer container and freeze until firm, 8 hours or overnight. Before serving, let stand at room temperature until slightly softened, about 15 minutes.
                    Makes 6 (½-cup) servings

Nutritional Information per Serving: *Calories: 134, Total Fat: 5 g, Cholesterol: 2 mg, Sodium: 205 mg*

Caribbean Freeze

Chocolate-Strawberry Crepes

CREPES:

⅔ cup all-purpose flour
2 tablespoons unsweetened cocoa
    powder
6 packages artificial sweetener or
    equivalent of ¼ cup sugar
¼ teaspoon salt
1¼ cups skim milk
½ cup cholesterol-free egg substitute
1 tablespoon margarine, melted
1 teaspoon vanilla
    Nonstick cooking spray

FILLING AND TOPPING:

4 ounces fat-free cream cheese,
    softened
1 package (1.3 ounces) chocolate
    fudge-flavored sugar-free instant
    pudding mix
1½ cups skim milk
¼ cup all-fruit strawberry preserves
2 tablespoons water
2 cups fresh hulled and quartered
    strawberries

1. To prepare crepes, combine flour, cocoa, artificial sweetener and salt in food processor; process to blend. Add milk, egg substitute, margarine and vanilla; process until smooth. Let batter stand at room temperature 30 minutes.

2. Spray 7-inch nonstick skillet with cooking spray; heat over medium-high heat. Pour 2 tablespoons crepe batter into hot pan. Immediately rotate pan back and forth to swirl batter over entire surface of pan. Cook 1 to 2 minutes or until crepe is brown around edge and top is dry. Carefully turn crepe with spatula and cook 30 seconds more. Transfer crepe to waxed paper to cool. Repeat with remaining batter, spraying pan with cooking spray as needed. Separate crepes with sheets of waxed paper.

3. To prepare chocolate filling, beat cream cheese in medium bowl with electric mixer at high speed until smooth; set aside. Prepare chocolate pudding with skim milk according to package directions. Gradually add pudding to cream cheese mixture; beat at high speed 3 minutes.

4. To prepare strawberry topping, combine preserves and water in large bowl until smooth. Add strawberries; toss to coat.

5. Spread 2 tablespoons chocolate filling evenly over surface of crepe; roll tightly. Repeat with remaining crepes. Place two crepes on each plate. Spoon ¼ cup strawberry topping over each serving. Serve immediately.

Makes 8 servings (2 crepes each)

Nutritional Information per Serving: *Calories: 161, Total Fat: 2 g, Cholesterol: 1 mg, Sodium: 374 mg*

Raspberry Sauce

2 cups fresh raspberries or thawed
    frozen unsweetened raspberries
1 tablespoon orange juice
1¼ teaspoons EQUAL® Measure™ or
    4 packets EQUAL® sweetener or
    3 tablespoons EQUAL® Spoonful™
½ teaspoon finely grated orange peel

• Place raspberries in blender container; blend until smooth. Strain through sieve; discard seeds. Stir orange juice, Equal® and orange peel into puréed berries. Serve over fresh fruit, frozen yogurt or cheesecake.

Makes 1 cup

Nutritional Information per Serving (¼ cup): *Calories: 35, Total Fat: 0 g, Cholesterol: 0 mg, Sodium: 0 mg*

Chocolate-Strawberry Crepes

Blueberry Triangles

1½ cups fresh or frozen blueberries, slightly thawed
3½ teaspoons EQUAL® Measure™ or 12 packets EQUAL® sweetener or ½ cup EQUAL® Spoonful™
1½ teaspoons cornstarch
2 to 4 teaspoons cold water
  Reduced-Fat Pie Pastry (page 325) or favorite pastry for 9-inch pie
  Skim milk
½ teaspoon EQUAL® Measure™ or 1½ packets EQUAL® sweetener or 1 tablespoon EQUAL® Spoonful™

• Rinse blueberries; drain slightly and place in medium saucepan. Sprinkle berries with 3½ teaspoons Equal® Measure™ or 12 packets Equal® sweetener or ½ cup Equal® Spoonful™ and cornstarch; toss to coat. Cook over medium heat, stirring constantly, until berries begin to release juice and form small amount of thickened sauce. (Add water, 1 teaspoon at a time, if bottom of saucepan becomes dry.) Cool; refrigerate until chilled.

• Roll pastry on floured surface to ⅛-inch thickness; cut into 8 (5-inch) squares, rerolling scraps as necessary. Place scant 2 tablespoons blueberry mixture on each pastry square. Fold squares in half to form triangles and press edges together to seal. Flute edges of pastry or crimp with tines of fork; pierce tops of pastries 3 or 4 times with tip of knife.

• Brush tops of pastries lightly with milk and sprinkle with ½ teaspoon Equal® Measure™ or 1½ packets Equal® sweetener or 1 tablespoon Equal® Spoonful™. Bake on foil- or parchment-lined cookie sheet in preheated 400°F oven until pastries are browned, about 25 minutes.

Makes 8 servings

Nutritional Information per Serving: *Calories: 147, Total Fat: 6 g, Cholesterol: 0 mg, Sodium: 134 mg*

Apple Strudel

1 sheet (½ of a 17¼-ounce package) frozen puff pastry
1 cup (4 ounces) shredded ALPINE LACE® Reduced Fat Cheddar Cheese
2 large Granny Smith apples, peeled, cored and sliced ⅛ inch thick (12 ounces)
⅓ cup golden raisins
2 tablespoons apple brandy (optional)
¼ cup granulated sugar
¼ cup packed light brown sugar
½ teaspoon ground cinnamon
2 tablespoons unsalted butter substitute, melted

1. To shape the pastry: Thaw the pastry for 20 minutes. Preheat the oven to 350°F. On a floured board, roll the pastry into a 15×12-inch rectangle.

2. To make the filling: Sprinkle the cheese on the dough, leaving a 1-inch border. Arrange the apples on top. Sprinkle with the raisins, then the brandy, if you wish. In a small cup, mix both of the sugars with the cinnamon, then sprinkle over the apple filling.

3. Starting from one of the wide ends, roll up jelly-roll style. Place on a baking sheet, seam side down, tucking the ends under. Using a sharp knife, make 7 diagonal slits on the top, then brush with the butter. Bake for 35 minutes or until golden brown.

Makes 18 servings

Nutritional Information per Serving: *Calories: 151, Total Fat: 6 g, Cholesterol: 8 mg, Sodium: 123 mg*

Blueberry Triangles

Index

A

Alpine Fettuccine, 258
Apple Sauce Irish Soda Bread, 293
Apples
  Apple-Cherry Crisp, 352
  Apple-Cinnamon Bread, 84
  Apple-Potato Pancakes, 288
  Apple Raisin Pancakes, 74
  Apple-Raisin Sour Cream Pie, 332
  Apple Slaw with Poppy Seed Dressing, 130
  Apple Strudel, 372
  Apple Stuffing, 292
  Baked Apple Crisp, 354
  Chocolate Peanut Butter Fondue, 364
  Chunky Spiced Applesauce, 274
  Curried Salad Bombay, 134
  Dreamy Orange Cheesecake Dip, 344
  Fruit Baked Apples, 346
  Glazed Stuffed Pork Chops, 178
  Grandma's Apple Crisp, 354
  Grilled Pork Tenderloin with Apple Salsa, 172
  Herb Chicken with Apples, 192
  Maple-Flavored Syrup, 89
  Mile-High Apple Pie, 328
  Oregon Hot Apple Cider, 53
  Shredded Carrot and Raisin Salad, 138
  Spiced Fruit Butter, 90
  Sweet and Sour Broccoli Pasta Salad, 142
Apricot-Almond Coffee Ring, 80
Apricot-Chicken Pot Stickers, 40

Artichokes
  Artichoke Dip, 17
  Artichoke-Pepper Torte, 60
  Chicken Caesar Salad, 122
  Chicken Diablo, 194
  Fresh Vegetable Lasagna, 244
  Fruit Antipasto Platter, 52
  Marinated Artichoke Cheese Toasts, 22
  Mediterranean Pita Sandwiches, 164
  Santa Fe Chicken Pasta Salad, 146
Asian Dishes
  Apricot-Chicken Pot Stickers, 40
  Asian Noodle Soup, 106
  Egg Rolls, 34
  Ginger Wonton Soup, 106
  Mandarin Pork Stir-Fry, 174
  Moo Shu Pork, 176
  Oriental Garden Toss, 260
  Oriental-Style Sea Scallops, 222
  Sesame Chicken Salad Wonton Cups, 38
  Shanghai Beef, 182
  Spiced Sesame Wonton Crisps, 38
  Szechwan Beef Lo Mein, 240
  Thai-Style Pork Kabobs, 172
  Vietnamese Beef Soup, 98
Asian Noodle Soup, 106
Asparagus
  Asparagus-Swiss Soufflé, 61
  Cold Asparagus with Lemon-Mustard Dressing, 262
  Grilled Steak and Asparagus Salad, 146
  Mustard-Crusted Roast Pork, 168

Asparagus *(continued)*
  Pasta Primavera, 244
  Rosemary Chicken with Asparagus Lemon Rice, 200
Athenian Rice with Feta Cheese, 278

B

Baked Apple Crisp, 354
Baked Corn Timbales, 275
Baked Vanilla Custard, 366
Bananas
  Banana Cream Pie, 335
  Banana Walnut Bread, 88
  Chocolate Peanut Butter Fondue, 364
  Fitness Shake, 92
  Fruit Antipasto Platter, 52
  Honey-Caramelized Bananas and Oranges, 346
  PB & J French Toast, 78
  Spiced Grilled Bananas, 350
  Triple Fruit Trifle, 348
Barbecued Cheese Burgers, 156
Barbecued Pork Sandwiches, 162
Beans
  Bean & Nacho Pinwheels, 32
  Bean Tortilla Pinwheels, 32
  Black Bean & Rice Burritos, 157
  Black Bean Bisque with Crab, 96
  Black Bean Pancakes & Salsa, 76
  Black Bean Quesadillas, 24
  Black Bean Salsa, 12
  Black Bean Tostadas, 28
  Chipotle Tamale Pie, 206
  Cowboy Caviar, 17
  Fajita Salad, 148
  Five-Layered Mexican Dip, 10
  Green Bean Casserole, 266

Beans *(continued)*
Grilled Tuna Niçoise with Citrus Marinade, 223
Herbed Green Beans, 268
Hot Three-Bean Casserole, 268
Hummus Pita Sandwiches, 164
Layered White Bean and Tuna Dip, 16
Meatless Sloppy Joes, 158
Mediterranean Chili, 116
Mediterranean Pita Pizzas, 24
Mediterranean Pita Sandwiches, 164
Mexican Strata Olé, 72
Pinto Bean & Zucchini Burritos, 166
Pork with Couscous & Root Vegetables, 174
Red Pepper & White Bean Pasta Sauce, 236
Roasted Red Pepper, Corn & Garbanzo Bean Salad, 140
Salmon and Green Bean Salad with Pasta, 126
Sesame Chicken Salad Wonton Cups, 38
Smoked Turkey Pasta Salad, 132
Southwest Corn and Turkey Soup, 110
Spicy Chick-Peas & Couscous, 276
Spicy Orzo and Black Bean Salad, 132
Spinach and Mushroom Enchiladas, 58
Spinach Tomato Salad, 136
Texas-Style Chili, 118
Triple Bean Salad, 140
Turkey and Bean Tostadas, 206
Turkey Chili with Black Beans, 118
Tuscany Bean & Pasta Soup, 103
Vegetable-Bean Chowder, 114
Vegetarian Chili, 116
Vietnamese Beef Soup, 98
Zesty Romaine and Pasta Salad, 128

Beef
Beef and Broccoli, 178
Beef and Caramelized Onions, 184

Beef *(continued)*
Beef & Vegetable Stir-Fry, 180
Beef Pot Roast, 180
Beef Stroganoff, 184
Down Home Barbecued Beef, 152
Fajita Salad, 148
Festive Stuffed Peppers, 270
Grilled Steak and Asparagus Salad, 146
Italian-Style Meat Loaf, 182
Kansas City Steak Soup, 98
Meatloaf Ring with Garlic Mashed Potatoes, 179
Mediterranean Chili, 116
Mini Beef & Potato Kabobs, 45
Pasta Meatball Soup, 103
Pasta Picadillo, 258
Shanghai Beef, 182
Southwest Barbecue Kabobs, 45
Spicy Beef and Onion Sandwiches, 162
Steak Jamaican, 179
Szechwan Beef Lo Mein, 240
Texas-Style Chili, 118
Vietnamese Beef Soup, 98
Bell Pepper Nachos, 27

Berries
Berry Good Dip, 17
Blueberry Bread Pudding with Caramel Sauce, 358
Blueberry Lattice Pie, 325
Blueberry Lemon Scones, 82
Blueberry Muffins with a Twist of Lemon, 84
Blueberry Triangles, 372
Brownie Cake Delight, 320
Chicken and Fruit Salad, 136
Chocolate Peanut Butter Fondue, 364
Chocolate-Strawberry Crepes, 370
Dreamy Orange Cheesecake Dip, 344
Fresh & Fruity Cobbler, 356
Lemon Raspberry Tiramisu, 342
Mixed Berry Topping, 76
Nectarine and Berry Pie, 338
Raspberry Sauce, 60, 320, 370
Rhubarb-Strawberry Pie, 330

Berries *(continued)*
Strawberry Jam, 90
Strawberry Margarita Pie, 330
Strawberry Sauce, 315
Strawberry Smoothie, 92
Triple Berry Breakfast Parfait, 73
Triple-Berry Jam, 89
Triple Fruit Trifle, 348
Berry Good Dip, 17
Beverages
Citrus Cooler, 52
Coffee Latte, 92
Cranberry-Lime Margarita Punch, 53
Fitness Shake, 92
Holiday Eggnog, 90
Orange Jubilee, 92
Oregon Hot Apple Cider, 53
Piña Colada Punch, 53
Strawberry Smoothie, 92
Biscuit Topping, 356
Black Bean & Rice Burritos, 157
Black Bean Bisque with Crab, 96
Black Bean Pancakes & Salsa, 76
Black Bean Quesadillas, 24
Black Bean Salsa, 12
Black Bean Tostadas, 28
Blintzes with Raspberry Sauce, 60
Blueberry Angel Food Cake Rolls, 322
Blueberry Bread Pudding with Caramel Sauce, 358
Blueberry Lattice Pie, 325
Blueberry Lemon Scones, 82
Blueberry Muffins with a Twist of Lemon, 84
Blueberry Triangles, 372
Bread
Apple-Cinnamon Bread, 84
Apple Sauce Irish Soda Bread, 293
Apricot-Almond Coffee Ring, 80
Banana Walnut Bread, 88
Cheese Twists, 46
Fruit Twists, 46
Italian Bread Sticks, 290
Maple-Walnut Bread, 88
Orange Fruit Bread, 86
Pineapple Zucchini Bread, 86

Bread (continued)
Roasted Pepper Focaccia, 293
Soft Pretzels, 46
Tex-Mex Corn Bread, 292
Whole Wheat Pita Toasts, 16
Breakfast Burritos with Tomato-Basil Topping, 58
Breakfast Strata, 70
Broccoli
Beef and Broccoli, 178
Broccoli & Cauliflower Stir-Fry, 264
Broccoli & Cheese Rice Pilaf, 276
Broccoli and Cheese Topped Potatoes, 284
Broccoli Lasagna Bianca, 252
Broccoli with Creamy Lemon Sauce, 264
Chicken Divan, 194
Chicken Stir-Fry, 192
Mediterranean Pasta Salad, 130
Oriental-Style Sea Scallops, 222
Pasta Primavera, 244
Sweet and Sour Broccoli Pasta Salad, 142
Triple-Decker Vegetable Omelet, 54
Turkey-Broccoli Roll-Ups, 34
Vegetarian Broccoli Casserole, 266
Zesty Romaine and Pasta Salad, 128
Brownie Cake Delight, 320
Brownies, 308
Bruschetta, 22
Burgers
Barbecued Cheese Burgers, 156
Turkey Burgers, 160

C

Caesar Salad, 140
Cajun Grilled Shrimp with Rotini and Roasted Red Pepper Sauce, 252
Californian, The, 158
California Rolls, 30

Canapés
Bruschetta, 22
Crab Canapés, 42
Crab Toasts, 22
Crostini, 20
Marinated Artichoke Cheese Toasts, 22
Smoked Salmon Appetizers, 36
Tuscan White Bean Crostini, 20
Caramelized Peaches & Cream, 350
Caramel Sauce, 358
Caribbean Cole Slaw, 144
Caribbean Freeze, 368
Caribbean Shrimp & Pasta, 230
Carrot and Parsnip Purée, 264
Cashew Chicken, 198
Catalan Spinach and Pasta, 256
Catfish with Tropical Fruit Salsa, 212
Celebration Pasta, 248
Cheese-Filled Poached Pears, 346
Cheese Tortellini with Tuna, 240
Cheese Twists, 46
Cherry Cobbler, 352
Cherry Lattice Pie, 332
Chewy Coconut Bars, 304
Chicken
Apricot-Chicken Pot Stickers, 40
Californian, The, 158
Cashew Chicken, 198
Chicken and Dumplings Stew, 112
Chicken and Fruit Salad, 136
Chicken and Spinach Salad, 128
Chicken Caesar Salad, 122
Chicken Diablo, 194
Chicken Divan, 194
Chicken Enchiladas, 202
Chicken Fajitas with Cowpoke Barbecue Sauce, 186
Chicken Florentine with Lemon Mustard Sauce, 188
Chicken Stir-Fry, 192
Chicken Tetrazzini, 238
Chicken with Brandied Fruit Sauce, 196
Cream of Chicken Soup, 110
Crispy Baked Chicken, 194

Chicken (continued)
Crispy Oven-Baked Chicken, 198
Egg Rolls, 34
Garlic Chicken Caesar Salad, 142
Healthy Choice® Tangy Oven-Fried BBQ Chicken, 188
Hearty Chicken and Rice Soup, 108
Herb Chicken with Apples, 192
Lemon Chicken with Herbs, 203
Maui Chicken Sandwich, 156
Mediterranean Chicken, 190
Paella, 214
Penne Pasta Salad, 138
Pepper Glazed Cajun Chicken, 203
Roast Chicken & Potatoes Catalan, 196
Rosemary Chicken with Asparagus Lemon Rice, 200
Santa Fe Chicken Pasta Salad, 146
Sesame Chicken Salad Wonton Cups, 38
Skillet Chicken and Rice, 200
Skillet Chicken with Garlic & Sun-Dried Tomatoes, 203
South-of-the-Border Nachos, 26
Spicy Marinated Chicken Kebabs over Rice, 202
Spicy Mesquite Chicken Fettuccine, 256
Sunburst Chicken Salad, 136
Sweet and Sour Stir-Fry, 190
Taco Chicken Nachos, 26
Tangy Chicken Breasts with Citrus Sage Sauce, 192
Tarragon Chicken Salad Sandwiches, 160
Vegetable-Chicken Noodle Soup, 108
Chile Scramble, 62
Chipotle Tamale Pie, 206
Chocolate
Chocolate Chip Cookies, 302
Chocolate Espresso Brownies, 310

Chocolate *(continued)*
  Chocolate Glaze, 318
  Hershey's 50% Reduced Fat
    Oatmeal Chip Cookies,
    296
  No-Guilt Chocolate Brownies,
    310
Chocolate Cheesecake, 314
Chocolate Cream Pie, 326
Chocolate Peanut Butter Fondue,
  364
Chocolate-Strawberry Crepes,
  370
Chunky Spiced Applesauce,
  274
Cider Glaze, 300
Cinnamon French Toast, 78
Cinnamon-Ginger Tortilla Sticks,
  362
Cinnamon-Raisin Roll-Ups, 30
Cioppino, 104
Citrus Cooler, 52
Citrus Marinade, 223
Cocktail Stuffed Mushrooms,
  40
Coconut Custard Pie, 335
Coffee Latte, 92
Cold Asparagus with Lemon-
  Mustard Dressing, 262
Country Kielbasa and Vegetables,
  248
Country Peach Tart, 340
Country-Style Mashed Potatoes,
  286
Cowboy Caviar, 17
Cowpoke Barbecue Sauce, 186
Crabmeat
  Black Bean Bisque with Crab,
    96
  Cioppino, 104
  Crab Canapés, 42
  Crab Toasts, 22
  Crustless Crab Florentine
    Quiche, 223
  Maryland Crab Cakes, 224
  Southern Crab Cakes with
    Rémoulade Dipping Sauce,
    42
Cranberry Gelatin Salad, 270
Cranberry-Lime Margarita Punch,
  53
Cranberry Sauce, 274
Cranberry Scones, 83

Cranberry Stuffing, 204
Cream Cheese and Jelly Cookies,
  298
Cream of Chicken Soup, 110
Creamy Garlic Dressing, 148
Creamy Macaroni & Cheese,
  274
Creamy Rice Pudding, 360
Creamy Tapioca Pudding, 358
Crispy Baked Chicken, 194
Crispy Oven-Baked Chicken,
  198
Crispy Topping, 354
Crostini, 20
Crown of Salmon Appetizer,
  44
Crustless Crab Florentine Quiche,
  223
Curried Salad Bombay, 134

D

Date Bran Muffins, 83
Date Cake Squares, 306
Dips & Spreads
  Artichoke Dip, 17
  Berry Good Dip, 17
  Dreamy Orange Cheesecake
    Dip, 344
  Five-Layered Mexican Dip,
    10
  Green Pea Mockamole, 12
  Layered White Bean and Tuna
    Dip, 16
  Nutty Carrot Spread, 20
  Olé Dip, 10
  Peach Preserves, 89
  Roasted Eggplant Spread, 18
  Señor Nacho Dip, 10
  Shrimp Dip with Crudités, 12
  Spiced Fruit Butter, 90
  Spicy Mustard Dip, 10
  Strawberry Jam, 90
  Triple-Berry Jam, 89
  Vegetable-Topped Hummus,
    18
Double Chocolate Mousse Pie,
  326
Double Corn, Cheddar & Rice
  Chowder, 114
Double Corn & Cheddar
  Chowder, 114

Down Home Barbecued Beef,
  152
Dreamy Orange Cheesecake Dip,
  344

E

Easy Brunch Frittata, 68
Easy Carrot Cake, 324
Easy Tex-Mex Bake, 250
Egg Dishes
  Asparagus-Swiss Soufflé, 61
  Baked Vanilla Custard, 366
  Blueberry Bread Pudding with
    Caramel Sauce, 358
  Breakfast Burritos with
    Tomato-Basil Topping, 58
  Breakfast Strata, 70
  Broccoli Lasagna Bianca, 252
  Chile Scramble, 62
  Cinnamon French Toast, 78
  Creamy Rice Pudding, 360
  Crustless Crab Florentine
    Quiche, 223
  Easy Brunch Frittata, 68
  Eggs Benedict, 72
  Eggs Santa Fe, 62
  French Vanilla Freeze, 368
  Ham and Cheese Frittatas,
    68
  Iowa Corn Pudding, 294
  Italian Omelet, 56
  Mexican Strata Olé, 72
  Mini Vegetable Quiches, 64
  Potato and Pork Frittata, 170
  Roman Spinach Soup, 102
  Salmon Quiche, 66
  Scrambled Egg Burritos, 73
  Spinach-Cheddar Squares, 73
  Spinach Quiche, 66
  Triple-Decker Vegetable
    Omelet, 54
  Turkey and Rice Quiche, 208
  Vegetable Quiche, 64
  Vegetable Strata, 70
  Western Omelet, 56
  Zucchini Mushroom Frittata,
    66
Eggplant & Orzo Soup with
  Roasted Red Pepper Salsa,
  102
Egg Rolls, 34

Eggs Benedict, 72
Eggs Santa Fe, 62

F

Fabulous Fruit Bars, 304
Fajita Salad, 148
Festive Potato Salad, 124
Festive Stuffed Peppers, 270
Fettuccine Alfredo, 242
Fish (*see also* **Crabmeat,
    Salmon, Shellfish, Shrimp
    and Tuna**)
    Catfish with Tropical Fruit
        Salsa, 212
    Cioppino, 104
    Crown of Salmon Appetizer,
        44
    Fish Creole, 220
    Grilled Fish with Pineapple-
        Cilantro Sauce, 218
    Herbed Haddock Fillets, 218
    Mediterranean Fish Soup,
        96
    Mustard-Grilled Red Snapper,
        216
    Orange Ginger Seafood,
        245
    Oven-Roasted Boston Scrod,
        214
    Pacific Rim Honey-Barbecued
        Fish, 224
    Red Snapper Vera Cruz, 212
    Snapper Veracruz, 216
Fitness Shake, 92
Five-Layered Mexican Dip, 10
French Breakfast Crepes, 60
French Vanilla Freeze, 368
Fresh & Fruity Cobbler, 356
Fresh Cranberry Relish, 270
Fresh Fruit Trifle, 348
Fresh Greens with Hot Bacon
    Dressing, 122
Fresh Plum Cobbler, 356
Fresh Tomato-Basil Salsa, 14
Fresh Vegetable Lasagna, 244
Fruit Antipasto Platter, 52
Fruit Baked Apples, 346
Fruit Twists, 46
Fudgey Chocolate Cupcakes,
    364
Fudge Brownie Sundaes, 366

G

Garden-Style Risotto, 280
Garlic Chicken Caesar Salad, 142
Gazpacho, 104
Ginger Wonton Soup, 106
Glazed Stuffed Pork Chops, 178
Grandma's Apple Crisp, 354
Granola Bites, 308
Greek Spinach-Cheese Rolls, 32
Green Bean Casserole, 266
Green Pea & Rice Amandine,
    276
Green Pea Mockamole, 12
Grilled Cheese 'n' Tomato
    Sandwiches, 154
Grilled Dishes
    Barbecued Cheese Burgers,
        156
    Grilled Fish with Pineapple-
        Cilantro Sauce, 218
    Grilled Honey Garlic Pork
        Chops, 178
    Grilled Pork Tenderloin with
        Apple Salsa, 172
    Grilled Steak and Asparagus
        Salad, 146
    Grilled Tuna Niçoise with
        Citrus Marinade, 223
    Grilled Vegetable Muffuletta,
        150
    Mini Beef & Potato Kabobs, 45
    Mustard-Grilled Red Snapper,
        216
    Pacific Rim Honey-Barbecued
        Fish, 224
    Shrimp and Pineapple Kabobs,
        228
    Southwest Barbecue Kabobs,
        45
    Spiced Grilled Bananas, 350
Guiltless Zucchini, 262

H

Ham 'n' Apple Rollers, 30
Ham and Cheese Frittatas, 68
Hawaiian Stir-Fry, 262
Hazelnut-Coated Salmon Steaks,
    216
Healthy Choice® Tangy Oven-
    Fried BBQ Chicken, 188

Hearty Chicken and Rice Soup,
    108
Herb Chicken with Apples, 192
Herbed Green Beans, 268
Herbed Haddock Fillets, 218
Herbed Potato Chips, 48
Hershey®s Basic Cocoa Baking
    Mix, 364
Hershey®s 50% Reduced Fat
    Oatmeal Chip Cookies,
    296
Holiday Eggnog, 90
Honey-Caramelized Bananas and
    Oranges, 346
Honey Glazed Carrots and
    Parsnips, 268
Honey Pumpkin Pie, 336
Hot Shrimp with Cool Salsa, 226
Hot Three-Bean Casserole, 268
Huevos Ranchwich, 158
Hummus Pita Sandwiches, 164

I

International Dishes (*see also*
    **Asian Dishes, Italian Dishes
    and Mexican Dishes**)
    Apple Sauce Irish Soda Bread,
        293
    Caribbean Cole Slaw, 144
    Caribbean Freeze, 368
    Caribbean Shrimp & Pasta,
        230
    Catalan Spinach and Pasta,
        256
    Curried Salad Bombay, 134
    French Breakfast Crepes, 60
    Grilled Tuna Niçoise with
        Citrus Marinade, 223
    Hummus Pita Sandwiches, 164
    Mediterranean Chicken, 190
    Mediterranean Chili, 116
    Mediterranean Fish Soup, 96
    Mediterranean Pasta Salad,
        130
    Mediterranean Pita Pizzas, 24
    Mediterranean Pita
        Sandwiches, 164
    Mediterranean Vegetable
        Sandwiches, 157
    Moroccan Lentil & Vegetable
        Soup, 100

International Dishes *(continued)*
Moroccan Pork Tagine, 170
Paella, 214
Pasta Picadillo, 258
Piña Colada Punch, 53
Red Snapper Vera Cruz, 212
Roast Chicken & Potatoes
    Catalan, 196
Roasted Eggplant Spread, 18
Snapper Veracruz, 216
Spicy Spanish Rice, 278
Steak Jamaican, 179
Tropical Bread Pudding with
    Piña Colada Sauce, 357
Vegetable-Topped Hummus,
    18
Venezuelan Salsa, 14
Iowa Corn Pudding, 294
Italian Dishes
Bruschetta, 22
Cioppino, 104
Crostini, 20
Garden-Style Risotto, 280
Italian Bread Sticks, 290
Italian Crouton Salad, 120
Italian Omelet, 56
Italian-Style Meat Loaf, 182
Pasta Carbonara, 256
Roasted Pepper Focaccia, 293
Roman Spinach Soup, 102
Seafood Risotto, 222
Spinach Parmesan Risotto, 280
Toasted Ravioli with Fresh
    Tomato-Basil Salsa, 14
Tuscan White Bean Crostini, 20
Tuscany Bean & Pasta Soup,
    103
Tuscany Cavatelli, 238

J

Jalapeño Coleslaw, 138
Jicama & Shrimp Cocktail with
    Roasted Red Pepper Sauce,
    36

K

Kabobs
Mini Beef & Potato Kabobs, 45
Peppered Shrimp Skewers, 44

Kabobs *(continued)*
Shrimp and Pineapple Kabobs,
    228
Southwest Barbecue Kabobs,
    45
Spicy Marinated Chicken
    Kebabs over Rice, 202
Thai-Style Pork Kabobs, 172
Kansas City Steak Soup, 98
Key Lime Pie, 328
Key Lime Tarts, 340

L

Lasagna Roll-Ups, 254
Layered White Bean and Tuna
    Dip, 16
Lemon Chicken with Herbs, 203
Lemon Raspberry Tiramisu, 342
Light & Luscious Chocolate Cake
    with Raspberry Sauce, 320
Linguine with Pesto-Marinara
    Clam Sauce, 242
Low Fat Devil's Chocolate Fudge
    Cake, 319
Low Fat Molasses Jumbles, 300
Luscious Chocolate Cheesecake,
    316

M

Mandarin Pork Stir-Fry, 174
Maple Caramel Bread Pudding,
    358
Maple-Flavored Syrup, 89
Maple Pumpkin Pie, 334
Maple-Walnut Bread, 88
Marbled Angel Cake, 318
Marinated Artichoke Cheese
    Toasts, 22
Marinated Tomato Salad, 126
Maryland Crab Cakes, 224
Maui Chicken Sandwich, 156
Meatless Sloppy Joes, 158
Meatloaf Ring with Garlic
    Mashed Potatoes, 179
Mediterranean Chicken, 190
Mediterranean Chili, 116
Mediterranean Fish Soup, 96
Mediterranean Pasta Salad, 130
Mediterranean Pita Pizzas, 24

Mediterranean Pita Sandwiches,
    164
Mediterranean Vegetable
    Sandwiches, 157
Mexican Dishes
Bean & Nacho Pinwheels, 32
Bean Tortilla Pinwheels, 32
Bell Pepper Nachos, 27
Black Bean & Rice Burritos,
    157
Black Bean Pancakes & Salsa,
    76
Black Bean Quesadillas, 24
Black Bean Tostadas, 28
Breakfast Burritos with
    Tomato-Basil Topping, 58
Chicken Enchiladas, 202
Chicken Fajitas with Cowpoke
    Barbecue Sauce, 186
Chipotle Tamale Pie, 206
Cranberry-Lime Margarita
    Punch, 53
Fajita Salad, 148
Five-Layered Mexican Dip,
    10
Huevos Ranchwich, 158
Mexican Roll-Ups, 27
Mexican Strata Olé, 72
Nacho Pinwheels, 32
Pinto Bean & Zucchini
    Burritos, 166
Scrambled Egg Burritos, 73
Spinach and Mushroom
    Enchiladas, 58
Stacked Burrito Pie, 294
Turkey and Bean Tostadas,
    206
Mile-High Apple Pie, 328
Mini Beef & Potato Kabobs, 45
Mini Vegetable Quiches, 64
Mixed Berry Topping, 76
Mocha Crinkles, 298
Mocha Marble Pound Cake,
    318
Mocha Sauce, 368
Mocha Yogurt Glaze, 318
Mock Hollandaise Sauce, 72
Mom's Lemon Meringue Pie,
    336
Moo Shu Pork, 176
Moroccan Lentil & Vegetable
    Soup, 100
Moroccan Pork Tagine, 170

Muffins & Scones
  Blueberry Lemon Scones, 82
  Blueberry Muffins with a Twist of Lemon, 84
  Cranberry Scones, 83
  Date Bran Muffins, 83
  Orange-Pecan Scones, 82
  Spicy Scones, 80
Mushroom Ragoût with Polenta, 290
Mustard-Crusted Roast Pork, 168
Mustard-Grilled Red Snapper, 216

N

Nacho Pinwheels, 32
Nectarine and Berry Pie, 338
New Orleans Pork Gumbo, 112
New York Cheesecake, 315
No-Guilt Chocolate Brownies, 310
Nutty Carrot Spread, 20

O

Olé Dip, 10
Onion Soup with Pasta, 102
Open-Faced Eggplant Melt, 154
Orange and Red Onion Salad, 146
Orange Chiffon Cheesecake, 314
Orange-Cranberry Sauce, 274
Orange Fruit Bread, 86
Orange Ginger Seafood, 245
Orange Jubilee, 92
Orange-Mango Dressing, 144
Orange-Pecan Scones, 82
Oregon Hot Apple Cider, 53
Oriental Garden Toss, 260
Oriental-Style Sea Scallops, 222
Oven-Fried Tex-Mex Onion Rings, 46
Oven-Roasted Boston Scrod, 214

P

Pacific Rim Honey-Barbecued Fish, 224
Paella, 214

Pasta Carbonara, 256
Pasta Meatball Soup, 103
Pasta Picadillo, 258
Pasta Primavera, 244
Pastitso, 245
PB & J French Toast, 78
Peach Preserves, 89
Penne Pasta Salad, 138
Penne Salad with Spring Peas, 124
Pepper Glazed Cajun Chicken, 203
Peppered Shrimp Skewers, 44
Piña Colada Punch, 53
Pineapples
  Citrus Cooler, 52
  Fruit Antipasto Platter, 52
  Grilled Fish with Pineapple-Cilantro Sauce, 218
  Hawaiian Stir-Fry, 262
  Maui Chicken Sandwich, 156
  Mediterranean Pasta Salad, 130
  Piña Colada Punch, 53
  Pineapple Upside-Down Cake, 319, 322
  Pineapple Zucchini Bread, 86
  Shrimp and Pineapple Kabobs, 228
  Sweet and Sour Stir-Fry, 190
  Tropical Bread Pudding with Piña Colada Sauce, 357
Pinto Bean & Zucchini Burritos, 166
Pita Pockets, 166
Pleasin' Peanutty Snack Mix, 52
Pork (*see also* **Sausage**)
  Barbecued Pork Sandwiches, 162
  Eggs Benedict, 72
  Ginger Wonton Soup, 106
  Glazed Stuffed Pork Chops, 178
  Grilled Honey Garlic Pork Chops, 178
  Grilled Pork Tenderloin with Apple Salsa, 172
  Ham and Cheese Frittatas, 68
  Ham 'n' Apple Rollers, 30
  Mandarin Pork Stir-Fry, 174
  Moo Shu Pork, 176

Pork (*continued*)
  Moroccan Pork Tagine, 170
  Mustard-Crusted Roast Pork, 168
  New Orleans Pork Gumbo, 112
  Open-Faced Eggplant Melt, 154
  Pork Chops in Creamy Garlic Sauce, 176
  Pork with Couscous & Root Vegetables, 174
  Potato and Pork Frittata, 170
  Sesame Pork Salad, 144
  Thai-Style Pork Kabobs, 172
Potatoes
  Apple-Potato Pancakes, 288
  Breakfast Burritos with Tomato-Basil Topping, 58
  Broccoli and Cheese Topped Potatoes, 284
  Chicken and Dumplings Stew, 112
  Country-Style Mashed Potatoes, 286
  Easy Brunch Frittata, 68
  Festive Potato Salad, 124
  Grilled Tuna Niçoise with Citrus Marinade, 223
  Herbed Potato Chips, 48
  Meatloaf Ring with Garlic Mashed Potatoes, 179
  Mini Beef & Potato Kabobs, 45
  Pork with Couscous & Root Vegetables, 174
  Potato and Pork Frittata, 170
  Potatoes au Gratin, 282
  Potato Latkes, 74
  Potato Skins with Cheddar Melt, 48
  Potato-Swiss Galette, 282
  Potato-Zucchini Pancakes with Warm Corn Salsa, 288
  Roast Cajun Potatoes, 286
  Roast Chicken & Potatoes Catalan, 196
  Spirited Sweet Potato Casserole, 284
  Sweet Potato Puffs, 286
  Turkey & Cheese Stuffed Potatoes, 208
  Vegetable Quiche, 64

Prune Purée, 83, 324
Pumpkin Harvest Bars, 302

Q

Quick Refrigerator Sweet Pickles, 272

R

Ranch-Style White Sauce, 266
Raspberry-Almond Bars, 306
Raspberry Sauce, 60, 320, 370
Red Pepper & White Bean Pasta Sauce, 236
Red Snapper Vera Cruz, 212
Reduced-Fat Pie Pastry, 325
Refrigerator Corn Relish, 272
Rhubarb-Strawberry Pie, 330
Rice
    Athenian Rice with Feta Cheese, 278
    Beef and Broccoli, 178
    Bell Pepper Nachos, 27
    Black Bean & Rice Burritos, 157
    Broccoli & Cheese Rice Pilaf, 276
    Cashew Chicken, 198
    Cream of Chicken Soup, 110
    Creamy Rice Pudding, 360
    Festive Stuffed Peppers, 270
    Garden-Style Risotto, 280
    Green Pea & Rice Amandine, 276
    Hazelnut-Coated Salmon Steaks, 216
    Hearty Chicken and Rice Soup, 108
    Mediterranean Chicken, 190
    Paella, 214
    Pork Chops in Creamy Garlic Sauce, 176
    Rice Pilaf with Dried Cherries and Almonds, 278
    Rice Pudding, 360
    Rosemary Chicken with Asparagus Lemon Rice, 200
    Seafood Risotto, 222
    Sesame Pork Salad, 144
    Shrimp Étoufée, 226

Rice (continued)
    Shrimp in Tomatillo Sauce over Rice, 228
    Skillet Chicken and Rice, 200
    Spicy Marinated Chicken Kebabs over Rice, 202
    Spicy Spanish Rice, 278
    Spinach Parmesan Risotto, 280
    Stir-Fry Shrimp and Snow Peas, 228
    Thai-Style Pork Kabobs, 172
    Turkey and Rice Quiche, 208
    Turkey Jambalaya, 210
    Vegetarian Broccoli Casserole, 266
    Wild & Brown Rice with Exotic Mushrooms, 275
Rich Chocolate Cheesecake, 312
Roast Cajun Potatoes, 286
Roast Chicken & Potatoes Catalan, 196
Roasted Eggplant Rolls, 35
Roasted Eggplant Spread, 18
Roasted Garlic & Spinach Spirals, 28
Roasted Pepper Focaccia, 293
Roasted Red Pepper, Corn & Garbanzo Bean Salad, 140
Roast Turkey with Cranberry Stuffing, 204
Rock 'n' Rollers, 30
Rolled Appetizers
    Bean & Nacho Pinwheels, 32
    Bean Tortilla Pinwheels, 32
    California Rolls, 30
    Cinnamon-Raisin Roll-Ups, 30
    Egg Rolls, 34
    Greek Spinach-Cheese Rolls, 32
    Ham 'n' Apple Rollers, 30
    Mexican Roll-Ups, 27
    Nacho Pinwheels, 32
    Roasted Eggplant Rolls, 35
    Roasted Garlic & Spinach Spirals, 28
    Rock 'n' Rollers, 30
    Sassy Salsa Rollers, 30
    Smoked Salmon Appetizers, 36
    Turkey-Broccoli Roll-Ups, 34
Roman Spinach Soup, 102
Rosemary Chicken with Asparagus Lemon Rice, 200
Rush-Hour Lasagna, 254

S

S'More Gorp, 50
Salmon
    Crown of Salmon Appetizer, 44
    Hazelnut-Coated Salmon Steaks, 216
    Salmon and Green Bean Salad with Pasta, 126
    Salmon Quiche, 66
    Salmon Steaks with Lemon Dill Sauce, 220
    Smoked Salmon Appetizers, 36
Salsa
    Black Bean Pancakes & Salsa, 76
    Black Bean Salsa, 12
    Chicken Enchiladas, 202
    Cowboy Caviar, 17
    Fajita Salad, 148
    Fresh Tomato-Basil Salsa, 14
    Mexican Strata Olé, 72
    Pinto Bean & Zucchini Burritos, 166
    Santa Fe Chicken Pasta Salad, 146
    Snapper Veracruz, 216
    Stacked Burrito Pie, 294
    Texas-Style Chili, 118
    Venezuelan Salsa, 14
    Warm Corn Salsa, 288
Santa Fe Chicken Pasta Salad, 146
Sassy Salsa Rollers, 30
Sauces & Dressings (see also **Toppings**)
    Caramel Sauce, 358
    Chunky Spiced Applesauce, 274
    Cowpoke Barbecue Sauce, 186
    Cranberry Sauce, 274
    Creamy Garlic Dressing, 148
    Fresh Cranberry Relish, 270
    Maple-Flavored Syrup, 89
    Mocha Sauce, 368
    Mock Hollandaise Sauce, 72
    Orange-Cranberry Sauce, 274
    Orange-Mango Dressing, 144
    Ranch-Style White Sauce, 266
    Raspberry Sauce, 60, 320, 370
    Red Pepper & White Bean Pasta Sauce, 236

Sauces & Dressings (continued)
Refrigerator Corn Relish, 272
Strawberry Sauce, 315
Sweet and Sour Sauce, 35
Tartar Sauce, 214
Sausage
Breakfast Strata, 70
Cocktail Stuffed Mushrooms, 40
Country Kielbasa and Vegetables, 248
Mediterranean Pasta Salad, 130
Sausage and Bow Tie Bash, 238
Turkey Jambalaya, 210
Scallop and Spinach Salad, 134
Scrambled Egg Burritos, 73
Señor Nacho Dip, 10
Seafood Risotto, 222
Sesame Chicken Salad Wonton Cups, 38
Sesame Pork Salad, 144
Shamrock Parfaits, 362
Shanghai Beef, 182
Shellfish (*see also* **Crabmeat and Shrimp**)
Cioppino, 104
Linguine with Pesto-Marinara Clam Sauce, 242
Oriental-Style Sea Scallops, 222
Scallop and Spinach Salad, 134
Sherry-Poached Peaches with Gingered Fruit and Custard Sauce, 344
Shredded Carrot and Raisin Salad, 138
Shrimp
Cajun Grilled Shrimp with Rotini and Roasted Red Pepper Sauce, 252
Caribbean Shrimp & Pasta, 230
Cioppino, 104
Hot Shrimp with Cool Salsa, 226
Jicama & Shrimp Cocktail with Roasted Red Pepper Sauce, 36
Paella, 214

Shrimp (continued)
Peppered Shrimp Skewers, 44
Seafood Risotto, 222
Shrimp and Pineapple Kabobs, 228
Shrimp & Snow Peas with Fusilli, 234
Shrimp Dip with Crudités, 12
Shrimp Étoufée, 226
Shrimp in Tomatillo Sauce over Rice, 228
Spicy Shrimp Puttanesca, 246
Stir-Fry Shrimp and Snow Peas, 228
Silver Dollar Pancakes with Mixed Berry Topping, 76
Skillet Chicken and Rice, 200
Skillet Chicken with Garlic & Sun-Dried Tomatoes, 203
Smoked Salmon Appetizers, 36
Smoked Turkey Pasta Salad, 132
Smucker's® Peachy Pear Crumble, 357
Snack Mixes & Chips
Herbed Potato Chips, 48
Pleasin' Peanutty Snack Mix, 52
S'More Gorp, 50
Southwest Snack Mix, 50
Spiced Sesame Wonton Crisps, 38
Snapper Veracruz, 216
Soft Apple Cider Cookies, 300
Soft Pretzels, 46
Southern Crab Cakes with Rémoulade Dipping Sauce, 42
South-of-the-Border Nachos, 26
Southwest Barbecue Kabobs, 45
Southwest Corn and Turkey Soup, 110
Southwestern Turkey, 210
Southwest Snack Mix, 50
Spaghetti with Marinara Sauce, 246
Spice Cake with Fresh Peach Sauce, 324
Spiced Fruit Butter, 90
Spiced Grilled Bananas, 350
Spiced Pumpkin Pie, 334
Spiced Sesame Wonton Crisps, 38

Spicy Beef and Onion Sandwiches, 162
Spicy Chick-Peas & Couscous, 276
Spicy Lentil and Pasta Soup, 100
Spicy Marinated Chicken Kebabs over Rice, 202
Spicy Mesquite Chicken Fettuccine, 256
Spicy Mustard Dip, 10
Spicy Orzo and Black Bean Salad, 132
Spicy Pumpkin Soup with Green Chili Swirl, 94
Spicy Scones, 80
Spicy Shrimp Puttanesca, 246
Spicy Spanish Rice, 278
Spinach
California Rolls, 30
Catalan Spinach and Pasta, 256
Chicken and Fruit Salad, 136
Chicken and Spinach Salad, 128
Chicken Florentine with Lemon Mustard Sauce, 188
Crustless Crab Florentine Quiche, 223
Eggs Benedict, 72
Fresh Greens with Hot Bacon Dressing, 122
Fresh Vegetable Lasagna, 244
Garden-Style Risotto, 280
Greek Spinach-Cheese Rolls, 32
Grilled Vegetable Muffuletta, 150
Roasted Eggplant Rolls, 35
Roasted Garlic & Spinach Spirals, 28
Roman Spinach Soup, 102
Scallop and Spinach Salad, 134
Spicy Orzo and Black Bean Salad, 132
Spinach and Mushroom Enchiladas, 58
Spinach-Cheddar Squares, 73
Spinach Parmesan Risotto, 280
Spinach Quiche, 66

Spinach (continued)
　Spinach-Stuffed Shells, 242
　Spinach Tomato Salad, 136
Spirited Sweet Potato Casserole, 284
Stacked Burrito Pie, 294
Steak Jamaican, 179
Stir-Fry Dishes
　Beef and Broccoli, 178
　Beef & Vegetable Stir-Fry, 180
　Broccoli & Cauliflower Stir-Fry, 264
　Cashew Chicken, 198
　Chicken Stir-Fry, 192
　Mandarin Pork Stir-Fry, 174
　Mediterranean Chicken, 190
　Moo Shu Pork, 176
　Oriental-Style Sea Scallops, 222
　Shanghai Beef, 182
　Stir-Fry Shrimp and Snow Peas, 228
　Sweet and Sour Stir-Fry, 190
Strawberry Jam, 90
Strawberry Margarita Pie, 330
Strawberry Sauce, 315
Strawberry Smoothie, 92
Summer Fruit Tart, 338
Sunburst Chicken Salad, 136
Sweet and Sour Broccoli Pasta Salad, 142
Sweet and Sour Sauce, 35
Sweet and Sour Stir-Fry, 190
Sweet Potato Puffs, 286
Swiss Cheese Sauced Pasta Shells with Crumbled Bacon, 234
Szechwan Beef Lo Mein, 240

T

Taco Chicken Nachos, 26
Tangy Chicken Breasts with Citrus Sage Sauce, 192
Tarragon Chicken Salad Sandwiches, 160
Tartar Sauce, 214
Tarts
　Country Peach Tart, 340
　Key Lime Tarts, 340
　Summer Fruit Tart, 338
Texas-Style Chili, 118
Tex-Mex Corn Bread, 292

Thai-Style Pork Kabobs, 172
Toasted Ravioli with Fresh Tomato-Basil Salsa, 14
Toppings
　Biscuit Topping, 356
　Chocolate Glaze, 318
　Cider Glaze, 300
　Crispy Topping, 354
　Mixed Berry Topping, 76
　Mocha Yogurt Glaze, 318
　Yogurt Topping, 316
Trail Mix Truffles, 50
Triple Bean Salad, 140
Triple Berry Breakfast Parfait, 73
Triple-Berry Jam, 89
Triple-Decker Vegetable Omelet, 54
Triple Fruit Trifle, 348
Tropical Bread Pudding with Piña Colada Sauce, 357
Tropical Fruit Cream Parfaits, 362
Tuna
　Cheese Tortellini with Tuna, 240
　Layered White Bean and Tuna Dip, 16
　Tuna Noodle Casserole, 236
　Tuna Salad Pita Pockets, 162
Turkey (see also **Sausage**)
　Barbecued Cheese Burgers, 156
　California Rolls, 30
　Chipotle Tamale Pie, 206
　Curried Salad Bombay, 134
　Easy Tex-Mex Bake, 250
　Italian-Style Meat Loaf, 182
　Lasagna Roll-Ups, 254
　Pita Pockets, 166
　Roast Turkey with Cranberry Stuffing, 204
　Rock 'n' Rollers, 30
　Sassy Salsa Rollers, 30
　Smoked Turkey Pasta Salad, 132
　Southwest Corn and Turkey Soup, 110
　Southwestern Turkey, 210
　Turkey and Bean Tostadas, 206
　Turkey & Cheese Stuffed Potatoes, 208
　Turkey & Pasta with Cilantro Pesto, 232

Turkey (continued)
　Turkey and Rice Quiche, 208
　Turkey-Broccoli Roll-Ups, 34
　Turkey Burgers, 160
　Turkey Chili with Black Beans, 118
　Turkey Gyros, 152
　Turkey Jambalaya, 210
　Turkey with Mustard Sauce, 204
Turtle Cheesecake, 316
Tuscan White Bean Crostini, 20
Tuscany Bean & Pasta Soup, 103
Tuscany Cavatelli, 238

V

Vegetable-Bean Chowder, 114
Vegetable-Chicken Noodle Soup, 108
Vegetable Manicotti, 232
Vegetable Quiche, 64
Vegetable Strata, 70
Vegetables with Spinach Fettuccine, 250
Vegetable-Topped Hummus, 18
Vegetarian Broccoli Casserole, 266
Vegetarian Chili, 116
Venezuelan Salsa, 14
Vietnamese Beef Soup, 98

W

Warm Corn Salsa, 288
Western Omelet, 56
Whole Wheat Pita Toasts, 16
Wild & Brown Rice with Exotic Mushrooms, 275

Y

Yogurt Topping, 316

Z

Zesty Romaine and Pasta Salad, 128
Zucchini Mushroom Frittata, 66

METRIC CONVERSION CHART

VOLUME MEASUREMENTS (dry)

1/8 teaspoon = 0.5 mL
1/4 teaspoon = 1 mL
1/2 teaspoon = 2 mL
3/4 teaspoon = 4 mL
1 teaspoon = 5 mL
1 tablespoon = 15 mL
2 tablespoons = 30 mL
1/4 cup = 60 mL
1/3 cup = 75 mL
1/2 cup = 125 mL
2/3 cup = 150 mL
3/4 cup = 175 mL
1 cup = 250 mL
2 cups = 1 pint = 500 mL
3 cups = 750 mL
4 cups = 1 quart = 1 L

VOLUME MEASUREMENTS (fluid)

1 fluid ounce (2 tablespoons) = 30 mL
4 fluid ounces (1/2 cup) = 125 mL
8 fluid ounces (1 cup) = 250 mL
12 fluid ounces (1 1/2 cups) = 375 mL
16 fluid ounces (2 cups) = 500 mL

WEIGHTS (mass)

1/2 ounce = 15 g
1 ounce = 30 g
3 ounces = 90 g
4 ounces = 120 g
8 ounces = 225 g
10 ounces = 285 g
12 ounces = 360 g
16 ounces = 1 pound = 450 g

DIMENSIONS

1/16 inch = 2 mm
1/8 inch = 3 mm
1/4 inch = 6 mm
1/2 inch = 1.5 cm
3/4 inch = 2 cm
1 inch = 2.5 cm

OVEN TEMPERATURES

250°F = 120°C
275°F = 140°C
300°F = 150°C
325°F = 160°C
350°F = 180°C
375°F = 190°C
400°F = 200°C
425°F = 220°C
450°F = 230°C

BAKING PAN SIZES

Utensil	Size in Inches/Quarts	Metric Volume	Size in Centimeters
Baking or Cake Pan (square or rectangular)	8×8×2	2 L	20×20×5
	9×9×2	2.5 L	23×23×5
	12×8×2	3 L	30×20×5
	13×9×2	3.5 L	33×23×5
Loaf Pan	8×4×3	1.5 L	20×10×7
	9×5×3	2 L	23×13×7
Round Layer Cake Pan	8×1½	1.2 L	20×4
	9×1½	1.5 L	23×4
Pie Plate	8×1¼	750 mL	20×3
	9×1¼	1 L	23×3
Baking Dish or Casserole	1 quart	1 L	—
	1½ quart	1.5 L	—
	2 quart	2 L	—